ALBUERA

Wellington's Fourth

Peninsular Campaign, 1811

GENERAL SIR WILLIAM BERESFORD

After the drawing by Thomas Heaphy
[The National Portriat Gallery]

ALBUERA

Wellington's Fourth Peninsular Campaign, 1811

PETER EDWARDS

THE CROWOOD PRESS

First published in 2008 by
The Crowood Press Ltd
Ramsbury, Marlborough
Wiltshire SN8 2HR

www.crowood.com

British Library Cataloguing-in-Publication Data
A catalogue record for this book is available from the British Library.

ISBN 978 1 86126 946 1

Edited by Martin Windrow

Typeset by S R Nova Pvt Ltd., Bangalore, India

Printed and bound in Great Britain by The Cromwell Press, Trowbridge

Contents

12 Back to Badajoz, 29 May–5 June
Beresford's health - Hill's return - Soult, Massena and Brent Spencer - Lumley's cavalry action at Usagre - Wellington at Badajoz - limitations of time and resources - Dickson and Fletcher - the plan - trenches opened - the castle - Fort San Cristobal - drooping muzzles, failing carriages, counterfire and thirst.

13 The Assaults on Fort San Cristobal, 6 & 9 June
6 June: the plan of attack - allocation of troops - the French garrison - Dyas' Forlorn Hope - the ditch cleared - inadequate ladders - casualties - the causes of failure - 9 June: the plan - the rubble cleared once again - the Chasseurs Britanniques throw down the ladders - failure - casualties - news of Soult and Massena - the siege adandoned - reflections - the effect of Albuera on French morale.

14 El Bodon, 25 September, and the Final Manoeuvres
Wellington concentrates - the two marshals - Badajoz provisioned - Dickson and the battering train - headquarters established at Fuenteguinaldo - the blockade of Ciudad Rodrigo - Marmont breaks the blockade - Picton at El Bodon: Montbrun's attack - the 5th and 77th form square - cavalry charges and counter-charges - retreat in marching squares - Wellington moves behind the Coa - Marmont goes into winter quarters - Wellington closes on Ciudad Rodrigo - the battering train is brought up - Napoleon milks Marmont's army for other fronts. Final assessments of the 1811 campaign - summary - a new French circumspection - Allied cavalry successes - Beresford - Wellington's moments of danger - his talents for logistics and intelligence - the British soldier.

Appendices

Sources and Further Reading

Index

Maps

Preface

*In our two battalions we had fifty officers present, and with the exception of eight all were
either killed, wounded or taken. Immediately after the action the 2nd Battalion out of 413
men had only twenty-five fit for duty. [Since then] almost all the prisoners have made their
escape and rejoined us: I now command a Company consisting of eight men, the poor remnants of more than fifty-nine soldiers... in a few days I hope my wounds will be quite healed.*
(Lieutenant William Woods, 2/48th Regiment, 29 May 1811)

ON a baking hot Friday in July 1809, at Talavera near Madrid in Spain, Sir Arthur Wellesley's small British army beat King Joseph Bonaparte's Frenchmen, and evaded – just –
a much larger force under Marshal Soult coming up behind. Of the many who were wounded
in the action, Sir Arthur necessarily had to abandon some 1,500 who could not march,
together with their few doctors, in the grim makeshift hospitals in and around the town.
Another 2,500 walking wounded endeavoured to follow their retreating regiments, but about
500 died en route. Talavera was indeed a hard, bloody victory, and everyone – from the newly
ennobled Viscount Wellington downward – knew that it was won by the skin of their teeth;
one more push from the French would have done for them entirely.

Both the 1st and 2nd Battalions of my own regiment, the 48th (Northamptonshire), were
there, and played an honourable part in that early Peninsula battle – which was my excuse for
writing a book on the Talavera campaign. Two years later, in May 1811, after many more
sweltering and freezing miles back and forth in Portugal and Spain, both battalions again
lined up opposite the blue coats of France, at Albuera near the frontier fortress of Badajoz. The
day's Despatch by the commanding general – Sir William Beresford – was hastily re-written
by Lord Wellington's aides as the story of a valiant victory; but it was another dreadful day
for the poor 48th, gallantly though both battalions fought to the bitter end. Their combined
strength in that earlier action at Talavera had been 1,374 bayonets. After Albuera, that figure
was officially reduced to 303; but Lieutenant Edward Close of the 2nd Battalion wrote in his
diary that, immediately after the action, the two battalions between them had only 125 men
fit for duty, while his brother-subaltern William Woods, quoted above, said that their own
2nd Battalion had just 25 fit men left – out of 413. Two-thirds of the officers were dead,
wounded or taken, both the 2nd Battalion's Colours – oh horror! – had been captured, and
eventually its few human relics were mercifully merged into the 1st Battalion. Our 2nd Battalion had ceased to exist.

According to painstaking calculations made in 1911 by Sir Charles Oman, the losses that
day on both sides totalled a staggering 14,178 men, of whom the French incurred an estimated
8,262, the British 4,159, the Spanish 1,368 and the Portuguese 389 – the more staggering in
that the action lasted just six hours, from 8 o'clock in the morning until 2 in the afternoon.
These losses were the heaviest suffered in all the Peninsula battles during Lord Wellington's
six years of campaigning, although the purely British casualties at Talavera were greater.

We shall try to see why, as the story unfolds. That Wellington was absent, that William Beresford was present but lacked lustre, that it rained, that the Polish Lancers ran amok on Dutch courage, that time was frittered away – all these are factors; but there was much more to it.

Wellington wrote 'if it had not been for me ... they would have written a whining report about it which would have driven the people in England mad.' In modern parlance, he saw the immediate need to spin the news of the 4,000 British battle casualties, set against the outcome – and the more especially since it followed only eleven days after his own expensive victory at Fuentes d'Oñoro, which according to Oman cost 2,063 men. His Fuentes Despatch to Lord Liverpool admitted that the losses came 'from the great superiority of force to which we have been opposed ... the actions were very severe, and our loss has been great.'

And Fuentes itself followed hard on the heels of another, only slightly less expensive victory: that won by Thomas Graham at Barrosa in the south of Spain. Barrossa had cost another 1,238 Allied casualties, of whom nine in every ten were British, and had come very close to being a tactical disaster, thanks again to another clown of a Spanish general.

To this story of three costly major battles in the space of a couple of months – one of them fought and won by Wellington, the other two fought for him by other generals, and nearly lost – must be added the two failed sieges of the mighty fortress of Badajoz. Together these five actions reduced the British strength in the Peninsula that summer by some 8,700 men – the equivalent of more than five infantry brigades. At this time the Peninsular Field Army comprised only eighteen British brigades in all, and, having just about expelled the French from Portugal, Wellington was looking to carry offensive operations forward into Spain at last. Men were ever in want, but never more so than now. That in the next twelve months he was triumphantly to lay siege to and capture the frontier fortresses of Ciudad Rodrigo and Badajoz, and then defeat 50,000 Frenchmen in the great victory at Salamanca, says much for his own determination and genius, and for his army's resilient powers of recuperation.

The fact that nearly three-quarters of Wellington's losses were incurred by others no doubt reinforced his innate reluctance to delegate any serious command. Similarly, his unforgettable experiences with Spanish commanders in 1809 had ensured forever a jaundiced view of their capabilities. It was Beresford's Spanish subordinate and Beresford's inadequate handling of him that contributed to Albuera's particular bloodiness; conversely, while Graham's Spanish superior was the complete cause of his near-disaster at Barrossa, his handling of the situation won Lord Wellington's approval, and Graham's subsequent elevation to command of a corps.

Many of those who had been present at Albuera resented Beresford's receipt of the Thanks of Parliament for his victory; they well knew not only that it over-stretched the definition of a victory, but also that the laurels truly belonged elsewhere. Dissent over Albuera, and over the earlier affair at Campo Mayor, broke poisonously into the open after the war, not least due to the third volume of Napier's great *History*, in which rather too much mud was flung – a man's honour in those days was a prickly thing. The animosity rumbled on – happily for future historians: during efforts to justify various events and decisions much information was generated, which is valuable today to those of us who try to unravel what went on.

There is indeed no shortage of ammunition for armchair generals aiming at William Carr Beresford for his actions both at Campo Mayor and Albuera; and in the background to these events there looms, of course, the shadow of our great hero Wellington. It is impossible to consider Beresford in isolation; we can be sure that he himself was all too conscious of that imperious shadow – a prospect few of us would enjoy. In his pioneering work *On The Psychology of Military Incompetence* (Cape, 1976), Norman Dixon itemizes certain common characteristics of incompetence demonstrated by army commanders over the centuries. Actual stupidity figures much more rarely than other personality traits. Simply, a man's nature inevitably colours his decisions, and Dixon's well-documented theory identifies a common thread linking all the perpetrators of the military blunders he examines. Its features include anxiety under stress, which encourages passivity or a lack of urgency; an inability to profit from past experiences; a strange aversion to reconnaissance; great physical bravery, but little moral courage; an apparent imperviousness to loss of life, yet a tendency to avoid risks, sometimes in favour of tasks so difficult that failure might seem excusable; and an obstinate persistence in a settled plan, despite strong new intelligence to the contrary.

Not all these characteristics fit William Beresford's behaviour at Albuera, but some do. That he presided over a serious waste of human resources is undeniable, and he thereby failed to observe one of the first principles of war – economy of force. Such wastage through administrative incompetence (as at Walcheren in 1809) or planning incompetence (as at Arnhem in 1944) does not apply to Albuera; but the third underlying common theme of waste – a seemingly deliberate policy of attrition – is more readily apparent. While certainly not in the same class as Napoleon, whose appalling boast was that 'A man such as I am is not much concerned over the lives of a million men', we shall see that Beresford was certainly careless in his husbanding of the fighting force with which Wellington had entrusted him. We must recall, however, that Beresford's given role with the Portuguese Army was its organization, training and administration; he received his first major field command - that of Hill's corps - only during and because of the absence of the latter in England. His uncertain handling of it at Albuera was the first and last time he was to be allowed effective command of a corps out of Lord Wellington's sight. He did not expect to fight Soult, after all, and nor did he want to, notwithstanding his apparent three-to-two superiority in numbers. The very different truth was that of every three men in his army, one was British, one Spanish and one Portuguese. And from the all-important cavalry point of view – for this was good horse country – the French outnumbered him by nearly four-to-one - 3,762 sabres in twelve regiments, to his 1,088 in three. Looked at in that way, the prospects before action was joined take on a different hue.

In fairness we must also recall that Beresford achieved his aim, and success is the great and final arbiter of all military arguments. It *was* a victory, however horribly hard-won, and not just because Soult was the first to quit the field, with the greater casualties. Soult had sallied forth, after all, to save Badajoz, and three days after Albuera the Allied siege of that fortress was renewed; Soult had failed in his purpose. Thus Wellington's instruction to his staff to 'Write me down a victory' was justified, even if it came about in spite of Beresford and due solely to the remarkable fighting qualities of the red-coated regiments that Wellington had put into his hands.

So Barrosa, Fuentes and Albuera are three exceedingly problematic encounters, resulting in the shedding of much blood and some reputations. Three more of the Emperor's marshals were duly scalped, for the second time – Victor, Massena and Soult – and thus joined Marshal Jourdan and King Joseph Bonaparte in receipt of their Emperor's scornful anger, and his inability to understand, yet again, what had stopped them beating the British. For the third and last time the French had been ejected from Portugal. Massena was returned whence he had come ten months before, for which he received the sack; Arthur Wellesley, Lord Wellington, received Parliament's Vote of Thanks; and the British and Portuguese army received the warmth of the rising sun in their faces, as they turned to invade Spain. The Peer's strategy could at last be carried forward into its next phase.

In 1810 Wellington had frustrated, before Torres Vedras, Napoleon's edict to kick the British out of Portugal, and in 1811 his eyes could reasonably gaze - as unlucky John Moore's had, before him - upon that long and vulnerable umbilical cord connecting the Emperor in Paris to his brother in Madrid: the great road over the Pyrenees through St Jean de Luz, Vittoria and Burgos. To take or threaten Burgos, where the cord conveniently bends to the west, was Lord Wellington's audacious strategic aim; but before sallying forth he cautiously decided that the prize of Portugal must first be securely locked away, with the keys of Ciudad Rodrigo and Badajoz safe in his pocket for any possible re-entry. The campaign season of 1811 was essentially devoted to his attempts to acquire those vital frontier fortresses, and our penultimate chapter covers his second, again unsuccessful attempt on Badajoz. It was as well that Wellington was a patient man, who could be frustrated by failure but never discouraged; it was all to be a lengthy journey.

This book begin with General Graham's battle against Marshal Victor at Barrosa, outside Cadiz, on 5 March 1811. For the present author it seems an appropriate beginning, since every one of the fourteen French battalions stepping out that day had fought, unsuccessfully, twenty months earlier at Talavera, against his own regiment (helped, of course, by some others, to say nothing of Sir Arthur Wellesley).

Author's Note on Military Designations   The following note is to confirm the styles used here for identifying British and French fighting units, since other conventions exist elsewhere. However, this book is written on the general assumption that the reader is already reasonably familiar with Peninsular operations, rank and staff structures, and terms in common usage.

In this text British infantry units are referred to as either e.g. 'the 48th', or 'the 1/48th', both meaning the 1st Battalion, 48th Regiment of Foot; or as e.g. 'the 2/66th', meaning the 2nd Battalion, 66th Foot. The 43rd, 52nd and 71st Regiments were designated as Light Infantry; the distinction between these and the other regiments lay solely in their training, and the open-order tasks they were sometimes given. (There was no significant difference in the performance of the weapons carried by all these red-coated Regiments of Foot: the Short Land or India patterns of smoothbore flintlock musket - 'Brown Bess'.) In all cases, these references to British infantry units are to a single battalion of ten companies, with an official establishment of approximately 1,000 all ranks. Actual field strengths were often a great deal lower – 500 was considered normal. The green-clad Rifle battalions (5/60th, and 1/, 2/, 3/ and 4/95th) are differentiated in the text; on the battlefield these units, which were armed with Baker rifles of superior accurate range to the Line infantry's musket, were routinely dispersed as skirmishers, sometimes in separate companies.

French infantry regiments are referred to as e.g. 'the 86e Ligne', or '9e Léger', meaning the 86th Regiment of the Line, or the 9th Regiment of Light Infantry. As with the British, the distinction between the two types of regiment was largely nominal and often had little reality on the battlefield. The Line and Light regiment were both officially units of four battalions each of six companies, with a full regimental establishment of just under 4,000 men. In practice regiments fielded only three (or sometimes, two) battalions, and battalion field strengths might be much lower than establishment; but the reader must bear in mind that any mention of, for instance, a single British 'regiment' (always meaning just one of its battalions) confronting a whole French regiment is describing a very unequal encounter.

Two picked companies of each battalion, either British or French, were designated as the 'light' and 'grenadier' companies. Theoretically the rankers for these 'flank' companies were selected from, respectively, the most agile, and the biggest and strongest men available, and their uniforms bore certain distinctions. In the French army these *compagnies d'élite*, and particularly the grenadier companies, might be detached from their parent units and grouped temporarily into composite battalions for tactical purposes. The British Army had routinely done the same in the American Revolutionary War. During the Peninsular War such Flank Battalions were less common, but the light companies of the three battalions in a British brigade might be grouped together temporarily for tactical tasks that required speedy movement and initiative at low levels of command.

Regiments of British light cavalry – Light Dragoons and Hussars – normally had an active service establishment of four squadrons, each of two troops. A regimental establishment was 905 all ranks, but field strength could be much less, depending on sickness, fodder and remounts.

The French light and medium cavalry were designated as either *Chasseurs, Hussards* or *Dragons*. The differences between the first two lay solely in their styles of uniform; both were armed with sabres, holster pistols and carbines. The dragoons carried heavier swords and also muskets; officially capable of fighting as mounted infantry, in practice they were employed in the Peninsula as all-purpose cavalry whose tactical use was almost indistinguishable from that of the light cavalry. In this text the style used for these designations is Roman rather than italic type, capitalized as for English (we assume that readers will not find the style e.g. 26e Dragons too distracting). Like their British counterparts, French cavalry regiments had squadron establishments of about 120 officers and men, and might field four to six squadrons, each of two troops. Again, their actual mounted numbers would fluctuate widely.

*   *   *

One more Charge, and then be Done.
When the Forts of Folly fall,
May the Victor, when He comes,
Find my Body near the Wall.

1
Barrosa, 5 March 1811.

IT is customary to quantify Lord Wellington's great victories in Portugal and Spain either with lists of beaten French generals, or the miles covered, or the numbers of Napoleon's troops put out of action. Thus, according to Sir Charles Oman's meticulous calculations, we can measure success in French casualties lost: at Rolica, 600; Vimiero, 1,800; Oporto, 4,000; Talavera, 7,300; Busaco, 4,600; Barrosa, 2,000; Fuentes d'Oñoro, 2,800; Albuera, 8,300; Ciudad Rodrigo, 2,000; Badajoz, 5,000; Salamanca, no less than 14,000; Vittoria, 8,000; in the Pyrenees, 12,600; at Nivelle, 6,000; Orthez, 4,000; and Toulouse, 3,000. Thus these major engagements alone cost Napoleon some 86,000 Frenchmen and their allies hors de combat - killed, wounded or taken - in the six-year campaign, to which we must add goodness knows how many more thousands lost to disease, starvation, desertion, and the constant attrition inflicted by the local guerrillas.

Those names are the battle honours awarded to the regiments of the Peninsular Field Army, and subsequently carried on their Colours. Yet there is one name missing, the one which accounted for more Frenchmen than any other single action: 'Torres Vedras 1810' - the greatest slayer and incapacitator of the entire war. There was no battle of that name, so there was no battle honour, and consequently it has enjoyed a relative lack of historical attention; it represents operations over several months and a wide stretch of the Portuguese countryside. Yet nearly 25,000 troops were lost to Marshal Massena's parade states as a direct result of the construction, provisioning and defence, through the winter of 1810/11, of that remarkable system of forts around Lisbon - and at negligible expense in British lives (though the 'scorched earth' policy outside the Lines sacrificed those of thousands of Portuguese peasants).

Massena marched into Portugal in September 1810 with 65,050 men (taking Oman's figures); but his strength on 15 April 1811 - a fortnight before notice of his dismissal finally arrived after Fuentes d'Oñoro - was down to 39,546 effectives. Between these dates he had received two reinforcement drafts totaling 3,225 men; and two columns of wounded, numbering together about 3,000, had been sent back to France. Oman's conclusion was that the total loss to Massena was 'just under 25,000 men or 38 per cent of his force'. He also lost nearly 6,000 of his 14,000 horses, and effectively all his wheels – he had a mere thirty-six wagons by the end. Some 2,500 of his men had died in battle, 8,000 had been captured in Coimbra's hospitals in October 1810, and another 4,000 were wounded elsewhere; but the bulk of the remainder were simply starved - starved into weakness, into the hospitals, or to be carved up by the peasantry. Wellington's long-sighted stratagem, set in train only weeks after his escape from Soult in the autumn of 1809, had struck Massena a devastating blow.

How he harried Massena out of Portugal altogether is summarized in the next chapter, but in the months of March and April 1811 these were not the only commanders striving in opposition. Marshals Soult and Beresford also danced to their partners, after a fifth general, Thomas Graham, had acted as the catalyst, which culminated, on 16 May, in their bloody

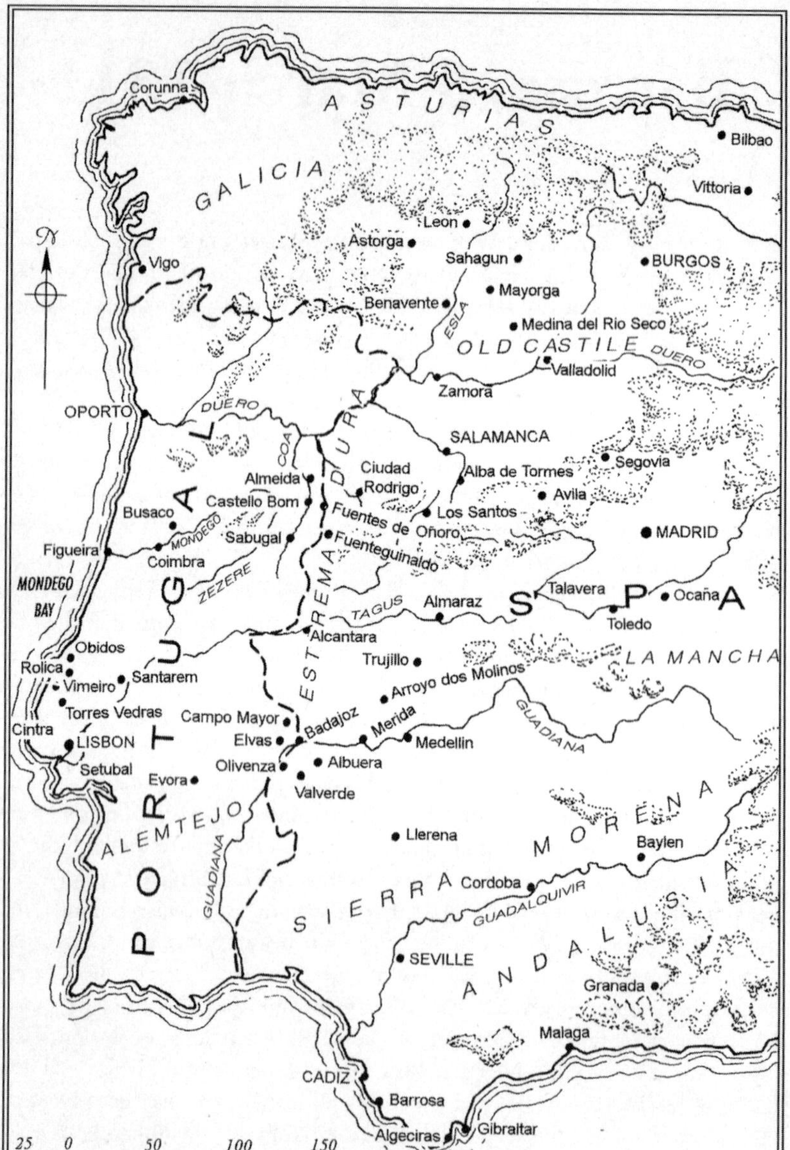

Map 1:
THE PENINSULA, 1811
Note: Only places mentioned in the text and a few
other major cities and features are named here.

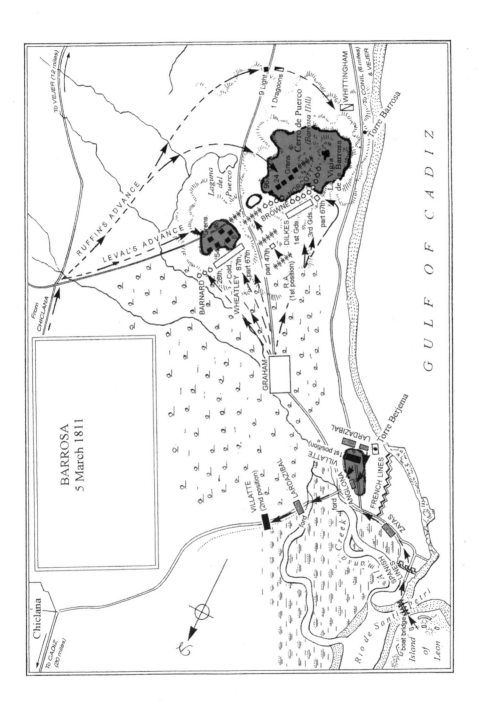

confrontation at Albuera. That he was able to do so arose simply because he happened to command the British garrison in Cadiz.

Of all Napoleon's many army corps in Spain – Victor's 1st around Cadiz, Suchet's 3rd near Tortoga, Sebastiani's 4th in Grenada, Mortier's 5th west of Seville, and Macdonald's 7th up at Gerona – it was Victor's that was mainly relevant to the other four corps that comprised Massena's Army of Portugal. Of course, all these commands were engaged in the work of suppression and looting normal to occupation troops the world over (for which all were paid back in relentless hostility by the local populations, and in a far bloodier coinage by the guerrillas); but most of these deployments were peripheral to the operations of Wellington's Peninsular Field Army. Victor was truly relevant, however, because he was engaged in a task that was acknowledged as hopeless – the blockade of Cadiz – while close enough to Massena's scene of operations to be safely stripped of some fighting units. In January 1811 Marshal Soult collected a force of 20,000 men to invade Estremadura, to take Badajoz and the other fortresses, and generally to come to the aid of Massena's now starving and retreating army. Soult raised most of his infantry from Mortier, but he also took from Victor two full infantry regiments and no less than half of the latter's cavalry; Victor was also required to provide further detachments to inland garrisons. Consequently his strength before Cadiz shrank by a quarter, from 24,000 men to 18,500; and this made him vulnerable, since the necessity of manning the encircling lines meant that if he had to take the field he must do so with fewer than those 18,500 bayonets. Since Mortier had been weakened to an even greater degree, along with the Seville garrison, the next nearest troop reinforcements were at Malaga and Granada, too far to come to Victor's support speedily if his blockade should be seriously threatened.

News of Victor's state was confirmed to the Allied commanders in Cadiz in the first week of 1811. The British had had a garrison there since the previous January, and in the meantime the original three battalions had grown to eight (including two Portuguese), plus two field batteries and two squadrons of the 2nd Hussars of the King's German Legion. General Graham was in command of nearly 6,000 men, which, added to 20,000 Spanish regular and militia troops, now easily outnumbered their besiegers of the French 1st Corps.

The physical situation of Cadiz was such that no land assault was likely to prevail, given that British command of the seas guaranteed provisions and reinforcements. All French efforts to overcome the landward defences - commenced in January 1810, and not finally abandoned until August 1812 - came to nought, while involving a commitment in men, artillery and administrative support that could usefully have been deployed more directly against Wellington's forces. Indeed, it is one of the puzzles of the entire Peninsular War that the French continued to sit outside Cadiz for quite so long. Confident in their near-island fortress, the Allied commanders inside Cadiz now discussed this first chance to strike at the newly vulnerable Victor. The diligence with which the French had maintained their blockading force during the past year suggested that if Victor could indeed be caught napping, this should provoke his further reinforcement, thus weakening French efforts elsewhere in Spain. With Soult now heading north with 20,000 men, including 4,000 cavalry, such an outcome would no doubt be much appreciated by Lord Wellington, who had been sent the captured original of Napoleon's despatch to Soult.

*   *   *

As will quickly become apparent, however, Graham was to fight heavily handicapped by his Spanish opposite number, one General Manuel La Peña - sadly not the world's sharpest military brain, nor the most upright of leaders. His nickname was 'Doña Manuela', and to say that he was irresolute, ambitious, self-serving and inadequate merely scratches the surface; but he was the senior Spanish general in Cadiz, and it was with him that Graham necessarily had to combine in this important joint endeavour.

Thomas Graham himself, although already aged 62, was a very different character. An incident in France twenty years earlier had turned a Scottish landowner and sportsman into a come-lately soldier dedicated to fighting the excesses of the French Revolution and, by extension, Napoleon's armies. While he was bringing the body of his beautiful young wife home for burial following her untimely death in southern France in 1792, the coffin was torn open by drunken Revolutionary officials in search of contraband, and he himself was arrested and nearly killed. His embittered outrage at the disrespectful treatment of his wife's body converted him into an ardent Francophobe and supporter of the war. On his return home he raised the 90th Regiment (Perthshire Volunteers) at his own expense, and from 1794 he served wherever the French could be found. He proved to be a soldier with fire in his belly; promoted major-general after Corunna, he now commanded the Cadiz garrison as a lieutenant-general. Graham would have been amongst the first to propose an expedition against Victor; he was not the sort to sit tamely under siege, especially when there seemed little imminent danger of the defences being challenged.

Cadiz presented really insuperable problems to the attacker. It was situated at the northern end of a 5-mile isthmus, 'in some places not more than a hundred yards across', according to William Surtees. Halfway down, the isthmus was strongly entrenched at the battery of San Ferdinando, and without command of the seas this was Victor's one and only entrance door. Nor was it even that simple: the isthmus was joined to the northern end of the island of Leon, some 7 miles long by 4 miles wide, itself cut off from the mainland of Andalusia by a substantial channel, bordered by salt marshes and crossed by just one bridge of boats. Once this had been removed, and batteries established along the channel to work in conjunction with a fleet of gunboats, it is no surprise that King Joseph – on receiving Victor's report that he could do nothing without boats and heavy artillery – wrote pathetically to his brother 'If Your Majesty could spare the Toulon Fleet, it might usefully be employed here'. That purely rhetorical plea had been made a year before, yet still Victor sat outside Cadiz.

Apart from 3,400 siege artillerymen, sappers and marines, Victor had 2,000 men in three infantry battalions garrisoning the Cadiz lines, and another 30 miles inland – 'towering in the mountains, the dazzling white town of Medina Sidonia shining in the sun' (Surtees) – he had deployed another five battalions, a Chasseur regiment and a field battery under General Cassagne, as left flank protection; a Spanish irregular brigade was making threatening noises in the mountains. These detachments left him with three weak divisions under Ruffin, Leval and Villatte, comprising 9,500 bayonets in seventeen battalions. He had 700 cavalry in two dragoon regiments, and two gun batteries. However, while he was indeed thin on the ground, these infantry units (led by the same divisional commanders) had all fought with Victor against the British at Talavera, twenty months earlier; they were experienced and fit campaigners, well-fed and not weakened by extended marches – although it remained to be seen if they had learnt any tactical lessons at Talavera.

It is not to be doubted, however, that General Graham's soldiers were to labour under some substantial handicaps. They were inferior to Victor's in battle experience and in health and, possibly, even in that vague thing called regimental spirit. By normal British standards Graham's force was quite a hotch-potch, and what he was about to achieve was all the more remarkable because of it. Of his fifty-nine British infantry companies, thirty-eight or two-thirds were organized as four normal Army List battalions, commanded by their own officers and trained over time in familiar groupings; but the other twenty-one companies were combined into provisional or ad hoc battalions put together solely for this operation, which therefore probably lacked the customary unit spirit and cohesion. This was a necessary side-effect from Graham's success in begging reinforcements from General Cameron, commanding on Gibraltar. The only recognizable brigade was Colonel Wheatley's, comprising the eight battalion companies of the 1/28th (Gloucestershire) from the Tarifa garrison, the 2/67th (Hampshire) and the 2/87th (Irish Fusiliers). The other brigade under Dilkes comprised the 2/1st Foot Guards, two companies from the 2/2nd (Coldstream) Guards, three companies from the 2/3rd Guards, and two companies of riflemen from the 2/95th. In addition, Graham constructed two small composite Flank Battalions: that under Lieutenant-Colonel Browne (28th), with the light and grenadier companies from each of the 1/9th (Norfolks), 1/28th and 2/82nd (Prince of Wales Volunteers); and a second under Lieutenant-Colonel Andrew Barnard (95th Rifles), with four companies of riflemen from the 3/95th and the two flank companies from the 2/47th (Lancashire). The rest of the Lancashires garrisoned the Cadiz defences. Finally, Graham also had the two flank companies of the 20th Portuguese; two squadrons of the 2nd Hussars KGL (about 170 troopers, under Major Busche); and two companies (ten guns) under Major Duncan of the Royal Artillery. The force that Graham was to lead against Victor thus represented a temporary coalition of eleven different 'cap-badges'.

More of a practical problem was the question of fitness. One-third of Graham's infantry, and his German hussars, had been among those evacuated, only a year earlier, from the pestilential island of Walcheren on the coast of Holland. Of the 35,000 British troops brought off in February 1810 more than 11,500 had been hospital cases, and we know that reinforcements reaching Wellington in July 1811, a year and a half later, still fell sick in droves from the recurring effects of 'Walcheren fever', whether of the malarial or typhoid type. It was to be hoped that nothing too taxing was on the horizon for these troops; what was proposed in theory should not prove too demanding, involving only a four-day approach march.

As fighting soldiers the French started as odds-on favourites, led by a marshal who had shown his mettle at Marengo, Saalfeld, Jena, Pultusk, Friedland, Ucles, Espinosa, Medellin and Talavera. The bulk of his force were first and second battalions of regiments from the illustrious Grande Armée, and they had more recent battle experience. The whole of Victor's 1st Corps had been blooded at Talavera, whereas only a quarter of Graham's fifty-nine infantry companies had fought on any meaningful Peninsular field. The four companies from the 2/95th Rifles and the 1/9th had been at Rolica and at Vimiero, and the 1/9th companies also at Busaco; all ten companies of the 2/87th had been in the chase after Soult following Oporto, and had fought with Donkin's brigade at Talavera, where they lost a third of their officers and men at the Casa de Salinas. Otherwise – with the the unfortunate exception of the Walcheren experience – Graham's men would be looking forward to their first real outing.

*   *   *

The plan was to land the joint Spanish-British force at the southernmost tip of Spain – at Tarifa not far from Algeciras, across the bay from Gibraltar. It would then march back to the north-west to threaten Victor's rear, and it was supposed that he would respond by moving forward in opposition – whereupon some 4,000 Spanish from the Cadiz garrison were to sally forth to overpower his reduced rear-party, and to destroy his forts and batteries. It was anticipated that the sea-borne movement would comprise 9,600 Spanish (including 1,600 irregulars, joining from the mountains) and 5,000 British. This combined Allied army should outnumber the French comfortably. General Graham ceded command to the Spanish general La Peña, on the grounds of contributing the smaller troop strength; this was correct protocol, but it quickly turned out to be a grave mistake.

Graham set sail on 21 February; powerful winds took his troop convoy past Tarifa to Algeciras, where he disembarked. After a 10-mile march back to Tarifa on the 24th, he assimilated the various companies lent him by Cameron from Gibraltar and Tarifa. The Spanish convoy disembarked on the 26th and 27th; La Peña had organized his expedition into two small divisions, one of five battalions under General Lardizabal, and one of six battalions under the Prince of Anglona. He had fourteen guns, and five squadrons of horse under Major Samuel Whittingham - the same English officer (with the rank of major-general in the Spanish service) who had served General Cuesta at Talavera. In view of what he was about to experience under General La Peña, he could be forgiven for feeling that despite his elevated rank he had made an unlucky choice of foreign employer.

On the last day of February the combined army marched 10 miles to Facinas, with Graham's division moving in reserve; it was agreed to concentrate his two KGL squadrons with Whittingham's five Spanish. At Facinas a choice of tracks now presented itself: one more westerly in from the coast via Vejer, which would lead to the rear of Victor's lines before Cadiz itself, and one more northerly via Casa Viejas and Medina Sidonia. Between the tracks lay the 7-mile plain of La Janda, at this time of year a very shallow lagoon. It was decided, quite rightly, to take the latter track; although not much better for wheeled traffic, this would directly threaten Victor's rearward communications with Seville as well as, by implication, his position before Cadiz. Victor could not but react to any substantial Allied presence around Medina Sidonia, and react quickly; he was unlikely to receive any assistance from General Sebastiani, who was then embroiled with local guerrillas near Marbella, a week's march away. So, on 1 March, Lardizabal's division began the movement forward, reaching on the 2nd the village of Casa Viejas, where they surprised and eventually routed (thanks to Graham's deployment of the 28th's Light Company) two French infantry companies. Overtaken by Whittingham's cavalry, these fired one volley before throwing down their muskets, but they were promptly and mercilessly cut down by the Spanish and German troopers.

General La Peña liked marching at night; but unfortunately, given their long incarceration in Cadiz, neither his staff officers nor his battalions had any recent training or experience in this difficult task. It was not unusual practice in the British Army, especially in hot weather, but because of the uneven terrain and a routine lack of maps and compasses it was restricted to easy or familiar routes. With the Spanish leading, progress by night around the soggy plain of La Janda had been painful, slow and fatiguing – Graham's division took nineteen hours to cover the first 13 miles. He wrote in his diary: 'Marched in the evening, very tedious from filing across water [the stream which fills the head of the lagoon of La Janda] and other difficulties. Misled by the guides on quitting the Cortigo de la Janda [the farm at the head of the lagoon]: the counter-march made a most fatiguing night... It was twelve noon before the troops halted, having been nineteen hours under arms'. They had passed a horribly cold night and morning in a biting easterly wind, and were quite 'done up'.

In the hands of Manuel La Peña the affair now deteriorated, although not yet quite descending into farce. Most generals with nearly 15,000 troops behind them would be warmly satisfied to find General Cassagne's 3,000 men in front of them, a full day's march from home and succour. These represented a quarter of Victor's field force, and could now easily be removed from the equation, leaving Victor with less than 10,000 bayonets in his three weak-ened divisions. Doubtless Victor would march to the rescue, and doubtless there would then be a battle - exactly the originally agreed purpose of the joint expedition. By then, win or lose – and the odds were surely heavily with the Allies – the Cadiz garrison would have blown up the besieging forts and batteries.

Instead, La Peña shied at the hazard before him, his indecision made worse by a report that Cassagne had been reinforced. Seeing only conflicting options, decisions to be made, respon-sibilities to be shouldered, 'Doña Manuela' would have none of it, curiously wilting at the prospect of an easy victory. He ordered the army to remain halted until 5pm, when it was to turn away south-west to Vejer, and there take the alternative coastal track to Cadiz; a battalion detachment and some irregular horse were to stay behind to watch Cassagne.

General Graham's opinion of this extraordinary decision may well be imagined: what factors in this situation could possibly dictate such a course of action? With restraint, he objected only to the prospect of another night march, commencing just five hours after the completion of the previous nineteen-hour ordeal. La Peña agreed only to a six-hour post-ponement – the march would go ahead at 11pm, in full darkness. Then came news that the new track was in any event partially flooded, and La Peña now ordered Graham to move off behind the Spanish at 6am the next morning, 3 March. The column eventually set off at 8am, but progress was slow and soon ground to a halt. By this time all too aware of the drawbacks of trying to act in concert with his allies, Graham galloped to the front of the column, where he found the Spanish hesitating at the edge of a waist-deep flood which rushed through a depression. William Surtees of the 95th Rifles wrote: 'I rode forward to ascertain the cause of our stopping for so long a time. The Spanish were going into the water one at a time – here one, and there one – while the creatures of officers were making the men carry them on their backs'.

Such lack of resolution could not be allowed to waste yet more hours out of the day: Graham called up the British guns and an escort of the 95th, whom he sent straight into the water and across in sections, as if on parade. 'My battalion led the van,' wrote Surtees, 'and marched right through it as if it had been plain ground, the water taking them generally about mid-deep. The rest of the British army followed, and were all through in less than half an hour; a one-horse cart stuck fast in the middle' - and Graham and his staff officers threw themselves off their horses, to put shoulders to the wheels. All this was watched by the increas-ingly shame-faced Spanish, who at last deigned to press on regardless. 'I set the example of going into the water,' Graham wrote in his diary, 'which was followed by Lacy, the Prince of Anglona, and others. The passage lasted three hours, and would have taken double that time but for the exertions made to force the men to keep the files connected.'

It was not until midnight on the 3rd that the column reached Vejer - fifteen hours to cover 12 miserable miles. The two legs of the march, overnight on 1/2 March and then on the 3rd, had taken a combined thirty-four hours to get forward 25 miles. (The actual distance marched would have been much greater, of course: a gruelling physical effort that sapped the strength of the fittest, never mind those who were still 'not right' after Walcheren.)

*   *   *

Victor's men – their shoes and muscles still quite intact – had yet to bestir themselves. He had received Cassagne's report concerning La Peña's approach to Casas Viejas late on 2 March; nearly two days later, before dawn on the 4th, he received a second contact report from the dragoon squadron on outpost duty at Vejer. Both reports specified large numbers of enemy, but 12 miles and a day apart. So were there two axes of advance? If not, why had the dangerous thrust towards Medina Sidonia – his greatest fear – not developed, but diverted to the south? It was a puzzle Victor no doubt shared with Graham. And in between the two reports, on the night of 2/3 March, the Spanish garrison, in accordance with the timetable laid down by La Peña before he set sail, had made their effort on Victor's forts and batteries. General Zayas could not know that La Peña was three marches away at Casa Viejas (the latter's counter-manding orders arrived only the next day); so, as arranged, he built the bridge of boats across the Santi Petri channel, and ran a battalion over to the mudflats on the isthmus facing the French entrenchments. They constructed a strong *tête-du-pont*, covered throughout by the many heavy guns on the island of Leon.

Determined to remove this thorn in his flesh, and lured by the possibility of capturing the bridge, the next night Victor made a last-light assault with six picked companies. The Spanish battalion was duly annihilated and 300 prisoners were taken; but the bridge was recovered by Zayas, at the cost of two sunken boats. It was now clear to Victor that the sally had gone off at half-cock, and could only have been part of some wider plan, presumably an attempt upon his rear along the coast road. Assuming that Victor knew his Spanish opponents' skills, he would doubtless have agreed with the view expressed by Robert Blakeney of the 28th: 'The proceedings of Zayas and [La Peña] offer a correct specimen of the manner in which combined movements were executed by Spanish generals; all acted independently and generally in direct opposition to one another.'

Victor's plan for dealing with La Peña was for Villatte's division – of five battalions, 2,500 bayonets in all – to sit as a blocking anvil across the Allied approach road from the south. The position chosen was just south of the junction with the road going north-east to Chiclana, 4 miles away, where Ruffin's and Leval's twelve battalions would be located. Their 6,400 infantry and 400 horse were to be the hammer; concealed by the thick woods between the coast road and Chiclana, they would advance south-westwards to fall upon the Allied flank. The Allies were expected, naturally, to make their approach up the coast road. Once contact with Villatte had occurred, the latter was immediately to withdraw a little way north on the Chiclana road, so that the anvil would not become caught between the advancing Allies and Zayas debouching from the Spanish lines. From Medina Sidonia, Cassagne was to rejoin Victor on the morning of 5 March, unless he could confirm that a substantial enemy force was still outside Casas Viejas.

This was a typically bold plan by Victor, particularly since he was misinformed as to the strength of his enemy: he understood there to be 26,000 in the joint army – 18,000 Spanish and 8,000 British (which was roughly twice the actual odds against him). Yet he was facing them with less than 10,000 men, rising to 13,000 should Cassagne get up in time. It may be, of course, that he did not feel outnumbered: perhaps he was making a judgement on the likely contribution of Spanish leadership, based on his experience at Medellin, Talavera and assorted lesser affairs.

First, La Peña had to lead his force into the trap Victor had prepared. He had arrived at Vejer at midnight on 3/4 March, and now decided upon his third consecutive night march, to commence at 5pm on the 4th. Graham thought he had persuaded his ally to go only the 8 miles to Conil so as not to weary the troops further, with a fight in prospect; such a short march could hardly go wrong even at night, for the road to Conil was easy to follow. It would take the Allies within 9 miles of General Zayas, and allow the opportunity for a timely reconnaissance on 5 March. But La Peña appeared to change his mind; on arrival at Conil, instead of halting he pressed his advance guard to hasten further – and of course a wrong turn was taken, towards Chiclana rather than Cadiz. The mistake was not discovered until dawn, by which time the head of the Allied column had gone several miles astray. Thomas Graham recorded the scene in his diary:

> Soon after it being reported that our columns were misled and were marching on Chiclana instead of keeping nearer the coast, I halted them [his battalions] and galloped on. Found they had followed the Spaniards, and coming up to the head saw the whole staff in the greatest confusion, from the contradictions of the guides. I could not help exclaiming rather improperly, *'Voila ce que c'est que les marches de nuit'* ['That's what comes of marching by night']. After some further rather ludicrous scenes of distress, several people of the country agreeing that a path to the left led through the heath towards Santa Petri, and that, the country being dry, the guns could move in all directions over the plain, it was agreed that the march could continue as I had originally recommended, by a flank movement left in front, forming lines of columns, the cavalry and rearguard on the right in first line, and so on. Our columns closed up, and the army proceeded in this way across the extensive heathy plain of Chiclana, making a remarkably pretty field day.

Accordingly, the force eventually came in sight of the beach to the west. The cavalry reported no enemy on Barrosa Hill, which dominated the coast road, but what looked like a strong brigade on a lesser feature 3 miles on – this, of course, was Villatte, at the road junction a mile and a half east of the site of the bridge of boats over the Santi Petri. As can be seen from the map, a wooded rise covers most of the half-mile width of the isthmus there, between the tower of Bermeja and the Almansa Creek. There Villatte's five battalions blocked any further progress, their flanks secured on the sea and the mudflats. The invitation was plain: if you want to come through, you must move us.

It was now some hours after first light. The previous five days had been spent covering a mere 50 miles, mostly in darkness, effectively in three marches lasting nineteen, fifteen and fourteen hours respectively. Had Graham's advice to halt the day before at Conil been heeded, a good night's rest and a two-hour daylight march up the 6 miles of coast road from there would have achieved the same concentration without a debilitating fourteen-hour diversion across country. Now there was no time to rest; there was a battle to be fought, and La Peña sent Lardizabal's leading division straight at Villatte.

It was 9am; Graham's battalions were just arriving on Barrosa Hill to the south, 3 miles behind Lardizabal's point. A patrol of German hussars went off to scout eastwards through the woods towards Chiclana. The British companies dropped packs, loosened their neckcloths, got out their waterbottles and sank to the sand; if the Spaniards were going in to bat first, good luck to them. The ripple of musketry came down the beach, echoing off the woods to the right.

Lardizabal's five battalions were exchanging fire with Villatte's five (we may assume line to line, since no record has come down to us); each suffered about 10 per cent casualties, or some 300 men. La Peña then reinforced with the leading brigade from Prince Anglona's division; and as General Zayas launched his bridge of boats again with excellent timing, Villatte wisely pulled away north-eastwards as planned. He crossed the ford over the Almansa Creek, and next to a mill beside the road he turned about to offer a new front, overlooking the mudflats. La Peña, perhaps disliking a wet deployment, made no further attempt to challenge Villatte. He had linked up with Zayas, and had thus secured a safe route back into Cadiz.

The forts and batteries could now be demolished at leisure, and at about noon La Peña sent word to Graham for the British to march from Barrosa to join him at Bermeja, Villatte's former position; presumably he was becoming nervous about having his army in two halves, separated by a 3-mile stretch of rocks and sand and with the sea at their backs – two other enemy divisions were as yet unlocated, and he had omitted to reconnoitre the wooded slopes above the coast road. But this order to close made no sense to General Graham, sitting as he was on the one dominating feature for miles around. If he gave it up, Victor could take it, effectively bottling the Allies between the sea, the woods and Almansa Creek, with nowhere to go but back into Cadiz. Graham had come out of Cadiz specifically to find and destroy the French, and all this unfortunate night marching must not be for nothing. He did not fear the 3-mile gap between himself and the Spanish, for any French force entering it to attack one half of the army could be taken in rear by the other. Besides, all the Spanish backpacks had been dropped off on the hill, and the army's baggage also lay there.

When he made these points to La Peña, a temporary compromise was agreed: a strong joint force would continue to hold Barrosa Hill, but only while Graham brought the rest of his battalions to join La Peña at Bermeja. Five Spanish battalions and Lieutenant-Colonel Browne's Flank Battalion would remain on the hill, while Whittingham's five squadrons of Spanish horse used the coast road. At mid-day Graham set off northwards through the pinewoods along a direct track. This was the alternative route from Conil, which passed across a low saddle on the eastern end of the Barrosa feature. It had earlier served Lardizabal's guns, so it was well marked and proven for wheels. Colonel Wheatley's brigade led, followed by Dilkes', then Duncan and his guns, then the Rifles and Lancashires of Lieutenant-Colonel Barnard, and a rearguard of two companies of the 2/95th Rifles under Lieutenant-Colonel Amos Norcott. Inside the woods visibility was very limited.

Presumably Marshal Victor's mental visibility was also somewhat clouded. We must remember that he believed he faced some 26,000 men, and at this stage – around 12.30pm – the numbers just did not add up. Cassagne reported no substantial grouping around Medina Sidonia (but also broke the bad news that he could not join for another two or three hours); Villatte reported some 3,000 Spaniards opposite the mill on the creek, and a like number around Bermejas; his cavalry reported that Barrosa Hill was lightly held, but not by the British (the redcoats of Browne's battalion were taking their rest on the reverse or southern slopes); and that the British who had earlier been seen on the hill were now moving through the wood, heading for the Spanish, actually across his front. These four reported bodies could not begin to total 26,000 men. Either his earlier estimates were wrong, or there was an uncommitted Allied force, conceivably on 'the other side of the hill'. Ever mindful of his Emperor's skill in striking suddenly at divided enemies before they could come together, Victor now decided not only to seize Barrosa Hill, but simultaneously to attack the elongated British column to his front.

*   *   *

His orders were firstly to the 1er Dragons, to get round the southern or seaward end of Barrosa Hill and seize the coast road; secondly, to Ruffin, to climb the eastern slopes; and thirdly to Leval, to take on the main body in the wood. He urged them not to lose a minute – once the latter had closed on the Spaniards at Bermeja the opportunity would be lost.

On the southern slopes of Barrosa, overlooking the coast road, 'Mad John' Browne's temporary battalion of six flank companies were now fast asleep. The German hussars, their horses with slack girths, were likewise dozing around the wagons containing the reserve ammunition – smoking, looking at horseshoes and feeling tendons. Commissary Henegan recalled: 'The men stretched themselves at ease on the slopes of the hill... We had been twenty hours under arms, and upwards of seventeen on the march, during which time no man had tasted food beyond the dry biscuit that his haversack contained, nor had one drop of brandy from his canteen revived exhausted nature on the wearisome route... throwing themselves in every direction on the green sward... the hussars dismounting for the same purpose, loosened the girths of their horses... slumber seemed at once to seal the eyes of the weary objects that lay around in profound repose.' La Peña himself was also sitting on his horse close by, together with his subordinate brigadiers Cruz Murgeon and Beguines, doubtless positioning the five Spanish battalions he had loaned. At that moment, without warning, a German hussar galloped over the crest: the French were coming! From the east – straight at us!

It is said that Ruffin's six battalions, on Marshal Victor's orders, were in full uniform of blue and red – an imposing sight even without the movement and colour of the three green-coated, brass-helmeted dragoon squadrons at their head, now cantering away to their flank and clearly hooking round to the very beach next to the wagons. All was pandemonium on the road and the slopes above; General La Peña set an unfortunate example, shouting and panicking, which quickly spread amongst his troops. Accompanied by a few shots from the two guns that he had placed on the hilltop (and which were promptly abandoned), there was much confused shouting of orders and scrabbling for packs and muskets. Shoes were retied, men jostled each other as they fell in, officers called for their horses; the hussars vaulted into the saddle, easing their sabres and tightening the chinstraps of their fur caps. La Peña or Cruz Murgeon (it is not clear which) immediately gave the order to retreat upon Cadiz – and without informing Colonel Browne of his intention. His five battalions closed up any-old-how on to the coast road, along with the baggage column, and stepped out hurriedly, spread across the rough track and the rocks and sand either side. Whittingham deployed his squadrons across the track just beyond the old lookout tower, to face the three French squadrons now thundering closer.

Lieutenant-Colonel Browne, aghast at the panic, tried to persuade Whittingham – as an officer in the Spanish service – to halt the abandonment of the heights; then he took his battalion up to the ruined chapel on the hill, preparing to make a fight of it by loop-holing the walls. However, when he saw the Spanish, covered by Whittingham's horse, hurrying north towards Cadiz, Browne gave up his untenable position. As Ruffin's six battalions swung right to climb the slopes, Browne set out to catch up with General Graham along the wooded track. Ruffin's approach march had swept wide to the south of a marshy area called the Laguna del Puerco; his two brigades came up in a single column of double companies, guns in the rear.

Another version of this confused story (retailed in General Whittingham's memoirs) has it that Browne was the first to flee, and that in his absence Whittingham actually got two Spanish battalions up on to the hilltop and two more down by the watchtower, where they drove away the first French dragoons plundering some of the baggage train. The most southerly of Ruffin's battalions was the 2/9e Léger who, according to Whittingham's version, pushed back this Spanish rearguard commanded by Beguines as far as the Casa de las Guardias, half way to Bermeja.

Be that as it may, it is certain that as Ruffin climbed the south-eastern slopes, Browne's battalion descended north-westerly, and were charged by a dragoon squadron. They quickly formed square – which says much for universal drills, since they were six companies from three different regiments – and prepared to volley. 'Be steady, my boys,' cried Colonel Browne; 'Reserve your fire till they are within ten paces, and they will never penetrate you.' At that moment, however, Major Busche's squadron of KGL hussars charged past the corner of the British square into the French dragoons and broke through them – Commissary Henegan again: 'so impetuous was the movement, that before the French could recover from the shock, the Germans had reined in their horses, wheeled round, and again broke the enemy's disordered line. The French dispersed in every direction'. Across in the pinewoods, according to the Rifle Brigade's historian:

> A sergeant of the German Hussars came galloping along the track through the forest and overtaking Norcott, who with his rearguard of Riflemen had marched about half a mile into the wood, asked for the British General, saying that the French were in great force on the right and were pushing on to seize the Barrosa ridge in rear. Norcott directed the sergeant to the head of the column and turning his men to the right-about, extended them over a front of about 600 yards and advanced through the fir trees towards the French. When Graham received word... he was at the head of his main body considerably over a mile and a half from the outskirts of the pine woods. He at once gave the order 'Right about face! Form as you can!' and galloped back.

Colonel Browne of the Flank Battalion entered the pinewood at a canter, well ahead of his companies, and not far into their shade he met Thomas Graham hurrying out. Having already turned his column, 'in order to support', as he wrote in his Despatch, 'the troops left for its [Barrosa Hill's] defence and believing the General [La Peña] to be there in person', Browne's appearance, and beyond him the sight of his battalion marching away from the foot of Barrosa, horrified Graham. The key position had been abandoned, and he knew now that he should never have left it. On clearing the treeline he could also see the retreating Spanish to his far right; the blue blocks of Ruffin's battalions moving on Barrosa; and Leval's up the track to his left, less than half a mile distant 'on the plain, on the edge of the wood, within cannon-shot'. The two French divisions had clearly marched divided, separated one from the other by about a mile, and were not yet reunited. Like Victor an hour earlier, Graham instantly saw the slimmest of chances to engage his enemies separately. The only alternative – to retreat upon the Spanish – seemed to be a recipe for a vulnerable disorder; it could lead at worst to defeat on the field, at best to an ignominious withdrawal into Cadiz. As he later wrote in his diary: 'A retreat in the face of the enemy who was already in reach of the easy communications by the sea-beach, must have involved the whole Allied army in the danger of being attacked during the unavoidable confusion, while the different corps would be arriving on the narrow bridge of Bermeja at the same time.'

Did Graham feel confident that he would not be alone in his attempt to retake the hill? He had left La Peña on Barrosa not half an hour since, and could surely count on at least some part of the Spanish force also marching towards the sound of the guns. The bayonet odds were three-to-two in Victor's favour (6,400 to 4,400); but both French divisions were on the march in columns, not drawn up in stationary lines, and nor were they expecting to be attacked. Against that, Graham had time neither for any reconnaissances by his subordinates nor for the issuing of any comprehensive orders; he had an inadequate view of the ground; his column was inside out, having been turned about hastily; and there was not much stamina left in his men.

It was a desperate decision, which a lesser man would have shirked: to attack a superior force in these fluid circumstances required the utmost confidence in the troops and vice versa. But that confidence might be misplaced, given the *ad hoc* groupings of the companies: take away many of the men's regimental commanders, and their Colours, and bundle them up with other cap-badges, and they might not pull their best together. In the main these troops were inexperienced in battle, and their enemies were veterans. It remained to be seen whether it would matter.

*   *   *

The more urgent of the two British attacks was that against Leval; Ruffin was already on the hill, and was not going anywhere. Graham had to gain time for his battalions to form; they would come out of the woods piecemeal, but must be committed together, in line and at the right angle. That meant stopping Leval quickly while they sorted themselves out. Fortunately, the nearest unit on the track was Andrew Barnard's Flank Battalion of four companies of the 3/95th Rifles and two companies of Colonel Bushe's 20th Portuguese – some 700 rifles and muskets – and these were ordered left off the track in the wood. Clearing the edge and shaking out into extended order, they saw Leval's six battalions not more than 400 yards away. It must have been a daunting sight for 700 men busy getting into a thin double line: Leval had 4,050 in two large columns, each of three battalions one behind the other, each column seventy-two men wide and twenty-seven men deep. Allowing a modest space between the two columns, their joint frontage might have been 200 yards across from end to end.

The near column comprised the 1/54e Ligne, then its 2e Bataillon, then a battalion of grenadier companies; in the further column were the 1/8e, then the 2/8e, then the 1/45e Ligne. Leval's gun battery was to his left rear. Andrew Barnard on his charger led his 400 greenjackets into the open to face the 54e Ligne, with Colonel Bushe's blue-coated Portuguese a little to his right opposite the 8e. Fire was opened early, to the great astonishment of the French; they had no skirmishers out in advance, and with no warning they took the galling fire immediately into their massed ranks. With the dark wood looming behind the crackle and smoke of 700 firelocks, which were undoubtedly getting closer, the French were confused and taken aback.

The commanding officer of the 2/8e, Vigo-Roussillon, says that a false alarm of cavalry was raised, so both battalions of his regiment and the 1/54e in error formed squares. These temporarily presented an admirable target not only to the riflemen, but also to Major Duncan's artillery pieces, which had by now cleared the wood. Seeing the situation at a glance, Duncan had immediately unlimbered and opened fire with common shell. This unnecessary and time-wasting formation of French squares was a marvellous bonus for Barnard, Bushe and Wheatley. It was probably caused by a misreading of Duncan's battery emerging into the open; ten guns meant eighty horses, and at the sight of the dust that that number would kick up, an apprehensive shout of 'Cavalry!' might easily go up. William Surtees, serving with the 95th in Barnard's battalion, described what he saw on leaving the woods:

When we reached the plain, and perceived the enemy, never did a finer sight present itself. They were manoeuvring on the high ground before us. Those immediately in front of my battalion were the famed 8th Regiment, and consisted of two battalions of 700 men each; one was composed of grenadiers, and the other of voltigeurs, or light infantry. The grenadiers had long waving red plumes in their caps, at least a foot in length; while the light infantry had feathers of the same length and make, but green, with yellow tops. The whole of the French army had on their best or holiday suits of clothing, with their arms as bright as silver, and glancing in the sun as they moved in column, gave them a really noble and martial appearance. We had no sooner cleared the wood than we inclined to our left, and immediately went at them. Major Duncan's guns commenced playing upon their column the moment he could get a clear piece of ground. The two companies of the 47th, attached to my battalion, were taken to cover and remained with the guns. Our people extended as we went up the hill, the Portuguese supporting us in the rear; and in a very short space of time we were hotly engaged with the fellows with the beautiful green feathers, many of which fell to the ground in a short time. As we advanced, the battalions to our right and in rear of us got formed in line, and moving forward in fine style, took up stronger ground in advance; the guns in the centre also moving onward, and causing dreadful havoc in the enemy's ranks.

Early in the action my horse was killed, being shot in the head, which ball, had his head not stopped it, would in all probability have entered my body. He fell like a stone. I then went on and joined the ranks, and finding a rifle of a man just fallen, (poor little Croudace's servant, who afterwards fell himself), I took a few shots at them in revenge for my horse. At this time the grenadier battalion of the 8th, with their waving red plumes, began to advance in close column, the drums beating all the time the *pas de charge*. They were supported by other columns in their rear, together with one, the French 54th, which they sent into the wood to try to turn our left. The 8th advanced, notwithstanding the galling fire kept up by our people and the Portuguese, every shot of which must have told, as they were in a solid body, not more than from 100 to 150 yards distance. Our people were of course compelled to give way to this imposing column.

The accurate and effective fire from the 95th, the Portuguese and the gunners were signal enough to Leval that he had indeed arrived upon Marshal Victor's chosen enemy in the woods. He accordingly swung right-handed from the track and started to deploy into his fighting formation and, in so doing, justified Graham's near-suicidal use of Barnard's battalion. For it all took time, during which Colonel Wheatley was able to get his brigade into assault formation along the edge of the wood.

The 20th Portuguese behaved particularly well, given that this was their first time in action. They had been in Cadiz as garrison troops ever since being raised in 1809, so to find themselves facing an advancing French division was a sharp contrast. For two companies to hold their ground, and keep off a French battalion for several long minutes, was commendable. Only when their commanding officer, Lieutenant-Colonel Bushe, was mortally wounded did they become a little shy and drift to the rear; and indeed, Barnard's riflemen also had to fall back, for with the French deployment completed Leval was advancing. Barnard himself had been wounded, with another sixty-four of his men, and a like number of the Portuguese – 121 men killed and wounded between the six companies deployed, or about one in every six men who had left the wood.

Wheatley's time had come. Leval had broadened his front and turned it to face the wood. He had four of his six Line battalions in line, two in reserve, and each of the four was in column of double companies: about seventy-two men wide and nine men deep. From his right to left they were the 1/54e, 2/54e, 2/8e and 1/8e – a frontage of 288 men or some 400 yards of ground, with his guns coming into action to the left. Leval's men had been at Talavera twenty months before: the 8e and 54e Ligne were in Lapisse's division south of the Medellin, and in the second wave attack they helped successfully, if temporarily, to rout both the 1/2nd (Coldstream) Guards and the 1/3rd Guards, until themselves held and beaten by the redoubtable 1/48th (Northamptonshire). Here at Barrosa the 8e and 54e Ligne, by a nice coincidence, were directly opposite the two companies of the Coldstream.

Barnard's riflemen and Bushe's Portuguese had given Wheatley time to sort himself out, before being pushed aside by Leval's advancing columns, and Duncan's guns continued to do considerable damage. Wheatley's line was adjacent to the guns, which were protected by the two flank companies of the 2/47th. Right of the line were the five right wing companies of the 2/67th under Lieutenant-Colonel Prevost; then the 2/87th under Major Gough; then the two companies of the 2/2nd (Coldstream) Guards under Lieutenant-Colonel Jackson, with the eight battalion companies of the 1/28th under Colonel Belson on the left of the line. Altogether Wheatley had some 1,557 bayonets, of which the 87th comprised nearly half and the 28th a quarter. Barnard's riflemen from the 3/95th formed up behind the 28th, the Portuguese behind the 87th.

'*Marchez! En avant!*' The French line of columns was a little ragged as it advanced down the slight slope. They fired as they came, using independent fire except for the 2/8e Ligne, which fired volleys by order; that unit thus made slightly better progress than the other three, and gradually forged ahead. The drums beat the *pas de charge*, pausing to let the men shout '*Vive l'Empereur!*' It is worth trying to picture the scene.

If it is correct to estimate, from standard drills, that Leval's frontage was 288 men or some 400 yards of ground, then they were confronted by a far wider red line stretching right across their front. Wheatley's 1,557 men (not counting the riflemen or Portuguese) would have a frontage of around 800 yards. Surtees says of the French 8e that 'They never yet got into line, nor did they ever intend to do so, I believe, but advanced as solid bodies, occasionally firing from their front.' It is said that the 2/54e, who were opposite the 28th (Gloucesters), did attempt to deploy from column of divisions (double companies) into line; but it was the 2/8e, with their slightly advanced position, who first made contact – unfortunately for them, with the Irish 87th. Colonel Vigo-Roussillon of the 2/8e said that they closed within 60 yards of the 87th; Major Gough, who was out ahead of his Irish Fusiliers and therefore feeling devilish close anyway, said it was 25 yards; both said that they held their men's fire to that point, whereupon one single volley thundered out from either side. Gough's men hammered away at least 664 balls, the battalion's bayonet strength, and probably many more (most would have loaded double balls); the French could only fire perhaps 200, from the first three ranks.

The 87th immediately charged, and the 8e recoiled behind the heaps of their dead and wounded; they would have broken, if there had been room to run, but they found themselves jammed by their sister battalion. The 1/8e in turn were routed by the guns and the five companies of the 67th, who were firing into their head and left flank. So the 1er and 2e Bataillons of the 8e Ligne, some 1,200 effectives before the volleys and now perhaps nearer 900, were dying together. 'As they were in column when they broke,' wrote Major Gough, 'they could not get away. It was therefore a scene of most dreadful carnage.' As the French had advanced, Duncan's guns likewise had moved up 600 yards to a second position, and their shrapnel shell and grapeshot were now truly destructive.

It is not clear to what extent the five companies of the 67th on Gough's right, and the two companies of the 2/2nd Coldstream on his left, joined in this furious bayonet fight. Fortescue says General Graham himself (on foot, his horse being shot from under him) led the Coldstream, shouting out, 'Men! Cease firing and charge!', and that they and the 87th charged together. However, Lieutenant Wright Knox of the 87th, writing two days after the battle (in an unpunctuated stream of memory that marvellously catches the rush of events), stated that the Coldstream were behind the 87th because

> General Graham... the bravest old fellow ever went into the field... after [we were] firing some time, gave us the order to charge... he followed our Regiment down waving his hat... we advanced rapidly accompanied or rather supported (for they were in rear of us) by two Companies of the Guards, they [the French] continued firing briskly on us and stood firmly until we were within 8 or 10 yards of them when finding they were not able to turn us, and without attempting to stand the Charge, they gave way, then commenced a scene of slaughter, all the Officers of the 8th French Regiment with some of the men got about the Eagle, and tried to get off with it, they were pursued by our men, here they made some resistance and every man of them was cut off, we returned over part of the field amidst shouts of victory from our soldiers glorying in exposing their bayonets covered with blood, but along with this we were obliged to hear the cries of thousands of wounded crying out for mercy. General Graham met us on the return, shaked hands with Colonel Gough, halted the Regiment and thanked them for deciding the fate of the day.

Hugh Gough had had 664 bayonets, the 67th had 260 and the Guards another 200. The French were 900 or less after the volleys, so if the Irish had help it was scarcely an even match. As always, their fighting spirit was formidable; they tore into the packed blue ranks with gusto, the mêlée lasting (according to Gough) about a quarter of an hour: 'Confused and flying as they were... they seemed so confounded and so frightened... they made while we were amongst them little or no opposition.' Colonels Autie and Lanusse were killed, Vigo-Roussillon wounded and taken; their total casualties were 726, or a shockingly high 50 per cent of the regiment's parade state that morning. The Irish were in no mood to take prisoners, it seems: there were only nineteen.

The 87th (Irish Fusiliers) took something much more precious, however: the Eagle standard of the 8e Ligne, which had been in the keeping of the 1er Bataillon. The colour party struggled heroically to keep it safe in the crush, but one of the 87th's subalterns, Ensign Keogh, slashed his way through and actually got a hand on the pike-staff before being killed (according to Oman, by two bayonet thrusts). His fellow subaltern, Lieutenant Knox, had a different version: 'Poor Ensign Kough was killed attempting to seize the Eagle, he was a very good fellow, and an excellent soldier, I was within 2 or 3 yards of him when he fell, the ball went through his heart, it was instant death.' Sergeant Patrick Masterson then skewered the standard-bearer, Sous-lieutenant Edme Guillemin, with his 9ft sergeant's pike; he seized the Eagle, allegedly with the immortal words 'Bejabers, boys, I have the cuckoo!', and made it his own – the first French regimental Eagle captured in the Peninsula, after two and a half years of war. Major Gough wrote: 'This sergeant never let it out of his hand until he delivered it to me, and afterwards carried it the remainder of the day between our Colours.' In due course it was taken to London and presented to the Prince Regent, who granted the 87th the right to bear an eagle and a laurel wreath above the harp on their Colours, and the title of the Prince of Wales's Own Irish Regiment. Masterson received a commission, and Gough was made brevet lieutenant-colonel. And many noticed the coincidence that enlivens this story of the 87th and the 8e Ligne's Eagle, as expressed by William Surtees:

> They [the 8e] were one of the regiments, it is said, which were engaged at Talavera, and were particularly distinguished; and it is further said, that the 87th was one of the regiments opposed to them, and over which they gained some advantage; that is, the French troops caused the British brigade, in which the 87th were serving, to retire with considerable loss; and that it was for their conduct in this action that Bonaparte had placed a golden wreath of laurel round the neck of the regimental eagle with his own hand. If such was the case, it is most remarkable that the very regiment by whom they should have obtained this honour, should be the regiment that deprived them of their eagle, which had been so highly honoured.

*   *   *

In the midst of this orgy of killing, Major Gough's attention was drawn by General Graham to the approach of Leval's reserve left wing battalion, the 1/45e Ligne.

> 'At this moment (when we could have taken or destroyed the whole 8th regiment,) the 47th [sic] French regiment came down on our right, and General Graham who was, during the whole of the action, in the midst of it, pointed them out and begged I would call off my men (I will not say "Halt" as we were in the midst of the French). With the greatest of difficulty by almost cutting them down, I got the right wing collected, with which we came to within about fifty paces of them, they (for us, fortunately) broke and fled, for had they done their duty, fatigued as my men were, at the moment, they must have cut us to pieces. We were therefore, after they broke, unable to follow them, but took the howitzer attached to them.'

One has to admire Gough's success in extracting five of his companies for this task, given the circumstances, and it says much for his company officers that their orders to disengage were obeyed by their excited men.

The French 45e, perhaps remembering their rough handling at Talavera, and with ten enemy companies now lapping around them (five 87th, five 67th), could be forgiven their lack of response to Leval's order to reinforce failure. Since these 700 men suffered only 55 casualties, among whom there was but a single officer, we may surmise that the battalion had been thoroughly demoralized by the collapse of the 8e right in front of them. And things were no better on Leval's right. At least the right hand of his two battalions of the 54e Ligne actually tried to manoeuvre, to turn Wheatley's left; curiously, however, having moved well out to approach via the woods, it took no further recorded part in the action – it either lost its way, or possibly was penned into the pinewoods by Barnard's riflemen and Bushe's Portuguese. Surtees says that 'The 54th by some means got entangled (in the woods); for, except their light company, no part of the regiment ever got into action again.' So the 2/54e was left alone, to face Lieutenant-Colonel Charles Belson's eight battalion companies of the 1/28th. One of his officers, the 21-year-old Captain Charles Cadell, wrote in his memoirs:

> We had formed line under cover of the 95th, and then advanced to meet [the French] right wing, which was coming down in close column – a great advantage – and here the coolness of Colonel Belson was conspicuous: he moved us up without firing a shot, close to their right battalion, which just then began to deploy. The Colonel then gave orders to fire by platoons from centre to flanks, and low; 'Fire at their legs and spoil their dancing.' This was kept up for a short while, with dreadful effect. The action now being general all along the line, we twice attempted to charge. But the enemy, being double our strength (since our flank companies were away), only retired a little on each occasion. Finally, giving three cheers, we charged a third time, and succeeded: the enemy gave way and fled in every direction... They had been beaten in every part of the field.

Compared to the 50 per cent casualties suffered by the 8e Ligne, it might seem that those of the 54e, at 24 per cent, were relatively light. However, if it is true that the 1er Bataillon in the wood was but little engaged, then the brunt of the regimental total of 323 casualties fell to the 2e Bataillon, which would be approaching half its strength. The remnants staggered back behind Leval's only remaining intact battalion – the composite right wing reserve of grenadier companies under Colonel Meunier – and joined the survivors of the 8e and 45e Ligne a little to the south-east of the track back to Chiclana. Wheatley had won. Compared to Leval's losses of 1,104 all ranks, his own casualties totaled 510, plus about another twenty for the wing of the 67th. Of the total, 173 belonged to the 87th, 137 to Barnard's riflemen and eighty-six to the 28th. It had been an action entirely reminiscent of Vimiero and Talavera: a defensive success again marked by British (Irish) readiness to offer the bayonet, and French reluctance to accept the challenge.

*   *   *

It is now necessary to turn the clock back an hour and a half to the commencement of this short, intense action, to see how Leval's fellow divisional commander Ruffin, who had just arrived on the top of Barrosa Hill, fared against Brigadier Dilkes.

As already recounted, 'Mad John' Browne and General Graham met just inside the wood. According to Browne's adjutant, Robert Blakeney, Graham greeted the colonel angrily: 'Browne, did I not give you orders to defend Barrosa Hill?' 'Yes, Sir,' said Browne, 'but you would not have me fight the whole French army with 470 men?' Graham was unimpressed: 'Had you not five Spanish battalions, together with artillery and cavalry?' 'Oh!' replied Browne, 'they all ran away long before the enemy came within cannon-shot.' Graham considered for a moment. 'It is a bad business, Browne; you must turn around immediately and attack.' 'Very well,' replied Browne. 'Am I to attack in extended order as flankers, or as a close battalion?' 'In open order,' said Graham, before returning to his troops in the woods. He must have reflected that while a line of skirmishers could hold Leval in check until Wheatley had deployed, something more was needed to occupy Ruffin, considering that Dilkes' brigade had farther to march before they could come into action; so he rode back to Browne, to order a manoeuvre that both must have known was hopeless. 'I must show something more serious than skirmishing,' said Graham; 'close the men up into a compact battalion.' 'That I will, with pleasure,' replied Browne, 'for it is more in my way than light bobbing.'

Browne's buglers sounded the call to reform line from skirmish order and, trotting forward to the front of his men, 'Mad John' raised his cocked hat, saying 'Gentlemen, I am happy to be the bearer of good news: General Graham has done you the honour of being the first to attack those fellows. Now, follow me, you rascals.' As he led his redcoats forward, from the saddle of his charger Browne broke into his favourite song, *Hearts of Oak*: 'Come cheer up my lads, 'Tis to glory we steer, To add something more to this wonderful year...'. Crossing a re-entrant, the Flank Battalion were briefly out of sight; then, in a double line the twenty-one officers and 468 men (according to Blakeney) emerged into full view of Ruffin's 3,108 men. The British were allowed to close to a perilously close range before Browne said, 'There they are, you rascals – if you don't kill them, they will kill you; so fire away!' His flank companies were then indeed fired upon, both by the three right-hand French battalions, and by the eight-gun battery assembling on the crest. Ruffin's three battalions were, from his right to left, the 1/96e, 2/24e and 1/24e Ligne, with two composite reserve battalions of grenadier companies a little in rear. (The 2/9e Léger was not in the line, having been sent off earlier with the 1er Dragons to the south end of Barrosa.)

Browne's men were terribly hard hit by the French fire: more than 200 went down in the first rushes, according to Blakeney – which is quite plausible, for the eight French guns were firing grapeshot in enfilade. Such losses were clearly the death-knell for any closer engagement between these two hugely disproportionate forces; to attack uphill an established enemy of six times greater strength is suicide. Since Ruffin was not going to quit his hill voluntarily, perhaps Graham should have ordered Browne not to attack alone and immediately, but to go forward only far enough to be ready to act as skirmishers, and to link up in the usual way with the main assault when it came forward? His Flank Battalion lost 236 of its 489 men in the space of a very few minutes – very nearly half its strength, and two-thirds of its twenty-one officers. One has to wonder if they might have achieved the same object – fixing Ruffin – merely by threatening an assault? The survivors of the battalion sought what cover they could find, behind trees, hillocks and bushes, and fired independently; but stand up and advance again they would not, nor did Browne try to make them.

At that moment there is no doubt that Ruffin could have dashed them away down the slopes, had he charged. That he did not was because he could now see, across the smoke-filled hillside, Dilkes' battalions forming up outside the wood. Blakeney recalled: 'Casting a glance behind we discovered the Guards emerging from the forest. They presented neither line nor column, a confused mass showing no order whatever... except the order to advance against the foe.' Dilkes' fighting formation was to be covered by the deployment as skirmishers of Amos Norcott's two companies from the 2/95th Rifles. Following in Browne's steps, they doubled out to the front and, sweeping a line right across the approaches of Barrosa, began engaging Ruffin's own sharpshooters, who were just then emerging. Duncan's guns now opened fire on the crest.

The first unit to clear the woods was the largest, the 2/1st Foot Guards, 600 strong; then came the three companies of the 2/3rd Guards, and then five companies of the 2/67th. The latter actually belonged to Colonel Wheatley's brigade – his rearmost troops; however, on the rapid turn-about inside the wood the wing had tagged on to Dilkes' brigade – this was no time or place to stop and dither. The two companies of the 2/2nd (Coldstream) Guards were extracted inside the wood by Dilkes, to escort Duncan's guns, although in the event that job was taken by the two companies of the 47th Lancashires. The Coldstream, as we have seen, fought with Wheatley – again, there was no time to unscramble things.

Because Dilkes' various units left the woods one behind the other, and because he led them rather right-handed to shake out down the westerly approaches to Barrosa, the brigade was effectively in echelon: the 67th to the right rear of the 3rd Guards, who were similarly to the right rear of the 1st Guards. The formation totalled 1,460 men, plus another 217 riflemen skirmishing with Norcott; these 1,677 British were facing Ruffin's 3,108 Frenchmen. They took up their dressing as they approached the re-entrant, which was a steeper proposition further to the west than it had been for Browne. As the line emerged out of the dip on to the lower slopes, Ruffin's artillery opened up for a second time, to great effect. In captivity after the battle, Ruffin told British officers that he had never seen men fall so fast, and that he expected the line to break and turn at every instant. But the Guards plodded on; seeing that the slightly steeper slopes to their right not only held more natural cover, but also presented a convex slope under which – at least for a while – they could climb beneath the guns' possible angle of depression, they gradually shifted in that direction. The line inevitably became irregular, in a fashion certain to have caused the NCOs apoplexy.

On coming up to the flatter ground in front of the French, whose guns could be brought to bear on them only briefly, the Guards were charged by the two battalion columns of the 24e Ligne, mostly angled to meet the 1st Guards. Slightly to their rear were the 1/96e and the two composite battalions of grenadiers. This was a daunting prospect for the exhausted Guardsmen. For several days now they had been on the march, on the lightest rations. That morning they had been rushed into the pinewood, and turned around in confusion, and rushed out of it again; they had climbed a 160ft slope, under fire; and now here came the French, fresh and twice their number, charging 300 yards downhill in a mass nine deep, and they just two ranks deep. The French could scarcely fail to roll right through them and out the other side; battalion columns were splendid for cohesion, control and collective courage.

Yet here, as at Vimiero, Talavera and Busaco, the chosen fighting formation of the French was a mistake. The red line halted and volleyed every musket, the lead balls hammering up the slope and into the packed blue ranks; they could not miss. The Guards' line lapped around Ruffin's two battalion columns in a semi-circle, firing into the side files as well as the leading ranks – 1,200 British muskets, to which the first three ranks of the two French columns could oppose only about 400. The first two volleys slowed the French, as men fell at the feet of those advancing behind, who had to stumble over their comrades. The third volley halted them – it usually did – and the surviving French officers belatedly tried to open out and give more of their men a chance to use their weapons. Seeing the 24e Ligne lose momentum, Marshal Victor himself now led forward Ruffin's two grenadier battalions to the left of the 24e, angling at the 3rd Guards and the 67th companies. Again they were brought to a bloody halt, this time only yards from the British, and again they sought to deploy and win the firefight. Failing, the whole French mass slowly edged backwards, recoiling under heavy fire all the way up the slope and over the brow. They were now almost encircled; the 300 or so remnants of Browne's Flank Battalion, temporarily forgotten by the French, had moved forward and engaged the 96e Ligne in flank, and Norcott's greenjackets were up on the right.

The Guards stepped forward over the French dead and wounded, and the wings closed in. A howitzer was captured on the crest by Browne's men, a gun by the 1st Guards, and 107 unwounded prisoners were rounded up. The French ran, edging north behind Leval's division, down the far slopes; Ruffin and his brigadier were left on the hill mortally wounded, and were taken. He had lost twenty-nine officers and 722 men – one-third of each. At Talavera, too, his 24e and 96e – all three battalions of each – had run, down another hill, the Medellin, pursued by the 1/29th (Worcestershire) and 1/48th (Northamptonshire); on that day, too, they had lost a third of their strength. There are historians who argue that the repeated failure of French battalion columns sent against British lines owed more to Wellington's skill in selecting reverse-slope positions than the simple arithmetic of musketry; the uphill charges at Barrosa would seem to be a sufficient answer. Compared to Ruffin's total loss of 751 all ranks, Dilkes' casualties totalled 591, plus about twenty-five for the wing of the 67th. Dilkes suffered at a higher rate than Wheatley, for Ruffin's established position on the hill was a much tougher prospect. As we have seen, Browne's *ad hoc* battalion of flank companies lost very nearly one in every two men, and the Guards one in three.

*   *   *

Victor took Ruffin's defeated battalions back towards the track to Chiclana, joined up with Leval and, unharried by Graham's exhausted troops, turned and attempted to form a fresh front. He still had ten guns; the 2/9e Léger, 1/45e Ligne and a grenadier battalion were all in reasonable shape, and were supported on the flanks by the 350 sabres of the 1er Dragons. Throughout the engagement the dragoons had been at the seaward end of the hill, keeping an eye on General Whittingham's squadrons; perhaps surprisingly, they had taken no part in either Wheatley or Dilkes' actions. But they now did a good job of covering Victor's withdrawal, several times threatening Dilkes' brigade – the 3rd Guards formed square more than once.

For the first time in this battle, Graham at last had his whole force formed in some sort of order – Wheatley's brigade on the left, Dilkes' on the right, guns central and skirmishers moving forward – on a front of about a mile, facing east. Duncan had pushed his guns forward to a third position, on a knoll on the summit of Barrosa ridge, whence he swept with his fire the gently sloping ground across which Leval had fallen back. One of the two KGL hussar squadrons now appeared from the right; they had followed the withdrawal of the 1er Dragons – not on the orders of the lethargic Whittingham, but at the urging of Graham's Assistant Adjutant-General (that same Major Frederick Ponsonby who had charged with the 23rd Light Dragoons at Talavera). At Barrosa he charged to rather greater purpose, since the Germans overthrew the dragoon squadron on Victor's left flank and drove it on to the infantry. The German hussars continued beyond, to the guns and beyond them again, into one of the infantry columns; but these mainly stood firm, and drove them off. None the less, this small initiative by a single squadron of horse proved just too much for the generally demoralized French infantry; they promptly made off towards Chiclana, leaving two more guns behind – which the hussars claimed.

Ten minutes later, Whittingham turned up with the other four squadrons. His earlier presence must surely have guaranteed many more French casualties; his absence was typical of what was criticized as his lacklustre leadership – the very reverse of what was usually expected of a thrusting cavalryman. His own account for his absence, in his Official Report to La Peña, leaves no room to doubt that he knew where his duty lay:

> The enemy, after finding himself repulsed from the heights, commenced his retreat in an orderly manner, covered by his cavalry. This was the moment in which I proposed to myself to collect together and act on the offensive with my 400 horse... when, upon the right of the whole line, there appeared a column of infantry of about 500 men, preceeded by a party of horse, and moving as if to turn our flank. It was indispensable to manoeuvre so as to keep them under observation, while a sergeant and six men of the squadron of carabineers reconnoitred them; and the opportunity thus escaped me of charging, with the whole of my disposable cavalry, the enemy who was retiring rapidly.

It was, said his son as editor of his memoirs, 'simply an accident over which he had no control, that delayed the advance of General Whittingham, after the successful charge of the British under General Graham.'

The wounded Captain Charles Cadell, commanding the 28th's Grenadier Company, wrote: 'We collected on the top of the hill, from which we had beaten the enemy, and saw the French retreating in great confusion, dismayed and crest fallen – we gave them three hearty British cheers, at parting.' And with those cheers in his ears, Thomas Graham let Marshal Victor go; he had no choice, given the state of his men. How badly now he needed the support of his ally: this was the moment – the most perfect, if not quite the very last – when La Peña should have emerged, trumpets blaring, from the woods upon the flanks of Victor's mauled and retreating column. It had not yet rejoined Villatte, nor had Cassagne's 3,000 men closed from Medina Sidonia: Victor was entirely vulnerable. As Graham wrote to the British ambassador in Cadiz, in the aftermath of the battle: 'Had the whole body of the Spanish cavalry with the horse-artillery been rapidly sent by the sea-beach to form in the plain, and to envelope the enemy's left – had the greatest part of the infantry been marched through the pine-wood in our rear to turn his right, what success might not have been expected from such decisive movements?' But La Peña was not the man for decisive movements.

The Spanish general had been fully aware of the two-hour progress of this action just 3 miles away – a ten-minute canter along the beach; yet he made no move to help, and his 10,000 men remained rooted. La Peña was clearly a man who was easily satisfied. His approach march from Tarifa had been laughable; he had failed to seize the opportunity to destroy Cassagne, and thus the chance to lure Victor away from Cadiz; he had failed to inform Zayas of the delayed march, thus allowing him to give the game away by attacking prematurely. He had pushed Villatte to one side, but left him intact; he had abandoned the vital high ground of Barrosa; and now he sat, as Fortescue charmingly put it, 'in tremulous security, like a squatted hare which the hounds have overrun... he gathered his skirts about him and with quivering anility, sat still.' ('Anility' is an archaic term meaning behaviour characteristic of an old woman.) Had he not already caused one of Napoleon's generals to withdraw? He had done enough, and was not going to leave the security of the drawbridge into Cadiz, now conveniently just behind him.

Thomas Graham's reaction to this lack of support, when next morning he led his British command over that drawbridge, was to inform La Peña in formal terms that he would take no further orders from him, but would act as he saw fit with the discretionary powers given him by London. In this he was supported three weeks later by Lord Wellington, who wrote 'I concur in the propriety of your withdrawing to the Isla on the 6th, as much as I admire the promptitude and determination of your attack on the 5th' – which is as handsome a compliment as any soldier could wish to receive.

There is no doubt that Wellington's sentiments were thoroughly sincere, even though the immediate importance of Graham's victory at Barrosa might have been greater. In truth, it had not been a clear-cut victory in terms of relative casualties, which was how these affairs were often seen at home in the press: Graham had lost 1,238 men (a 24 per cent casualty rate), whereas Victor lost 2,062 (29 per cent), but although Graham prevailed against far superior numbers, the relative losses were not dissimilar. In addition, it was true (and very welcome, for home consumption) that Victor had lost Generals Ruffin, Rousseau and Bellegarde, Colonels Autue and Lanusse killed, and one of his ADCs, six pieces of cannon, an Eagle and 500 prisoners – and it was he who had quit the field of battle. However, Lord Wellington's pleasure probably lay more in the further doubt cast on the French claim to be Europe's dominant warrior race: how he must have smiled, to hear that those very same battalions who had attacked him at Talavera in columns had attacked Graham in those same old columns – and with the same old result. French doctrine had not changed, it seemed, and that was all to the good. And we must also note that, unlike at Talavera, where the line had occasions to conquer column only in defence, on Barrosa ridge Dilkes' line proved equally superior in attack. This experience, and the inevitable postmortem chat around the camp fires, would spread further confidence among Graham's redcoats for the future.

Lord Wellington had another reason to smile on receiving Graham's Despatch, and that was Graham himself. Here, it seemed, was a general with whom Wellington could do business – as far as we know, they had not served together before. Barrosa had demonstrated in him those qualities required in Wellington's lieutenants: an eye for ground; a character resolute, determined and fearless in action; speed of decision, and an ability to inspire his troops with both confidence and enthusiasm. Accordingly, when he joined the main army that summer from Cadiz, Thomas Graham was given command of the 1st Division, and he would soon become a corps commander with the addition of the 6th and 7th Divisions. Graham's corps was to provide part of the covering force for the final siege of Badajoz in March 1812, and shortly thereafter he was given a further two brigades of cavalry for the advance to Salamanca. Although an eye infection took him back to England he returned in time for Vittoria, where he commanded some 20,000 troops.

Barrosa had produced a dependable right hand for Wellington, and also a colleague who shared his informed contempt for the traditional Spanish military hierarchy. In his personal (and we must hope private) letter of congratulation to Graham after the battle, Wellington included this eloquent judgement:

The conduct of the Spanish throughout this expedition is precisely the same as I have ever observed it to be. They march the troops night and day, without provisions or rest, and abusing everybody who proposes a moment's delay to afford either to the famished and fatigued soldiers. They reach the enemy in such a state as to be unable to make any exertion, or to execute any plan, even if any plan has been formed; and then, when the moment of action arrives, they are totally incapable of movement, and they stand by to see their allies destroyed, and afterwards abuse them because they do not continue, unsupported, exertions to which human nature is not equal.

*   *   *

Although perhaps not readily apparent, the strategic outcome of Barrosa was arguably not to Wellington's disadvantage. The negatives and the might-have-beens are easy to list. Had La Peña contributed as handsomely as he should have, and had Victor consequently been handled more severely, it might have led to the blowing-up of his forts and entrenchments – perhaps even to the sucking-in of reinforcements from Sebastiani and Godinot, thus encouraging the insurgency in Granada and Cordova. Marshal Soult would effectively have had to reconquer Andalusia, and to rebuild the lines before Cadiz from scratch. As it was, Victor re-occupied them just three days after the battle; he had lost 2,000 men and much reputation, but the siege of Cadiz duly recommenced.

Yet was this a bad thing? While it might seem that little had been accomplished, we should ponder the advantages to the Allied cause of the French thus continuing to tie up vast resources in this hopeless task. Had the forts been destroyed following a substantial Allied victory, French policy towards Cadiz might well have been reviewed, and future operations there down-graded, thus releasing men and provisions for more worthwhile activities – such as the pursuit of Wellington. As it was, the siege was to continue for another seventeen pointlessly expensive months. Soult certainly rushed back to Andalusia, fearing the worst, upon receiving news of Barrosa. He had already captured Badajoz, on 11 March, so the news of Graham's expedition came just too late to save that place; but Soult's move south facilitated Beresford's advance to Badajoz against what was now relatively light opposition, prior to laying siege to it himself.

So what did Barrosa achieve? It gave the French a bloody nose, which was good for everyone's morale; ironically, thanks to La Peña, it prolonged the wasteful French siege operations at Cadiz; it diverted Soult for many weeks, and eased Beresford's passage; and it brought Sir Thomas Graham into the mainstream of the Peninsular Field Army, to the undoubted benefit of British arms.

2
Campo Mayor,
25 March

SITTING just across the border in Spain, the French held the two pivotal frontier strongholds: Ciudad Rodrigo on the northern route from Portugal and, 130 miles to the south, Badajoz. Portugal could never be free from the threat of renewed invasion, nor could Wellington move further into Spain, while these fortresses remained under the *tricolore*.

To take Ciudad Rodrigo would require the prior capture of Almeida, 20 miles to its west, which the British were already blockading. Its garrison was vulnerably low on provisions (Napier says just a fortnight's rations), having supplied Massena's famished regiments as they passed eastwards on their retreat. It was located just too far west from the main French concentration areas around Salamanca, and any replenishment convoys would need strong protection. So Almeida could probably be starved out without battle casualties, so long as it could be kept isolated for a short while.

In early March, while Marshal Massena was withdrawing north-east along the Mondego river, from way to the south came the news of Soult's retaking of Badajoz. Word reached Wellington on the night of 13/14 March; and a couple of days later he sent to confirm his delegated orders to Marshal Sir William Beresford: 'You had better lose no time in moving up to Portalegre, and attack Soult, if you can, at Campo Mayor, and again to besiege Badajoz.'

Beresford was already en route with nearly 20,000 men, a corps command which he owed – in Rowland Hill's absence – to the rigid system of seniority that governed such appointments. A tall, massively-built Anglo-Irishman, the bastard son of a marquis, William Carr Beresford was a courageous veteran of battles on three continents, and a former commanding officer of the 88th Regiment (Connaught Rangers), whose milky and ruined left eye added to his soldierly presence. He had been a brigadier in the British Army three years earlier; he now held the local British rank of lieutenant-general – but he was also a Marshal of the Portuguese Army, to whose reform he had brought great talents and energy since February 1809. However, his largest previous field command was a brigade, at Corunna under Sir John Moore.

He would not be meeting Soult just yet, however: the 'Duke of Damnation' had recently left for Andalusia and Seville, on hearing of the French defeat at Barrosa. He had left Marshal Mortier with 11,000 men in five brigades of infantry and two of horse, to reduce the other three frontier fortresses between the Guadiana and Tagus rivers: Campo Mayor, Albuquerque and Valencia di Alcantara. All were taken by 21 March, and Mortier returned to Badajoz leaving General Latour-Maubourg at Campo Mayor, with just 2,400 men, to dismantle the fortifications there and to recover the siege train cannons and any from the walls which might be usable. Latour-Mauburg's little force comprised 300 troopers of the 2e Hussars, 350 of the 10e, just 150 of the 26e Dragons and some eighty Spanish Chasseurs – say 880 horse in all. His main strength was the two battalions of the 100e Ligne, some 1,200 strong, with assorted engineers, drivers, and a half-battery of horse gunners.

Having heard of Soult's departure for the south, Beresford approached Badajoz with confidence. He neared Campo Mayor, some 10 miles to its north-west, late on 24 March, to find two or three French hussar vedettes suitably deployed a couple of miles in advance. Beresford's formidable corps comprised four divisions: the cavalry under Brigadier Robert Long, the 2nd and 4th Divisions under Major-Generals Stewart and Cole respectively, and Hamilton's Portuguese infantry division. The horse were in two brigades: Colonel Grey led eight squadrons of the 3rd Dragoon Guards and the 4th Dragoons, and Colonel Otway five (albeit weak) squadrons of the 1st and 7th Portuguese Cavalry. In addition, about 230 sabres of the 13th Light Dragoons were under Beresford's direct control, in five troops.

The 4th Division was moving some 2 miles in rear of the main body, so Beresford had immediately to hand around 16,000 men. His superiority over Latour-Maubourg's 2,400 was thus not in doubt, nor the surprise of his arrival. The story of the next few hours is plainly that of a minor affair, the outcome in no doubt; yet it was a story that was to be long-remembered. The controversy over Robert Long's cavalry charge at Campo Mayor, coupled with later events at Albuera, was to rumble on for many years. The relevance to our main story of Albuera is that Beresford was implicated in similar ways on both occasions, with Campo Mayor subsequently seen as a sort of prologue. This spendidly apoplectic passage in William Napier's Volume VI of his great *History*, published nearly thirty years after the events, gives a flavour of the ferocity then still simmering:

> My Lord, you will never hide your bad generalship at Campo Mayor… you had an enormous superiority of troops, the enemy were taken by surprise, they were in a plain, their cavalry were beaten, their artillery-drivers cut down, their infantry, hemmed in by your horsemen and under the play of your guns, were ready to surrender; yet you suffered them to escape and to carry off their captured artillery and then you blamed your gallant troops. The enemy escaped from you, my lord, but you cannot escape from the opinion of the world.

Nor can Wellington himself escape some responsibility for what happened, for William Beresford's state of mind that morning was strongly conditioned by his lordship's personal caution as to the employment of the cavalry arm. The following was written on 20 March, when Wellington was way up on the Mondego, and probably reached Beresford on the 22nd or 23rd when he had reached Arronches, just one march from Campo Mayor – so it must have been uppermost in his thoughts:

> I recommend to you to keep your troops very much en masse. I have always considered the cavalry to be the most delicate arm we possess. We have few officers who have practical knowledge of the mode of using it, or who have ever seen more than two regiments together; and all our troops, cavalry as well as infantry, are a little inclined to get out of order in battle. To these circumstances add, that the defeat of, or any great loss sustained by, our cavalry, in these open grounds, would be a misfortune amounting almost to a defeat of the whole; and you will see the necessity of keeping the cavalry as much as

possible en masse, and in reserve, to be thrown in at the moment when an opportunity may offer of striking a decisive blow.

Wellington cannot have been easy in his mind about having delegated a major command to Beresford, seeking battle so far to the south; it was simply not in his nature to delegate. Like a worried parent concerned for the safety of an elder son entrusted with half the family treasure, he would stress his main fears; woe betide the son who did not listen, and we may be sure that Wellington's strictures were only too alive in Beresford's memory as he advanced to Campo Mayor. The going was, after all, turning into quite brilliant horse country – according to the gunner Alexander Dickson 'perfectly open, with gentle rises and falls, and excellent for the operation of cavalry.'

At 10.30am on 25 March, in persistent rain, on the east side of the flat road from Arronches to Campo Mayor, the four light companies of Lieutenant-Colonel Colborne's Brigade – those from the 1/3rd (Buffs), 2/31st (Huntingdonshire), 2/48th (Northamptonshire) and 2/66th (Berkshire) – were making their best speed across the plain. The 'light bobs' were preceded by two squadrons of the 13th Light Dragoons and two of the 7th Portuguese Cavalry. This advance guard was commanded by the 33-year-old Colborne in person; the remainder of his brigade, that is the battalion companies of his four units, were on the road itself, together with another troop of the 13th, and Colonel Grey's Heavy Brigade – the 3rd Dragoon Guards and 4th Dragoons. Away to the east of the road was Hamilton's Portuguese infantry division, and Colonel Otway's other Portuguese cavalry squadrons. In rear, on the axis of the road, was the balance of Stewart's 2nd Division (Houghton's and Lumley's brigades), and further back still Cole's 4th Division. The rate of advance at this point was that of the infantry. One man who was up the sharp end with one of the light companies, Lieutenant Edward Close (2/48th), wrote in his diary:

> March 25th – Moved towards Campo Mayor in three divisions. The major part of the 13th Light Dragoons, some Portuguese cavalry, and the light companies of our brigade were on the left. A troop of the 13th Light Dragoons, and the Buffs and the other regiments in the centre. The right column was chiefly composed of Portuguese [sic]. We commenced our march to a hill in our front, on which the French showed some cavalry, and on which, it was supposed, they would stand an attack. The left moved round the hills in flank. The centre went directly on, upon the road, towards a windmill. The right a little to their right. The enemy, however, saved us the trouble and retired until we got close to Campo Mayor.

At some point in this progression the order of march was adjusted, to take account of the going. General Long wrote a month later that:

> the enemy's pickets were found placed upon a height that... forms the boundary of the open country into which we were about to debouche... the order of march was completely changed... I proceeded to move, and was soon ordered to the front with all the cavalry... on reaching the open country... the cavalry was here divided... . I moved with the light portion of my division, and the infantry marched supported by the heavy brigade.

The 13th's regimental history conveys this most vividly:

> Orders came for all the cavalry to gain the front – the country proving sufficiently open
> ahead for cavalry operations. This was done by traversing at a gallop some bad rocky
> ground. The 13th, and the 1st and 7th Regiments of Portuguese Cavalry on gaining the
> front, formed contiguous columns of half squadrons at half distance – occasionally, by
> the nature of the ground, going from either flank by threes, and forming up again. These
> light regiments were followed by the brigade of heavy cavalry. The columns moved forward
> at a brisk trot, and the infantry followed as quickly as possible [i.e. fell further behind].

It is said that the French vedettes thus pushed back included a reconnaissance party led by
General Latour-Maubourg. He had come up to assess reports of Beresford's approach, received
the previous day but quite discounted, since the Frenchman had had no official word of
Massena's latest withdrawal or warning of the closeness of the Allies. We may presume his horror at confirmation of the imminent arrival of an enemy force seven times the strength of his
own. Latour-Mauburg had no choice but to rush back to his headquarters in Campo Mayor,
shout the few words needed to start a hurried withdrawal, and pray for the best. He at least
had the consolation that at first light he had seen off to Badajoz a long, slow mule convoy,
including sixteen heavy cannons from the siege train, his stores and ammunition, some sick
(and no doubt the usual loot), all lightly escorted and by now a few miles down the muddy
road towards Badajoz, with each gun and cart drawn by eight mules. The garrison was pretty
much ready to move, and in preparation to abandon Campo Mayor horse and foot were soon
paraded on the glacis to the south of the main gate.

Marshal Beresford sat his horse on a low ridge above the town and watched the French column emerge from the gate prior to forming up. Ahead of him, also watching and waiting for
orders, was his cavalry commander. Robert Long later wrote: 'I trotted away with the light gentry, and having driven the enemy's picquets from the positions they occupied, I at length
passed over a considerable plain which brought me to a small ridge, from whence I looked
down on the town of Campo Mayor, distant about 1,200 yards. Here I first saw their cavalry
(a part of them at least) drawn up in line of battle under the protection of the works. I immediately formed my line and waited further orders, not knowing what were the Marshal's intentions.' It was about 1.30pm when Beresford sent to tell Long (as he put it in his Despatch)
'to turn the enemy's right, to delay the enemy's force until some infantry could come up.'
Long set off with Otway's Portuguese leading, the 13th Light Dragoons following, and with
Beresford in his wake, slowly bringing on the eight squadrons of the Heavy Brigade.

The countryside around Campo Mayor and down across the Spanish border is mostly
rolling grassland, with distant views and little cover; but it is criss-crossed by streams that run
down from the relatively higher ground to the east of the road. Some of these had boggy bot-
toms, and of course they also provided areas of dead ground; when actually in such lower
ground the limit of visibility was necessarily the next crest ahead. Long had to skirt wide of
the town initially, to keep well away from Fort St Jean, which extended the fortifications to
the east of the Badajoz road. It may be that he trotted wider still, to get around the heads of
the streams. In any event, Beresford felt compelled to send a staff officer – Henry Hardinge,
his DQMG – to move Long closer in. Long did not comply to Beresford's satisfaction, and

Hardinge was sent a second time 'to express the Marshal's displeasure'; we may assume that even by this early stage neither Long nor Beresford was in the best of tempers.

In Beresford's case, this minor annoyance irritated a mind already concerned over what he seemed to be initiating. 'You will see the necessity of keeping the cavalry as much as possible en masse, and in reserve', saith the Lord; yet here he was, already with his precious horse divided. At least he could console himself that the Heavy Brigade was in reserve, and that Wellington had clearly written that the purpose of cavalry was 'to be thrown in at the moment when an opportunity may offer of striking a decisive blow.' That is effectively the reply he had given to Long earlier that morning as the advance to contact had commenced: that Long should not attack a superior force, but should rather 'wait for the infantry to come up if he were in any doubt; yet if the opportunity to strike a blow occurs he must avail himself of it.'

Looking down at the road to Badajoz, Long could count around 900 horse in the French column; they were now nearly 2 miles along the road, and making all best speed. He himself had, he thought, 1,200 sabres, and so he clearly felt he was being presented with the opportunity to strike, as defined. Glancing right along the shallow valley that the road paralleled, he could see his two dragoon regiments a quarter-mile in rear, a little nearer the road than they had been. It would be fourteen squadrons against eight in his favour; and anyway, with the infantry slogging over the wet plain some way behind, there was no other way to prevent the French reaching Badajoz.

General Latour-Maubourg was an experienced cavalry commander (his division had kept Cuesta's Spanish well bottled up at Talavera), and once it was plain that the British meant business he put the 100e Ligne into battalion squares – or rather, rectangles – still marching for all they were worth, and protected front and rear by two squadrons of the 10e Hussards. The three squadrons of the 2e Hussards went forward to complement the three from the 26e Dragons, who were covering the front of the infantry's left or exposed flank. He formed the 2e Hussards – curiously – at right-angles to his dragoon squadrons, thereby presenting Long with a teasing challenge: a single charge against either dragoons or hussars would expose his flank to the other. Since the solution had to be a simultaneous assault on both, Latour-Maubourg had thus forced Long to split his command. Long rightly accepted the challenge, although with rather too much confidence: he had arrived in the Peninsula only three weeks earlier, and on this morning of 25 March he had had command of Beresford's cavalry for just six days. Never having seen them under fire, he was hardly conversant with the variable quality of Portuguese horse – an arm which had benefited far less than their infantry from Marshal Beresford's energetic reforms.

Long's plan was for Colonel Otway with two squadrons of the 7th Portuguese to get round forward and behind the French hussars, to cut off their retreat towards the Badajoz road; he himself and three squadrons of the 1st Portuguese would attack the leading hussars directly, and the 13th Light Dragoons would take the 26e Dragons in flank. It is not clear what – if any - orders Long had specifically given to Colonel Grey of the Heavy Brigade. Captain Carlo Doyle (87th), his DAQMG, went to the charge with and at the request of Colonel Head of the 13th Light Dragoons. During the long-running postmortem into the affair, Doyle wrote in a letter of June 1833 that in riding forward with Head he observed 'from the rising ground, over which we passed, the Heavy Brigade was advancing in our rear just before the charge.' Further, he assumed that orders had been passed to Colonel Grey 'to follow in support and I have no doubt Colonel Head acted under the same impression.' The commanding officer of the 4th Dragoons later wrote that he 'had seen shortly before the attack the light brigade at about 500 yards in advance, and from a direction more to the left than the heavy brigade', just as they went right-handed 'over a small ridge of heights, whence it immediately descended into the bottom on the Badajoz road, whence the charge against the enemy took place.'

Head's right-hand squadron commander, Lieutenant-Colonel Patrick Doherty, tells us that Robert Long had ridden up to Head and said 'There's your enemy – attack him', adding 'and now, Colonel, the heavy brigade are coming up on your rear, and if you have an opportunity, give a good account of these fellows.' Colonel Head replied 'By gad, Sir, I will.'

Long spurred forwards to take Otway's rear three squadrons, and Head took the 13th away to the right, giving the order 'Threes Right!' and then wheeling them to face the green-clad French dragoons while manoeuvring into two lines.

Immediately, Colonel Count Chamorin pivoted his three squadrons of the 26e Dragons, from being parallel to the road, to meet the British; whereupon (to confound Long's plans almost instantly) the three squadrons of French hussars closed up behind them. According to Colonel Head, the 13th now suddenly faced four separate ranks of enemy troopers. His own double line comprised Patrick Doherty's squadron on the right, made up of Captains Bowers and Buchanan's troops; and Lieutenant-Colonel Joseph Muter's squadron on the left, made up of the troops led by Captain Joseph Doherty (on the left) and Lieutenant Major (on the right). In addition, about twenty men under Lieutenants Moss and Doherty – the third Doherty in the regiment – arrived at the last minute from skirmishing duties, anxious to miss nothing. The 13th's regimental history puts their charging strength at between 222 and 232 men.

The two formations started about 200 yards apart. The French dragoons, having no wish to be sitting ducks, dug their heels back; and so did the 13th, the momentum gathering on both sides as the trumpets took them up through the usual gear-changes of walk, trot and canter. As Head cantered his squadrons past the 100e Ligne on the road they received a couple of volleys; several men were hit, including Lieutenant Smith of the right-hand squadron, who took a musketball in the stomach. With his two squadrons attacking three, Colonel Head had to decide which two to hit; he chose the French centre and left, leaving alone the squadron to his left, where he knew General Long was operating.

It is rather unclear how the French were formed at that moment. Colonel Head states that they were four deep, and he should know. The French dragoon line being longer than the British, despite relative strengths of 150 to 230, this could only confirm that the latter were indeed in two ranks, but the 26e Dragons in one (hence the overlap on the French side). It also presumably means that the second, third and fourth French lines were made up of the three hussar squadrons of the 2e and 10e.

In any event, once 'Charge!' rang out, at a closing speed of between 30 and 40 miles per hour the clash was indeed literally shocking, with saddles emptied on both sides – many not by wounds, but simply by unbalanced horses under unbalanced riders being brought about, and brought up, by the kinetic energy of the impact. As an article in the RUSI *Journal* of February 1900 put it: 'Many riders and horses were overthrown and stunned by the shock.' The right-hand squadron commander, Patrick Doherty, said that 'Every horse was let out and the men cheered; the enemy did the same. The crash was tremendous; both parties passed each other, and at a short distance in rear of the enemy, the 13th came about; the enemy did the same, and a second charge took place with equal volume, when the conflict became personal with the sabre.'

We must remember that the opposing lines were riding with minimal spacing between individual horses – just 6inches, according to the British drill. It was indeed remarked at the time how unusual it was to pass through one another, although easier to see it happening on the second or return charge. As the RUSI article put it, 'Equally exciting... when, a short distance in rear, the 13th wheeled smartly round and reformed – a movement which, with the better command they maintained over their horses, they performed more quickly than the French, who rode with a loose rein... both forces for a second time hurled themselves against each other.' But Beresford himself for some reason later refused to accept that the second charge had happened at all, saying that the 13th 'never rallied to bar the enemy's advance. They never drew up, nor indeed ever stopped... the whole of this tale is suppostitious' [that is, hypothetical].

None the less, Patrick Doherty's account is supported by a sapper officer, Lieutenant John Burgoyne: 'The 13th went through them; the enemy closed and faced to the right about, the 13th rode through them again.' And as Ian Fletcher quite rightly points out in his fascinating chapter on Campo Mayor in *Galloping at Everything*, 'there must have been a second charge' (that passed through), 'otherwise the French dragoons would have been trapped on the wrong side of both their supports and the road to Badajoz'.

Once the individual combats commenced on the second coming-together, the advantage lay with the 13th's curved sabres: the French 26e had a long but straight sword designed for thrusting, which is best combined with forward motion. In a static, whirling mêlée slashing with the curved blade was quicker, and the French blade's extra 5-odd inches was if anything an encumbrance. Again, there is an interesting comment in the 1900 RUSI *Journal*: 'The point was the *cheval de bataille* of the French, but it failed, as the 13th parried with ease.' That said, of course, the three French hussar squadrons also carried sabres.

An unidentified officer of the 13th wrote in the *Courier* three weeks after the action: 'The French sustained three [sic] charges of our cavalry without breaking... [they] certainly are fine and brave soldiers, but the superiority of our English horses, and more particularly the superiority of swordsmanship our fellows showed, decided every contest in our favour.' The same officer also covered the episode when Corporal Logan of the 13th killed Colonel Count Chamorin of the 26e Dragons (the original spelling is preserved):

> Yesterday (the day after the action) a French Captain of Dragoons brought over a trumpeter, demanding permission to search among the dead for his Colonel; his regiment was a fine one, with bright brass helmets, and black horse hair, exactly like the old Romans are depicted with; the Captain was a fine young man, and had his arm in a sling. Many of us went with him – it was truly a bloody scene, being almost all sabre wounds, the slain were all naked, the peasants having stripped them in the night; it was long before we could find the French Colonel – he was lying on his face, his naked body weltering in blood, and as soon as he was turnd up, the Officer knew him, he gave a sort of scream, and sprung off his horse, dashed his helmet on the ground, nelt by the body, took the bloody hand and kissed it many times in an agony of grief; it was an affecting and awful scene [the officer was the count's brother]... The French Colonel I have already mentioned, was killed by a corporal of the 13th; this corporal had killed one of his men, and he was so enraged, that he sallied out himself and attacked the corporal – the corporal was well mounted and a good swordsman, as was also the Colonel – both defended for some time, the corporal cut him twice in the face, his helmet came off at the second, when the corporal slew him by

a cut which nearly cleft his skull asunder, it cut in as deep as the nose through the brain. The corporal (Logan) is not wounded.

Logan was a member of Lieutenant Major's troop, the right-hand troop of Lieutenant-Colonel Muter's squadron. This anonymous account of the injuries suffered by Colonel Chamorin is confirmed by Lieutenant Moyle Sherer of the 34th Regiment, who wrote in 1823:

> I remember well, among the events of this day, having remarked one fine manly corpse very particularly; it lay a few yards from the road side, alone, naked, the face and breast downwards, and on the back of the head a deep and frightful cleft, inflicted by the sabre; all around the spot where it lay the ground was deeply indented with the print of horses' feet, who appeared to have gone over it at a furious pace. The sky was cloudy, and the wind high; the body was cold and pale, the fine-formed limbs stiff and motionless; the spirit, which had animated it, not an hour before, had indeed fled; yet, I know not how it was, the very corpse made a forcible appeal to the feelings, and seemed to suffer, it looked so comfortless, so humbled, so deserted. An English dragoon, leading a wounded horse, and conducting two prisoners, one of whom had sabre-cuts on the cheek and shoulder, passed me while I was contemplating the scene. 'Do you recollect,' said I, 'friend, what took place here?' 'Yes, sir; they shewed us a front here, and we charged and drove them; but this man, who was an officer, tried to rally them, and was cut down by our adjutant, as I think.' At this moment, one of the French horsemen, leaning down, exclaimed, '*C'est le Colonel.*' '*Comment diable,*' said the other. '*C'est bien lui,*' said his comrade; '*il est mort. Ah! Qu'il etait brave soldat, ce villain champ de bataille n'est pas digne d'un tel victime.*' They passed on. What! This carcase, on which the flies were already settling, which lay, all spurned and blood-stained, on the rude and prickly heath, had been, but one short hour before, a man of rank, perhaps also of talent, fortune, courage, whose voice breathed command, whose eye glanced fire, whose arm shook defiance: – even so, such is war!

The unassailed French dragoon troop on the right of their line, the Grenadier Troop, 'wheeled inwards, upon the rear of (Captain Joseph Doherty's) troop', according to Captain Doyle, but were beaten off. 'The impetuosity of Colonel Head's charge had so completely broken and appalled the other squadrons, that the cool steady conduct of that young officer and his elite was of no avail. And they were hurried away, mixed up in the mass of fugitives, the whole flying on the road leading towards Badajoz. It is not impossible that this circumstance may have occasioned the silly report of the 13th having been bodily taken' – that is, that an observer from the north would have seen the Grenadier Troop completely surround and get behind the British. In this mixed-up mass of pursued and pursuers it might well appear that the British were being driven off by the French.

It may also very well be that Count Chamorin's death triggered his dragoons' flight, the more so given his reputation as a good swordsman; in any case, off they went down the road to Badajoz, abandoning the 100e Ligne, chased enthusiastically by the 13th Light Dragoons, all disappearing over a ridge to the south.

Robert Long was on the left flank of the Light Dragoons as they charged, with three squadrons of Portuguese; his plan to attack the French hussars was now redundant. 'I felt myself obliged to detach two squadrons of the Portuguese to support and rally them [the vanishing 13th], under the orders of Colonel Otway.' Now these too broke away in pursuit – Captain Doyle saw them 'at some distance to the left, at a gallop'. They were entirely in hand, according to Lieutenant-Colonel Henry Watson, commanding the 7th Portuguese squadrons under Colonel Otway: 'The fact is that the support was conducted in the most regular manner nearly to Badajoz by the 7th Portuguese cavalry *in columns*' – a picture rather spoiled by an entry in the 13th's regimental history: 'During the pursuit the men of the 13th had considerable trouble with their Portuguese allies, who could with difficulty be persuaded to give quarter. Many an unfortunate Frenchman's life was saved through the interference of the privates of the regiment.'

The Portuguese caught up with Colonel Head's 13th Light Dragoons, most of whom had drawn to a halt north of Fort San Cristobal, over the river from Badajoz. They had caught up with Latour-Maubourg's convoy of sixteen heavy guns, ammunition wagons, stores, sick men, baggage and spare horses and mules from Campo Mayor. The rear drivers and gunners quickly surrendered, but those nearing Badajoz attempted to make a run for it, and were sabred. The Portuguese, not surprisingly in view of the inferior condition of their ponies, commandeered the draught horses and any loose cavalry mounts they came upon. Some effort was made to turn the guns but, pursuit being the priority, it was continued down to and past Fort San Cristobal on the north bank of the Guadiana. Some casualties were suffered from the fort's grape and canister fire, and they drew rein at the fortifications protecting the end of the bridge itself. The 13th's historian reports that only about twenty fugitives made it over the bridge and into the sanctuary of the fortress; the many others they had overtaken had all thrown down their weapons, or been cut down.

Colonel Head and his officers, being the best mounted, gathered together in a knot out of musket range of the *tête-du-pont* garrison, while their troopers gradually came up, men and horses heaving for breath; of course, they were all absolutely jubilant. Only twenty French had escaped them – therefore hundreds remained behind them from the six squadrons they had originally charged and dispersed, and were now presumably trapped by the Heavy Brigade, the infantry and the gunners. Colonel Head and his officers had every reason to swap excited stories as they turned, chattering, and walked their foamed-up horses back along the road towards Campo Mayor. Eight miles, someone said! And just think of that convoy and its rich pickings – all they lacked was an Eagle, but doubtless by now someone had got that of the 100e Ligne.

Returning to the convoy, by dismounting troopers and putting them up as drivers the victorious 13th turned the guns, and set off cheerfully with their prizes and their rounded-up prisoners, expecting any minute to see dragoons from the Heavy Brigade advancing, to take over what their historian rightly calls 'the fruits of its gallant fight'. Five slow miles and over an hour later, a solitary horseman appeared before them. It was one of their own dragoons with a message from Lieutenant Holmes, Colonel Head's adjutant who, badly cut in the sword hand during the charge, had remained behind. His message was obviously mistaken: it said that the entire body of the French infantry and hussars had been permitted to proceed unmolested, and were even now approaching along the road. Colonel Head flatly refused to accept that this could be so; not for the first time, somebody had clearly mistaken the blue of Portuguese uniforms for that of the French, and he expected soon to see support coming up in the form of Hamilton's Portuguese division. But then a second lone courier clattered over the horizon, again from the adjutant: the first message was confirmed, with the addition that the 100e

Ligne was now accompanied by those horsemen previously surrendered, whom the marching column had met on their way, and who had since picked up their sabres and remounted.

Colonel Head had no time to ponder over the inexplicable; his small, blown force was quite inadequate to block the road, still less to continue with their prizes, if two battalions and 600 or 700 horse – he could only guess – should loom over the crest. He was down to about 130 dragoons, and far fewer of the Portuguese; their horses were done up, and there was no mention in Holmes' messages of the prospects of support. The only course of action was to go cross-country to rejoin the main force, abandoning the guns, the captured baggage and all the prisoners. They circled to the east, almost immediately seeing to their left the French, whose escorting hussars formed up to attack. Head faced them, drawing his diminished force into line, but the French pulled away. This threatening cover-play was repeated, but it was plain that Latour-Maubourg wished only to press on south; Head turned his back, and about 6.30pm he reunited his drooping regiment with the main body. To his pain and astonishment Colonel Head was coldly and formally received by Beresford, who concluded his chastening remarks (about courage not being the only requisite, either for troops or officers) by asking: 'And I suppose, Sir, if the gates of Badajoz had been open, you would have galloped in?' Head is reported as replying, 'Indeed, Sir, of that you may feel quite certain' – a retort described by one of his squadron commanders as characteristic of the ardour of the plucky Irish colonel.

Thus ended what Sir John Fortescue avers 'would no doubt have become a classic in the annals of cavalry' had the 13th Light Dragoons been supported; 'I know of nothing finer in the history of the British cavalry' is an unarguable accolade from the greatest historian of the British Army. As it was, Latour-Maubourg duly met up with Marshal Mortier, who had rushed out from Badajoz to the rescue with 2,000 infantry and a cavalry regiment; all the convoy's wagons and all the guns except one 6in howitzer and six ammunition caissons got safely across the bridge.

*   *   *

So where were the Heavy Brigade? And the brigades of Allied infantry, and the guns? What had Robert Long been doing; and where was Marshal Beresford in all of this? It was plain that Long and Head had disrupted a superior cavalry force, the prime escort to a mere two battalions of foot, miles from help, surprised, dislocated and marching for their lives – and that they had now been spared. It was a disgrace to British arms; Campo Mayor's garrison, with its cavalry escort mostly dispersed, should have been shelled to bits by the gunners, scattered, ridden down by the Heavy Brigade, and the remnants captured by the infantry. In examining what went wrong, historians face the inevitably partial and self-justifying accounts by major participants, anxious to protect their reputations at the expense of others'. At least the controversy provides the rare bonus of multiple accounts by eyewitnesses, although it has to be said that what follows is only one possible interpretation of those accounts.

Towards mid-day on the 25th, Lieutenant-Colonel John Colborne was initially commanding the infantry-heavy advance guard, until the country opened out on the approaches to Campo Mayor. Beresford then decided that the advance to contact must become cavalry-heavy. Brigadier Robert Long was brought up to the front with the Light and Heavy Brigades, and Colborne found 'the whole of my advance guards disposed of, and placed under the immediate command of Sir Wm. Lumley, with the exception of a squadron or troop of cavalry, and the 66th Regiment.' That is, the light companies of Colborne's brigade were for the moment to move with Lumley's battalions, at this stage the leading infantry brigade. Colborne was not unemployed for long:

> Sir Wm. Stewart, perceiving that I had received no orders to advance, rode up to me and desired me to ascend the hill with the cavalry and the 66th Regiment to the right of the town. I immediately hastened up the hill with Major Boyce in command of the squadron, and ordered the 66th to follow. I had patrolled up this hill a few hours before daylight, and alarmed a picquet of the enemy, and was, therefore, persuaded that the town was evacuated. On reaching the summit of the hill southward of Campo Mayor, accompanied by the squadron of cavalry, I observed a column of French infantry, protected by cavalry, marching rapidly towards Badajoz, abandoning from time to time two or three horses or mules, apparently loaded with baggage. The head of the column was a very short distance from Campo Mayor. I moved through some enclosures to the southward, and ordered the 66th Regiment to follow the cavalry under my command, as rapidly as possible. While we were greatly excited, and the commanding officer of the 66th receiving my instructions, an Aide-de-Camp from the General commanding the brigade came from the northward of the town, and delivered me a message that I was separating too far from him. I hastily said, Tell the General I can see better than he can from this ground; and proceeded through a small ravine or valley, at a gallop, til we found ourselves on the flank of the enemy's column, and, perhaps, at about six or seven hundred yards from it. I think we must have been in this situation not more than a quarter of an hour after we had separated from Sir Wm. Stewart. We halted when the French column formed square, and their cavalry trotted towards Col. Head's squadrons to receive their charge.

So this narrative takes us back to Colonel Head, accompanied by Robert Long's DAQMG, Captain Doyle, going forward to the charge. After the charge, Colborne continues: 'The French retired, pursued by our cavalry, and, from the ground we occupied, the Portuguese Skirmishers and the Heavy Brigade appeared to be advancing in the form of a crescent.' Colborne does not specify a distance from the French, but for him to identify the shape of the line they must have been lower down than him, towards the road. We may also deduce the distance not to be very great – not, certainly, anything like a mile and a half, which later was to be the adamant opinion of Robert Long. Beresford himself stated in a letter of 1834 that 'after the charge... on reaching the field, I found the Heavy Brigade 500 yards in the rear of the enemy, and the 13th Light Dragoons not anywhere within sight.' Similarly, as we saw earlier, Colonel Charles Dalbiac, commanding the Heavy Brigade's 4th Dragoons, wrote of seeing 'shortly before the attack the light brigade at about 500 yards in advance', and to the left of the Heavy Brigade. And Doyle, also already quoted, saw 'the Heavy Brigade in our rear just before the charge', and by implication close enough 'to follow in support' of the light cavalry.

All these accounts reasonably fix the position of the eight squadrons of heavy dragoons at the time of Colonel Head's charge as adjacent to the rear of the French column on the road, say 500 yards back. What about the infantry? The received opinion seems to be that Lumley's leading brigade was at this stage still a long way off, perhaps 2 miles. Beresford stated this to be so, quoting later letters from Henry Hardinge (his DQMG), Count de Villa Real (his ADC) and Robert Long. But there was one battalion well in advance of Lumley's troops, sent forward by the divisional commander himself, with the squadron of Portuguese cavalry under Major Boyce, in the hands of Lieutenant-Colonel Colborne: the 2/66th.

This mixed battle group was advanced by General Stewart behind the all-cavalry advanced guard under Brigadier Long, but ahead of Lumley's battalions on the road – Colborne, as we have seen, was told at one point that he was getting too far in advance, but he none the less pushed on 'at a gallop' right up to the flank of the French column behind Long and Head. He sent back word to Lieutenant-Colonel Goldie of the 66th to hurry up and join him: 'To the commanding officer of this regiment I constantly dispatched instructions to hasten on, and follow our route' – in other words, across country. The distances were not great – Colborne said that less than a quarter of an hour elapsed between his getting his orders from Stewart to take forward the 66th, and his own arrival on the flank of the French column (even if some of the ground was covered at a gallop). The 66th behind him could not have been too far away; and this may explain a curious statement by General Stewart's ADC, Captain Gabriel, which went against the common remembrance that all the infantry were 2 miles in rear – that 'The head of the infantry column was a few hundred yards (about 4 or 500) in rear of the heavy brigade', while 'the enemy's column was in sight.' So perhaps it was the 2/66th that Gabriel saw, and he mistook them for Stewart's division?

Of course, had they been visible to Colborne when he saw the Heavies looking like 'a crescent', he would have said so, for their absence was very much part of his later disappointment at what happened. But perhaps they were just too far back – or were held back by someone, just out of his reach? Colborne said that Goldie told him the 66th 'had been halted three times, when making every effort to carry into effect my orders.' We must also note the curiosity contained in a letter to Beresford of June 1832 from Lumley, at Campo Mayor the leading infantry brigade commander: 'being at the head of the column of infantry forming the advance, and moving on as rapidly as circumstances would permit, I observed Lord Beresford dismount for the moment and surrounded by a group of officers. I galloped up, and was then informed that a staff officer had just reported the 13th Dragoons to have been all taken prisoners.' Most of us, reading the above, would say that the leading infantry could not have been above half a mile away if William Lumley (at their head) was in a position physically to observe his general dismount.

It is pertinent at this stage to ask, where is Beresford? As Napier cuttingly expressed it, 'To profit from sudden opportunities, a general must be constantly with his advanced guard, in an offensive movement.' Yet Beresford was not well up with his advance; he was therefore unable to see Colonel Head's charge develop, nor its result; and thus accepted too readily a misdeduction of what someone thought he had seen.

And what of the guns? Major Hartmann (KGL) tells us that 'the whole brigade of artillery... [was] immediately in the rear of the advanced guard.' We may assume that this means on the Badajoz road, for ease of movement; and we might presume, on pragmatic tactical grounds, that they were in advance of Lumley's battalions, but certainly behind the Heavy Brigade. Beresford, however, defines Hartmann's 'of the advanced guard' not as the cavalry, but as 'of the advance of the infantry... [therefore] about two miles in the rear' – which would be a strange place to move his fire support.

In summary, then: when Colonel Head charged, it would seem that the Heavy Brigade were perhaps a quarter of a mile in rear; the guns (bar two, which were somewhere behind those eight squadrons) were 2 miles away; and – with the exception of the 2/66th, which may have been near the two forward guns – the infantry battalions were 2 miles, or nearly an hour's march away (unless Lumley was nearer the mark). Beresford himself and his staff were almost certainly somewhere in a dip, behind the Heavies.

*   *   *

Back now to Robert Long who, seeing the 13th disappear, was left in a muddle; he sat his horse at the head of three Portuguese squadrons, cheated of a charge, and now halted on the road in front of the marching enemy column. He described what happened next in a letter written three days later:

> I followed as rapidly as I could to support this attack, still supposing the heavy brigade in my rear, occupying the attentions of the remaining part of the enemy's force, but, to my utter astonishment, when, at the point where I first met the Badajoz road, I halted, and looked around to see what was next to be done, I found they had quitted altogether the line of direction I had pointed out, and at the suggestion of one of Marshal Beresford's aides-de-camp, had marched by their right to the other side of the valley and road, and were halted a mile and a half off, on the opposite and elevated ground, quite abandoning me to myself, and completely oversetting all my plans.

If that was not enough, Long now found that a party of French hussars – he thought two squadrons' worth – had rallied on the road 200 yards to his left. Since the French marching column was approaching from his right, led by another squadron of hussars, he was sandwiched. He made to charge clear through the hussars to his left, but 'some of the enemy's infantry advancing and flankers firing, and a troop of their cavalry advancing and shouting, my Portuguese friends got alarmed, broke away and fled in disorder.' His DAQMG, Captain Doyle, had just arrived back up the road from accompanying Colonel Head's charge and pursuit as far as the spot where the battering train was captured. He helped Long collect and steady the Portuguese, who lost six men killed and wounded and, shamefully, twenty-eight taken. 'After a little difficulty the Portuguese were rallied and brought back in good order', and they continued south within 200 yards of the French column, marching parallel – it was plain to Long that it would be foolish to venture the Portuguese horse in any further attempt on the column's cavalry escort.

The obvious solution was to get the Heavies up. 'It was only necessary', says Long, 'to charge and beat, and throw into confusion the cavalry at their head and rear (and which if the British dragoons could not do they have no business here) and the object was accomplished.' Doyle went off to order up Long's absent Heavy Brigade, passing the French infantry – then in close column again and marching for all they were worth, with Long and the nervous Portuguese keeping pace just out of musket range on their left flank.

Further in rear, Beresford's ADC, the Count de Villa Real, says that before they met Doyle coming back, 'We rode on quickly and coming up with the heavy brigade, the Marshal inquired what was going on in front. He was told there had been some charges in which it appeared the French cavalry had been broken, but having seen only part of the light cavalry, and learning that the 13th light dragoons had been taken prisoners, the Marshal, expecting the infantry to be up soon, desired the Hon. Colonel Grey to take position on the left of the road, until he could know what had occurred in front.'

At this point Doyle, on his way to take Long's summons to the Heavy Brigade, met Beresford: 'having passed the column of French infantry I certainly then found Marshal Beresford and his staff, with two of Major Hartmann's guns, contiguous to the Badajoz road, and not above 300 yards from the enemy.' Beresford demanded to know where the 13th Light Dragoons were, to which Doyle replied 'that they had charged and broken the French cavalry, and were pursuing them on the Badajoz road. I then learnt [presumably to his amazement] that the 13th, whom he had only recently left in victorious pursuit, 'had all been cut to pieces or bodily taken, and it was by the Marshal's order the heavy dragoons were in the position in which Brigadier-General Long then saw them. I of course returned and acquainted the Brigadier-General of what I had been told.'

Beresford's ADC, the Count of Villa Real, wrote:

> As the French continued to retreat at a quick pace, the Marshal sent instantly back to the artillery that some guns should come rapidly forward, and ordered also the heavy cavalry brigade to advance upon the right of the French as they retreated. Two guns having arrived, fired a few rounds upon the French, but with little effect, though at a short distance. They moved on after the enemy upon the road as they continued to retire. I was then sent to Colonel de Grey to desire him to charge the French infantry as soon as he should see it broken by our artillery, or that he considered he might do so with advantage, as we had already lost one British regiment of cavalry.
>
> Expecting to join Colonel de Grey in the charge, I rode along with him at a jog-trot to keep up with the French, with which we found ourselves in line, and not further from them than about 100 yards. He asked me whether the infantry were advancing. I said that it had been ordered so. We could not help regretting the bad effect of our guns, of which not a single shot struck the French column; and observing at the same time how well they kept together, though we were so close upon them, and they were moving at such a quick step. I accompanied Colonel de Grey more than a mile, until he received orders to halt, in consequence of the artillery not being able to move any further. The allied infantry was then very far in the rear, and not much in advance of the town of Campo Mayor.

Two guns, out of the six in the KGL brigade behind the advanced guard, had been brought forward and opened fire down the road on the rear of the marching column. However, they fired only a few roundshot 'at too long a range' according to Major Hartmann, one of the officers with these guns. Doyle watched the effect: 'the 100th Ligne behaved with coolness, Hartmann's guns killed a few men, but they kept firm in their formation.' Hartmann said of the guns that 'They were prevented, by an express order from Marshal Beresford to halt, from advancing close on the French column... to bring the enemy under a more effectual range for case shot.' Cleeve's KGL brigade were equipped with light 6-pounders, for which the case shot was effective out to about 350 yards. So when Hartmann wrote that 'Three or four hundred yards more trotting would have done the business as far as the guns were concerned', it seems that the two guns could not have been closer than about 700 yards, which sits uneasily with our earlier conclusion that the Heavy Brigade were 500 yards behind the French column, and even more so with Doyle's observation that the guns were 'not above 300 yards from the enemy'.

Why did the guns unlimber so far in rear, and try roundshot, when another minute at the trot would have put them up with the cavalry and within canister range? Hartmann later denied, as did his officers, that the two guns' team horses were too fatigued, blown or distressed 'to urge them forwards' (as claimed by Beresford's DQMG Henry Hardinge) or 'to move any further' (as claimed by his ADC the Count de Villa Real), since 'We only came that morning from Monte Regengo, and the animals at that period of the campaign, were still in excellent order' (Captain Mielmann, KGL). Monte Regengo was only 8 miles from Campo Mayor. Hartmann wrote 'The horses of the artillery were not by any means fatigued or distressed. The officer commanding the two guns brought up, Captain (now Lieutenant-Colonel) De Rettberg [it was in fact Cleeve] of the Royal Hanoverian Artillery of Stade, and myself, present on the spot, were only prevented, by an express order from the Marshal to halt.' And anyway, why only two guns, when more were available? Hartmann stated that he proposed bringing the whole of Cleeve's battery forward, but the offer 'was not granted'. Beresford stated that he had 'not the slightest recollection of ever receiving any such suggestion'; presumably, therefore, Hartmann spoke to one of his staff. Beresford also said that, on the contrary, 'the officer reported that his horses could proceed no further. I did not desire to expose the only cavalry that remained entire to the risk of loss [in a charge]; and it was only when the guns could be no longer kept up with the troops, that I commanded the whole to halt.'

And so this whole strange episode entered Alice in Wonderland territory. According to Robert Long, writing three days later, he:

> soon after saw them [the Heavies] in motion at a very slow pace in two lines, keeping to the right of the road on which the enemy were retreating. At length they approached the right flank of the enemy's column, indicating an apparent intention to attack, bringing up at the same time two pieces of artillery, which no earthly obstacle prevented firing into the French column at such a distance as they chose. I hung upon their left flank with my valiant runaways. The country was beautifully open and favourable for the movements of both artillery and cavalry. The enemy still had several miles to go to their point of retreat, and between them were interposed the four squadrons of British and Portuguese... In such a state of things I did not conceive it possible for the enemy to exist for ten minutes longer... had they been summoned, an immediate surrender would have taken place. After parading and escorting them in this manner for some distance, *judge my astonishment at seeing all the troops, artillery etc., halted, and the enemy permitted to retire without molestation*... the defeat of the enemy's column would have wound up as brilliant a little field-day as fortune could have delighted my heart with.

*   *   *

And that was that. The French went gratefully into Badajoz, and the British into Campo Mayor, 'for rest and refreshment', in Beresford's words. The allied casualties were about 170 killed, wounded and taken, of whom the 13th Light Dragoons lost some sixty – a quarter of their charging strength. The French suffered a good many more; imprecise figures ran between 300 and 600. The 26e Dragons, according to Martinieu, lost eight out of their sixteen officers and 100 troopers; but interestingly, a Spanish officer who escaped from Badajoz a few days later said that while the enemy had only fifteen prisoners from the 13th, they took in upwards of 400 of their own cavalry wounded, 'and all with sabre cuts'. This figure was also quoted by Colonel D'Urban in his journal four days later: 'The enemy's loss was considerable on the 25th. He has carried into Badajoz above 400 wounded. All his Artillerymen who had been employed in the siege of Campo Mayor were sabred.'

The true worth of Campo Mayor to the British was not measured in bodies; it was the moral superiority again established by their cavalry. As after Sahagun, Villada, Mayorga and Benevente, the word spread that a British charge was a dreadful thing to face; French cavalry thereafter were that touch more apprehensive. After all, two squadrons in two lines overcame six squadrons in four lines, and the French turned and ran – moreover, they ran knowing that they were deserting the 100e Ligne: dishonour was added to defeat.

The greater dishonour, of course, may have belonged to William Beresford. In the furious pamphlet wars of the 1830s he was never quite accused of lying about Campo Mayor, or of getting his staff officers to lie on his behalf, for in those days to call a gentleman a liar was a worse charge than murder. All the same, doubt seems to hang over so many aspects of 25 March: Long's original orders, the movements of the Heavy Brigade and the infantry, the location and halting of the guns, the state of their team horses, the report of the 13th's capture, Beresford's own inadequate movements – and all these compounded for decades afterwards by his desperate, detailed denials and the endless attention he paid to the proving of his case. The specifics are perhaps trivial when set against his central failings – of enterprise, and moral courage. His passivity in halting the follow-up that should have destroyed the French force; the supine withholding of any attempt to block the road with his heavy dragoons, or to shell the French into opening up so that they could be charged, or even just held until the infantry got up – all these point to a dangerous indecisiveness. There is also a lack of moral courage about his eagerness to heed Wellington's strictures on the irreplaceability of his cavalry; fear of that disapproval seemed uppermost in his mind, colouring his judgment at the least hint of a threat.

That he failed to move to where he could himself see the vital ground was nobody's fault but his own. Nor was his apparently unquestioning acceptance of Tripp's ludicrous report (or was it Long's?) that a whole cavalry regiment in open ground had been captured and apparently driven away, like a herd of sheep – so instantly accepted, it was almost as if he welcomed it, as if it gave him an excuse not to commit the Heavy Brigade. And then his curious passivity over getting more guns forward – indeed, even seeming to look for reasons not to do so.

The truth was that in senior command Beresford was ineffectual, and the absent Hill's British regiments soon knew of his incompetence that day, even though they had been kept out of battle. They sided with the 13th Light Dragoons when the inevitable reprimand came whistling in from Wellington's headquarters; the 13th's consolation, as Napier wrote, was 'the unsparing admiration of the whole army', and sympathy too, in equal measure. It was as well that none of them knew what Beresford's failings would cost them, seven weeks later, at a place called Albuera. We end this rather prophetic chapter with another corrosive judgement on Beresford from William Napier: 'History, my Lord, deals with very great men, and you sink in the comparison... when she looks at Campo Mayor and Albuera, she will not rank you amongst the great commanders.'

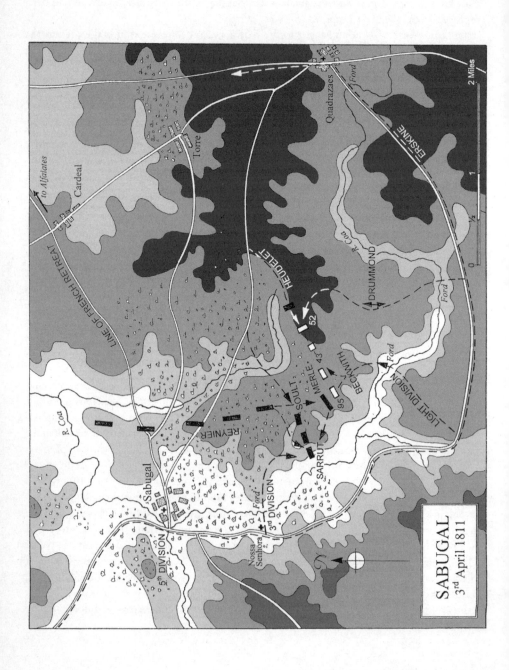

SABUGAL
3rd April 1811

3
Following Massena to Sabugal, 5 March– 3 April

AT the time of the battle of Barrosa, and far to the north, Marshal Massena was already well into his withdrawal from facing the British in front of their Lines at Torres Vedras. The bones of the story are that Massena, repulsed at Busaco the previous September and frustrated before the Lines, had been forced by the need for food into a retreat to Santarem in November 1810. As the cold of winter gripped harder the condition of his hungry army had worsened, as had its treatment of the wretched peasantry. Eventually, on 5 March 1811, Massena began to retreat once more – 200 miles up to and along the line of the River Mondego, to Celorico, Almeida, and thence across the frontier into Spain to Ciudad Rodrigo.

Vengeful Portuguese irregulars ranged like wolves along the flanks and tail of the retreat – they had much to avenge; and as they struggled north and east Massena's army lost many thousands to starvation, sickness and Portuguese knives and pitchforks. They responded in kind, and the grim route of their retreat was marked by burning villages, butchered and tortured civilians, abandoned loot and equipment, and mules and horses hamstrung when they could no longer keep up. A typical reaction to these many outrages was expressed in a letter of 15 April by Captain William Stothert, 3rd Guards:

> The most barbarous excesses were committed by the enemy throughout his whole line of march, and the inhabitants who from age or sickness, were unable to quit their houses, became victims to the horrid brutality of the French soldiery. There is no atrocity of which these unprincipled ruffians have not been guilty; every crime that stains the black catalogue of human cruelty having been committed on the persons and property of the poor wretches who had the misfortune to fall into their hands. The prospect of the advanced guard, was always that of burning villages, of plundered cottages, of murdered peasants. The roads were covered with the dying and the dead – with cannon, baggage and ammunition, which the enemy could not carry off; with mutilated cattle, with everything, in short, that could create horror and disgust, that could make the heart feel sentiments of indignation against the barbarous enemy, and of pity for the suffering and ravaged natives.

Sharp local actions between French rear- and British advance-guards were fought at Pombal, Redinha, Condeixa, Cazal Nova, Foz d'Arouce, and at Sabugal on the Coa. Rifleman Ned Costello, 1/95th, was at Condeixa and Cazal Nova:

In the course of the noon we passed through the pretty town of Condeixa, which the enemy had fired in several places. The main street was completely blocked by the flames darting across the road from the opposite houses. To enable the troops to pass, we were obliged to break a way through some dry walls. This caused a temporary halt, during which the chief part of the division gallantly employed themselves extricating the unfortunate inhabitants from the burning houses. Tom Crawley made use of his great strength to some purpose, and chucked some five or six old people, whom he had brought forth over his shoulders, over a wall as he supposed, out of immediate danger. Tom, however, who should have looked before he made the old ones leap, was not aware that close to their descent was a large well, into which, to their great terror, he had very nearly dropped the terrified and screeching sufferers.

Having cleared the houses away, we proceeded to Casal Nova, where we came up with the incendiaries, whom we found perfectly prepared to receive us. The country all about was greatly intercepted by old walls, and afforded excellent facilities for skirmishing. In a few seconds some of our division was observed moving upon our right, and we were ordered to extend, and at it we went. After several hours hard fighting, kept up with great spirit by both sides, we compelled the enemy to retire, but not before we had lost an excellent officer in the person of Major Stewart, who received a shot through the body. He was led by two buglers to the rear, where he died shortly after. The death of this officer gave a step to my old Captain O'Hare, who obtained the majority.

In this skirmish Lieutenant Strode also received a severe (mortal) wound. This officer in action always carried a rifle, for the skilful use of which he was celebrated. A man in our company named Pat Mahon received three balls on the hip at the same instant, and so close together that a dollar might have covered the three holes they made.

The enemy still continued the retreat, their skirmishers, at times, making short stands to keep our rifles in check, and a few of their rear sections occasionally pouring a running fire into us. We drove them, however, through the village of Casa Nova. Some of the French for a few minutes here availed themselves of pieces of dilapidated walls, but as soon as we commenced outflanking them, they all retired, with the exception of one man, who, to our surprise, remained loading and firing as if he had a whole division to back him. I scarcely know what could have induced me to fire at this poor fellow alone, and exposed as he was to at least twenty other shots; but my blood was up, through his having once aimed at me, his ball whizzing close by as I approached. Be that as it may, I had got within fifty yards when I fired. In an instant I was beside him, the shot had entered his head, and he had fallen in the act of loading, the fusil tightly grasped in his left hand, while his right clutched the ramrod. A few quick turns of the eye as it rolled its dying glances on mine turned my whole blood within me, and I reproached myself as his destroyer. An indescribable uneasiness came over me, I felt almost like a criminal. I knelt to give him a little wine from a small calabash, which hung at my side, and was wiping the foam from his lips, when a heavy groan drew my attention aside, and turning my head I beheld, stretched near him and close to the wall, another wounded Frenchman, a sergeant. '*Helas,*' exclaimed the wounded man, the big tears suddenly gushing down his sunburnt countenance, as he pointed with his finger to my victim, '*vous avez tue mon pauvre frere*', and indeed such was the melancholy fact.

The sergeant, a stout heavy man, had fallen, his thigh broken by a shot. The younger brother, unable to carry him off the field, had remained, apparently with the intention of perishing by his side. We halted for the night on an adjacent hill, about a mile in advance. The French also took up their position opposite us. The picquets of both armies occupied a beautiful ravine, that sloped between us. I took advantage of the few moments leisure our position afforded to return to the French sergeant. But I found him and his brother both as naked as they were born, perforated with innumerable wounds, no doubt administered by the Portuguese. I turned back to the camp, but in a very poor humour with myself, though I could not well close my eyes to the magnificent scene around me. The sun had set, its light had been supplanted by burning villages, and fires that on vale and mountain correctly pointed out where the hostile divisions were extended.

Second Lieutenant John Kincaid of the 95th Rifles also saw the flames:

Our post that night was one of terrific grandeur. The hills behind were in a blaze of light with the British campfires, as were those in our front with the French ones. Both hills were abrupt and lofty, not above 800 yards asunder, and we were in the burning village in the valley in between. The roofs of the houses were every instant falling in, and the sparks and flames ascended to the clouds. The street were strewed with the dying and the dead – some had been murdered and some killed in action – which, together with the half-famished wretches whom we had saved from burning, contributed in making it a scene which was well calculated to shake a stout heart.

Rifleman Costello again:

The following morning the French continued their march of havoc, and we closed after them, village after village giving flaming proofs of their continued atrocities. Passing through one (Miranda do Corvo) which had been fired by reason, as we were informed, of it having been the quarters of Marshal Ney and staff, an appalling instance of vengeance here occurred. The parents of one of our Cacadores had lived in this village, and immediately we entered, he rushed to the house where they resided. On reaching the doorway, the soldier hesitated a few seconds, but the door was open, and stretched across the threshold he beheld the mangled bodies of his father and mother, the blood still warm and reeking through the bayonet stabs, while an only sister lay breathing her last, and exhibiting dreadful proofs of the brutality with which she had been violated. The unhappy man staggered, frenzied with grief, and stared wildly around him; till suddenly burying all other feelings in the maddening passion of revenge, he rushed forth from what had probably once been a happy home. His first act was to dash at some French prisoners that unfortunately were near the spot, guarded by some of our dragoons. These he attacked with the fury of a madman. One he shot and another he wounded, and he would have sacrificed a third, had not the guard made him a prisoner. On the circumstances being made known to the General, he was liberated.

Confirmation of British attempts to save French prisoners from Portuguese revenge at Miranda do Corvo comes from 2nd Lieutenant George Simmons, 95th:

The rascally French had plundered this place, and committed every sort of wanton atrocity upon the inhabitants, and then left many of their helpless countrymen for the infuriated inhabitants to wreak their vengeance upon. Luckily for these poor wretches, we followed the French so rapidly that they fell into our hands, and were put in charge of British soldiers, or they would have been butchered indiscriminately.

Two days later Auguste Schaumann, Deputy Assistant Commissary with Wellington's cavalry, saw another perspective:

On the 17th March a thick mist prevented us from marching before midday, as it was impossible to discover the road the enemy had taken. We marched across the battlefield to the narrow pass through which the enemy had been forced across the small bridge over the Ceira. We found the bridge blown up, and the river, a foaming forest stream, roaring along and swollen with the rain, its bed so full of large, smooth flints, that it was dangerous to ride through it. Here we began to see evidences of the appalling consequences of a too hasty flight. Prisoners assured us that the crowd on the bridge was so thick at the time it was blown up that a number of men had been flung into the air, and about 500 had been drowned in crossing the river. The banks were still covered with dead bodies. A number of exhausted donkeys, horses and mules, which had not been able to wade across the large smooth stones of the roaring stream, and which the barbarians had made unfit for use either by hamstringing them or twisting their necks, were still writhing in the mud, half dead. Among them lay commissariat carts, dead soldiers, women and children, who had died either from want and cold, or through the explosion. Over the whole of this ghastly confusion of bodies, our cavalry and artillery now proceeded to march without mercy, until the whole was churned into a mess of blood and slush. Never during the whole of the war did I again see such a horrible sight,

 Our hussars came back with a number of prisoners, and in a chapel we found a poor Portuguese peasant, probably a guide, who for some reason or other had been cruelly cut to pieces. After following the enemy for two [leagues], we camped out in a pine wood close to the road. Death and destruction, murder and fire, robbery and rape, lay everywhere in the tracks of the enemy. Every morning at dawn when we started out the burning villages, hamlets and woods, which illuminated the sky, told of the progress of the French. Murdered peasants lay in all directions. At one place, which contained some fine buildings, I halted at a door to beg water of a man who was sitting at the threshold of the house, staring fixedly before him. He proved to be dead, and had only been placed there, as if he were still alive, for a joke. The inside of the house was ghastly to behold. All its inmates lay murdered in their beds, but their faces were so peaceful that they looked as if they were sleeping, and some were even smiling. They had probably been surprised in the night by the French advanced guard and murdered. The corpse of another Portuguese peasant had been placed in a ludicrous position in a hole in a garden wall, through which the infantry had broken. It had probably been put there in order to make fun of us when we came along.

 As on the 19th March we thought the enemy were still occupying their strong position on the Ponte de Murcella, our baggage was sent to the rear, and we marched to the attack at dawn. But we had made a mistake. The enemy had gone and the bridge had been destroyed. The sappers were already engaged in building a light wooden bridge for the passage of our infantry. The cavalry and artillery had to go through the roaring stream, on the stony bed of which many a horse fell. We halted on the opposite bank and waited until a portion of our infantry had crossed, and then continued our pursuit, and found the plain covered with stragglers, dead Frenchmen, arms and baggage. Gradually they were compelled to abandon upon the high road all the silver, gold, valuables, silks and velvets, costly ecclesiastical vestments, monstrances and crucifixes, which they had plundered from the churches, convents and private houses; and as the Portuguese peasants cut the throats of all the Frenchmen they encountered, the Light Division became the heirs to all their abandoned treasure. The villages through which we marched were nothing but heaps of debris. We followed the enemy over five [leagues], and Captain Aly, who commanded the advanced guard, made 600 prisoners. In the afternoon we caught sight of some French cavalry, but they vanished again. Late in the evening we camped close to a swamp in which several enemy soldiers and animals had sunk and perished. A few that were still alive were rescued. Among other things our booty consisted of 1,000 bullocks, cows, goats and sheep, which were handed over to me. The rest of the plunder was either sold at auction that night, or else bartered away. In addition to other things, I bought two very sharp amputating knives out of the instrument case of a French surgeon, who was a prisoner; and for a long time used them as carving knives at table.

When we continued our march we found the small town of Galliges completely burnt and deserted. The ravages of the French on this road had again been terrible. In one of the villages lying in a hollow to our right, they had drowned some of the inhabitants by first binding them hand and foot, and then laying them head foremost in a stream. We marched on to Cea. As I was riding towards the place over some rocks surrounded by bushes I heard a piteous cry, and when I reached the spot whence it came I found a Frenchman, whom a few peasants had stripped quite naked and now proposed to beat to death. The Frenchman dropped on his knees before me and implored me to save his life. The peasants on the other hand begged me urgently to allow them to cut his throat. Of course, I did not allow this, but took him with me to Cea, where he was placed among the prisoners.

Two days later, beginning on 22 March, there followed an extraordinary week for the retreating French, in which Marshal Ney, long-time commander of the 6th Corps (which he had raised in 1804), was relieved of that command and sent home to France. His gross but justified insubordination exploded against a new plan, now crazily conjured up by Massena, to retreat not conveniently to the store-houses of Almeida only about two marches away, but south, 70 miles across the bare mountains into Spanish Estremadura, and thence back into Portugal via the upper Tagus. It may be that Massena held some vain hope of saving face with his Emperor not only by evading Wellington's pursuit but also by not quitting Portugal altogether. The prospect of this march so appalled his generals, and their rejection was so adamant, that he changed his mind; but Ney's excessive outspokenness led to his replacement by General Loison – much to the army's horror, for Ney was greatly admired for his dashing leadership in action, while Loison was simply a butcher.

The retreat continued, and by 3 April Massena was behind the Coa. What then transpired had all the makings of a classic Wellingtonian victory, and the little-known combat of Sabugal – it did not rate a battle honour – is well worth retelling.

*   *   *

The line of the Coa is the last water obstacle before the Spanish frontier, 15 miles to the east of Sabugal. Although it offered plenty of fordable sites for foot and horse, none the less it was not easily passable everywhere, particularly for wheels. From Sabugal north to the bridge at Sequeiro is about 12 miles as the crow flies, but nearer 20 miles as an obstacle requiring observation and deployment for defence. Massena had some 37,000 men, leaving aside D'Erlon's 9th Corps and Montbrun's cavalry, who were back near Almeida (busy consuming some of the fourteen days' provisions held there by Brennier). Junot's 8th Corps were 10 miles behind Sabugal at Alfayates, reached on the last day of March when they were close to the last extremities of starvation and fatigue. They were now within reach of the frontier, and two days' march from the provisions at Ciudad Rodrigo.

Loison's 6th Corps had Marchand's division at Sequeiro, and Ferey's and Mermet's at Bismula to the south – 8 miles from the right of Reynier's 2nd Corps, also behind the Coa at Sabugal. These locations remained unchanged during the first two days of April. Thus in summary Massena had two corps forward on a 20-mile river line (Reynier left, Loison right) and one back (Junot), with a fourth really out of contention around Almeida (D'Erlon).

This loose grouping made Massena vulnerable, especially given the weakened physical state of both men and horses. Rapid marches to reinforce – or indeed to do anything – were quite out of the question. Massena would have done better to follow in the steps of Junot and D'Erlon, if he could not hold a tighter grip on his other corps. But he did not, and Wellington saw his chance to encourage the French to slink out of Portugal at last.

In brief, he would arrange to occupy Loison's 6th Corps on the French right, while slipping a force round behind Reynier's 2nd Corps on the left to cut his escape to Alfayates and Ciudad Rodrigo – and would then attack Reynier's two divisions frontally with four British. That would see 22,000 bayonets concentrated against Reynier's 10,000, with another 5,500 men of the Light Division and two brigades of cavalry in place behind. If done at first light with no warning, then neither Loison nor Junot would be able to provide support in time. Wellington intended nothing less than the destruction of Massena's 2nd Corps, and both the ground and his plan were such that the result seemed a foregone conclusion. This masterly and positive interpretation of his enemy's situation shows Lord Wellington's military brain working at its best: it was the equivalent of the boxer, well ahead on points over a tiring opponent now backed into a corner, who sees the man's guard become loose, low and wide.

Loison's 6th Corps was to be approached but not engaged by Campbell's 6th Division, beyond Rapoula, with a battalion from Hoghton's recently formed 7th Division doing the same further north at Sequeiro. That is, since Loison could reasonably assume he was first choice to be assaulted, they were to give him every encouragement in that belief without quite making it so. Similar threatening gestures were to be made at D'Erlon's 9th Corps, to the north of Almeida, by the Portuguese militia brigades under Trant and Wilson.

Reynier's left front was to be attacked forcibly by Picton's 3rd Division, over the ford a mile upstream of Sabugal near the chapel of Nossa Senhora, with the 5th Division later entering the town itself via its bridge, and then climbing the front of the French-held ridge. Behind them, ready in reserve on the road from Guarda, would be Spencer's 1st Division and the rest of Houghton's 7th. These formations moved into position on 1 and 2 April; Reynier's pickets, such as they were, were gently urged backwards over the river line by cavalry. Tomkinson of the 16th Light Dragoons noted in his diary, 'April 2nd – the enemy has only a small picket on our side, which withdrew on our sending a party to drive it over.'

The turning movement upstream of Sabugal was necessarily given to Sir William Erskine, temporarily in command of both the Light Division and the two cavalry brigades (their own generals, Crauford and Cotton, being on leave). The cavalry was to move over the Coa and turn north to Quadrazaes and Torre, thereby blocking Reynier's route back through Souto to Alfayates. The Light Division was to cross by a nearer ford, to get behind his regiments on the ridge. Wellington stressed that he wanted to see Reynier actually commence his withdrawal, following pressure by the Light and 3rd Divisions on his rear and left flank, before the 5th launched itself in the centre. He himself would be on the conical hill a half-mile west of Sabugal town, which would give him an excellent line of sight to the 3rd and 5th Divisions across the river but not more than about 3 miles upstream.

The ground surrounding Sabugal was a maze of wooded slopes clustering either side of the course of the Coa. In many places the adjacent hillsides rose steeply from its ravine, with a multitude of small watercourses marking the re-entrants between the spurs. There were a few fords joining various primitive tracks, which naturally tended to follow the spines of the major spurs. The hill and plateau system to the east of the river began a mile from the town, and ran south quite close to the river, climbing still higher towards Quadrazaes. The access road south from Guarda via Sabugal ran to the west of the river, in full view to Reynier for a good 3 miles. The road then turned east, partially hidden behind a parallel ridge beneath the river. Reynier's divisions were deployed north to south, on the ground dominating the approaches from the town, but extending no more than a mile and a half below it. It was this deployment, together with the discovered crossing places beneath and beyond the hill feature, which Wellington now sought to exploit. He issued his orders on the night of 2 April, for an attack next day.

Across the river, Reynier took note of the allied cavalry activity during the day and the campfires after nightfall. This did not bode well, and he applied to Massena for orders. The obvious deduction was initially doubted, but then there was a change of mind, and Massena ordered Reynier to send his guns back to Alfayates, and strongly suggested that he follow suit with his entire corps. Since it was now about 2am on the morning of the 3rd, Reynier decided that he had insufficient remaining darkness to pull out surreptitiously, and would do so the next night. He did, however, belatedly send out a dragoon regiment to his south, and light infantry pickets to the ford above the town at the chapel of Nossa Senhora.

First light came through a curtain of rain and mist, with thicker fogs swirling around the damp slopes of the river valley. A similar fog unfortunately covers much of what then happened at the river crossings, since the accounts vary. Some cavalry appear to have crossed very early, since Reynier's withdrawing column of guns en route to Alfayates, the other side of Souto (4 miles distant from Quadrazaes) were set upon, unsuccessfully; a fleeing driver took the news to Reynier, who shortly afterwards also got word of a column in red coats being seen at one of the fords. The main body of British horse presumably moved later, together with Major-General Erskine, and it would have been proper practice for him to have both brigades of the Light Division in tow, so that he or his staff officers could then direct where and when he chose the brigades to peel off for the earlier fords, as he continued on to the higher crossings.

Unfortunately, Beckwith's 1st Brigade – the 1/43rd, 1/95th Rifles and one company from the 2/95th (it is almost certain that the 1st Cacadores were not present that day) – were left behind in the fog, without orders. Drummond's 2nd Brigade had moved with Erskine. At some point Erskine sent an ADC to right the matter – it is said that he spoke in a highhanded fashion – and Colonel Beckwith promptly marched off, presumably left to his own choice as to the crossing-place. He chose one some 4 miles upstream from Sabugal, a little further by road and track, and which was directly beneath, rather than in rear of, the north–south line of Reynier's battalions. It can be seen from the map that it was the next upstream ford, another mile further on, which would have taken him to his objective. It was now around 10am on the morning of 3 April. Rifleman Ned Costello was serving in 2nd Lieutenant George Simmons' company of the 1/95th: 'After crossing the river, we advanced up the hill on the other side. Under a fleecy shower of rain, we soon became hotly engaged with the French.'

Lieutenant Simmons himself wrote in rather more detail:

> Colonel Beckwith's brigade crossed the river Coa; the sides steep; the 95th led. It was deep and came up to my armpits. The officer commanding the French pickets ordered his men to fire a few shots and retire...
>
> As soon as the riflemen crossed, they extended and moved up the steep hills, covered with mountain heath and brushwood. On approaching the first chain of heights, the enemy commenced skirmishing. By this time the 43rd Light Infantry and Cacadores had joined us. The enemy were driven from one chain of hills to another for two miles, when suddenly, on gaining the top of a third chain of hills, our whole line in skirmishing order came in contact with seven columns of French. The company I was leading on... owing to the situation of the ground, came literally within twenty yards of a column before we could see it. Guess my astonishment! The most hideous yelling assailed my ears, the French drumming, shaking their bayonets, and calling out 'Long life to the Emperor Napoleon!'

It would appear that Beckwith followed the track through a small chestnut wood, up the spur from the river, which led left towards the main slopes. The French pickets fell back across the open ground, giving the alarm; and Beckwith's men came upon Reynier's left-hand regiment, the 4e Léger. This regiment, part of Sarrut's brigade, comprised three battalions about 1,100 strong in all, which were advancing in columns of double companies. Sarrut's other two regiments – the six battalions of the 2e Léger and 36e Ligne – were some way further back, along the flatter slopes of the plateau.

Since Beckwith had crossed the Coa too soon and too close to the French, and in difficult visibility, much confusion now arose, and for quite some time no help could be expected. With one bayonet battalion, the 43rd, and four companies of riflemen, Beckwith was in effect challenging 12,000 Frenchmen, complete with supporting cavalry and guns (not all of the latter having been sent back). It was fortunate that the fog obscured the fact that he was outnumbered almost exactly ten-to-one.

The first contact was with the skirmishers of the 4e Léger, who proved ineffective against the riflemen, but the latter were in turn driven back by the following columns, on to the flanks of the 43rd's line. There the 4e Léger were held, however; the limited fire of the first three ranks of their 1,100-strong columns were no match for 750 muskets and 350 rifles, and after a few volleys Beckwith charged, pushing the 4e back through a small wood of chestnut trees. But on the far side he came up against the rest of Sarrut's brigade, whose three-to-one superiority drove him back to the protection offered by the stone walls of some enclosed fields. Sergeant Anthony Hamilton of the 43rd Light Infantry wrote that: 'In this charge, twenty-seven of my own company were cut down, thirteen of whom were killed, and the others, myself among the number, wounded. Under these circumstances the leading battalion would probably have been sacrificed, had not Colonel Beckwith with great promptitude, retreated behind some stone enclosures, which enabled him to maintain his ground.' It is appropriate to quote Napier of the 43rd – his prose is unmistakable:

> Scarcely had the riflemen reached the top of the hill, when a compact and strong body of French drove them back upon the forty-third; the weather cleared at that instant, and Beckwith at once saw and felt all his danger; but he met it with a heart that nothing could shake. Leading a fierce charge he beat back the enemy, and the summit of the hill was attained, but at the same moment two French guns opened with grape at the distance of a hundred yards, a fresh body appeared in front, and considerable forces came on either flank of the regiment... The musketry, heavy from the beginning, now increased to a storm; the French sprung up the declivity with great clamour, and it was evident that nothing but the most desperate fighting could save the regiment from destruction.

A new force of French infantry now approached, curiously on the road from the east. These were the 2,000 men of the 17e Léger and 70e Ligne, Godard's brigade in Heudelet's division. The story is now best handed over to one Lieutenant John Hopkins, aged 24, commanding the right flank company of the 1/43rd. Beckwith later declared that, so far as it was possible for a man in command of one company to decide an action, Hopkins had decided the combat of Sabugal. Here is Hopkins' account:

> Early in the morning of the 3rd April, during heavy rains, the 43rd Regiment was formed in column of companies at their alarm post, close to the miserable Portuguese village in which they had passed the night. They were kept a considerable time under arms, awaiting orders for crossing the river Coa. At last an officer of the Staff rode up, and in a hasty, petu-lant manner asked Colonel Beckwith, who commanded the brigade, why he had not marched to the ford. The Colonel replied that he had not received any instructions from the General, Sir William Erskine, for that movement. On this, however, the Colonel marched us rapidly towards the ford. We advanced right in front; four companies of the 95th led. We all crossed the Coa, which from incessant rains had become so swollen as to render the passage difficult and dangerous. The bank on the further side of the river was steep in ascent, covered with thick underwood. We soon gained its summit, halting in front of the brow of the hill to avoid the torrents of rain, fast pouring down, with the wind at our backs. The officers sat themselves, with their backs against a low stone wall. The enemy in position at Sabugal discovered us, and fired several shot. Colonel Beckwith laughingly said, 'Gentlemen, you have an extraordinary taste, to prefer shot to rain.' He ordered the 95th to advance to the town, which was some distance to our left front. They advanced in skirmishing order, under a sharp fire from the enemy, many of the shot reaching us. The atmosphere was greatly darkened by the bad weather.

The firing on the Rifles became incessant, but they gained their ground up to the French position. Colonel Beckwith sent the 43rd forward in support of the Rifles; they descended towards the river, into a sort of plain, interspersed with trees and underwood. As we approached, the heavy fire of the French marked their line of battle; and the riflemen retired upon us in good order. Colonel Beckwith having gone some distance towards the left, in order to reconnoitre the position of the enemy, Colonel Patrickson was left in the entire command, and close upon the enemy. He gave the orders for an instant advance and charge against the line in our front, which was on an eminence. At this moment a slight clearance from the rain enabled me, who was in command of the company on the extreme right of our line, to perceive that, at some distance towards our right rear, a strong detachment of the French from Rovena were directing their march to the ford. I saw all the danger of our being so turned, and immediately requested Captain Duffy, commanding the next company, to allow me to take mine to oppose the attempt of the enemy, who were gaining fast upon our rear. He replied he could not take upon himself such a responsibility as allowing the separation of my company from the regiment. I said no time should be lost, and that I would take the responsibility at such a moment upon myself; and instantly I marched off the company, by bringing up their left shoulders, advancing rapidly to the right towards an eminence at some distance, on which I placed the company in position, fronting the enemy, who were marching round the right flank: I was now quite separated from the Regiment, which was fiercely engaged with the French. I had above 100 men in the company; as several of Duffy's men had followed. The two subalterns with the company were William Freer and Henry Oglander, both most excellent officers.

The body of French, who were marching towards the Coa, halted on seeing us, and dispatched a body of infantry against us. I reserved my fire until they neared the summit of the hill, when I opened upon them, causing them to retire in some disorder to the plain. They again formed, and advanced as before, but were checked, retreating to a greater distance. At this time Colonel Beckwith rode up; I reported all that had occurred, and that the French had brought up two guns in rear. I requested his instructions. He spoke most handsomely to me, approving and thanking me for what I had done, and said that he should give me no orders, but leave me to act entirely on my own judgement, in which he had perfect confidence; that he would not forget me, and that he would bring me to the notice of Lord Wellington. On his leaving, Sir John Elley, who commanded the cavalry, came up and I begged that some dragoons might reinforce me. He made no reply, but rode off, shaking his head as if unable to comply. During this time the enemy were forming in greater strength; they advanced with the drummer beating the *pas de charge*; the officer in command, some paces to the front, leading his people to the hill. William Freer asked permission to go forward and personally engage him; this of course I refused, as his presence with the company was more important.

The French bravely stood our fire, and their two guns were brought to bear on us. I ordered a charge, which was done with great spirit, driving the enemy to some distance. Whilst these attacks were made, the Regiment was constantly engaged at Sabugal. The firing was severe and continuous, never receding nor slackening, thus affording me the utmost confidence; for had not the French left been so severely attacked, they would have been able to detach a body against my rear or on my left flank, which would have compelled me to retreat upon the troops now advancing to our support.

It was at this time the captured howitzer was left under command of the fire of the 43rd and Rifles, as every attempt of the French to carry it off was ineffectual, causing severe loss in both cavalry and infantry.

Hopkin's foes were Heudelet's 17e Léger and 70e Ligne. They came up as Beckwith retreated to the stone walls adjacent to Hopkins, who was a half-mile to the right. The new pressure was from Sarrut's 2e and 36e Ligne, and from Heudelet's pair of howitzers. The attack formed in three columns but was stopped dead in its tracks by the 43rd's volley fire. Charging, they and the riflemen tumbled the French back beyond the single howitzer once more; but now two squadrons of Pierre Soult's horse counter-attacked on their right, and rallied the 4e Léger on their left, driving them back yet again to the walls, over which there now developed a close-quarter firefight. The French dragoons came off worst in this encounter; behind their advance, however, Sarrut's infantry came forward again and sought to rescue the lonely howitzer. Good shooting persuaded them otherwise, and left the howitzer sitting 50 yards away in a fire-swept gap between the two sides. Colour-Sergeant Garrety, 43rd, wrote:

> A second and stronger column of infantry rushed up the face of the hill, endeavouring to break in and retake the howitzer, which was on the edge of the descent, and only fifty yards from the wall. But no man could reach it and live, so deadly was the 43rd's fire. One of my comrades, having previously passed the howitzer, took a piece of chalk from his pocket, as he said, marked it as our own, and we were determined to keep it.

In all this, Colonel Beckwith led from the front, wounded and with blood dripping down his face (Tomkinson wrote that 'he was hit by a musket ball on the outside bone of the right eye'), personally taking the companies forward into the charge and judging when to give ground. Garrety again: 'One of our company called out Old Sidney is wounded. Beckwith heard the remark and instantly replied, but he won't leave you: fight on, my brave fellows; we shall beat them.'

There is a record of Sydney Beckwith's verbal mannerisms at this time, described as calming yet spirited, and the orders themselves given not as in the drill manual, but conversationally. This immensely popular comander – also nicknamed 'Old "What's this?"', from his habitual opening remark – was reputed to know most of his men by name. One of his subalterns, 2nd Lieutenant Johnny Kincaid, aged 23, tells us:

> Beckwith himself was the life and soul of the fray... and his calm, clear, commanding voice was distinctly heard amid the roar of battle, and cheerfully obeyed. He had but single companies to oppose to the enemy's battalions; but, strange as it may appear, I saw him twice lead successful charges with but two companies of the 43rd, against an advancing mass of enemy... Beckwith's manner of command on those occasions was nothing more than a familiar sort of conversation with the soldier... seeing the necessity for immediate retreat, he called out, 'Now, my lads, we'll just go back a little if you please.' On hearing which every man began to run, when he shouted again, 'No, no, I don't mean that – we are in no hurry – we'll just walk quietly back, and you can give them a shot as you go along'... and regulating their movements by his, as he rode quietly back in the midst of

them, conversing aloud in a cheerful encouraging manner... A musket ball had, in the meantime, shaved his forehead, and the blood was streaming down his countenance, which added not a little interest to his appearance. As soon as we had got a little way up the face of our hill, he called out, 'Now, my men, this will do – let us show them our teeth again!' This was obeyed as steadily as if the words halt, front, had been given on parade, and our line was instantly in battle array, while Beckwith, shaking his fist in the faces of the advancing foe, called out to them, 'Now, you rascals, come on here if you dare!'... as soon as they came near enough, another dash by Beckwith, at the head of the 43rd, gave them the coup de grace.

For an hour – and a long hour it must have felt – this one-sided fight continued, and if Sir John Fortescue says it was a fight 'which has hardly a parallel in our military annals except that of Inkerman', who are we to argue. Sir John Moore should have been alive to see what the 43rd and the 95th did that day. John Hopkins of the 43rd again:

> The enemy were still at some distance, and appeared to be reinforced, and intending another attack; and I perceived the 2nd Battalion of the 52nd advancing rapidly. I went to the commanding officer, pointing out the enemy near, and we agreed it would be best for him to form his regiment on the right of my company, and make an immediate advance upon the French, which we did. As we advanced, they retired, forming themselves into the line perpendicular to our left, and in continuation of their line to Sabugal, where their chief body was posted. I therefore brought up my right shoulders to front them, extending all my men as skirmishers; the 52nd doing the same to my right, we all commenced skirmishing amid the trees in unabated rain.

Drummond's brigade had crossed the Coa more than a mile beyond Beckwith, with a climb of another 2 miles to get to the sound of the guns, distances that would comfortably fill the solitary hour of the 43rd and 95th. Another mile, and surely Beckwith's 1st Brigade would have perished. Sir William Erskine, however, added further lustre to the contempt in which he was widely held, by trying actually to stop Drummond – for what reason (as with much that he attempted), nobody knew. Fortunately, the staff officer sent with the order and Drummond together agreed in the obvious circumstances to read it with a Nelson's eye.

Drummond's brigade comprised both battalions of the 52nd, the Portuguese 1st Cacadores and four companies of the 4/95th Rifles. The 2/52nd, as we see from Hopkins, took right flank to his company, the rest of the 2nd Brigade coming up in support of the 43rd and the companies of the 1/95th. French cavalry were again cutting in to the scattered redcoats – the 43rd's company and the 2/52nd were all deployed in skirmishing order, out of the protection of a conventional line – and one of the 52nd's Colours was nearly taken. However, a squadron of the 16th Light Dragoons then joined the action, and the French horse were driven off. Captain Tomkinson of the Dragoons wrote: 'We were sent far away to the right at the time; a squadron of the enemy was annoying our infantry. Sergeant Proctor of the 16th, with two men, saved an officer of the 52nd from being taken.' It would be of events at about this stage that Major-General Miles Nightingall, in a letter of 8 April, painted the little cameo that only foxhunting people will find remotely hilarious: 'Colonel Ross of the 52nd very narrowly escaped being taken when the French cavalry charged our skirmishers. The latter were forced to retire behind a wall and it was with difficulty that Ross could get his horse over before the enemy got up close.' Lieutenant Hopkins of the 43rd also wrote about this phase of the action:

> The French showed fight, in their new line, mingling several dragoons with their skirmishers; their sudden debouch from behind the trees at first shook ours and severely wounded several. One man, close to me, was cut in the face, but he would not leave the field. A marksman, of the name of Cassan, was taking his aim at a dragoon riding towards him, when another horseman appearing suddenly on his right, he turned his firelock and shot him dead, the other dragoon instantly galloping away. Colonel Mellish, of the Staff, rode along the line; he was to be seen in every post of danger, loudly and gallantly cheering the men to stand fast against the enemy. Our whole line preserved their ground for some time, until a few horsemen getting amongst the skirmishers on the right, a sudden cry, 'The cavalry! The cavalry is in the midst of us!' caused the 52nd to retreat in confusion.
>
> I was with the skirmishers on the left, and did not retire my men, seeing that the horsemen who had got into the line were so few. Some men of the 52nd remained on the left with my company. It was fortunate that we remained skirmishing, as it prevented one of the Colours of the 52nd falling into the hands of the French, owing to the firmness of the men. The officer bearing the Colour came up to thank me, at the same time highly praising the gallantry of my men.

The following nice anecdote comes from the 52nd's regimental history:

> When the French cavalry dashed in upon the 52nd, Private Patrick Lowe, a well-known character for hardihood, was in advance with the skirmishers, and being a little stout man, and not one of the fastest runners, particularly when forced to turn his back, was soon almost overtaken by a French trooper. Finding that he had no time to get to the walls behind which the greater part of his comrades were now making cover, he took refuge behind the stump of a tree; came to the right about down on one knee, and deliberately covered the trooper with his piece on rest, and the butt to his cheek. The dragoon at once reined up, and not liking the look either of Patrick or of his muzzle, began to curvet right and left, hoping to induce him to throw away his fire. Lowe, however, remained as steady as a rock, and cool as on parade, still covering his man. Some of his comrades from the wall wished to bring down the dragoon, but were stopped by others, who called out that he was Pat's lawful game, and ought not to be taken away from him. Almost immediately the regiment in perfect order advanced, and to the surprise of everyone Lowe allowed his friend to ride off unharmed. When he was roundly taxed by the leading officer for such conduct, as being 'a fool not to shoot him', the reply was irresistible: 'Is it shooting ye mane, Sor? Sure how could I shoot him when I wasn't loaded?'

It is said that it was about this stage in the action when the fog lifted sufficiently for both Lord Wellington and Marshal Massena to be able to read their situations. Neither can have been pleased. The former would see his two light infantry brigades on the hillside now out-numbered five-to-three, and in the process of being outflanked on their left. The latter would see the British 3rd and 5th Divisions – 10,000 bayonets – crossing the Coa, while he had only Arnaud's brigade of eight weak battalions (say 3,300 men of the 31e Léger and 47e Ligne) to oppose them, the rest of his corps being committed already.

Napier, who was there, says:

> At this critical period, the fifth division passed the bridge of Sabugal, the British cavalry appeared on the hills beyond the enemy's left, and General Colville with the leading brigade of the third division issued out of the woods on Reynier's right.

Which raises a key question about the combat of Sabugal: why was Beckwith left so long unsupported? Drummond cannot be censured: he could scarcely have arrived sooner over the route he had to take. He must be allowed some period of indecision when he first heard the contact a mile to his left, echoing in the fog, and even more for the inexplicable delay to his release imposed by Erskine. The lack of substantial cavalry support, whose speed across country would have brought them up in no time, can safely be ascribed to Erskine's mismanagement. But a question mark does hang over Sir Thomas Picton: since there is no suggestion that his 3rd Division was anything other than correctly placed at dawn, ready to cross the ford near the chapel of Nossa Senhora, then why did he not cross sooner? After all, noise travels further under fog, and the continuing racket of 7,000 muskets just a mile away must have been channeled audibly along the valley of the Coa. This was clearly no transient affair of pickets, but the sought-after engagement that showed that Reynier's left was, as planned, now fully occupied – sooner than expected, of course, but there was no mistaking what was afoot. The descriptions of Beckwith's various movements, the charges, counter-charges and periods of wall defence surely imply an action lasting well over an hour (Fortescue gives his opinion that 'the fight was maintained for a full hour' even before Drummond arrived).

Oman tells us that Picton, and Dunlop commanding the 5th Division, both sent to Wellington ('who was close by') for orders on seeing the dawn fogs, having because of them 'resolved not to move'. We can take it, therefore, that their decision to sit tight was confirmed by his lordship – and by extension, that it remained his prerogative to change that decision when he wished to do so. The puzzle therefore leads us to him. In a letter the very next day to Beresford, he wrote: 'These combinations for engagements do not answer, unless one is on the spot to direct every trifling movement. I was upon a hill on the left of the Coa, immediately above the town, til the 3rd and 5th Divisions crossed, whence I could see every movement on both sides, and could communicate with ease with everybody, but that was not near enough.' This is very curious: Wellington is here acknowledging a fault in the co-ordination of the movement of his divisions, and that he could see it all – and yet Beckwith was left to fight alone for so long and with so nearly tragic consequences. Could Wellington really have thought Picton's advance a 'trifling movement'?

In any event, an anecdote from a sergeant in the 3/1st in Hay's brigade of 5th Division blames tardy action by Dunlop as the cause of Reynier's escape. The latter's route via Cardeal to Alfayates lay along the ridge to the north, which passed not only the ingress of Picton's 3rd Division but also Dunlop's 5th, beyond the town of Sabugal. Sergeant John Douglas wrote:

> As we advanced, the enemy retired. A long and narrow bridge, leading to the town, might have been defended with success, at least for some time, but so great was their hurry that

they abandoned it without firing a shot, leaving their kettles on their fires with their dinner nearly cooked. This you may imagine was no affront for as we double quick'd it over the bridge the fires were soon left bare, the men snatching the kettles off as they passed. We dashed through the town and ascended the hill. This also might have been defended a length of time, but they fled leaving their tents standing. During this time the right was hotly engaged. Cannon and musketry were hammering away in great style. The first notice we had of how the play went on the right was the French retreating in the utmost confusion, while there we stood idle spectators (except a few 9-pounders), letting them pass with all the plunder of Portugal. There never was in my opinion so fine an opportunity lost as this. It is my firm belief that had we been allowed to have attacked the enemy at that time the army of Massena would have been easily annihilated. General Hay rode up to General Dunlop, who commanded the Division, and demanded why he did not attack the enemy. His reply was, 'I am waiting for a guide.' 'There's the enemy, there's your guide,' exclaimed Hay. He then wanted his own brigade to lead the attack, but 'No'; on which sheathing his sword with madness, he exclaimed in front of the Division, 'I shall report your cowardice to Lord Wellington this night,' and I believe he was as good as his word, as the General went off to England in a few days and did not make his appearance for several months.

So it sounds as if Massena's thanks should stretch beyond the morning's fog and Picton's leaden feet, to embrace Dunlop's shyness? It seems Lord Wellington's displeasure was indeed provoked, for Dunlop was later to go on leave of absence, never to return to the Peninsula, nor to receive any honours for the campaign.

*   *   *

Reynier's casualties at Sabugal totalled 760, of whom 186 were taken, plus one gun. Heavy rain coincided with his withdrawal, and the subsequent lack of pursuit suggests that this high proportion of prisoners – a quarter of the losses – must indicate a demoralized attitude. A lack of fighting spirit may also be deduced from the high proportion of officer casualties: of the total killed and wounded, one in ten were officers – twice the usual ratio. They doubtless fell while out in front, showing that example that is so necessary when leading on the reluctant. Given the greatly increased misfire rate that would have been caused by the continuous rain, and which must have severely degraded the usual British superiority in line volley fire, it is surprising that French columnar shock action still failed. Their hearts cannot have been in it that day if even John Hopkins' hundred, on his little knoll, were not swept away. Wellington's casualties were a fifth of the French – just 162, of which half were in the 43rd and another quarter shared between the 1/52nd and 1/95th Rifles. Picton's 3rd Division lost just 25 men.

So all in all, and particularly bearing in mind this trivial butcher's bill on both sides, the French had been humiliated rather than hurt. The amazingly doughty performance by the troops of the 1st Brigade of the Light Division was the feature of the day, and owed much to the able and inspiring leadership shown by Sidney Beckwith; his cheerful energy made up for the impossible odds, and added extra shine both to his own name and to his soldiers'. In contrast was the limp leadership of Sir William Erskine, who failed – or whose staff failed – to point one of his two foot brigades in the right direction; who failed to get his cavalry up in meaningful support; who was himself notable by his absence throughout; but whom Lord

Wellington – who had long since identified him as a sort of madman – still seemed unable or unwilling to sack. Erskine killed himself two years later, jumping out of a window.

The conventional view of Sabugal is that had the fog cleared with the dawn Wellington's success would have been greatly enhanced, with Reynier suffering not just a 7 per cent casualty rate but seeing his entire 2nd Corps put in the bag. There was a rumour that Picton in fact set off in good time that morning, and then got lost in the fog, but the close and clamorous noise of battle makes this a lame excuse. Was his lordship himself the cause of Beckwith's unsupported solitude? Well, to direct 'every trifling movement', he said, one needed to be on the spot, whereas he was 'upon a hill... whence I could communicate with ease... but that was not near enough.' We do not know exactly what he felt was lacking, but it may have been an ability to instill a proper sense of urgency into Picton.

However, all's well that ends well; and three days later Wellington wrote to Captain Chapman, RE: 'We have given the French a handsome dressing, and I think they will not say again that we are not a manoeuvring army. We may not manoeuvre as beautifully as they do; but I do not desire better sport than to meet one of their columns en masse, with our lines. The poor 2nd Corps received a terrible beating from the 43rd and 52nd.'

The action at Sabugal concluded Lord Wellington's chase after Massena. For the third and final time, he had ejected the French from Portugal, bar a thousand men bottled up in Almeida. Massena had retreated skilfully in the main, but after Sabugal his army were thoroughly (if temporarily) beaten; they were as disorganized as they had been two years earlier, when Wellington had chased Soult out of Portugal after bundling him from Oporto. The general view in the army was probably fairly expressed a month after Sabugal by Beresford's chief gunner, Major Alexander Dickson, who wrote:

> Massena's army have I understand gone into quarters at Zamora, Toro, &c., and will probably not be able to undertake anything of consequence for some time. The retreat the French have made is the admiration of every one for its compactness and skill in executing, for I am told there remained no stragglers or fatigued men, but their loss in cavalry and artillery horses with other means of transport for stores, &c., must have been immense, and they will require a great supply to enable this army to commence active operations. Further attack upon this country I think out of the question until reinforcements are received from France.

This letter of Dickson's was dated 1 May; his final confident prediction was to be disproved just two days later, at a place called Fuentes d'Oñoro.

4
Villa Real, Olivenza and Los Santos, 26 March–16 April

WE have seen how General Graham defeated Victor at Barrosa, and so caused Soult to abort his invasion of Estremadura – but not before Soult had captured Badajoz; how Marshal Beresford capitalized on Soult's withdrawal to Seville in his approach to Badajoz, and his part in the curious affair at Campo Mayor; and how Massena retreated into Spain via the Almeida-Ciudad Rodrigo corridor after the fight at Sabugal in the first days of April. In the next chapter we will see Massena return through that corridor a fortnight later, to meet Wellington at Fuentes d'Oñoro between its Spanish and Portuguese gates. First, however, we must return to Beresford's corps, facing Badajoz in the southern corridor.

The story of the six weeks that separated the minor engagement at Campo Mayor and the hugely more important battle at Albuera is one of frustrations and uncertainties suffered by Beresford. It also includes the first British attempt in April–May 1811 to take the mighty fortress of Badajoz, using a plan laid down by Lord Wellington – a necessary and fascinating prologue to the second and third attempts of May–June 1811 and April 1812. The period also encompasses a little-known affair at Los Santos, whose cast featured precisely the same names that we met at Campo Mayor, and which provided another entertaining outing for the British cavalrymen.

* * *

The day after the Campo Mayor affair, the only Frenchmen on the north side of the Guadiana were the small party at Badajoz's *tête du pont,* and the garrison inside the adjacent Fort San Cristobal. Taking them and the main garrison into account, Marshal Mortier – left behind earlier by Soult to complete the capture of the lesser fortresses – would not be able to field more than about 10,000 men. Beresford could therefore advance across the river with confidence and easily push him away to the south, thus creating a safe space in which to lay siege to Badajoz. Speed was called for, to get to Badajoz before the newly captured fortress could be put back in good order; at the time of Campo Mayor the French had been in possession for only a fortnight, the breach was still open, the siege works and batteries had not been filled in, and the garrison had few provisions and not much ammunition. Beresford therefore sent William Stewart's 2nd Division and Hamilton's Portuguese promptly to Elvas, just down the road to the west, on 26 March; Cole's 4th Division were allowed a further day's rest at Campo Mayor, having no shoes left worth the name.

Elvas was to be Beresford's base on his line of communications back to the main army. It was only 15 miles from Jerumenha, where the Guadiana offered passable fords and a bridging site; Wellington had stipulated that Beresford should cross there, in a letter written five days before Campo Mayor: 'Lay down your bridge, and make a *tête du pont* opposite Jerumena; and in the first instance invest Badajoz on the left bank of the Guadiana, doing the same with the cavalry only, or Spanish troops, or militia, on the right. You might also make the Spaniards seize the bridges of Merida and Medellin.'

There was a road from the Jerumenha fords to Badajoz via Olivenza, some three marches all told from Elvas; the alternative bridge at Merida – 50 miles away to the east from Campo Mayor, across appalling country, and then 40 miles back to Badajoz – would have been a week's hard work. Not only were most of Beresford's infantry in no state for prolonged marching, lacking shoes, but time was of the essence: General Phillipon was fast repairing the walls of Badajoz.

Regrettably, on Beresford's arrival at Jerumenha it quickly transpired that neither there nor at Elvas – contrary to Wellington's information – were there enough pontoon boats to span the Guadiana. Twenty were required for the 180-yard river, there 4ft to 5ft deep; but only five Spanish wooden boats and four pontoons were available – at Elvas. And by ill-luck, Wellington himself had that January ordered the destruction of all river craft when Soult invaded Estremadura. There had been two sets of boat bridges stored at Badajoz, but these were now in French hands. The tin pontoons left Elvas on the evening of 29 March, and the five Spanish boats on the afternoon of the 31st, together with a party of infantry and sailors ('to be employed in the Engineer department', according to Dickson, the chief gunner). That night two of the wooden boats overturned on the road, and needed repairs.

On 1 April, Cole's 4th Division arrived at Elvas; by the 3rd all the materials for the bridge had been collected at Jerumenha, and Captain Squire, the local chief engineer, set about constructing a timber trestle-bridge either side of a necessarily shortened bridge of boats – but overnight his work was hit by a flash flood caused by melting snows up in the mountains. The river rose 3 feet, the cavalletti cross-members were washed away, and the precious boats were landed once more only with difficulty. On Thursday 4 April, Hamilton, Cole, Stewart and the cavalry had all concentrated as a corps, in the olive groves and cork forests adjacent to the river, with nowhere to go. The longer the frustrating delay at the Guadiana, the more risk that the French would oppose the eventual crossings.

Squire, as a good sapper, constructed in some haste the best practicable solution with what lay to hand: two 'flying' bridges, or ferries on ropes, one using three of the wooden boats and the other using two; and two stages or rafts, using each pair of pontoons. The ferries, according to Charles Cadell of the 28th, could lift 100 men or twenty-five horses – so seven or eight lifts would be needed to get a battalion, its officers' chargers and ammunition mules across the river; the rafts could with difficulty take sixteen soldiers, so long as they kept very still. It was a desperately slow crossing. Dickson tells us that 'The army commenced crossing on the afternoon of the 5th, and continued without intermission until the whole cavalry, infantry and artillery had passed, for which purpose it took about 72 hours.' By 6 April the river had fallen somewhat, but was still 3ft deep at the fords; and by this time the French at Badajoz, under their active governor Phillipon, had taken advantage of Beresford's delay to fill in the trenches, rebuild the breach and get in supplies.

Beresford was inevitably vulnerable to attack in the early stages of the crossings, with no retreat for any units broken up on the far bank; but he had no choice other than to press on and, amazingly, the French let him off the hook. Mortier had been recalled to Paris a week before, and it was Latour-Maubourg who missed this trick; he had troops at Olivenza, only one march away, yet it was the night of 6 April before he took action. When he did so, however, the Gods of War clearly wished to tease him – he came as near as could be to capturing Beresford himself, his entire staff and his headquarters, which were in the village of Villa Real, about 3 miles east of the river. The story has been related in various versions, but the most authoritative is undoubtedly to be read in the 13th Light Dragoons' regimental history:

> The squadron consisting of Captain Serle's and Captain White's troops, under the command of Major Morres, had been detached on April 5th, having crossed the Guadiana in advance of the rest of the army. Their orders were for an immediate advance, and the men had not time to finish cooking before they marched, and consequently went without any provisions.
>
> On the 6th, as the remainder of the regiment was in expectation to move any moment, and to join the advanced squadron, no provisions were sent out. Late in the evening, however, when it was known that the army would not advance, an Assistant Commissary undertook to conduct a train of mules with supplies to Major Morres, though the exact position of the advanced squadron was not accurately determined. He reached Major Morres at about 10pm.
>
> The advanced squadron on crossing the Guadiana on the 5th had taken up a position in front of that part of the army which marched with General Lumley, by whom the rest of the British force was joined later. Major Morres placed his vedettes and outposts in the most advantageous positions to watch any movements of the enemy from Olivenza. He continued to hold that post until the evening of the 6th, when he was relieved by a squadron of Portuguese cavalry under Count Penefield, who was accompanied by a British officer, Major Foljambe, 20th, who acted as AAG. Major Morres gave up his posts to the Portuguese and placed their vedettes. From Major Foljambe he received orders to fall back with his squadron and bivouac in the small wood before mentioned. Conceiving that his front was perfectly secured by the Portuguese pickets which were there posted, he only thought it necessary to establish a post on his right flank, which was the most exposed, as that flank of the army was uncovered. Thence he threw out a few pickets with occasional patrolling parties. These arrangements being made, and such others as he deemed needful, the men not immediately on duty tied up their horses, and the officers took possession of the small house or hut which was but a few yards away. At this juncture the Assistant Commissary arrived with the mules and provisions, and by men who had eaten nothing since April 4th those provisions were sadly needed and very welcome. Fires were lighted and food cooked, a meal was eaten, the men lay down by their horses, and the officers in their cloaks occupied the floor of the hut.
>
> For his actions Major Morres has been blamed, we think unjustly. It had been urged that he should not have permitted fires to be lighted. But what were the facts? He was not on outpost duty. He had been regularly relieved and had fallen back to nearly the position of the army. He had even sent Cornet Macrea to General Stewart with a report of his being relieved, by whom, and the manner in which he had delivered up his post. His men were faint from want of food, and it was impossible to say how soon they might be

called upon again to turn out, and to turn out at a time when there would be no chance of cooking a meal. The fires which were lighted were lighted in the rear of his position and towards that occupied by our troops.

Now the enemy in the course of his retirement by the second road mentioned came upon the embers of the camp-fires and speedily located the position of the squadron. In dashed the French cavalry among the sleeping men and, taking them for Portuguese, used the sabre without mercy. On discovering them to be British, however, they 'were less ferocious and more intent on taking them prisoners.'

The troopers of the 13th, aroused from sleep, with their sabres hung for the most part on the holster-pipes of their saddles, were totally unprepared for resistance. The officers, aroused from their cabin-floor beds by the cries and shouts, rushed for the door. Lieutenant Doherty and Lieutenant King managed to get outside. The former reached his horse, mounted, gave it its head and the spur, and though pursued by French dragoons dashed out into the night, in what direction owing to the darkness he was unable to determine. By luck he rode towards a British vedette, by whom he was challenged.

In this way the news of the surprise reached the army. Lieutenant Doherty immediately made a report of the circumstances to Marshal Beresford and Sir Lowry Cole, after which he rejoined his regiment. Lieutenant King jumped into the stream near the wood, and though fired at (the top of his cap being pierced), got clean over and escaped. Cornet James Macrea had not returned from his mission and thus escaped.

Major Morres and Lieutenant Moss were taken prisoners, together with 1 sergeant-major, 5 corporals, 2 trumpets, 2 farriers, and 40 privates. Sixty troop horses and 2 camp-kettle mules were captured. Lieutenant Doherty lost three horses and all his baggage. Lieutenant King a like amount. Cornet Macrea lost two horses and his baggage, and the whole of the horses and baggage of Major Morres and Lieutenant Moss fell into the hands of the enemy. The wife of one trooper was also amongst the prisoners. Only twenty men escaped, and three wounded were left on the ground.

Other accounts relate how Beresford, Stewart and Long all had narrow escapes in the village of Villa Real, losing not only horses but also a decent night's sleep. It was an embarrassing episode, but it could have been a great deal worse. In his report to Wellington, Beresford not only blames Morres entirely, rather than his own staff, but asserts that he, Beresford, knew in advance of the French's 'meditated attack' and had issued a warning 'before sunset' on 6 April 'of such an attempt':

the cavalry piquet allowing itself to be surprised; and which I cannot account for, as I had, and gave information during the preceeding evening of the meditated attack. The commanding officer of the piquet being a prisoner, he has it not in his power at present to assign the cause of this surprise, and I can only therefore say that it was so complete, that although fully informed of the probability of such an attempt, even no alarm was given by this piquet: and we had no information of the enemy's advance till he was amongst our infantry piquets, in front of our line.

Five days later, in a letter of 12 April, Robert Long also referred to prior knowledge: 'I... went to get my horse fed and watered ready for anything that might occur after daybreak, a report having been circulated by the Enemy [sic] that they intended to attack us.' But did Long warn Morres, we wonder? Twenty years later, of course, this small episode provided D'Urban and Beresford with another stick with which to beat Robert Long. From the pamphlet *Further Strictures*, almost certainly written by D'Urban:

> On the morning of the 6th, Marshal Beresford was informed by several persons coming from Olivenza, that the enemy, entirely ignorant of the state of affairs near Jerumenha, had assembled 2,000 infantry, 500 cavalry and three guns at Olivenza, and intended during the night to attack the covering corps on the left bank. The hour when this effort was to be made was distinctly stated... The Marshal before sunset communicated to the principal officers the intended attack... The squadron of the 13th he had ordered to be withdrawn before dark, and to be placed in rear of General Stewart's division. From some mistake or other, which occurred in giving or carrying Major-General Long's orders, this movement was not executed. At the hour which was intimated, somewhere about midnight, the enemy made their attack; but after the capture of the squadron of the 13th Dragoons, on approaching our line, and finding the troops on the alert, they retired.

Clearly Beresford's warning did not reach Major Morres. It remains a curious episode, very embarrassing for Colonel Head and the 13th (whose triangular involvement with Long and Beresford was not yet over, as we shall see).

*   *   *

The French were now in an uncomfortable spot. The British needed but one march eastwards to put themselves the same distance south of Badajoz (the small garrison in Olivenza could be by-passed); and another march would then see them across the main chaussee to Seville, and thus astride Latour-Maubourg's communications to Soult. If they were quick about it, they could even force Latour-Maubourg into Badajoz: that would never do, since above all he must keep the line open to Soult. So he decided to turn his back on Badajoz, leaving its newly-repaired walls in the reliable hands of General Phillipon and his 3,000-strong garrison. Concentrating 16 miles south at Albuera, Latour-Maubourg set off down the chaussee, heading for Santa Marta and destinations south. He left 400 men as garrison in Olivenza.

Beresford promptly by-passed Olivenza, quite correctly; when his summons to the garrison to surrender was declined he left them to the shoeless 4th Division. We are fortunate to have a letter, written a week later, by Major Alexander Dickson of the Portuguese Artillery, in command of the guns at Olivenza. It both describes what happened, and introduces us – at a low and almost trivial level – to the arcane business of taking a fortress, which will stand us in good stead when we reach Beresford's abortive siege of Badajoz a month later:

> On the 9th April the army advanced in two columns on Olivenza, which we expected the enemy to evacuate, as it was known they had a very small garrison in a large place, with very little artillery or stores, but on our approach we found it the contrary, as they fired from the place with artillery on our cavalry that patrolled to the front. The Marshal then sent a verbal summons and was answered that all communications must be in writing. He then wrote to summon the place, and was answered by the Governor, a Colonel named Neboyer, that he was determined to hold out; that if his garrison was small, he could

(nonetheless) depend upon it, (this was alluding to an expression in the summons) but the letter was worded in a polite manner.

I should have mentioned before, that Marshal Beresford at Juromenha called upon me to give my opinion what was necessary to reduce Olivenza in case the enemy held out, and I stated to him that I thought six heavy guns with 300 rounds each, under the circumstances we supposed the place to be in, would be sufficient, by bringing a good battery as near the place as possible and battering in a breach. At the same time having formerly visited Olivenza, I mentioned a point from whence I thought this might be done – the same where the battery was afterwards placed.

As soon as the enemy's reply to the summons was received, the Marshal sent for me and desired me to proceed immediately to Elvas to prepare for the attack. I reached Elvas that night. On the 10th I fitted out six heavy brass 24 Prs. with 300 rounds a gun. On the 11th they marched by way of Juromenha and reached our camp at Olivenza on the 13th, and I assure you it cost us some labour to get the guns on, as they were rather heavier than our brass 42 Prs. To serve this artillery I got a Portuguese company from Elvas.

On the night of the 14th I got four of these guns into a battery which had been constructed about 240 yards from the counterscarp, and on the morning of the 15th I begun to batter a curtain close to a flank, and in four hours the breach was nearly practicable, and the French garrison so alarmed that they surrendered at discretion being about 460 in number.

Soon afterwards whilst the place was taking possession of, I had the pleasure to see the peasants, who were not permitted to enter the gate, get into the town up the breach. In two hours more it would have been fit to assault... The enemy had 13 guns mounted in the place, but no calibre higher than a 12 Pr. They kept up a brisk fire upon us during our attack, but I lost only one artillery man killed with 3 wounded.

The day afterwards, General Cole wrote to Beresford:

Having succeeded in getting the guns into the battery during the night, and got everything ready before daybreak on the 15th, and also established 2 flanking batteries of field pieces, I sent a summons to the Governor, a copy of which I have the honour to enclose with his answer, which being a refusal to accept the terms I offered, our fire immediately commenced, and was returned with some spirit from the town. At eleven o'clock a white flag was hoisted by the enemy, and an officer came out with a letter from the Governor, a copy of which I have the honour to enclose with my answer and the governor's reply, to which I sent none, and recommenced our fire. After a few rounds, a white flag was again raised, and they surrendered at discretion.

One has to say, with respect to this rather long-winded seven-day operation, that from Dickson's narrative it is plain that the whole thing was a great waste of time, energy and resources. The six 24-pounders and all the ammunition wagons, which could be drawn at no more than 1 mile each hour, would have been more sensibly drawn the 17 miles direct to Badajoz, not twice that distance via Olivenza – where their work was so brief, yet which took so long to arrange. Colonel Neboyer played his hand neatly throughout. He would be well pleased to march out after six days, with his eight officers, 357 men under arms and ninety-six sick, leaving on the walls his fifteen ancient guns, ill-mounted on ox-carts. It has been said (by Oman and others) that Beresford 'was not aware of the weakness of the garrison... [else] he would have swamped it at once by an escalade.' Certainly, 357 bayonets defending a mile of walls would not seem too difficult to overcome, even without any ladders immediately to hand. Yet Colonel Neboyer's answer to Beresford's summons, clearly implying that his garrison was small, makes one wonder why Beresford seemed to ignore the obvious deduction: put in a couple of diversions, and try a quick assault. D'Urban and Long suggest that he was well aware of the garrison's size. Possibly Major Dickson's journal entry for 9 April helps us:

> The Marshal sent for me (after receiving Neboyers' answer) and we went together to the right. I pointed out to him an old work near the place, where I thought a battery might be placed with the greatest effect, and *strongly recommended* that the heavy artillery should be brought up without delay. He then ordered me to proceed immediately to Elvas for this purpose.

Beresford would surely have asked Dickson for an indication of the time needed to get his guns up, and the answer would have been in days, not hours. Add to that the unknown time required to effect the breach, and it is clear that the Marshal felt no sense of urgency – either at Olivenza or, more intriguingly, in respect to the mightier walls of Badajoz. These should have been his top priority: 'You had better lose no time... again to besiege Badajoz' were his orders from Lord Wellington, not three weeks before. Could it be simply that he was unduly swayed by a mere major's professional advice? Granted, he and his army were prompt in pressing on after Latour-Maubourg, to create the unthreatened space he would need to deal with Badajoz; but committing to Olivenza substantial resources which should already have been on their way to Badajoz was not a wise move, and it smacks – once again – of over-caution.

After the frustrations of the Guadiana crossing, and the need to do something about Olivenza, Beresford hoped that he could press on after Latour-Maubourg as soon as may be. Yet another problem now arose, in the shape of the empty provision stores at Estremoz, a Portuguese depot 20 miles west of Juromenha that had been allocated to him by Lord Wellington. Unfortunately, a British commissary there, called Thompson, had earlier allowed the Spanish under Mendizabal to eat their fill. He was promptly sacked, but his misjudgement further delayed Beresford's advance – which had reached Albuera on 11 April – until alternative supplies came up on the 13th. On 15 April, Cole's 4th Division in their new shoes limped in to rejoin at Santa Marta, and on the 16th the army at last marched together for Zafra.

At this point we need to bring into the picture those Spanish units that were in the area, for they are to play a part at Albuera. Wellington had suggested that the bridge at Merida should be left to them, and General Xavier Castanos captured it on 10 April. He and Beresford had conferred on 30 March, prior to which he had been operating north of the Guadiana, retaking the minor fortresses of Valencia d'Alcantara and Albuquerque. On 11 April his cavalry swept another 30 miles south to Almendralejo, on the road to Zafra – that is, he was moving to the east of the British on a nearly-converging axis. It had been agreed that the Spanish would move on the line Merida–Ribera–Usagre–Llerena, and the British on the more westerly line Albuera–Los Santos–Fuentes Cantos–Monasterio.

At about this time Beresford heard that a further 10,000 Spaniards, with 1,100 horse, were on their way: two divisions from Cadiz led by Generals Zayas and Lardizabal, and 3,500 men brought north by General Francisco Ballasteros, all to be under the overall command of General Joachim Blake. Ballasteros had been chased across the hills for twelve days by Soult's

General Maransin, emerging at Fregenal on 12 April, and two days later he had been pushed to Salvatierra. Maransin was under the impression that he was shepherding the Spaniards towards Latour-Maubourg; now, since Salvatierra was only one march from Santa Marta, and Maransin being totally unaware of Latour-Maubourg's retreat and of Beresford's advance, an opportunity arose instead for the British: to put Maransin's 4,500 men in the bag. On 14 April he was at Xeres, one march behind Ballasteros, who was visited that day by Beresford's QMG, Colonel D'Urban. A plan was agreed:

> Proposed to Ballasteros to do his utmost to draw D'Arenberg [the Allies thought the latter was commanding, not Maransin] after him so that the Marshal may cut off his retreat. He agrees and will fall back if attacked upon Nogales – making a good show of resistance not to excite suspicion. If D'Arenberg takes the bait he must be lost altogether; if he halts at Xeres to consider for only two days we ought to also get hold of him.

For this purpose, therefore, Beresford's march for Zafra was designed to come between the two French generals, with a view to cutting beneath the unsuspecting Maransin. However, Latour-Maubourg foresaw the dangerous trap developing, and sent warning letters to Maransin; these were intercepted by guerrillas, but he got the news anyway via a collaborating Spanish citizen of Xeres, and hastily retired south and east, to tuck himself beneath Latour-Maubourg at Llerena, on the road to Guadalcanal. This latter place was 90 miles below Badajoz, and 70 miles above Seville, right up against the Sierra Norte de Sevilla, so it can be seen to what extent Latour-Maubourg had back-pedalled away from Beresford, to close on Soult. Beresford had indeed rapidly created a safe space in which to make his attempt on Badajoz.

With his usual innate grasp of timing, it is appropriate that we now find Lord Wellington riding south from Sabugal to make his reconnaissance of Badajoz. However, before going north with Beresford to their meeting at that fortress, we should consider the cavalry clash at Los Santos, 2 miles from Zafra.

*   *   *

It will be readily anticipated, since the major players in this scene were William Beresford and Robert Long, that all was not sweetness and light; the acrimony between these two that characterized the aftermath of Campo Mayor continued unabated. (Beresford's rooted animosity towards Long, and his anxiety to be rid of him as his cavalry commander, would be demonstrated when in due course Wellington proposed Sir William Erskine, not Long, for command of the new second cavalry division: 'You will find him more intelligent and useful than any body you have. He is blind, which is against him at the head of cavalry, but very cautious.' Erskine was the man described the previous year by the Military Secretary at Horse Guards as 'no doubt sometimes a little mad, but in his lucid intervals he is an uncommonly clever fellow; and I trust he will have no fit during the campaign, though he looked a little wild as he embarked.' The preferred appointment of a half-blind madman gives some measure of Robert Long's abrasiveness.)

To return to 16 April – the Count de Villa Real, on Beresford's staff, would write:

> The army had halted at a very short distance from Los Santos, while the Quarter-Master-General was marking the ground it was to occupy. Headquarters was established at Zafra,

where they were arrived, when a Spanish officer came in great haste to report to Marshal Beresford, that a column of French cavalry was advancing on Los Santos. This information came totally unexpected. The Marshal got immediately on his horse, and in a few minutes reached the ground upon which the cavalry were halted. It was still dismounted. The Marshal ordered General Long to mount immediately, and to keep under the high ground in order not to be perceived by the enemy.

Robert Long, writing to General Le Marchant nine days later, said:

> We halted about two miles off [from Zafra], in a valley, whilst the ground in front was reconnoitring, and I received orders to feed the cavalry, and even cook. The first I acceded to, and we filled ourselves with green forage and water previously, as we concluded, to our taking up our ground.

Lieutenant Charles Madden, 4th Dragoons, stated that they had come off a march of 20 miles without corn, so the horses would by then be in dire need of sustenance, even green grass, inadequate though it would be. Long again:

> In about a couple of hours information was brought that 600 of the enemy's cavalry were advancing rapidly upon Los Santos. I was ordered forward. The fire of our skirmishers soon announced their proximity, and I trotted the column round the village till I got upon the Seville road.

The Count de Villa Real continues:

> A party of the French showed itself on our side of the village; but, on perceiving our cavalry, they retired immediately. The Marshal having seen them, then desired General Long to make the dispositions he thought proper to advance quickly. General Long said that the Portuguese cavalry having their left in front, he thought he must bring their right to the front, and asked whether he was to move right or left in front, adding something about the time it would take. The Marshal replied briskly not to lose time in whatever he did, lest the opportunity of acting might escape him. I consider that our cavalry was not above two hundred yards from Los Santos.

The column comprised the 13th Light Dragoons, followed by two Spanish guns, Otway's Portuguese horse and then Grey's Heavy Brigade of the 3rd Dragoon Guards and the 4th Dragoons. Since the 13th were to suffer no casualties that day, and one month later at Albuera had a strength of twenty-three officers and 380 troopers, it would appear that the regiment (now in four squadrons) was at twice the sabre strength it paraded at Campo Mayor, even allowing for their losses near the Guadiana crossings. The regiment joined the Seville road in line of march, the leading or right squadron commanded by Major Boyse; the troop constituting his left half-squadron was led by Lieutenant Drought, with the right half under command of Captain Macalester. Behind Boyse came the other three squadrons, commanded by Lieutenant-Colonels Patrick Doherty and Muter and Lieutenant George Doherty respectively. The latter's squadron was, as he later wrote, 'only composed of the remains of the squadron that had been surprised near Olivenza a few days previously'. His temporary command – vice the captured Major Morres – was surely a matter of intense satisfaction to the lieutenant, even if it numbered little more than a weak troop.

Lieutenant-Colonel Head commanded the whole, with Lieutenant-Colonel Patrick Doherty his second-in-command. The latter remembered 'the regiment moving on at a brisk trot to the ground of formation.' The enemy were, as at Campo Mayor, the 2e and 10e Hussards, said to be 600 strong; however, a fortnight later at Albuera they paraded 550 all ranks, and since in this present affair they were reported to have lost nearly 300 men one way and another, on the morning of the 16 April it is not inconceivable they were actually nearer 800 sabres. The Count de Villa Real once more:

> The Marshal, after giving orders to General Long to advance, rode on towards the village with the officers of the staff. He entered it, and stopped in the street waiting for the cavalry, which I was desired to go and hurry on. General Long said he was manoeuvring; and would advance the moment he got the cavalry in order. Upon my delivering General Long's answer, Marshal Beresford, not seeing the cavalry come up yet, sent me back again to General Long impatiently to order him to come up without any further delay, as the French would be off before he arrived.
>
> The 13th Light Dragoons being in motion, the Marshal proceeded farther on; and, on getting out of the village, we saw the French cavalry halting in column fronting us, at about two hundred yards beyond it, among some stony ground and low walls, which only left a narrow open space before them.

Brigadier Long stated that:

> The rising of the ground prevented my seeing them, till I reached the top of the rise, where there was a narrow debouche into a triangular and open space, beyond which I observed the enemy posted in column of squadrons.

It seems clear that the Seville road, from the French point of view, disappeared over a crest; therefore, when Long brought up the 13th and halted to survey the scene, they would have no way of knowing how strong a body lay behind it – except by sending a squadron forward to find out. This was put in hand straight away. Unfortunately, Marshal Beresford and his staff being out ahead of the 13th, and understandably keen to scramble back to safety, Long later could not hold back the acid remark that 'the retreat of the *troupe dorée* [gilded band] on the enemy's advance having distracted the men's attention, created some little confusion.'

One of the French squadrons deployed into line immediately Colonel Head's leading squadron came into sight over the rise, and advanced to attack. George Doherty wrote 'We only had time to wheel into line, when the leading squadron of the enemy moved to the charge.' Lieutenant Jeffreys, the serefile officer behind Patrick Doherty's right centre squadron, wrote that '[Our] troop was not clear of the narrow lane or pass when I saw Captain Macalister's troop [the leading troop] wheel up and charge.' Macalister himself said 'the squadron was scarcely formed when the order to charge was given by Boyse. The left half squadron [Boyse's] could scarcely have got clear of the narrow lane, when my troop formed up, and immediately on forming, charged.'

So only Boyse's squadron charged, in some sort of scarcely-formed rough order on the left, with the other three squadrons moving into line as they came up out of the narrow ground. Boyse went at the charging French, whose commander was cut down. Easily dispirited, his troops broke and turned; Boyse pursued for 300 yards, sabring the slower of the French, who rallied behind the other watching squadrons. Boyse and his squadron halted and reformed. Villa Real again:

> The Marshal was very anxious that the cavalry should act, and pressed General Long to be quick, and to attack the enemy; but, though he remained a while in presence, there was no charge from our cavalry, except that already mentioned of the squadron of the 13th. The French, however, seeing our cavalry advancing, opened from the rear, and went off. Upon this the Marshal ordered one of the squadrons of the 13th to disperse, and to pursue. He rode himself with the remainder of the regiment.

George Doherty wrote that the whole of the French then 'immediately gave way, and went off in close column, at a rapid pace'. He himself was called forward by Colonel Head and ordered 'to pursue with my squadron and cover the front of the regiment as skirmishers, which continued to advance in line.' Young George Doherty had the joy of evening the scores with the very troopers who had surprised his squadron near Olivenza, and 'many were cut down', according to the 13th's history. His under-strength squadron (the left squadron) was supported by Colonel Muter's left centre squadron, while Boyse and Colonel Doherty moved forward by threes from the right, Beresford and Long placing themselves in the van. Villa Real was with his chief:'I saw the soldiers of the 13th getting in the rear of the French column, cutting down and taking prisoners many of the French soldiers in the ranks. The French finally broke, and galloped off in confusion.'

It was presumably prior to this stage that the delay occurred, since Doherty would have needed to thread his squadron forward through Boyce's, and then to shake out into skirmish line, while Boyce rallied the two halves of his own squadron and formed column, with Robert Long bringing up Otway's Portuguese squadrons to form a second line – all through the narrow lane, before getting into the open. At some point Long also sent Grey's Heavy Brigade to the right, to endeavour to cut the enemy's retreat. Both Beresford and his QMG, D'Urban, were later to complain of the time Long took to organize the chase. Beresford in his Despatch remarks mildly enough that 'we were certainly long in arranging formations for the pursuit, by which [the enemy] got a little start'; but during the paper campaign of 1833, D'Urban would write to Beresford:

> Much precious time was lost by General Long's indecision, until you, yourself, were at length obliged to ride up to him, and urge him to charge; that he still galloped about calling for his guns; and that in the end they were charged by the 13th Light Dragoons (the regiment then in front of the column, upon somewhat narrow ground), by your own personal order to the commanding officer. Nay, (if my memory serves me), so strong was the impression on your mind at the time of the vacillation which had before prevailed, and of the crisis to which it led, that you said to Boyce, 'Charge them, or they will charge you'.

So there was no love lost there; and for Robert Long the sense of rancour must have been deepened by Beresford's behaviour in riding with the 13th's squadrons. Almost certainly he was right when he wrote that it was the marshal's presence, which of itself imposed restraint on the chase:

> We pursued, but in the strictest order. The consequence was, that to preserve the regularity we could not gain ground upon them sufficiently to make a charge or cut them off... General Beresford desired me not to let them escape. I observed that this could not be prevented, unless the whole of the 13th dragoons were let loose on them. This could not be permitted, consequently we could not overtake them, having already a start of a quarter of a mile, and going as hard as they could lay their heels to the ground.

The pursuit along the Seville road went on for about 10 miles. In the words of the 13th's regimental history:

> At first the enemy, having so much ground of us, halted regularly, fronted, and discharged their carbines, and while the 13th were forming up put about their horses and retired at a gallop. But by degrees the 13th closed upon them and their formation was lost; they became completely broken, and a general rout took place. Those of the enemy who, on being overtaken, did not surrender were cut down.

Beresford eventually realized that, since the Heavy Brigade had been unable to hook around behind the French, and horses were beginning to drop from fatigue, no more could be done. 'Marshal Beresford ordered the pursuit to cease. The regiment was halted and dismounted, and from the Marshal received a handsome compliment on their behaviour.' Robert Long put the French losses at four officers (one killed), and 150 men and horses killed, wounded or taken; D'Urban made it three officers and 200 men; but the 13th's history says 'One officer killed and two taken, 107 prisoners brought in by the 13th; and some Spanish cavalry which chanced to be on the ground collected 170 more.' Among the horses taken – and very welcome – were seven of Major Morres' unfortunate picket, now recaptured. Long lost no men, but 'twelve horses, chiefly old blacks, died that night of fatigue'. A 10-mile gallop/canter followed by another 10 miles back to Los Santos, all on empty stomachs bar some snatched green forage, would not have helped.

Of course, the allusion made in Beresford's Despatch to Long's apparent indecisiveness would almost certainly have been pressed home verbally to Lord Wellington when he met him shortly afterwards at Badajoz. As for Long himself, his own bitterness showed raw when he later wrote:

> Never was there such a fox chase, but I did not enjoy it, because I knew that the 'ignorans' expected us to take every man of them, which I knew was impossible, without disbanding every soldier I had in pursuit; and this, after the thanks I experienced at Campo Mayor, I did not feel inclined to do. Had I had my will, I should have detached a corps to the left by a road which intercepted the line of the enemy's retreat, and would infallibly have been fatal to them. But here again I was over-ruled. Thus success is not left at my disposal, but I shall be made amply responsible for all failures.

It should be noted that Long's somewhat pathetic reference to being overruled on a wished-for left hook, as opposed to the movement of the Heavies already moving on his right, is nowhere mentioned in the private memorandum he wrote (it is thought, as an addendum to his letter to General Le Marchant) only nine days after the affair.

Since Los Santos followed just three weeks after Campo Mayor, both the French and the Allied cavalry units involved would have much to talk about around their subsequent camp-fires. On both occasions the French were already back-pedalling, and therefore revealing a less than robust attitude. At Campo Mayor the abject failure of their initial charge in such superior numbers had been followed by shameful flight and the abandonment of the 100e Ligne, and now at Los Santos another long flight with tails between their legs must have left them feeling belittled and thirsty for revenge. The next few weeks would provide several opportunities.

Beresford's cavalry were quite done up, and were rested the next day. However, the Spanish horse of Penne-Villemur to the east progressed as far as Usagre, where they picked up intel-ligence that Latour-Maubourg was at Llerena, two marches south-east of Beresford, whereas the direct Seville road ran due south; there was therefore a slim chance that a rapid thrust down the latter might cut him off. But early on 19 April, Penne-Villemur sent news that he himself had arrived the previous day in Llerena, and that Latour-Maubourg was reportedly approaching Guadalcanal; so he had the Sierra Norte de Sevilla behind him, and was by now 90 miles or a week's march from Badajoz.

Marshal Beresford decided to accept this scenario; it was a fine achievement to have pushed Latour-Maubourg out of Estremadura, without the loss of a man since Major Morres' picket had been taken, nearly 100 miles back. So Beresford turned at last, and marched his infantry north towards Badajoz, leaving Colborne's brigade to make faces at Latour-Maubourg. Robert Long and the cavalry stayed around Zafra, the Spanish horse around Llerena; and when, a few days later, the force under Zayas from Cadiz had joined Ballasteros, Blake deployed them to guard against Soult's use of the main Seville road. One way or another, Beresford had ensured that early warning of any aggressive moves by either French commander, together with some opportunity for delaying tactics, was now in place. He himself now set off to meet Lord Wellington, to reconnoitre the siege of Badajoz.

5
Fuentes d'Oñoro,
3–5 May

WE left Lord Wellington at Sabugal on 3 April, with the defeated and apparently exhausted Marshal Massena retreating into Spain at last. At that stage, Marshal Beresford was staring in frustration at the swollen Guadiana, prior to pushing Latour-Maubourg well away from Badajoz; and Soult was safely down in Seville, his communications to the north in poor shape. Wellington went south on 16 April to reconnoitre Badajoz, whose capture was, of course, Beresford's main task.

After his return north, Wellington received some surprising news – that Marshal Massena's 6th and 8th Corps (commanded by Loison and Junot respectively) had reached Ciudad Rodrigo on 26 April. Astonishingly, just a fortnight after quitting Portugal, Massena was back, marching to relieve Almeida. No wonder Wellington in later years was to judge André Massena 'the ablest after Napoleon'; when up against him he had always to be wary, for 'I found him oftenest where I wished him not to be'. Massena was a Mediterranean, born in Nice and once a penniless cabin boy; physically slight, energetic, with an animated face and flashing dark eyes, he was utterly corrupt and an enthusiastic looter and letcher, but these voracious appetites never blinded him – in Napoleon's court his cynical realism was said to be second only to that of Talleyrand. He must have believed – wrongly – that he had one last chance to restore himself in the eyes of his Emperor: on the very same day (20 April) that Napoleon signed the Despatch sacking him and appointing Marmont in his place, Massena wrote demanding help from Marshal Bessières – commanding the Army of the North – since he 'was bound in honour to march to the relief of Almeida'.

What Wellington's chief spy in Salamanca, Father Curtis, seems not to have passed on to him was the quantity of rations, ammunition, shoes, clothes, cash, and above all reinforcement drafts, which had for months been accumulating in the French depots. Thiebault, then the governor of Salamanca, states in his memoirs that at one stage during the late winter of 1810/11 he had no less than 18,000 men in his care – detachments belonging to Massena. So the army that marched out westwards, two weeks after it had staggered eastwards, was much larger, and better fed, rested, clothed, equipped and paid. It was short of guns, and Massena had had to beg Bessières for cavalry; the rest and recuperation had been too brief to build up his men for any extended operations; but Massena was able to concentrate four infantry corps with supporting arms and services at Ciudad Rodrigo – 42,000 bayonets, 4,500 sabres and thirty-eight guns, in all some 48,000 men.

These were veterans, and like their leader they were looking for revenge. They had suffered not only the privations of the recent retreat but also, for the majority, several earlier defeats at the hands of the British. Seven of the eighteen battalions in D'Erlon's 9th Corps had been at Talavera; the other corps were at Rolica, Vimiero and Oporto; no less than fifty-four battalions were at Busaco just seven months previously – altogether sixty of Massena's eighty-three battalions had been in one or more of these battles, and in other innumerable affairs and skirmishes. We know from the retreat to Corunna how badly Sir John Moore's infantry battalions had wished only for a chance to turn, stand and fight, just once, for their honour and for the satisfaction of clawing their enemy; it seems probable that Massena's battalions felt no differently.

Against Massena's 42,000 infantry in eighty-six battalions, Wellington could field 34,000 in sixty-five, of whom 23,000 were British, in forty battalions; so in French-versus-British terms he was outnumbered nearly two-to-one. The twenty-five Portuguese battalions took him up to a deficit of some 8,000 men, or a fifth fewer bayonets overall. He was more seriously outweighed in cavalry, however, for against Massena's 4,500 horsemen he could deploy only 1,850 – odds of worse than two-to-one – and with the country east of the Coa opening up into an undulating plateau running away towards Ciudad Rodrigo, this deficiency might be crucial. It was scarcely offset by his slight advantage in artillery (forty-eight guns to Massena's thirty-eight).

*   *   *

The Portuguese fortress of Almeida, with Massena's small garrison bottled up by Pack's one British and five Portuguese battalions, lay a couple of miles east of the Coa river. The main road to Almeida from Ciudad Rodrigo ran through the Spanish frontier post of Fort Concepcion, 6 miles further east and just 300 yards from the border. The fort sat on a long north–south ridge; 9 miles down this feature, and a mile in front of it, lay the village of Fuentes d'Oñoro. A minor track joined Fuentes to Ciudad via the hamlet of Carpio, about 9 miles away. Half way between the main road and the Fuentes track via Carpio, another track ran from Ciudad via Marialva and Gallegos, meeting the Dos Casas river a mile away to the east at Alameda. So there were in fact three routes from Ciudad, all crossing the Dos Casas.

Either side of the north–south spine of the ridge ran two rivers, the space between being about 2 miles wide; the westerly river was the Turon, the easterly the Dos Casas. Where the chaussee from Ciudad crossed the latter, the fort sat some 300 feet above on the ridge, and half of that height may be termed a ravine. To the north of the chaussee, the ravine was impassable to formed bodies of troops. To the south the ravine continued down to Fuentes, but while it got less precipitous, the climb up to the ridge remained – around 300 feet opposite Alameda, falling to 160 feet at Fuentes. Nearing that village, the river had dwindled to little more than a stream and was no obstacle.

It is clear that Lord Wellington's appreciation had concluded that – unless Massena came forward with an unexpectedly large force – he faced merely an attempted relief of Almeida, an effort of no great substance or duration. His intelligence was certainly sufficiently accurate to know Massena was not coming to invade Portugal; and he was entirely confident that he could prevent the blockade from being raised. He wrote to Lord Liverpool on 1 May that:

> I do not intend to allow them to relieve this place, unless I should be convinced that they have such a superiority of force as to render the result of a contest for this point doubtful. The enemy may be stronger than they were when they were obliged to evacuate Portugal, and they may have been reinforced by detachments of troops, particularly the Guards,

under the command of Marshal Bessières; but I still feel confident that they have it not in their power to defeat the allied army in a general action.

Massena's purpose being to get his relief convoy of provisions into Almeida, Wellington surmised that the chaussee would be his prime route; but also that he was unlikely to open it up frontally via Fort Concepcion, since that position had rather too great a resemblance to the ridge at Busaco, and such a choice would invite the British to roll down upon the French flank. What Massena needed to do was to get the British away from Fort Concepcion so that his convoys could pass through. This could be achieved by attacking further south on easier ground, and either beating them and then turning north, or causing Wellington to shift significant formations from the north into that more southerly action. That this was Wellington's reading of the situation is shown in a letter to General Spencer as early as 14 April: 'It is probable that they will move their whole army, or the greatest part of it, upon Ciudad Rodrigo from whence they would turn the heads of the ravines of the... Dos Casas and Turon.'

A fortnight later, on 30 April, George Murray, Wellington's Quartermaster General, issued a warning order for the army to occupy the line of the ridge behind the Dos Casas, down to the hamlet of Nave de Haver another 4 miles south beyond Fuentes, although 'the body of the army will be drawn towards the left.' That is, with little specifically stationed at Nave de Haver – and therein lay the seeds of much future trouble for all concerned. In outline, the British deployment was Erskine's 5th Division of eleven battalions on the ridge adjacent to Fort Concepcion and dominating the chaussee; Campbell's 6th Division of eight battalions on the ridge astride the track coming in from Alameda; and the 1st, 3rd, 7th and Light Divisions behind Fuentes itself. There was to be no deployment south beyond Fuentes bar a small mixed infantry/cavalry guerrilla band under Julian Sanchez, at Nave de Haver. (Sanchez, nicknamed 'El Charro', was a former regular infantry private and ensign of volunteer cavalry from the Ciudad Rodrigo area. Hungry for revenge for his murdered family, he became one of the best guerrilla leaders in the whole Peninsula, leading perhaps 700 uniformed cavalry and 1,000 infantry. Wellington came to know him well, and valued his assistance; but – as we shall learn from Captain Brotherton of the 14th Light Dragoons – it was unwise to trust guerrillas to defend fixed positions.)

Before we consider the various troop movements, it has to be said that, for a plan clearly thought out at Wellington's leisure, in two respects it was scarcely a Staff College solution to his situation. One of these he could nothing about, beyond crossing his fingers and trusting to his brigadiers; the other he proved to have got right, by the skin of his teeth (rather as he had two years before, regarding the threat to his left flank at Talavera from the north plain).

The flaw he hoped would not arise concerned what one might call his Plan B: that is, what to do if it all went wrong. Any retreat westwards would come up, after 7 miles or so, against the north–south ravine of the Coa river, the sides of which made those of the Dos Casas appear trifling. Whilst foot and horse can cross the Coa in various places (though by no means everywhere), artillery and wagons would effectively be forced to use one or more of just three bridges. The chaussee bridge west of Almeida was 8 miles from the northernmost British troops; that at Ponte Sequeiro, the other side of Villa Mayor, was 10 miles south-west from the southernmost; and in the centre, that near Castello Bom was 6 miles west from the church at Fuentes. In his orders of 2 May, with respect to the possibility of a retirement plan,

Lord Wellington proposed to march to the southern bridge at Ponte Sequeiro, south-west via Malhada Sorda and Villa Mayor. But if the reason for such a retirement was that Massena had turned his southern flank, this bridge would not be an available option. And since the chaussee bridge approach road actually passed adjacent to the fortifications of Almeida, and the bridge itself – previously broken by the French – had been rather hastily repaired, that route might well be a hazardous and unreliable alternative. This would leave Wellington with the one bridge near Castello Bom as his sole escape route for wheeled traffic. Unfortunately, that bridge was narrow and the access track winding, and one shudders at the prospect of a wagon toppling over and jamming on the way down to it.

The prospects for Massena's turning his right, however, appeared all too likely, and this brings us to the second feature of Wellington's overall plan that causes raised eyebrows. To understand this, it is necessary to describe the ground to the south of Fuentes.

The village itself lies to the west of the Dos Casas stream; the cottages sprawl nearly a mile from north to south, at the foot of two gentle spurs running down from the ridge a mile above. Prominent on the slope of the north spur is the church and churchyard; on the other spur there is a stone cross on a large rock. The track to Freineda, Castello Bom and Almeida climbs away from the village between the two spurs, having approached from Ciudad Rodrigo down a similar mile-long slope to the Dos Casas. This slope comes off another low north-south ridge, about 2 miles long, and the same height as Wellington's ridge: that is, Fuentes actually sits in a river valley about 2 miles wide, with modest ridges either side. This short easterly ridge provides a deal of dead ground behind it, from the Fuentes side.

The village is stone built, with narrow alleys, tight gardens and small enclosures. The south side overlooks the upstream Dos Casas, and a series of stone walls on that flank are eminently defensible against a turning attack – as indeed is the entire place, given stout infantry. It is a maze of jumbled houses, with small windows; the narrowness of the alleys would channel attacking movement, while the many blind corners would provide useful ambush sites for the defenders. Any fighting would be short-range infantry stuff, favouring those not afraid to rely upon their bayonets.

South of the village, the stream runs through meadowland for a mile, then divides; one arm heads through swampy ground, and the wood-enclosed hamlet of Poco Velho, towards a re-entrant in the ridge system – the hamlet is at the open end of a horseshoe of higher ground. The other rivulet – called the Ribeira del Campo – carries on through further areas of bog, to the hamlet of Nave de Haver, 2 miles south of Poco Velho and rather higher up on the other side of the horseshoe spur. There is a swampy plateau beyond the hamlet to the south-west, while to the north-west the plateau swells downwards to the Turon river, and thence becomes Wellington's north–south ridge beyond Fuentes. To the east of Nave de Haver, slopes, streams and small spurs run confusingly in all directions, the lower slopes dropping down to the east side of the Ribeira del Campo stream amongst bog and woodland. Broken woods continue for 3 miles north, to behind the short ridge to the east of Fuentes.

This detailed description of the ground, in conjunction with the map, shows the scope presented to Massena for turning Wellington's right – one could almost say, presented by Wellington himself. Wellington would not have been ignorant of the dead ground and covered approaches, nor of Massena's superiority in cavalry. There was a surprising contrast between, on the left hand, the strength of his whole position running south down the ravine from Fort Concepcion, and, on the right hand, the openness of the 3 miles from Fuentes down to Nave de Haver. Yet, as with his left at Talavera, he seemed unperturbed enough merely to wait and see.

*   *   *

On 2 May, Massena led his army across the Agueda at Ciudad Rodrigo, on two axes: the southerly one to Fuentes via Espeja, and the other towards Alameda via Marialva and Gallegos. By the evening, Reynier's 2nd Corps together with Solignac's division (from Junot's 8th Corps) had reached Gallegos, Loison's 6th Corps were at Espeja, and D'Erlon's 9th near Carpio. Each corps' cavalry brigade had led the advance, the country being mostly undulating plateau; in the process they drove back Wellington's screening force, comprising the Light Division and his four cavalry regiments (1st Dragoons, 14th and 16th Light Dragoons and 1st Hussars KGL), who all passed the night adjacent to Gallegos and Espeja.

Early on 3 May the screening force was driven in to the lines at Fuentes, as the French, now on three axes, closed up to the British positions. Reynier deployed north of Alameda, Solignac to its south, and the bulk of Massena's force – Loison's corps and Montbrun's cavalry division – approached Fuentes itself, with D'Erlon's corps in reserve. Behind the 2nd Corps, back at Gallegos, came the object of it all – the convoy of provisions for Almeida. Montbrun's horse took post in the woods south of Fuentes, opposite the British cavalry.

So Massena thus presented five of his eight infantry divisions – 27,000 men – adjacent to Fuentes, where at that moment Wellington had some 2,260 men from twenty-eight light companies, and the 2/83rd. Behind the village he had drawn up the 1st and 3rd Divisions (from whence came the light companies), with Spencer's 1st Division the right of the line, and Picton's 3rd to his left. Behind Spencer was Houston's 7th Division, and Crauford's recently arrived Light took post behind Picton. In all Wellington had 24,000 bayonets and less than 1,500 sabres facing Massena's 27,000 and 3,500 in and around Fuentes.

It is not clear if the British were, as usual, back on the reverse slopes. In a letter five days later Charles Stewart, Wellington's Adjutant-General, describes the line as 'very much exposed'. However, Sir Charles Oman states firmly that the line was behind the crest 'in accordance with [Wellington's] usual practice', and that therefore Massena could not 'make out the disposition of the allied troops'. We should perhaps ponder the likelihood of Wellington holding some 21,740 men a mile in rear of 2,260, whom he had told off to hold a village against a force twelve times stronger. Even at double quick time, it would take ten minutes to get reinforcements into action. Probably, the 7th and Light Divisions were indeed out of sight, and some part of the 1st or 3rd as well – we just do not know what force Wellington kept as his immediate reserve.

The French halted before Fuentes in the early afternoon of 3 May, and it is held that, as at Busaco, Massena launched a frontal attack almost immediately, and without due reconnaissance. Certainly his remark, in a letter four days later to Berthier, that '*Ce village etait caché per les accidents du terrain*', indicates that he could not have gone forward of the short ridge a mile east of Fuentes, or he would have had it in full view beneath him. With the relief column behind him at Gallegos he needed to open the route through the village, and rightly rejected any serious attempt across the ravine further north; but he sensibly ordered Reynier to make suitable noises in that direction, in hopes of drawing off some of the defenders. He succeeded magnificently. Wellington responded beyond all expectations: he sent the Light Division, and Colville's brigade of the 3rd Division, to support Campbell and Erskine.

In the event their services were not required, but Wellington did not recall them until last light on 4 May – Massena had the great satisfaction, therefore, for the next twenty-four hours, of having fooled the great Lord Wellington into reducing his bayonet strength at Fuentes by a quarter, from 24,000 to 18,200. Could Massena's infantry, now approaching the stone foot-bridge in the village, take advantage of this excellent start? Sergeant Joseph Donaldson, of the 94th's Light Company, was watching: 'The French advanced on our position in three columns, about 3 o'clock in the afternoon, and detached a strong body of troops against Fuentes'. These were a brigade of 1,700 men from Ferey's division of Loison's 6th Corps (three battalions of the 26e Ligne, and a battalion each from the Hanoverian and Midi Legions). They were preceeded by cavalry, with whom some of Arentschildt's 1st Hussars KGL now became involved. Sergeant Donaldson again: 'The [French] skirmishers were covered in their advance by cavalry, in consequence of which ours were obliged to fall back, for greater safety, to some stone fences on the outskirts of the village, while a party of our German hussars covered their retreat. The cavalry now commenced skirmishing, the infantry keeping up an occasional fire.' In fact the cavalry on both sides were Germans, and 'volleys of insulting language, as well as shot, were exchanged between them.'

Ferey's brigade forced their way through the village, right up to the rising ground and the church; but a counter-attack by the light companies, assisted by Portuguese Cacadores held in reserve by Colonel Williams (5/60th Rifles), commanding in the village, drove them through the streets and out the other side. Because of the labyrinthine nature of the buildings and walled spaces William's force was now well scattered. Ferey put in a second brigade on two axes, comprising 2,300 men in five battalions (66e and 82e Ligne). The new assault again made progress through the streets to the upper outskirts, 'in spite of the unparalleled bravery of our troops, [who] were driven back contesting every inch of ground' (Donaldson). French cavalry, too, were entering the narrow streets, and confusion reigned. This was partly caused by the 400 men of the Hanoverian Legion who, as Donaldson said, were 'dressed in red uniforms, [and] at first taken for a British regiment, and they had time to form up, and give us a volley before the mistake was discovered.' Fortunately, some pressure was taken off Colonel Williams when – according to Massena's ADC, Baron Marbot – the 66e Ligne, following behind the Hanoverians, fired into their backs. (Moral: never wear your enemy's colours.)

Colonel Williams was badly wounded in this second assault, and Wellington sent down another 1,800 bayonets from Spencer's 1st Division to retake the village. These were the 1/71st (Glasgow Highlanders) and 1/79th (Cameron Highlanders), with the 2/24th (Warwickshire) in support. 'On our retreat through the village', says Sergeant Donaldson, 'we were met by the 71st regiment, cheering, led on by Colonel Cadogan, which had been detached from the line [above] to our support. The chase was now turned... the French were so eager on keeping their ground... that many of their cavalry had entered the town, and rushed furiously down the streets [yet] all their efforts were in vain: nothing could withstand the charge of the gallant 71st.' Eight years later, an anonymous soldier of the 71st wrote his recollections:

> On the 3rd May, we stood under arms until 3 o'clock, when a staff officer rode up to our Colonel and gave orders for our advance. Colonel Cadogan put himself at our head, saying, 'My lads, you have had no provision these two days; there is plenty in the hollow in front, let us down and divide it.' We advanced as quick as we could run and met the light

companies retreating as fast as they could. We continued to advance, at double quick time, our firelocks at the trail, our bonnets in our hands. They called to us, 'Seventy-first, you will come back quicker than you advance.' We soon came full in front of the enemy. The Colonel cries, 'Here is food, my lads, cut away.' Thrice we waved our bonnets, and thrice we cheered; brought our firelocks to the charge, and forced them back through the town.

The French... lost a great number of men in the streets. We pursued them about a mile out of the town, trampling over the dead and wounded; but their cavalry bore down on us and forced us back into the town, where we kept our ground, in spite of their utmost efforts. In this affair my life was most wonderfully preserved. In forcing the French through the town, during our first advance, a bayonet went through between my side and clothes, to my knapsack, which stopped its progress. The Frenchman to whom the bayonet belonged fell, pierced by a musket ball from my rear-rank man. Whilst freeing myself from the bayonet, a ball took off part of my right shoulder wing and killed my rear-rank man, who fell upon me. Narrow as this escape was, I felt no uneasiness; I was become so inured to danger and fatigue.

During this day the loss of men was great. In our retreat back to the town, when we halted to check the enemy, who bore hard upon us in their attempts to break our line, often was I obliged to stand with a foot upon each side of a wounded man, who wrung my soul with prayers I could not answer, and pierced my heart with his cries to be lifted out of the way of the cavalry.

This last paragraph confirms the active presence, on the far bank of the Dos Casas, of French cavalry; there are also the interesting references to the rear-rank man, and to 'our line', both of which show that the 71st formed and fought conventionally – at least part of the time – rather than by the looser individual fire-and-movement normally associated with 'fighting in built-up areas'.

Massena made a third and last effort, with four battalions of Marchand's division, but got no further than the stream; it would seem that the 79th and 24th Regiments were now also well forward, and the British firepower was just too heavy. Donaldson wrote: 'The French, enraged at being thus baffled in all their attempts to take the town, sent forward a force composed of the very flower of their army; but they gained only a temporary advantage, for being reinforced by the 79th regiment, although the contest remained doubtful until night, we remained in possession of it, with the exception of a few houses on the rise of the hill on the French side.'

The light companies were withdrawn, and the 71st and 79th were the nightwatchmen, again with the 24th in support. The anonymous soldier of the 71st wrote:

We kept up our fire until long after dark. About one o'clock in the morning, we got four ounces of bread served out to each man, which had been collected out of the haversacks of the Foot Guards. After the firing had ceased we began to search through the town, and found plenty of flour, bacon and sausages, on which we feasted heartily, and lay down in our blankets, wearied to death. My shoulder was as black as a coal, from the recoil of my musket; for this day I had fired 107 rounds of ball-cartridge. Sore as I was, I slept as sound as a top til I was awakened by the loud call of the bugle an hour before day.

Soon as it was light the firing commenced and was kept up until about ten o'clock, when Lieutenant Stewart, of our regiment, was sent with a flag of truce for leave to carry off our wounded from the enemy's lines, which was granted; and, at the same time, they carried off theirs from ours. As soon as the wounded were all got in, many of whom had lain bleeding all night, many both a day and a night, the French brought down a number of bands of music to a level piece of ground, about ninety or a hundred yards broad, that lay between us. They continued to play until sunset, whilst the men were dancing and diverting themselves at football. We were busy cooking the remainder of our sausages, bacon and flour.

*   *   *

This music, during the daytime of 4 May, would have been the band practice sessions for the parade to be held that evening. (Such a long pause in the middle of a battle seems strange to modern eyes, and was uncommon, though not unknown, even in those days.) In a nice touch, perhaps rather than playing football, Marshals Massena and Bessières decided to hold a review and inspection of the cavalry brought down that day from the latter's Army of the North. These two small brigades included six squadrons of the Imperial Guard, a total of some 1,600 sabres; they made an entertaining spectacle, especially for Wellington's horsemen. Ensign John Cowell, 1st Coldstream Guards, watched:

> In the cool of the evening a parade took place of the cavalry and infantry of the Imperial Guard. In their rear and on their left flank were considerable woods of cork-trees and of the ilex or southern oak; in front of these our enemy stood out in strong relief and martial array, their bands playing as they passed in review before Marshals Massena and Bessières. It was a noble sight to behold within our reach these armed men, our nation's foe, surrounded by 'all the pomp and circumstance of war'... On our side we had no reviews; the bands of the German Legion (belonging to our Division) raised their strains in answer to the French, and gave back note for note, as on the morrow we did shot for shot. The moon rose, the bivouac fires were trimmed, the cigar smoked, and our soldiers sank to rest. [Trust the Guards to have cigars...]

Oman calculates that the first day's fighting in Fuentes had cost Wellington 259 casualties, Massena 485 with another 167 taken prisoner. A minority of the troops on both sides were involved on 3 May, yet by that night Massena knew that he had to try some other approach. Accordingly, on the 4th, while the bands played and he reviewed Bessières's troopers, he sent his cavalry commander, Montbrun, further south into the woods and beyond, to Poco Velho and Nave de Haver, to find the British formations that he presumed were acting there as flank guards, and to report on the tracks and going. Massena clearly still believed – rightly – that there was no real future in exploring downstream; and perhaps there were, after all, too many painful memories of Busaco ridge.

When Montbrun made his report in the afternoon of the 4th, Massena immediately conceived a bold stroke, one that would involve no less than half his army – 20,000 men – marching round Wellington's right flank and rolling him up from the south. For Montbrun brought the surprising news that beyond Fuentes, apart from the usual screen of cavalry picquets, there lay nothing but a bunch of guerrillas right down at Nave de Haver. The land was perfectly open to cross, notwithstanding the woods around Poco Velho and some areas of bog near Nave de Haver; there was a 2-mile gap between these two hamlets that was perfect cavalry country. That was the place to turn in, then sweep north up Wellington's ridge, to join forces with the divisions hopefully breaking out of Fuentes.

This scenario was so enticing that Massena, of all generals, must surely have sniffed for the the smell of a rat – was the great Lord Wellington laying some sort of trap? Nevertheless, the textbook solution seemed to be to strike hard in the centre at Fuentes, at the same time as turning the flank, and Massena accordingly issued his orders: 14,000 men in three divisions (Ferey's and two of D'Erlon's) were to capture Fuentes, with a diversion again by Reynier up near Fort Concepcion, while another 17,000 men in three divisions (Marchand's, Mermet's and Solignac's) were to turn the flank. Importantly, the latter thrust was to have three-quarters of all the cavalry – 3,500 sabres, under Montbrun. It was crucial that the timing of the Fuentes assault should draw in Wellington's reserves as the turning movement developed, and itself also demanded the deployment of reinforcements. All the preparatory movements were to be made and completed under cover of darkness on that night of 4/5 May, and the assault on the guerrillas at Nave de Haver was to go in at dawn.

Montbrun accordingly set out in the darkness, together with a detachment of engineers to improve the paths across the boggy ground. He placed one brigade beneath the hill of Nave de Haver, and the other four to the east of Poco Velho. At 2am the infantry followed on, towards Poco Velho, in the order of Marchand's, Mermet's and Solignac's divisions (the latter, of course, had moved off much earlier, to cover the additional 5 miles from its previous location near Alameda). 'At 3 o'clock in the morning of the 5th, our advanced parties sent in to state, that the enemy's columns were in motion; and before 6 they had commenced a desperate attack', wrote Wellington's AG, Charles Stewart.

*   *   *

During the previous day Wellington, having received reports of Montbrun's reconnaissance to his right flank, and feeling no concerns for his left, decided upon two responses. He fanned out as far as he could the twelve squadrons of his four horse regiments, across the 4 miles down to Nave de Haver; and he sent Houston's 7th Division to the slopes of the ridge in rear of Poco Velho. Two battalions – the 85th (Bucks Volunteers) and Portuguese 2nd Cacadores – went to the hamlet itself, since the whole purpose was to extend his line. With due hindsight, in his later Despatch he wrote: 'Imagining that the enemy would endeavour to obtain possession of Fuentes d'Oñoro and of the ground occupied by the troops behind that village, by crossing the Dos Casas at Poco Velho, I moved the 7th Division to their right, in order to protect, if possible, that passage.' We know from his 14 April appreciation that he expected the French to 'turn the heads of the ravines of the Dos Casas and Turon', and he was now seeing this anticipated grand tactic come to pass.

Why, then, did he send the inexperienced 7th? This was his smallest and newest division, formed two months previously, with only 20 per cent of British troops – the 2/51st (West Riding) and the 85th, both fresh-landed at Lisbon. The other seven battalions were five Portuguese, the Brunswickers, and the sometimes unreliable (French) Chasseurs Britanniques? The division was, after all, to move nearly 3 miles away from his line, into open country, with a clear and overwhelming cavalry threat in the offing. Wellington's reasoning here has always remained a puzzle, however concerned he was for his rearward communications; we can only suppose that he underestimated the likely magnitude of Massena's intentions. That it was a mistake he himself acknowledged, according to Larpent, who recorded him as saying in March 1813 that he had 'committed a fault by extending his right too much to Poco Velho; and that, if the French had taken advantage of it, there might have been bad consequences, but that they permitted him to recover himself and change his front before their face.' For it was not just his choice of the 7th Division that was questionable – it was risky enough to send anyone at all into that distant plain. We know how things finished up: with the refused tight line west–east at right angles between Fuentes village and the ridge, the whole line strengthened with trenches and earthworks. That the morning began so differently is surely a mark of Wellington's supreme confidence in his troops, and in his own sixth sense and ability to react quickly. That confidence was about to be thoroughly tested.

Lieutenant Francis Hall, 14th Light Dragoons:

> On the afternoon of the 4th May we were in the woods of Dos Casas, our horses just turned out to graze, and ourselves looking out for the thickest trees under which to pass the night, when the troop to which I belonged received orders to march in support of Don Julian Sanchez, whom Lord Wellington had, to use his own expression, 'prevailed on to occupy Nava d'Aver' – on the extremity of our right. We again saddled and set out as it was growing dark. We reached Nava d'Aver before midnight, but as it was needful our horses should eat, we had to move down to the low grounds of the Turon to find pasture for them. About three hours were spent in this way, and we returned to Nava d'Aver at daybreak. (May 5th) Considering the uncertainty of our next meal, we now endeavoured to procure breakfast. We had a little chocolate and biscuit with us, and burnt some broken doors to boil it with, but the old proverb was fearfully verified. It bubbled in the tin boiler, when the assembly sounded. The word was given, 'Mount your horses'. I mounted mine, holding the tempting fluid in my hand.

Captain Thomas Brotherton, in command of two squadrons of the 14th, in which Francis Hall was a troop commander, gives the bigger picture:

> I commenced the battle of Fuentes by running away with two squadrons for about two miles, pursued by a brigade of French cavalry. I had been sent the night before to the village of Nave d'Aver, which was occupied by that humbug, Don Julian Sanchez, with his corps of infantry and cavalry. It was a strong post, on an eminence, surrounded by stone wall enclosures, similar to those in Ireland, and no cavalry alone ought to have carried it. I arrived there late at night, and could not see what arrangements Don Julian had made for defence; but he assured me all was secure, and that he meant to defend himself most obstinately, before he retired. Just at daybreak in the morning, however, I requested Don Julian to show me where his pickets were placed. He pointed out to me what he said was one of them, but I observed to him that in the dusk of morning it looked too large for a picket. The sun rising rapidly dispelled the fog, and the illusion at the same time, for Don Julian's picket proved to be a whole French regiment dismounted. They now mounted immediately and advanced against us. I still thought the Spaniards would make a stand, as cavalry alone ought never to have carried the village; but the brave Don Julian took

himself off immediately with his whole force to the mountains, and left me with my two squadrons to shift for myself.

Francis Hall again:

> A large column of French cavalry appeared from the opposite wood, and Don Julian's people began to move off in commotion. I moved [the pan of chocolate] to my lips – in vain – the heated metal defied my endeavours, and unwillingly I relinquished my hold. We moved over an open plain towards the right of our position, throwing out skirmishers to our rear; the enemy followed us, doing the same to his front, and a brisk though undestructive firing began on both sides, we trying to get off, and they to intercept us.

These were the three weak regiments of Chasseurs in Fournier's brigade, some 800 sabres – more than enough for Sanchez and his men, who fled, and also for the 200 or so troopers of the 14th. They fought a hopeless delaying action back across the 2 miles to Poco Velho, repeatedly being outflanked every time they turned and showed a front. The Chasseurs' pursuit was stopped in the wood outside the hamlet, when the right-hand pickets of the 7th Division fired a volley. Lieutenant Hall continues:

> By the time we got to the edge of the woods of the Das Casas, we began to be pressed by a squadron of chasseurs, when a picket of the 85th Regiment, which lay among the trees, poured a volley into its centre, several men and horses dropped, and it was some moments before the gap closed. They immediately went about, and a few of the 2nd Portuguese Cacadores now crept behind some rocks, and began to fire on them. [Brotherton tells us that the 85th were here facing the French for the first time, and initially hesitated to open fire, calling out 'Are they the French? Are they the French?']

Montbrun's main force was also to hit Poco Velho, a little later. They were seen away to his right by another of Brotherton's officers. Lieutenant George FitzClarence, ADC to Lord Wellington's Adjutant-General Charles Stewart (who predictably was also well involved with this morning's work) wrote as follows:

> On its route, this [Brotherton's] squadron was the first to witness the threatening demonstrations of the French. It was a glorious sight. The morning was beautiful; the sun was gradually dispelling a thick mist which had prevailed during the night, and which seemed yet in lower grounds to dispute the solar influence. The silence of the morning was scarcely broken by the hum of the neighbouring armies, when the French advance upon our right was observed at the distance of about half a mile. The nearest columns of cavalry were only seen in parts, the continuity being broken by the partial fogs; beyond them the valley seemed filled with troops, parts of the columns only becoming visible for a moment as the mist cleared off. Farther to the right, the enemy were on higher ground. The sun had gained the ascendancy, and shone upon the accoutrements of the squadrons; and again the view was impeded by the fog, and the sequel left to the imagination. Enough, however, had been seen to authorize the report sent in, that the French were moving upon the right in great force.

Two more of Wellington's line-of-observation squadrons, from the 16th Light Dragoons and 1st Hussars KGL, under Major Meyer KGL, were caught by the steamroller – Wathier's brigade of Chasseurs, 750 strong – in a defile between two woods outside Poco Velho. The 16th charged first, followed by the Germans, both valiantly but vainly; the 16th lost their squadron commander taken prisoner (he had arrived from England only the night before) and a sergeant and six men killed trying to rescue him. Captain Tomkinson later wrote:

> Captain Belli's squadron, with one of the Hussars, was in advance; and the enemy having sent forward two or three squadrons, Major Meyers attempted to oppose them in front of a defile. He waited so long and was so indecisive, and the enemy came up so close, that he ordered the squadron of the 16th to charge. The enemy's squadron was about twice their strength, and waited their charge. This is the only instance I ever met with two bodies of cavalry coming in opposition, and both standing, as invariably, as I have observed it, one or the other runs away. Our men rode up and began sabring, but were so outnumbered that they could do nothing, and were obliged to retire across the defile in confusion, the enemy having brought up more troops to that point.

Francis Hall was also on the scene:

> Part of their column (of Chasseurs) was charged by a squadron of the 16th Light Dragoons, and Captain Belli, who had arrived from England but the evening before, was made prisoner. We were near enough to hear the clink and clash of their swords, but were prevented by a small marsh from seconding their attack.

The outnumbered troops fell back to join Brotherton's squadrons adjacent to Poco Velho, where they were gradually joined by the other eight squadrons of Wellington's four horse regiments. The sheer mass of Montbrun's force was quite overwhelming. As Tomkinson of the 16th wrote in his diary: 'The 7th Division in the wood had waited too long, and Lord Wellington thought it was all over with them, the enemy's cavalry being on each of their flanks, and they had ground to pass on which cavalry could act.'

An hour after daybreak the French infantry emerged from the woods in column of double companies and attacked Poco Velho. Marchand's division cleared the pickets from the wood before the hamlet and drove straight through, eleven battalions pushing Houston's 85th and 2nd Cacadores out the other side, into the arms of a waiting Chasseur regiment, who took seventy prisoners and killed and wounded another eighty-five – total casualties of 20 per cent of their joint strength. Far worse would have happened but for a charge by two squadrons of the German Hussars. The survivors began to make their way back to the 7th Division, a mile away on the slopes across the plain. Francis Hall again:

> Being joined by a troop of the Royal Dragoons, we again advanced a little, but the enemy's infantry already occupied the road, and in their turn fired a volley upon our detachment, which induced us to retire upon the main body of the army. The action was now commencing. The pickets were driven in in front of our right, which Massena evidently designed to turn by means of his great superiority in cavalry, which was now advancing under General Montbrun in heavy columns over the plains. Our scanty line formed to

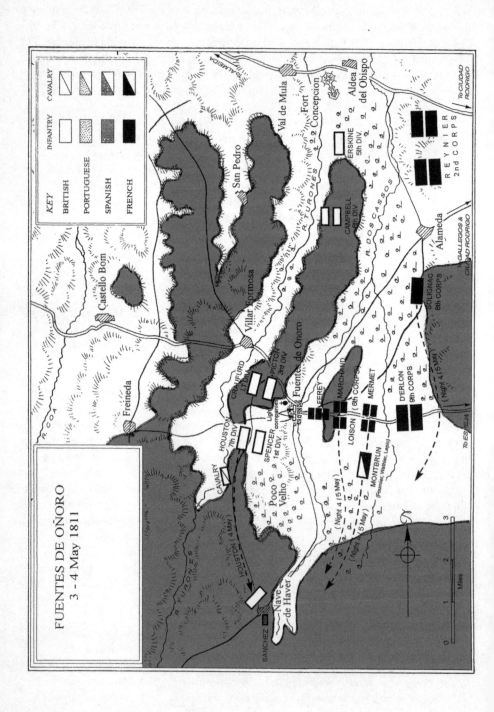

FUENTES DE OÑORO
3 - 4 May 1811

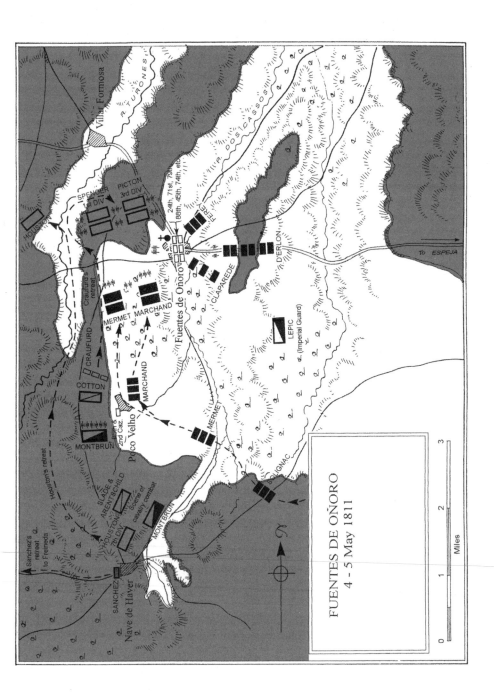

FUENTES DE OÑORO
4 - 5 May 1811

receive their advanced squadrons. Horses whose riders had been killed or overthrown ran wildly across the field, or lay panting in their blood. Two heavy Dragoons were in the act of felling a Chasseur with their broadswords; his chaco [sic] resisted several blows, but he at length dropped. Another was hanging in the stirrups, while his horse was hurried off by a German Hussar, eager to plunder his valise. Some were driving two or three slashed prisoners to the rear: one wretch was dragged on foot between two Dragoons, but as he was unable to keep pace with their horses, and the enemy were now forming for a second charge, he was cut down.

At about this time Brotherton was ordered by the fire-eating Adjutant-General, Charles Stewart, to lead his squadron in a charge, without support, which Brotherton regarded as 'an injudicious order... a dangerous step'. As he trotted forward he met Lord Wellington, who 'rode up to me and asked me where I was going. I told him of the orders I had received from Major-General Stewart. He made no further observation than "Go Back!"' This is the only account of Wellington's location at first light; it is important, for it shows once again his ability to be where decisions needed making. It may well be that the tail-end of Solignac's division was spied moving south, the dawn mists suddenly lifting, just as they did for FitzClarence. Drawn by the sounds of battle, Wellington rode out to see for himself, to get Crauford's Light Division quickly on the move to somewhere near Houston's 7th, for whom he would immediately be much concerned. We may assume that at the same time he took the other necessary decision, to form a new front at Fuentes. Spencer's 1st Division was to face south on the west side of the ridge, with Ashworth's Portuguese brigade on the top and Picton's 3rd Division on the east side, down towards Fuentes. The ground was dominating to the south, where it fell gently away, and from here it would not be subject to enfilade fire, being set back out of sight behind an intermediate crest.

It would take 'Black Bob' Crauford and his Light Division nearly an hour to cover the 4 miles to Houghton's position (wherever it had got to by the time he arrived) – an hour that Oman describes as 'a very dangerous one'. Three days later, FitzRoy Somerset wrote to his brother in Badminton House that 'the consequence (of the dawn irruption) was that there was a general, I might say, flight, but the disorder was really terrible, and it was at one time to be decided that during this disorder the enemy's cavalry might advance and not only destroy ours but put our infantry out of a situation to resist them.' The French infantry divisions, once clear of the woods and formed in heavy columns, were capable of an attack within that hour on the old right flank at Fuentes, the new one not yet being formed, and certainly capable, together with their cavalry, of getting between Houston and home.

Fortunately, after taking Poco Velho the French infantry seemed devoid of a sense of urgency. Their protecting cavalry was otherwise engaged, so they might well hesitate to debouch unguarded on to the open plain; and for this happy development the Allies could thank the untiring efforts of the twelve defending squadrons. These sat their horses 1,000 strong, together with six 6-pounders from Bull's Troop of horse artillery, between Montbrun's nearly 3,000 sabres and the 700 survivors of the 85th and Cacadores falling back to join Houston a mile or so away. Montbrun could not get through to cut the fleeing infantry down, even though he made ground throughout. The British and German regiments took turns by squadrons to charge and retire, charge and retire, until the plain was crossed and the two battalions were safe. The British cavalry then took post on the slopes to the left rear of the 7th Division, and the

French cavalry closed up and sought any unprotected flanks of the various battalions – without success. Tomkinson observed: '[The 7th Division] had got away into the rocks, and the enemy's advance charged up the rising ground on which our horse artillery was posted, and passed two guns of Captain Bull's Troop. Their advance was not well supported.'

That is, they were alone, without infantry, and volley fire kept them out. In a surprise encounter over a stone wall, one attack by a dragoon brigade was seen off by the Chasseurs Britanniques, and another charge, at the 2/51st, was also driven back by musketry. Again, the British cavalry dashed out at every chance to catch the French horse off balance. William Wheeler, a private with the 2/51st, wrote this in a letter a fortnight later:

> The enemy came down on our right in an immense body of cavalry, we had to throw back our right wing to oppose them. We had only two Portuguese guns, one of these the enemy dismounted the first round they gave us, and the Portuguese very prudently scampered off with the other for fear it would share the same fate.
>
> Our position after throwing back our right wing was about twenty paces under the brow of a gentle descent, beyond which was a large plain covered with the enemy. A little distance in our rear the ground began to rise rather abruptly, it was covered with cork trees, rocks and straggling bushes, there was also a long wall behind us. On the high ground this was occupied by the Chasseur Britanniques Regt and the Portuguese Brigade. We had some men in our front skirmishing, but they were soon driven in and formed with us, thus situated we anxiously waited the attack.
>
> An officer of Huzzars soon showed himself on the brow, he viewed us with much attention then coolly turned round in his saddle and waved his sword. In an instant the brow was covered with cavalry. This was a critical moment, the least unsteadiness would have caused confusion. This would have been followed by defeat and disgrace. The enemy had walked to the brow, and their trumpeter was sounding the Charge, when Colonel M— gave the words 'Ready, Present, Fire.' For a moment the smoke hindered us from seeing the effect of our fire, but we soon saw plenty of horses and men stretched not many yards from us.
>
> The C.B.Regt now opened fire, as did the Portuguese over our heads. It was a dangerous but necessary expedient, for our fire was not sufficient to stop the cavalry, so we were obliged to lay down and load. The confusion amongst the enemy was great, and as soon as the fire could be stopped a squadron of the 1st Royals and of the 14th Light Dragoons gallantly dashed in amongst the enemy and performed wonders, but they were soon obliged to fall back – for the enemy outnumbered them twenty to one or more; we now sorely felt the want of artillery and cavalry.

And Montbrun sorely felt the want of infantry, for it was now becoming less clear that his superiority in cavalry could alone break the 7th Division, inexperienced though they were. But Marchand and Mermet had not followed him to the west: they were heading north, for Wellington's new south-facing line at Fuentes.

At this juncture Houston received the welcome orders from Wellington to withdraw, as Craufurd at last brought up the Light Division to act as a screening force. The 7th Division were to pull back up the Turon to extend the new line west from Fuentes, continuing it to include Freineda, another 2 miles or so west of the river. Private Wheeler:

The enemy had formed again and was ready for another attack, our force was not sufficient to repel such a mass, so the order was given to retire independently by regiments. We retired through the broken ground in our rear, crossed the wall, and was pretty safe from their cavalry, but they had brought up their guns to the brow and was serving out the shot with a liberal hand. We continued retiring and soon came to a narrow rapid stream, this we waded up to our armpits and from the steepness of the opposite bank we found much difficulty in getting out. This caused some delay so the Regiment waited until all had crossed, then formed line and continued our retreat in quick time; it was now the division was suffering much from the enemy's fire, the Portuguese in particular, the C.B. regiment came in for their share.

Thanks to Colonel Mainwaring we came off safe, although the shot was flying pretty thick, yet his superior skill baffled all the efforts of the enemy, he took advantage of the ground and led us out of a scrape without loss. I shall never forget him, he dismounted off his horse, faced us and frequently called the time 'Right, Left' as he was accustomed to when drilling the regiment. His eccentricity did not leave him, he would now and then call out 'That fellow is out of step, keep step and they cannot hurt us.' Another time he would observe such a one, calling him by name, 'Cannot march, mark him for drill, Sergeant Major... I tell you again they cannot hurt us if you are steady, if you get out of time, you will be knocked down.' He was leading his horse and a shot passed under the horse's belly which made him rear up. 'You are a coward', he said, 'I will stop your corn three days.'

Wheeler here catches a flavour of the truly eccentric John Mainwaring, his commanding officer, who seemed so needlessly keen for his battalion to keep in step when fleeing at the double across (presumably) rough open country. He was later sent home in disgrace by Lord Wellington, for the more unforgivable eccentricity of ordering the 51st's Colours to be burnt, just as the action at Fuentes began.

Amazingly, Houston brought his 7th Division back with few casualties – Oman calculates a total of ninety-two out of the 3,800 strength of those seven battalions not at Poco Velho. Of these only nineteen were taken prisoner, indicating that the French cavalry never truly got amongst them at all, thanks to the British cavalry. It is probable that the dozen French guns did them more damage.

Crauford's five battalions had now to extricate themselves, and the ever-supportive cavalry squadrons, back to the Fuentes line nearly 3 miles away. Crauford formed the battalions in close column of companies, at quarter distance, which could form square very quickly. They retreated with the cavalry and six guns of Bull's Troop in the intervals. The infantry marched, the gunners unlimbered to fire a few rounds before a quick hook-in and catch up, the cavalry made brief squadron charges, the infantry forming their squares – some say seven times in all – whenever the French came forward. This they did repeatedly, hovering in great clouds, nearly 4,000 riders waiting for their gunfire to cause any exploitable disorder amongst the Allied infantry. 'Many times Montbrun made as if he would storm the light division squares, but the latter were too formidable to be meddled with', says Napier; 'yet, in all this war, there was not a more dangerous hour for England.' Such was the officers' confidence in their men that at times the static squares recommenced their movement, remaining in their box formations but facing forwards in the direction of march, and halting to face outwards with their bayonets when the French again looked likely to try their luck.

In their hearts the French horsemen must have known that only the largest slice of luck would open a British square, yet still they travelled hopefully. The prize was obvious, the means was present, but what was lacking was the ability to co-ordinate the means. Napier has it in a nutshell, albeit not expressed in his most flowing prose:

> The whole of that vast plain as far as the Turones was covered with a confused multitude, amidst which the squares appeared but as specks, for there was a great concourse, composed of commissariat followers of the camp, servants, baggage, led horses, and peasants attracted by curiosity, and finally, broken piquets and parties coming out of the woods. The seventh division was separated from the army by the Turones, five thousand French cavalry, with fifteen pieces of artillery, were close at hand impatient to charge; the infantry of the eighth corps was in order of battle behind the horsemen; the wood was filled with the skirmishers of the sixth corps, and if the latter body, pivoting on Fuentes, had issued forth, while Drouet's divisions fell on that village, while the eighth corps attacked the light division, and while the whole of the cavalry made a general charge; the loose multitude encumbering the plain would have been driven violently in upon the first division, in such a manner as to have intercepted the latter's fire and broken their ranks.

Second Lieutenant George Simmons, 1/95th Rifles, implies that their disciplined movement alone inhibited the French squadrons:

> A large body of cavalry had debouched some distance to our right. When clear of the wood, they wheeled to their right so as to intercept our retrograde movement. The enemy's skirmishers then followed us up, keeping up a smart fire until we left the wood. We formed column at quarter-distance ready to form square at any moment if charged by cavalry... a body of cavalry hovered about us, but from our formidable appearance and the steady manner in which the movement was conducted, the enemy did not charge us.

The Light Division's progression across the plain must indeed have been an awesome, heroic sight and, for those 3,800 men involved, a memorable experience; surely never before had such a fighting withdrawal been carried out so smoothly, by so many, in the face of an equal number of enemy sabres. It is impossible in such circumstances to believe that anyone other than these battalions of Moore's, instructed at Shorncliffe in 1803, would have had the necessary training, discipline and leadership – at all levels. It was a remarkable achievement; it was also cheaply done, with only sixty-seven casualties in the whole division. Sir John Fortescue did not exaggerate when he wrote 'No more masterly manoeuvre is recorded of any general; no grander example of triumphant discipline is recorded of any regiment in the history of the British Army.' William Napier was present, not with his 43rd, but as brigade major of Craford's Portuguese brigade. His able pen describes the famous extraction by Captain Ramsey of the two 6-pounders of Bull's Troop:

> A great commotion was observed amongst the French squadrons; men and officers closed in confusion towards one point where a thick dust was rising, and where loud cries and the sparkling of blades and flashing of pistols, indicated some extraordinary occurrence.

> Suddenly the multitude was violently agitated, an English shout arose high and clear, the
> mass was rent asunder, and Norman Ramsey burst forth sword in hand at the head of his
> battery, his horses breathing fire and stretching like greyhounds along the plain, his guns
> bounding like things of no weight, and the mounted gunners in close and compact order
> protecting the rear, heads bent low and pointed weapons, in desperate career.

Ramsey's Troop 'regained our lines in full view of the 43rd', according to their regimental history. He had obviously lingered to fire one or two rounds too many, and found himself flanked by grateful Chasseurs. However, Napier unfairly makes no mention of the help Ramsey received from the cavalry. Captain Brotherton had kept an eye on him, fortunately, and turned his squadron of the 14th, together with one of the Royals, to cut back and tangle with the Chasseurs, to buy time for Ramsey as he limbered up – another instance that day of mutual co-operation between the arms, but especially of the professional involvement of the cavalry. Time and again, references to their successful actions point to the squadron (or possibly two) as the level of unit concerned, with a noticeable lack of reference to the cavalry 'getting out of hand' – so commonly the criticism thrown at Wellington's horsemen in the Peninsula. Lieutenant Francis Hall took part in one of Brotherton's charges:

> We again formed in line, and a second charge was led by Captain Brotherton... He rode
> at the French officer, who was in front of his men, but the latter made a few steps on one
> side and politely let him pass. We were soon completely intermixed. Our men had evi-
> dently the advantage as individuals. Their broadsword [sic], ably wielded, flashed over the
> Frenchmen's heads, and obliged them to cower to their saddle bows. The alarm was,
> indeed, greater than the hurt, for their cloaks were so well rolled across their left shoulders,
> that it was no easy matter to give a mortal stroke with the broad edge of the sabre... many,
> however, turned their horses, and our men shouted in the pursuit; but it was quite clear
> that, go which way they might, we were but scattered drops amid their host, and could not
> possibly arrest their progress. We again, therefore, went about, and retired towards the
> Guards, who were formed in squares on the right of our line of infantry.
>
>   My military glories had here nearly been extinguished. I was galloping with the rest,
> when Captain Brotherton called to me to look behind, and on turning my head, I per-
> ceived a French dragoon, of no very friendly aspect, with his sword raised, close to my
> horse's crupper. I was lucky enough to parry his blow, which certainly, but for this friendly
> caution, had made 'worm's meat' of me.

Rifleman Costello of the 95th gives another useful eyewitness account of a charge, by the Royals, which nearly made him the owner of a French horse during the retreat across the plain:

> A loud cheering to the right attracted our attention, and we saw our 1st Heavy Dragoons
> charge a French cavalry regiment. This was the first charge of cavalry most of us had ever
> seen and we were all very much interested in it. The French skirmishers extended against
> us seemed to feel the same, and by general consent both (infantry) parties suspended firing
> while the affair of dragoons was going on.

The English and French cavalry met in the most gallant manner, and with the greatest show of resolution. The shock of the first collision seemed terrific, and many men and horses fell on both sides. Having ridden through and past each other, they now wheeled round again and a second charge followed, accompanied by some very pretty sabre-practise, by which many saddles were emptied. English and French chargers galloped about the field without riders. These occupied our attention, and the French skirmishers and ourselves were soon engaged in pursuing them, each nation endeavouring to secure the chargers of the opposite one as legal spoil. While engaged in this chase we frequently became intermixed, and laughed at the different accidents that occurred in our pursuit. I secured a very splendid charger when, chancing to turn my head, I perceived that the French were playing a deep game and had moved a regiment of infantry, and some cavalry, through the wood in our rear. The alarm was immediately given. I was obliged to part with my horse as our company, which was foremost, had to run for our lives into a square formed by the 52nd, who were close to the foot guards.

Despite these repeated encounters the casualties suffered by the British and German squadrons were surprisingly light. The return shows a total of 149 all ranks *hors de combat*, evenly spread across the four regiments. That only five men were taken prisoner shows that the squadrons were never really caught napping. While the parade states suggest that Wellington's sabre strength at the outset was 1,542, several of those present complain at the numbers doing duty away from their squadrons as orderlies and escorts. FitzClarence notes further that a whole squadron of the Royals was detached (he does not say where), but reckons 'the number of sabres present at Fuentes did not exceed 1,200 [and] we doubt whether it was so great'. Tomkinson of the 16th believed that 'our two brigades of cavalry scarcely amounted to 900 and those in bad condition'. If we take FitzClarence's estimate, then the casualty rate was 12 per cent. On the French side, the loss to Montbrun's cavalry of 359 was a rate of 10 per cent, as one would expect given their relative superiority in numbers.

*   *   *

One disaster did befall the Guards in Stopford's brigade. The 1/2nd (Coldstream) and 1/3rd Foot Guards had a picket line forward under Lieutenant-Colonel Hill of the latter regiment, extending along the lower slope. When the Light Division passed through into safety, Hill gathered his men into a 'hive' or small square, easily fending off the attentions of the following French cavalry. However, Hill foolishly extended them again too soon and, quick as death, the 13e Chasseurs roared in and over the three companies, killing and wounding eighty and capturing Hill and another twenty men. Lieutenant Francis Hall wrote:

During the afternoon the enemy's cavalry made a dart at the pickets of the 1st Division, with the expectation of sweeping off the line before our cavalry could support them. They succeeded in part, by coming up unexpectedly, but when they were perceived the men, by collecting into a knot (or 'hiving' as it is called) repulsed them with the bayonet. A troop of the 14th Light Dragoons under Captain Knipe, with a party of the Royals were ordered to skirmish, and suffered some loss in endeavouring to get possession of two field pieces.

Ian Fletcher, a chronicler of the Guards in the Peninsula, tells us that during the fight Captain Home of the 3rd Guards was attacked by three of the Chasseurs, one of whom grabbed his water bottle, the strap of which snapped, while another tore an epaulette from his uniform. The third Frenchman thrust at Home with his sabre, but the Guardsman almost pulled the man from his saddle. As the Frenchman recoiled to ride off Home snatched from his chest the man's prized cross of the Legion of Honour, before turning to his cheering comrades with his trophy.

We do not know much about the artillery duel, only that there was one, albeit brief. Oman says that the French took forward twenty-four of their thirty-eight guns with Marchand and Mermat's divisions (eighteen of their own, and six of Montbrun's cavalry). That is, these were on the plain before Wellington's reconstituted right flank, and bringing such fire to bear on the British line as was visible. Fortescue states that the cannonade was conducted at long range; while Commissary Schaumann notes that the French 'usually fired salvos of six', presumably meaning a whole troop or brigade 'volley'. Wellington had superiority in numbers, deploying thirty-six of his forty-eight pieces to support the 1st and 3rd Divisions and the troops defending the village. These were Bull's Troop of 6-pounders of horse artillery (two of which had figured in Norman Ramsey's dramatic escape); Lawson's Brigade of 9-pounders of foot artillery; Thompson's Brigade of 6-pounders, also of foot; and three Portuguese brigades each of 6-pounders. Since Wellington did not employ artillery concentrated for counter-battery work, it is likely that at Fuentes the six individual units would have been deployed as separate batteries in the intervals between his battalions. In a lecture at the Royal Artillery Institution, Oman referred to two Portuguese batteries being in front of the 3rd Division, and there is separate reference to one being to the flank of one of the Guards battalions; while Sergeant Donaldson of the 94th refers to the guns above the village, which did great execution in the final defence.

*   *   *

Not only did the British guns subdue the French artillery, but from the casualty figures for Marchand and Mermet it would appear that their columns were also well within range – Oman estimates a loss of more than 400 men in their divisions during the hours when they stood, waiting for the key to be turned in the lock of Fuentes village.

Generals Marchand, Mermet and Solignac were last seen leading 17,300 bayonets in columns heading for Wellington's new line at Fuentes. All the action, bar the earlier quick clearance of Poco Velho, had been in the hands of the French cavalry – which, it must be said, had caught out the British defence magnificently, overwhelming a dubious deployment by Wellington and coming close to surrounding one of his divisions. That Montbrun's cavalry could not deliver a total miracle was largely down to his lack of infantry when he needed it. To understand why these three divisions now stood idle before Picton's 3rd Division, we must note that there were three phases to Massena's plan. The first was to turn Wellington's right, now successfully accomplished; the second, dependent upon that, was for Ferey and D'Erlon then to try their luck again at Fuentes village; the third, in turn dependent on success in the village, was for Marchand, Mermet and Solignac to assault up from the south.

The reason Massena needed Fuentes in his hands first had to do with the shape of the line, and the ground, which Wellington had cunningly chosen. The L-shaped line overlooks all the approaches, part of which is a mini-ravine, while the plateau behind allows troops to be held back well protected until required. Wellington's superiority in artillery, the solid flanks and the bent line all made difficulties for the French, the L-shaped salient in particular meaning that enfilade fire would be a real threat to any force closing for battle. Finally, the shape of the line – which Commissary Schaumann well describes as 'a sort of wedge' – was delineated by a trench, with sloping parapet. He gives no details other than that 'our troops took up their position behind these works'; while Costello of the 95th Rifles refers to 'The Guards of the 1st Division entrenched behind the town of Fuentes'. Since other references talk of the earthworks being thrown up later that night or on the morning of 6 May, these may have been but the first shallow traces. In any event, Massena was not going to climb any such hill, certainly not if he could not see over it – not until he had his own men rolling up the British line from Fuentes to the east.

We now turn to the bloody events in the village. Some two hours after Montbrun's turning movement was seen to be making ground somewhere on the west side of Poco Velho, and while the Light Division was rescuing the 7th (say between 8am and 9am), General Ferey's men surged once more into the narrow alleyways. The day now depended on the outcome they could produce. It is to be noted that with the Light and 7th Divisions now some 3 miles off, Massena had caused Wellington to reduce his force at Fuentes to the 13,000 bayonets of the 1st and 3rd Divisions, against whom he now unloosed the nearly 14,000 men of the divisions of Ferey, Claparede and Conroux. He had acquired a slight local superiority, albeit inadequate in the event.

The positioning of the defenders was as follows. Ashworth's Portuguese brigade was astride the ridge, in the angle of the wedge; Spencer's 1st Division, in a double line, ran down overlooking the Turon, and Picton's 3rd Division to Fuentes village, also in two lines – Mackinnon's brigade being in rear of the village itself. The houses and alleys were held by the 1/71st from Howard's brigade, and the 1/79th and 2/24th from Nightingall's. The French held the chapel and farm buildings to the east of the stream. The anonymous soldier of the 71st wrote:

> A deserter told us that there were five regiments of grenadiers picked out to storm the town. We lay down, fully accoutred as usual, and slept in our blankets. An hour before day we were ready to receive the enemy. About half-past nine o'clock a great gun from the French line, which was answered by one of ours, was the signal to engage.

Ten battalions of Ferey's division crossed the stream and, familiar with the village from the unsuccessful fighting on 3 May, dashed between the houses. William Grattan, with the 1/88th (Connaught Rangers) just above the village, observed that they advanced 'with the characteristic impetuosity of their nation, and forcing down the barricades which we had hastily constructed as a temporary defence, came rushing on, and, torrent-like, threatened to overwhelm all that opposed them'. They quickly surrounded two companies of the 79th in some buildings near the Dos Casas and, all the officers being wounded, forced their surrender; they took ninety-four prisoners. The soldier of the 71st again:

> Down they came, shouting as usual. We kept them at bay, in spite of their cries and formidable looks. How different their appearance from ours! Their hats, set round with feathers, their beards long and black, gave them a fierce look. Their stature was superior to ours; most of us were young. We looked like boys; they like savages.... A French dragoon, who

was dealing death around, forced his way up to near where I stood. Every moment I expected to be cut down. My piece was empty; there was not a moment to lose. I got a stab at him, beneath the ribs, upwards; he gave me a back stroke, before he fell, and cut the stock of my musket in two. Thus I stood unarmed. I soon got another and fell to work again.

The French gradually forced the two battalions of Highlanders back to the top of the village; however, gathering together, catching their breath and joining with the 2/24th posted there in reserve, they came down again through the streets, pushing Ferey's men back to the bottom levels. Some 650 men or 15 per cent of Ferey's 4,200-strong division had already been lost in the fighting on the 3rd; his remaining men would now be growing disenchanted with the whole idea of entering Fuentes yet again.

General D'Erlon gathered all eighteen grenadier companies from his two divisions, and formed them into three *bataillons d'élite*. These picked troops now became the second wave of attacks to hit the village. Dressed in their red-plumed bearskin caps, they were readily mistaken for Imperial Guard troops by the Highlanders, who doubtless felt suitably flattered and probably fought the better for it. But for the second time, at around noon, the three British battalions were driven back up to the houses at the top of the village, and to the church above. Wellington, close by, necessarily reinforced the critical point; he called for the same light companies who had held Fuentes two days before, and the whole of the 6th Cacadores were also put in – but all to no avail. D'Erlon also reinforced, with another ten battalions from Conroux's and Claparede's divisions. Francis Hall of the 14th Light Dragoons recounts what he was presumably told by others:

> Sometimes the enemy obtained a partial lodgement, and the combat thickened from house to house and wall to wall. The church in particular, which was a kind of key to the possession of the village, was repeatedly stormed. The walls and doors were riddled with loop holes, through which each party fired muzzle to muzzle.

It is not clear how long this most dangerous phase lasted, with the initiative repeatedly shifting among the cottages, walled gardens and alleys, in a chaos of running soldiers stumbling over piled corpses, and casualties frantically dragging themselves towards what cover they could find. Buildings were now on fire from the shelling, filling with smoke the confined lanes where crowds of shouting, wild-eyed men of both sides struggled, utterly mixed up and often beyond any control save that of individual junior officers and sergeants. The 18-year-old Ensign William Grattan commanded the company in the 1/88th that was to lead the ultimate counter-attack, and he paints a vivid picture:

> Every street, and every angle of a street, were the different theatres for the combatants; inch by inch was gained and lost in turn. Wherever the enemy were forced back, fresh troops, and fresh energy on the part of their officers, impelled them on again, and towards midday the town presented a shocking sight; our Highlanders lay dead in heaps, while the other regiments, though less remarkable in dress, were scarcely so in the numbers of their slain. The French Grenadiers, with their immense caps and gaudy plumes, in piles of twenty and thirty together – some dead, others wounded, with barely strength sufficient to move; their exhausted state, and the weight of their cumbrous appointments, making

it impossible for them to crawl out of the range of the dreadful fire of grape and round shot which the enemy poured into the town. Great numbers perished in this way, and many were pressed to death in the streets.

Most of the British dead were Scotsmen; the regimental history of the 79th (Cameron Highlanders) says that 'A fierce and bloody hand-to-hand combat was maintained with the French grenadiers, the Highlanders in numerous instances clubbing their muskets and using them accordingly, instead of acting with the bayonet, so close and deadly was the nature of the strife maintained.' From the top of the village, young William Grattan watched the street-fighting:

> It was now half-past twelve o'clock, and although the French troops which formed this attack had been several times reinforced, ours never had; nevertheless the town was still in dispute. Massena, aware of its importance, and mortified at the pertinacity with which it was defended, ordered a fresh column of the 9th Corps to reinforce those already engaged. Such a series of attacks, constantly supported by fresh troops, required exertions more than human to withstand; every effort was made to sustain the post, but efforts, no matter how great, must have their limits. Our soldiers had been engaged in this unequal contest for upwards of eight hours [sic]; the heat was moreover excessive, and their ammunition was nearly expended.

Then came a real blow for the 79th to bear:

> A French soldier was observed to step aside into a doorway and take deliberate aim at Colonel Cameron, who fell from his horse mortally wounded. A cry of grief, intermingled with shouts for revenge, arose from the rearmost Highlanders, who witnessed the fall of their commanding officer, and was rapidly communicated to those in front.

Colonel Cameron had been shot through the neck. Back to William Grattan's account:

> The Highlanders were driven to the churchyard at the top of the village, and were fighting with the French Grenadiers across the tomb-stones and graves; while the ninth French light infantry had penetrated as far as the chapel, distant but a few yards from our line, and were prepared to debouch upon our centre.

The tipping-point had come: it seemed that the French were on the lip of breaking out after all. The fresh men of the 9th Corps' heavy column had brushed aside the exhausted defenders, to stand at last on the plateau. As the soldier of the 71st wrote, with an emphasis on the first four words: '*Notwithstanding all our efforts*, the enemy forced us out of the town, then halted and formed close column betwixt us and it'. Any further progress would be the signal for Massena to unloose Marchand, Mermet and Solignac towards the main British line. The 9th Corps column had to be stopped. The surviving soldiers of the 71st and 79th stood in open files, biting cartridge, pouring, ball down, crashing the butt on the ground to seat the load – never mind the ramrod at this range, anything to speed up the next shot. On their flank, cannons spewed case loaded on top of roundshot into the French, tearing bloody corridors through the close-packed blue ranks. The soldier of the 71st: 'While they stood thus, the havoc amongst them was dreadful. Gap after gap was made by our cannon, and as quickly filled up. Our loss was not so severe, as we stood in open files... firing at each other as quick as we could, [and when later] we passed over the ground where they had stood, it lay two and three deep of dead and wounded'.

Mackinnon's brigade was in reserve behind the 71st and 79th, on the high ground above the churchyard. Lieutenant-Colonel Alexander Wallace, in command of the 1/88th (Connaught Rangers), was 'attentively looking on at the combat which raged below', says William Grattan:

> Sir Edward Pakenham galloped to him, and said, 'Do you see that, Wallace?' – 'I do,' replied the Colonel, 'and I would rather drive the French out of the town than cover a retreat across the Coa.' 'Perhaps,' said Sir Edward, 'his lordship don't think it tenable.' Wallace answering replied, 'I shall take it with my regiment, and keep it too.' 'Will you?' was the reply; 'I'll go and tell Lord Wellington so; see, here he comes.' In a moment or two Pakenham returned at a gallop and, waving his hat, called out, 'He says you may go – come along, Wallace'.
>
> At this moment General Mackinnon came up, and placing himself beside Wallace and Pakenham, led the attack of the 88th Regiment, which soon changed the state of affairs. This battalion advanced with fixed bayonets in column of sections, left in front, in double quick time, their firelocks at the trail. As it passed down the road leading to the chapel, it was warmly cheered by the troops that lay at each side of the walls, but the soldiers made no reply to this greeting. They were placed in a situation of great distinction, and they felt it; they were going to fight, not only under the eye of their own army and general, but also in the view of every soldier in the French army; but although their feelings were wrought up to the highest pitch of enthusiasm, not one hurrah responded to the shouts that welcomed their advance. There was no noise or talking in the ranks; the men stepped together at a smart trot, as if on a parade, headed by their brave colonel.

The 79th's history recorded the arrival of the Irishmen, just as the lamented Colonel Cameron was carried to the rear:

> 'The 88th Regiment arrived in double quick time... The men were now at the highest pitch of excitement... A charge being ordered by Brigadier-General Mackinnon, the enemy was driven out of the village with great slaughter.' It was the teenage Ensign William Grattan who led the Rangers into the fight:
>
> It so happened that the command of the company which led this attack devolved upon me. When we came within sight of the French 9th Regiment, which was drawn up at the corner of the chapel, waiting for us, I turned round to look at the men of my company; they gave me a cheer that the lapse of many years has not made me forget, and I thought that that moment was the proudest of my life. The soldiers did not look as men usually do going into close fight – pale; the trot down the road had heightened their complexions, and they were a picture of everything that a chosen body of troops ought to be.
>
> The enemy were not idle spectators of this movement; they witnessed its commencement, and the regularity with which the advance was conducted made them fearful of the

result. A battery of 8-pounders advanced at a gallop to an olive-grove on the opposite bank of the river, hoping by the effects of its fire to annihilate the 88th Regiment or, at all events, embarrass its movements as much as possible; but this battalion continued to press on, joined by its exhausted comrades, and the battery did little execution.

On reaching the head of the village, the 88th Regiment was vigorously opposed by the French 9th Regiment, supported by some hundred of the Imperial Guard [sic], but it soon closed in with them and, aided by the brave fellows that had so gallantly fought in the town all the morning, drove the enemy through the different streets at the point of the bayonet, and at length forced them into the river that separated the two armies. Several of our men fell on the French side of the water.

About one hundred and fifty of the Grenadiers of the Guard, in their flight, ran down a street that had been barricaded by us the day before, and which was one of the few that escaped the fury of the morning's assault; but their disappointment was great, upon arriving at the bottom, to find themselves shut in. Mistakes of this kind will sometimes occur, and when they do, the result is easily imagined; troops advancing to assault a town, uncertain of success, or flushed with victory, have no great time to deliberate as to what they will do; the thing is generally done in half the time the deliberation would occupy. In the present instance, every man was put to death; but our soldiers, as soon as they had leisure, paid the enemy that respect which is due to brave men. This part of the attack was led by Lieutenant George Johnstone, of the 88th Regiment.

This same Lieutenant Johnstone is recorded by James Grant 'climbing to the summit of a stone cross, in a square near the river, and taking off his cap, waved it in defiance of the enemy', although whether this was before or after he had led the butchery described by Grattan is not known.

As Grattan and his fellow company commanders in the 88th went down through the village, they had the 45th (Nottinghamshire) in support behind, and the 74th Highlanders on their left – some 1,800 bayonets, and on this occasion that conventional term was grimly apt. The fighting was at close quarters and therefore savage. The two sides had won and lost these blood-greased alleyways too many times to give quarter, and the fighting turned into a terrible game of hide and seek – officers frantic at the confusion and lack of control, bellowing at their battle-mad soldiers not to leave alley-mouths and doorways unchecked as they surged on beyond; small parties of redcoats peeling off to scour through houses and enclosures; Frenchmen trying to climb away up chimneys but being pulled down by the heels, while the better shots stationed themselves at upper windows to peer around for blue-coated targets. Finally, the last half-hearted French counter-attacks at the bottom of the village petered out, and once again it was a case of renewing barricades and positioning the first line of muskets.

* * *

So ended the battle at Fuentes d'Oñoro. As an attempt by Massena to save his command, it failed; that decision had already been taken, and just five days later Marshal Auguste Frederic Louis Viesse de Marmont, Duke of Ragusa, arrived to take over the army. This minor aristocrat was a hero of Marengo, but at just 37 years old he probably owed his baton and his dukedom of Ragusa to the fact that he was a fellow gunner who had been a close personal friend and ally of Napoleon for many years.

That Massena gave Wellington a fright cannot be in doubt (nor that the Peer's habitual imperturbability prevented him from showing it). There is a convincing ring to Larpent's report of Wellington's reply, as he paused in his shaving on the morning of 5 May to hear the news that prisoners had divulged the awesome size of Massena's attack on his right: 'Oh! They are all there, are they? Well, we must mind a little what we are about' (one must admire the 'a little', in the circumstances). But he would already have decided on the principle behind his reaction: he was not going to conjure up more troops by moving Erskine's 5th or Campbell's 6th Divisions from their job of covering Almeida. The continuing blockade of that stronghold was his aim, and he was not going to be manoevred out of it by a threat, however substantial, to his right flank.

This showed great trust in his army, for the threat was not just proximate to his defensive position, but extended – or could extend, should Massena so decide – to his rearward communications to Garda and Sabugal via the bridges at Ponte Sequeiro and Castello Bom. A cavalry raid to the bridges was one thing, and could be ignored as a minor irritation; but should his army fail him, a cavalry raid with infantry and artillery support would be quite another. With those bridges gone, he would have a hazardous fighting withdrawal on his hands. So here is a classic example of the prime military axiom: maintenance of the aim. That morning, as he shaved and pondered his position, Lord Wellington knew he could not both block Almeida and keep his right flank communications across the Coa. As he wrote three days later in his Despatch, thanks to Massena's boldness these two purposes 'were become incompatible with each other. I therefore abandoned that which was the less important.' Hence he formed the new line with the wedge in it, sent the Light Division to bring in the 7th, and defied Massena to do his worst.

Overarching the blockade of Almeida, however, lay a greater imperative – maintaining the Peninsular Field Army in being. Had Wellington had any real doubts concerning his enemy's strength, morale or leadership – had Bessières brought 10,000 men of the Imperial Guard – then he would simply not have offered battle. Three days before the engagement he had written as much to Lord Liverpool: that he would 'allow them to relieve this place... if the enemy have such a superiority of force as to render the result of a contest for this point doubtful.' Almeida, and still less its garrison of a couple of battalions, was not worth an unequal confrontation, with poor odds, dependent on too many things going right. Imagine another 10,000 Frenchmen and twenty more guns at Fuentes.

Yet while applauding this pragmatic adjustment to his military aims, hindsight must question his decision to send Houston and his green 7th Division out on such a limb. On the face of it, to place a force of 4,000 foot and 1,400 horse in the way of 20,000 Frenchmen is such madness – on the part of the greatest battlefield commander of his time – that the only explanation is ignorance. Wellington had no way of knowing the size of Massena's turning movement when he had dispatched the 7th the previous day. Massena had therefore 'humbugged' Wellington, who had clearly assumed a lesser force with which the 7th Division could safely tangle. This is not apparent from his Despatch, however, as Ensign John Mills of the Coldstream noted in a letter of 27 June; the less said the better, perhaps, but the troops usually know the score:

> The French completely turned our right; Lord Wellington in his dispatch slightly notices it, and would lead you to think that the troops on the right were withdrawn, rather than as was the case, driven in.

Quite how Houston got away with it is still not clear, apart from a lot of luck and the admirable skills of the Light Division. Before their arrival, however, Montbrun enjoyed a three-to-one superiority over Houston's only defenders, the four Allied cavalry regiments. It is perhaps easier to picture them in their twelve squadrons each of a hundred sabres, and the French as thirty-five such squadrons. It is inconceivable that such superiority did not give the French many opportunities to trap or channel the British – suddenly to overwhelm an isolated squadron with five of theirs, say, or to tempt a Captain Brotherton into charging an apparently soft target before racing to cut off his escape. Yet the Allied cavalry suffered quite trivial casualties in all this – 144 killed and wounded, and only five captured. It was indeed an impressive performance on the one side, and either great ineptitude, or that and poor leadership, on the other. And this in spite of the French horses being mostly superior in condition, according to Wellington.

Nor did Massena have any excuse for the absence of infantry support to Montbrun's cavalry. It would have been all up with Houston's 7th Division if Marchand and Mermet's divisions had caught him before Crauford arrived. Massena said in his Despatch that they 'followed the movement of the cavalry as much as was possible for infantry in column to do'. But wherein lay the difficulty? The accounts are quite clear: eleven French battalions attacked Poco Velho and pushed the 85th and 2nd Cacadores out the other side, where they were caught by a waiting Chasseur regiment. They in turn were counter-attacked by two squadrons of KGL Hussars; the depleted 85th and Cacadores then crossed the plain to the 7th Division a mile away, protected from Montbrun's horse by their own twelve supporting squadrons. Why could the French infantry not simply follow hard on the heels of the 85th and the Portuguese, whom they had just dispersed within musket range – they could not have been more than 70 yards apart? They had thirty-five cavalry squadrons as protection, but they did not follow on, presumably lingering in Poco Velho before turning north. One wonders if, in later years, Massena ever thought it might have been a better idea to have accompanied his 20,000-strong turning movement himself. He certainly joined Marchand later, beneath the British line, for we have an account by Pelet, one of his ADCs:

> The Marshal came to the front when this sort of defile had become almost impregnable; a *tiraillade* was already established; he threw himself off his horse and, accompanied by myself, walked several times up and down the front of the line, to look for a point where he could break in. But the whole position seemed equally strong; the fire of the enemy upon Fuentes, and the reinforcements which he had sent into the village, drew in that direction the bulk of the French divisions. Everything had come to turn upon the *affaire de poste* in that direction. It was necessary to force the village and the ravine at its back, where all the ground was in favour of the enemy. The day slipped by in vain attacks.

We do not know whether in his younger days Massena – 'with the sparkling eye, the changeable face, the intensive figure' (General Foy) – would have thought of a solution. Certainly Thiebault reckoned that by 1811 'his tenacity alone was left, but not a single inspiration'. Three full divisions had been mauled in Fuentes village, and without opening that front door he dare not send Marchand and Mermet knocking on the side – not after what had happened at Busaco the previous autumn. It seems possible that his infantry rather let him down in

Fuentes, anyway; the historian Jac Weller suggests that they did not adapt as well as the British to the close and fluid conditions of street-fighting. Perhaps the mental conditioning of fighting in column, and the many hours' close-order drilling that that required, had bred a reluctance to act individually.

The casualty figures give pointers: Oman calculates that in the village the French lost 1,300 men to Wellington's 800. Napier, as brigade major of the Light Division's Portuguese brigade, was in charge of burying the dead in the village after the battles of 5 May; he says that he counted some ninety French corpses and forty British. Major-General Miles Nightingall says 'the enemy left 400 dead in the village and his loss cannot be much less than 1,200 in these different attacks' [on the village].

Since the total casualties for each side on the 5th were 2,192 and 1,452 respectively, it can be seen that in both cases over half the butcher's bill was paid in the narrow alleys of Fuentes itself. Elsewhere, the French lost 359 cavalrymen on the plain, and 400 infantry of Marchand's and Mermet's divisions – mostly when standing in their columns under the Allied artillery. British losses included 237 men of the 7th Division, at Poco Velho and later; 100 Guardsmen caught out of square; 149 cavalrymen and 100 horses on the plain; and – amazingly – just sixty-seven men of the Light Division during its withdrawal. The only two battalions to suffer bad losses were the Highlanders of the 71st and 79th, whose figures were 127 and 256, out of some 400 and 900 respectively. (The detailed casualty figures by regiments are reproduced in Appendices II and III at the end of this book.)

Perhaps a pointer to the curious overall ineffectiveness of Montbrun's horse, and of Ferey's and D'Erlon's infantry in Fuentes, is their very high officer casualties. As remarked with regard to Sabugal, these were usually suffered while setting an example, when those behind were a little shy of following on. At Fuentes the French loss in officers was nearly three times that of the British – twenty-eight killed as opposed to nine, 151 wounded against fifty-seven.

It is also interesting that at one stage, for the street-fighting, D'Erlon chose to put in eighteen grenadier companies, while Wellington chose twenty-eight light companies and riflemen. Further, there are three comments, two of them by a light infantryman and a rifleman, to the effect that British battalion companies – those of the 71st, 79th and 24th – were not as good in such circumstances as the light troops, being prone to fight 'shoulder to shoulder'. Firstly, Napier of the 43rd wrote that the three British regiments, being 'little accustomed to the desultory fighting of light troops, were pierced and divided' – desultory being used here in its true meaning of 'leaping' – from place to place and target to target. In street-fighting marksmanship against individual, close-range targets is paramount, in contrast to the volley fired by many towards a massive, easy target. Rifleman Ned Costello said 'The 79th Highlanders had suffered very severely here, and the place was strewn about with their bodies. The poor fellows were unused to skirmishing, and instead of occupying the houses in the neighbourhood, and firing from the windows, I heard they had exposed themselves by firing in sections' – that is, standing conventionally in the open, shoulder to shoulder. Finally, Commissary Schaumann recounts one incident where 'a detachment was skirmishing, and a young Highlander concealed himself behind a rock, and from this cover shot bravely at the enemy. The moment one of the older Highlanders saw this he cried to him indignantly: "Since when have Scotsmen fought in that cowardly manner?" and seizing the younger man by the collar, he pushed him into the middle of the field, exposed him to the enemy's fire, with the words, "When Scotsmen fight they look straight into the enemy's eyes!"' (Of course, to be fair to the

Highlanders and their well-worn muskets, sniping at individuals is a great deal easier with a Baker rifle.)

*   *   *

Grattan of the Connaught Rangers said that by 2pm on 5 May:

> the town was comparatively tranquil... and toward evening the firing ceased altogether... about 5 o'clock the Light Division was selected [to take over in Fuentes village] and passed us... every precaution was resorted to to strengthen the town; temporary walls were thrown up at the bottom of the streets, carts and doors were put into requisition to barricade every pass...
>
> The next day, the 6th, we had no fighting; each army kept its position, and Villa Formosa continued to be the receptacle for the wounded... I had little difficulty in finding out the hospitals, as every house might be considered one... my attention was arrested by an extraordinary degree of bustle, and a kind of half-stifled moaning, in the yard of a *quinta*, or nobleman's house. I looked through the grating, and saw about two hundred wounded soldiers waiting to have their limbs amputated, while others were arriving every moment. It would be difficult to convey an idea of the frightful appearance of these men: they had been wounded on the 5th and it was now the 7th; their limbs were swollen to an enormous size. Some were sitting upright against a wall, under the shade of a number of chest-nut trees, and many of these were wounded in the head as well as limbs. The ghastly countenances of these poor fellows presented a dismal sight. The streams of gore, which had trickled down their cheeks, were quite hardened by the sun, and gave their faces a glazed and copper-coloured hue; their eyes were sunk and fixed, and what between the effects of the sun, of exhaustion, and despair, they resembled more a group of bronze figures than anything human – there they sat, silent and statue-like, waiting for their turn to be carried to the amputating tables. At the other side of the yard lay several whose state was too helpless for them to sit up; a feeble cry from them occasionally, to those who were passing, for a drink of water, was all that we heard.
>
> A little further on, in an inner court, were the surgeons. They were stripped to their shirts, and bloody. Curiosity led me forward; a number of doors, placed on barrels, served as temporary tables, and on these lay the different subjects on whom the surgeons were operating; to the right and left were arms and legs, flung here and there, without distinction, and the ground was dyed with blood.
>
> Dr Bell was going to take off the thigh of a soldier of the 50th, and he requested I hold down the man for him. He was one of the best-hearted men I ever met with, but, such is the force of habit, he seemed insensible to the scene that was passing around him, and with much composure was eating almonds out of his waistcoat-pockets, which he offered to share with me, but, if I got the universe for it, I could not have swallowed a morsel of anything. The operation upon the man of the 50th was the most shocking sight I ever witnessed; it lasted nearly half an hour, but his life was saved.
>
> Outside this place was an immense pit to receive the dead from the general hospital, which was close by. Twelve or fifteen bodies were flung in at a time, and covered with a layer of earth, and so on, in succession, until the pit was filled. Flocks of vultures already began to hover over this spot, and Villa Formosa was now beginning to be as disagreeable as it was the contrary a few days before. This was my first and last visit to an amputating

hospital, and I advise young gentlemen, such as I was then, to avoid going near a place of the kind, unless obliged to do so.

While Ensign Grattan was extending his understanding of the realities of warfare, his general completed the entrenchments above Fuentes in case Massena should come again. Miles Nightingall tells us that 'The 6th and 7th May passed without any movement on our side, and were occupied in strengthening our right, by throwing up some breastworks covering our cannon and making *trous-de-loups* ['wolf-holes' – leg-breaking boobytraps] against their cavalry.' But Massena in fact had no aggressive intent; he sent instructions to General Brennier in Almeida to blow the place up and make his escape, while he himself thinned out his troops on the night of 7/8 May and headed east – to his supercession by Marmont.

   Much to Lord Wellington's fury and frustration, Brennier succeeded on the night of 10/11 May both in destroying the fortifications and evading his encirclers, to get out with 1,000 men at the cost of 300 and his baggage. Campbell's 6th Division had completely mishandled the blockade, and the episode understandably brought down a damning condemnation by the army commander: 'the most disgraceful military event that has yet occurred to the British army in the Peninsula'. The shame of amateurish incompetence and botched chances hung over all concerned; Wellington wrote four days later:

> Possibly I have to reproach myself for not having been on the spot, but really... having employed two divisions and a brigade, to prevent the escape of 1,400 men, who I did not think it likely would attempt to escape, the necessity of my attending personally... did not occur to me... I certainly feel, every day, more and more the difficulty of the situation in which I am placed. I am obliged to be every where, and if absent from any operation, something goes wrong.

It was a humiliation that much detracted from his success on the 5th, leaving his army looking flat-footed, and it reflected corresponding credit on the French; but in truth, Wellington found little satisfaction in his victory. Captain Cocks wrote in his journal:

> 'I heard Lord Wellington say afterwards at his table he thought he had never been in a worse scrape'. It had been altogether too close to a disaster, and he was angry with himself: he wrote to his brother William that Lord Liverpool was quite right not to move thanks [in Parliament] for the battle at Fuentes, though it was the most difficult one I was ever concerned in. We had very nearly three to one against us engaged; above four to one of cavalry; and moreover our cavalry had not a gallop in them; while some of that of the enemy was fresh and in excellent order. If Boney had been there, we should have been beaten.

Napoleon's new appointee, Marshal Marmont, wisely withdrew the various corps towards Salamanca, where for the next several weeks he would be busy refitting the Army of Portugal, and re-shaping its organization and command structures. And we ourselves will withdraw from following the fortunes of Lord Wellington, which have now taken us into May 1811, and revert to those of Marshal Sir William Beresford. We left him down south of Badajoz a couple of weeks earlier, being summoned to meet Wellington for a reconnaissance of that fortress.

6
The First Siege of Badajoz, 8–12 May

THE day Olivenza fell, Beresford's chief sapper Captain Squire and chief gunner Major Dickson dutifully set out to catch up with him, to request fresh orders. Covering nearly 50 miles in two days, they rejoined his headquarters at Zafra on 17 April – the day after the skirmish at Los Santos, and thus the day before he himself, also in search of fresh orders, was to move north to meet Lord Wellington. 'Return to Elvas and make preparations for the siege of Badajoz' was his obvious if belated instruction, according to Dickson, who also received the happy news that he was appointed chief of artillery for that purpose. Squire would be supernumary to Lieutenant-Colonel Fletcher, Wellington's chief engineer. The two officers returned post-haste, reaching Villa Real on the 19th, and on to Elvas where, the next day, they met Lord Wellington newly arrived from his own, more serious hack down from Sabugal (150 miles in four days, reputedly killing two of his horses en route, and with two dragoons of his escort washed away and drowned crossing a torrent).

Much effort now went into collecting transport, mules and horses to move guns and ammunition to Badajoz from both Elvas and Olivenza, and some 400 artillerymen, mainly Portuguese, from the various local companies at Abrantes, Olivenza, Juromenha and La Lippe. Lord Wellington had no formal capacity in either gunnery or engineering skills for prosecuting sieges, and had to do the best he could with what he could scrape together. As a consequence, in gunnery, he was to be largely dependent on such large-calibre Portuguese and Spanish pieces as were available on the walls of Elvas.

There were just twenty-four guns (sixteen 24-pounders and eight 16-pounders) and ten howitzers (two 10in and eight 8 inch). These were listed by the unhappy Dickson as 'brass Portuguese guns of the time of John IV and his son Affonso, bearing dates 1646, 1652, 1653 etc; also some Spanish guns of Philip III and IV, dates 1620, 1636 etc'. The bores of these 200-year-old museum pieces were so worn that Dickson had to hand-select shot to fit individual barrels: 'You could put your fingers in between the shot and the bore... [and] many of the gun carriages are in a rotten state and require repair... Here [Elvas] there is only the means of transporting three heavy pieces at a time.' It was 17 miles to Badajoz, and 1 mile an hour was good going. Only three truck carriages for transporting guns were available at Elvas for the eighteen guns there, and another six carriages and the requisite mules and bullocks were with the other six guns at Olivenza. It can readily be seen that Major Dickson earned his pay, simply in working out a convoy system to assemble his train.

The forward planning necessary for all this was, as one would expect of Lord Wellington's headquarters, well in hand from an early point. Two days after Campo Mayor (27 March) he had written to Beresford that 'Elvas must supply the means [for the siege] if possible: if it has them not, I must send them there; this will take time, but that cannot be avoided'. Upon receipt of this, Beresford (then at Elvas, of course, not yet having crossed the Guadiana) sent for Dickson 'to prepare a return by which might be seen in one view the natures of ordnance, quantity of ammunition etc. The reason of this return as the Marshal told me was for the information of Lord Wellington, and I think evidently shews the idea of a probable siege.'

Dickson produced the return the next day, and it doubtless crossed – on the road to Wellington's headquarters – a further note from him dated on 6 April: 'I am most anxious to receive the accounts of what Elvas can supply, that I may order up from our battering train the deficiency'. He wrote again on the 10th, presumably having now received the Elvas return, listing those items his chief engineer Fletcher 'thinks ought to be prepared to be taken out [from Elvas] for the siege of Badajoz', and listing separately those additional stores he had ordered from Lisbon. These lists would have reached Beresford at Albuera, which he quit on 13 April, and would therefore have been passed to Dickson and Squire at Zafra on the 17th.

Beresford joined Wellington at Elvas late on 21 April, and next morning the two commanders and their staffs crossed the Guadiana below the Caya. Escorted by two light battalions of the KGL, recently landed at Lisbon, and two Portuguese squadrons, they approached the walls of Badajoz from the south. Along the road from Valverde they bumped a French working party returning from cutting timber, and so alarmed Governor Phillipon at what he thought was an attempt to capture his men that he sallied out with a brigade some 1,500 strong, in two columns, including cavalry and two guns. The KGL history records that one advanced towards the staff, the other against Captain Bosewiel's company of the 2nd Light Battalion; at the same time the convoy from the wood which instead of being one hundred, proved to be four hundred strong, appeared in the rear... the detached company was overpowered... the French convoy entered Badajoz, leaving five killed, eight wounded and thirty-six taken.

Wellington continued a minute study of the walls, past Fort Picurina and on to the river opposite Fort San Cristobal, whence he returned to Elvas satisfied and turning over the possibilities in his mind. The next day, 23 April, he wrote a detailed one-page memorandum on the way he wished the siege to proceed, for the eyes of Beresford, Colonel Fletcher and Major Dickson. Fletcher was also at Elvas, of course, and, having conferred with Lord Wellington before, during and following the reconnaissance, he saw Dickson and confirmed that he would 'require about five heavy guns and three howitzers for San Cristobal and the operation of this side... and that (for the artillery depot) any convenient situation at a distance of two miles from the Picurina south east of Badajoz will be preferable... the direct road from Olivenza will do well'. This was Wellington's Memorandum of instructions for the investment and siege of Badajoz:

> Elvas, April 23, 1811
> 1st. The cutting tools having been sent to Olivenza this morning, a body of troops to be stationed tomorrow morning in the wood between Olivenza and Badajoz to cut materials.
> 2nd. As soon as a sufficient quantity of materials will be cut, Badajoz to be invested on the right as well as the left banks of the Guadiana.
> 3rd. If the weather should become settled before the materials will be cut, the place to be invested, as stated in article 2nd, as soon as the weather will be so settled as that the Troops

may be kept out without inconvenience. The importance of the early investment of the place will be observed from what follows hereafter.

4th. On the day the place will be invested the following measures to be adopted:

First. The flying bridge to be fixed on the Guadiana below the junction with the Caia.

Secondly. The guns & stores for which there are conveyance to be moved up from Olivenza to the station fixed upon for the formation of the Depot on the left of the Guadiana.

Thirdly. The Engineers' stores to be moved from Olivenza, Elvas, & Juromenha to the same place, & to the place fixed upon for the depots on the right of the Guadiana, in their due proportion.

Fourthly. The materials made at Elvas, Campo Mayor, &c, for which there may be conveyance to be moved to the ground fixed for the depots of stores on the ground on the right of the Guadiana.

Fifthly. The materials prepared at Olivenza in the wood & at all places on the left of the Guadiana, be moved to the ground on the left of that river.

Sixthly. The Ordnance and stores which there may be means of moving to be sent from Elvas to the ground on the right of the Guadiana.

5th. On the day after the place will be invested the carriages & cattle [i.e. draught oxen] to return to Elvas from the stations on both banks of the Guadiana for more Ordnance & stores, & go back to those stations respectively each on the 3rd day; and the same to be repeated on the 4th and 5th day from the investing of the place till all the Ordnance & stores required will be collected in the proper deposits.

6th. Ground to be broke for the attacks on Pardaleras, Picurina and S. Cristobal on the night of the day the materials will be in deposits on the ground.

7th. As soon as the British troops will be in possession of S. Cristobal the flying bridge placed below the junction of the Caia, to be brought to a station above the town, & if possible below the junction of the Gevora, & with this view it is recommended that the ford & passages of the river above the town should be well reconnoitred as soon as the place will be invested.

8th. When the British army will be in possession of S. Cristobal, La Picurina, and Pardaleras, Marshal Beresford will determine upon the point at which he will attack the body of the place. It is believed however that upon the whole one of the south faces will be the most advantageous.

Modern staff officers will read the above with some astonishment, since nine-tenths of it is statements of the obvious which merely diminish the local commanders' role. It is, however, a useful reminder that Lord Wellington's renowned attention to detail could sometimes get the better of him, and also of his reluctance to delegate.

As to the plan of attack, Oman's view has invariably been followed: that Lord Wellington was advised wrongly by Colonel Fletcher to attack the three forts equally and simultaneously, and that the plan was frustrated both by lack of resources and the approach of Marshal Soult. The alternative is put forward by Lieutenant-Colonel John Jones in his epic *Journals of Sieges etc.* of 1813: the advice was to attack Fort San Cristobal only, prior to attacking the weak castle walls on the north-east perimeter.

Jones stated that Wellington would contemplate 'any plan of attack... which should not require more than sixteen days open trenches, as in that period, and the time required to complete the necessary preparations for the siege, it was calculated that Marshal Soult would be able to collect a force equal to its relief.' Lord Wellington himself – like Soult in March – favoured one of the southern fronts, as expressed in the last sentence of his Memorandum. Yet those walls were defended by Fort Pandaleras; and Colonel Fletcher would not undertake to complete such an operation in less than twenty-two days of open trenches, even given unlimited resources. Beresford's guns and stores being totally inadequate for such a regular siege, therefore, Wellington's time limit of sixteen days might well have to be doubled. Since this was clearly unacceptable, Colonel Fletcher proposed an ambitious alternative.

Badajoz castle overlooks the town, which has no defences; seize the castle, dominate the town, and there can be no further resistance. The inside of the castle is similarly overlooked from Fort San Cristobal, and (Jones says) 'no body of troops could stand in it for the defence of a breach in its walls, without the erection of traverses, and other cover, requiring a degree of labour much beyond the power of the garrison to bestow during a short attack.' The castle walls were seemingly of old masonry and had not been modernized since the Moors had built them; Fletcher believed that they could be breached in three or four days – that is, from batteries on the north bank. So his plan was to carry Fort San Cristobal by assault, erect batteries in and around it to overwhelm the interior of the castle, and on the second night to work forward for the placement of breaching batteries. 'To conceal this plan of attack', wrote Jones, 'false attacks [would be made] against the other detached works.'

Then there was the role of Beresford's Spanish allies to consider. Lord Wellington set out his requirements unambiguously, insisting that they operate directly under the marshal, and itemizing where and how they should function – even to the locations of the various headquarters and advance posts. There must be no question of mere co-operation, even if that word was used as a courtesy. Fortunately, Castanos as senior Spanish commander had already agreed to accept Beresford's overall command. Wellington's concern was not in the context of the siege, of course, but in regard to the anticipated movement by Soult to frustrate it – what force Soult might muster remained unknown, and Beresford might well need all the help he could get. So the Spanish under Castanos, Ballasteros and Blake were required to join Beresford, should Soult re-invade Estremadura, from their immediate positions of observation; they were not, absolutely not, to attempt to engage the French themselves. Together they led 15,000 troops and, supposing they could get to the field of battle in good time, should transform Beresford's prospects.

Wellington gave Beresford clearly to understand his opinion that when the investment of Badajoz reached French ears, Soult must march to its relief. It would then be for Beresford to decide whether to fight him off, or to abandon the siege and retire behind the Guadiana:

> Marshal Beresford will consider... the chances of success, according to a view of the relative number of both armies, and making a reasonable allowance for the number of the Spanish troops which will cooperate with him... if he should think his strength sufficient to fight a general action to save the siege of Badajoz, he will collect his troops to fight it. I believe that, upon the whole, the most central and advantageous place to collect the troops will be at Albuera... All this must of course be left to the decision of Sir William Beresford. I authorize him to fight the action if he should think proper, or to retire if he should not.

The commander of a detached corps could hardly hope for a less ambiguous definition of his degree of freedom of action – and of his personal responsibility. (On your head be it, Sir William....)

On 23 April the River Guadiana rose – by various accounts – between 7 and 10 feet, and ruined the bridges and ferries at Jerumenha. Wellington instructed Beresford to change front so that his back was adjacent to the old Roman bridge at Merida, while as far as possible continuing the preparations for the siege. He then left, on the 25th, to rejoin his northern army, hearing en route of Massena's remarkable return to activity, which a week later was to bring them face to face at Fuentes d'Oñoro.

The river returned to normal levels on 29 April, and by then news had come up from the south, confirming some French movement back into Estremadura – foraging parties in the main, but also a hesitant probing by Latour-Maubourg. Beresford therefore sent Colonel John Colborne to see them off, a mission that he achieved admirably: with only his own brigade of four battalions, a couple of guns and two squadrons of Portuguese horse, he marched amazingly far and wide. Apart, of course, from the lack of mountains, the equivalent would be to cover a quadrilateral from Maidstone to London, then to Northampton, back down to Oxford, then to Guildford and finally back across to Maidstone. It was described in his diary by Lieutenant Edward Close, 2/48th, quoted below. The miles marched (in brackets) are the present author's estimates, necessarily 'as the crow flies' from a modern map. The distances seem to total 270 miles in the fortnight 29 April–13 May; with two rest days on the 8th and 12th, that gave an average day's route of 22 miles, or seven to eight hours' marching. Close's fellow subaltern William Woods, in a letter of 29 May, reckoned that the battalion covered 300 miles: 'The Brigade was so exhausted that nearly half the men were brought in on cars, or any conveyance we could procure.' The 66th's history made it 250 miles in eleven days. It was a remarkable sustained effort, and it is interesting to note – apropos La Peña's unfortunate night marches before Barrosa – that Colborne made good use of darkness:

April 29th – Our brigade, under Colonel Colburne of the 66th, marched to Ribiera from Almendralejo (18 miles), and got in at nine at night.

April 30th – Moved from this again at four in the morning, and at ten o'clock reached Lera (15 miles). Started again that evening at sunset, and passed through Valencea (5 miles), and halted in a wood near Margarilla.

May 1st – Marched at eleven o'clock at night, and

May 2nd – Reached Granja (25 miles), from thence, after a two hour halt, to Azuaga (5 miles), where we had a skirmish with the enemy, who continued to effect their escape in spite of the rapidity of our movements. Halted here for a few hours, and marched at four in the morning.

May 3rd – To Beranga (10 miles).

May 4th – To a wood a league from Granja (10 miles), halted a few hours, and marched to Fuente Ovejuna (15 miles), and encamped on a hill.

May 5th – Marched at two o'clock to a wood 2 leagues, and after a few hours halt moved to a wood about 3 leagues off.

May 6th – Reached Belalcazar (30 miles) where we found the enemy in possession of an old Moorish castle, extremely beautiful. We summoned the garrison, but we could not induce them to surrender. The commandant came out in his dressing gown to reply to our summons. We remained here the greater part of the day, and in the evening, to the great disappointment of the inhabitants of the town, who seemed very tired of their French neighbours, we moved off, and at length reached Cabeca de Buey (12 miles). The country we had passed over lay chiefly at the foot of the Sierra Morena mountains.

May 7th – Marched to Campanario (35 miles) after halting at Cabeca de Buey a few hours. The men were completely knocked up, and we halted a day to recruit [i.e. to rest].

May 9th – To La Haba (10 miles).

May 10th – To Guerina (20 miles).

May 11th – To Almendralejo (25 miles). All miserable places in a most abominable country; but tolerably cultivated, and the wheat remarkably fine. On our return we found the rest of our southern army had been investing Badajoz. We halted on the 12th.

May 13th – To Valverde (35 miles). We were here joined by the rest of our division.

Following the 'skirmish' at Azuega on 2 May, Latour-Maubourg was so convinced that he was facing a major British force that he quit Guadalcanal for the Sierra Norte de Sevilla – not far short of a hundred miles from Badajoz. John Colborne's hard-marching brigade had certainly cleared the decks for the attempt on that fortress.

On 3 May, Colonel Fletcher reported that his stores were assembled, and over the next five days the infantry brigades came up to invest the fortress. Colonel Jones tells us that on the 4th, with a view to the attempt on the castle, 'an officer (Lieutenant Forster, RE, to be killed in the second siege) this night examined the Rivillas, and ascended the rocky height of the castle nearly to the foot of the wall: he reported that the fords of the Rivillas had not been touched, nor the ascent of the castle hill rendered difficult'. The trenches were started on the night of the 8th, but at the crucially important San Cristobal they immediately ran into trouble: beneath a 3-inch skin of soil lay solid rock. The plan at that spot was to dig in three 24-pounders and two howitzers, at a range of only 450 yards from the wall. Therefore, to shelter the 400-strong working party, artificial walls of gabions (earth-filled wicker baskets) were laid out. The French naturally objected fiercely to this development, as recounted by an anonymous soldier of the 27th:

> Then with a slow and silent pace came an engineer heading the working party, with picks, spades and shovels; these were followed by others carrying gabions, which they laid down in rows a little in advance of where we were crouched. The engineer now pointed out the intended works, afterwards called the grand battery, and the massy picks struck the earth; but never shall I forget the terrific noises that followed the breaking of that ground. For a time our ears and senses were alike astounded by the conflicting peals of the artillery and musketry, which burst at once on the stillness of the night, gave such an appalling shock to us who were inactive spectators, as the oldest veterans had never experienced in their numerous conflicts.

In the darkness, lit by lanterns, the flying picks and shovels rose and fell dangerously in the confined space, sparking and skidding against the rock. The entrenching was desperately slow, and the men, working in relays, hated it; British infantry had never cared for digging. By daylight there was little to show for all the effort: a dozen yards of trench earmarked for the battery, and perhaps three times that to accommodate a mere thirty or so men of the covering party, away to the right. The guard on the trenches, drawn from a covering party totalling some 800 men, were therefore placed behind the slope of the hill, in rear of the battery.

By nightfall on 9 May one of the nine engineer officers had been killed and two wounded, and likewise many of the 400 diggers provided by Kemmis's brigade and the 17th Portuguese. French defensive fire from Fort San Cristobal and from across the river was continuous, and the protection afforded by the 3-foot-high gabions was necessarily limited. The trenches made little progress. At 7am on the 10th the French made a sortie; Phillipon sent over the bridge a fresh 700-strong battalion with two guns, who briefly got into the battery trenches, held only by a light company. The guard reacted quickly, however, turning the French out again with little loss after less than five minutes. Unfortunately they then got carried away; pursuing too far, they were themselves caught really badly by grapeshot and musketry from the *tête-du-pont* and San Cristobal – somewhat inexplicably, 400 British and thirty-eight Portuguese were killed or wounded, while the French lost only half as many, in what Wellington in his Despatch called 'a gallant but imprudent advance to the glacis of San Cristobal'.

That same day, according to Fortescue, William Beresford received the first reports that a corps under Marshal Soult was marching to relieve Phillipon's garrison; accordingly, that night work on a new battery was hurriedly begun, enfilading the bridge, while the original battery of five guns commenced firing at San Cristobal at 4am on the 11th. French counter-battery fire proved superior, however – presumably much to the chagrin of Major Dickson, who remains silent on the point – disabling four of the five pieces during the course of the day. It also killed another engineer officer and wounded two – leaving just three of the original nine positioned at Cristobal. That night, to replace the lost firepower, a third battery position was commenced immediately to the east and, on 12 May, new entrenchments were ordered for that night, to face the castle, on the plain bordering the left of the Guadiana. Some 1,400 men paraded for work, and 1,600 as a covering party. But at midnight on 12/13 May a report was received that Soult had moved north quickly; on the 10th he had covered 35 miles to Santa Ollala on the Seville road, and Latour-Maubourg on his right reached Llerena on the Cordoba road. This proved too much for Beresford, who prudently abandoned the siege – Llerena was but three forced marches away.

Total casualties in this first abortive attempt at Badajoz were a rather unnecessary 733, all but seven being in Kemmis's brigade and the 17th Portuguese Regiment outside San Cristobal. Captain Squire perhaps spoke for many when he wrote five days later: 'Doubt and indecision had... governed all our operations... Both officers and men were exhausted, mind and body; they felt and saw that they were absurdly sacrificed.'

This experience at Badajoz in May 1811 showed up the Peninsular Field Army's lack of trained engineers, lack of stores, lack of heavy calibre guns and trained gunners, and – in this instance – lack of time: for given time, all things were possible for Wellington's soldiers. But there was also under-estimation of the fortress' innate strength, and of the quality of the French defence – which was active and robust, and would continue to be so. This error on the part of his lordship and of Colonel Fletcher was understandable at this early stage of their learning curve in Peninsular siege warfare. As Fortescue reminds us, Badajoz in 1811 was the British Army's first attempt at taking a major fortress since the successful storming of Drogheda and Wexford back in 1649 (if we discount India, or Monte Video and Buenos Aires in 1807); it follows that engineer officers and commanders were totally inexperienced in the practicalities.

In retrospect, this failure was surely a blessing. Soult was approaching all too fast, and Beresford had long since run out of time. Lord Wellington's Memorandum was written on 23 April, and he left for the north on the 25th; he left Beresford with the clear prediction that the moment Soult heard of the siege, he would march to its relief. Wellington had stipulated sixteen days of open trenches: well, six days had been lost with the river flooding, then nine days passed after it returned to normal before the investment was complete, and Soult forced the abandonment after only four days of 'open trenches'. As it was, Beresford got his Allied army to Albuera ahead of Soult only by a margin of hours. Had he by some miracle, or some French treachery, actually broken into the fortress on 14 May, he really could not have fought at Albuera, as his lordship had effectively commanded. Indeed, given the need to put in a garrison of say two brigades, and to disarm and guard Phillipon's 3,000 men, and with the impassable Guadiana behind him, and Soult only a six-hour march away at Albuera (which he reached early on the 16th), then in such circumstances Beresford's generalship would indeed have been somewhat tested.

As it was, this brief episode ended in frustration. Major Dickson saw his guns wend their slow route back to Elvas, and Captain Squire back-loaded his stores, pausing only to burn his fascines and gambions under Phillipon's no doubt smiling gaze. The infantry brigades, glad enough to be done with digging, got on the march for Albuera, covered by the 4th Division and the cavalry. The Spanish generals Blake, Ballasteros and Castanos were firmly requested to conform. Soult's strength was held to be only 23,000 men, whereas Beresford reckoned he had 35,000 – some 10,000 each British and Portuguese, and 15,000 Spaniards. He would fight; he had no option.

As Beresford closed upon Albuera on 13 May, Marshal Soult joined forces with Latour-Maubourg at Fuente de Cantos, pushing his advance guard to Los Santos. The French were just two steady marches away.

7
The Roads to Albuera, 8–16 May

WHEN Soult had invaded Estremadura with 20,000 men in January, he had necessarily milked Victor's 1st and Mortier's 5th Corps to raise the necessary force. After his return south following news of Barossa, and hearing of Beresford's difficulties crossing the Guadiana, he felt in no immediate hurry to set out north again – there was then nothing to be done to help Massena in the short term, especially once reports arrived of the action at Sabugal and Massena's retreat back beyond Ciudad Rodrigo. In fact, during the fortnight that followed, when Massena was hectically refitting before his final fling at Fuentes d'Oñoro, Soult was in any case right out of the picture. Beresford's advance against Latour-Maubourg, and Colborne's domination of the country down to the Sierra Morena, had effectively cut Soult's communications with Badajoz and beyond from about 10 April. He did not start forming another army for a second move north until the last week of April, when Massena was approaching the Portuguese border once more.

It took Soult two weeks to collect his force at Seville – by about 8 May, when Beresford was opening his rocky trenches above Fort San Cristobal. Clearly Soult must march forthwith to relieve Badajoz; if he were quick about it, he might even cut off Colborne, or Blake, or both. Convinced that the latter could not possibly join Beresford before he would interpose himself, Soult reckoned Beresford was commanding no more than about 16,000 men, including the Portuguese and Castanos' and Ballasteros' troops; some 25,000 Frenchmen could therefore do the job comfortably – especially 25,000 Frenchmen led by Jean-de-Dieu Soult, Marshal of the Empire and Duke of Dalmatia. Then aged 42, Soult had started his military career as a 16-year-old infantry private; twenty years later, as a corps commander in 1805, he had led the masterstroke that won Austerlitz for Napoleon, who considered him France's finest tactician.

Latour-Maubourg's 5th Corps (Mortier had been recalled to Paris) was around Constantina and could produce 10,000 men; Victor's 1st Corps outside Cadiz would send four battalions and two regiments of horse; Sebastiani's 4th Corps the same, but with an extra cavalry regiment; and Godinot's independent garrison division in Cordova could move across virtually complete, with its nine battalions and two cavalry regiments. Soult placed the non-5th Corps battalions into two formations: nine battalions under Werle and six under Godinot. He thus effectively created a corps of three-plus divisions – Girard's and Gazan's of the 5th Corps, plus Werle's, with a fourth, weaker division commanded by Godinot. The horse numbered over 4,000 sabres and were formed in three brigades. Finally, Soult scraped together forty-eight guns in eight batteries, of which ten were 9-pounders; in weight of metal and effect, his artillery was therefore to be double the size of the Allies'.

Unfortunately for his battle prospects, although all his thirty-five battalions had much experience in the Peninsula, few had any against the British. One battalion each of the

40e, 64e, 88e, 100e and 103e Ligne had been present at Fuentes, but (according to Oman) had remained in reserve. The 100e had also encountered Beresford, of course, but without too much stress, on the road from Campo Mayor to Badajoz. One battalion each of the 16e and 28e Léger had fought in the streets of Fuentes. The 3/12e Léger had been with Solignac when he climbed the eastern ridge at Vimiero, only to be sent to the right-about with heavy losses. Otherwise, Soult's main pool of battle-hardened troops lay in the six battalions of the 58e Ligne and 16e Léger, who had fought with such élan but to no avail at Talavera. So just nine battalions – a quarter of Soult's infantry – had meaningful experience of facing the British on other fields, and twenty-six had not. Further, only three of his twelve cavalry regiments had crossed sabres – the 2e and 10e Hussards and the 26e Dragons, all at Campo Mayor; the Polish 1st Vistula Lancers had been present at Talavera, but unengaged (which may partly explain their later excess of enthusiasm at Albuera).

On 8 May the marshal reviewed his army corps to the north of Seville, and afterwards briefed his officers; he was a tall, commanding figure, and they certainly listened with close attention to his harsh, grating voice. They were to march at midnight the following day, to relieve Badajoz and push the British out of Estremadura. Four days later this clear and helpful message was relayed to Beresford by Seville's patriots, via the vedettes of Ballasteros, at a time when the siege of Badajoz was not going well; the French advance guard was now well beyond Monasterio, where ground contact was made with those vedettes. The next day, the 13th, Latour-Maubourg's 5th Corps came in from Llerena, pushing back Penne-Villemur's Spanish cavalry and joining Soult at Fuente Cantos, with the advance guard at Los Santos, just 33 miles from Albuera.

As we have seen, Beresford abandoned the siege works at midnight on 12/13 May. The British and Spanish cavalry screens being well in touch with the advancing French, he went forward 15 miles to Valverde, which lay 8 miles west of Albuera. He had with him 7,000 men: William Stewart's 2nd Division, Hamilton's Portuguese, and three batteries of artillery, while the rest of his army remained screening Badajoz, whence his siege guns and stores were gradually returning to Elvas.

At Valverde in the afternoon of the 13th Beresford discussed the situation with Captain-General Joachim Blake, who had ridden up from Barcarrota, 15 miles beyond Albuera, and with General Xavier Castanos. In truth, Beresford had not yet quite decided what to do; he needed up-to-date news on which way Soult would advance from Los Santos. Soult could get to Badajoz via Valverde, certainly, but the obvious and direct route was up the middle via Albuera – or possibly more easterly, via Solana and Talavera Real. He was perhaps unlikely to choose Valverde (which makes one question why Beresford was himself there, rather than in the middle), because Soult would thereby be putting himself on a flank march between Beresford and Blake, inviting the obvious. However, Beresford was not yet entirely committed to fighting at all. In the nervous-seeming letter he wrote to Wellington two days later, it almost seems as if he had tried to persuade Blake that retreat would be prudent: 'We are now in that position that has already made me so uneasy, and from which I have not been able to extricate myself. General Blake would not listen to crossing the Guadiana.'

There is a suggestion that at this conference Blake and Castanos blackmailed Beresford, firstly by saying that their men would 'desert and disperse' if taken into Portugal; and secondly by raising the political implications if Beresford abandoned his allies and if Blake were to fight alone and be annihilated. Blake certainly gave both Beresford and D'Urban the impression that the Spanish would fight Soult, alone if they must. This threat, if indeed it was more than a bluff, came on top of the other known considerations – the poorer provision of supplies north of the Guadiana; the strategic value to the French of again having a major power base for future operations into Portugal, via the Badajoz bridge; the threat to the base at Elvas; and the possibility of the Guadiana rising again, to block the movement of stores and troops.

There was also the question of the effect of a retreat on the spirit of the army. Beresford was aware that half his British troops had not been in a good scrap for two years – back at Talavera – while his 2nd and 4th Divisions had been present at Busaco, on the right and left wings respectively, but without seeing any action. Neither had fought at Sabugal or Fuentes d'Oñoro. Napier says that one of Beresford's staff officers told him 'strongly and unceremo-niously' that if he were to retreat, 'a very violent and unjust clamour would have been raised against him' by the impatient temper of his troops, whose 'burning thirst for battle' Beresford thereupon assuaged by giving way. Napier, who believed that Albuera was an unnecessary battle, bluntly argued that neither Lord Wellington nor Sir John Moore would have fought it, since they would have had the moral courage to reject this appeal – moral courage which he implied was lacking in those with 'second-rate minds'. But one has to say that Napier surely flatters the average British soldier, in suggesting that he should be so clamorous to die.

Beresford made his decision; and the ever-loyal Colonel D'Urban wrote later, as any sup-portive staff officer would, 'Having then maturely weighed all these considerations, he deter-mined to give battle. His confidence in his troops was unbounded, and the results proved he was right.'

Consequently, Blake agreed to get to Albuera by noon on 15 May, having united with Ballasteros the previous day, while Castanos's three battalions would join with the other Allied formations remaining around Badajoz. Accordingly, on the 14th, Blake set off from Barcarrota towards Almendral, still with no sign of the French on the westerly approach to Valverde. Beresford sent to Brigadier Madden, commanding two Portuguese regiments of horse, to redouble his efforts in covering the wide sweep of country – 300 miles or more – lying on the eastern approaches to Badajoz between Talavera Real and Almendralego, in order to cover the other option; and himself moved to block the central approach, as indicated three weeks earlier by Lord Wellington – at Albuera. He called forward Alten's independent brigade of the two Light Battalions KGL from Badajoz, and a temporary brigade of three Portuguese battalions under Colonel Collins. This left Myer's brigade still south of Badajoz, and Kemmis' brigade on the north bank – both from Cole's 4th Division. However, Kemmis' plan to cross the Guadiana at a ford below the fortress was negated by a flash flood on the night of 15/16 May; and since the flying bridge at the mouth of the Caya had been taken up once Squire's stores had moved to Elvas, Lowry Cole was to fight without Kemmis – hard though the latter marched the 30 miles via the bridge at Jerumenha. (We may reasonably imagine that the rank and file of his 2/27th, 1/40th and 97th may not have been too disappointed at their lateness when they did finally arrive on the corpse-strewn field of Albuera.)

On 13 May, as Beresford pondered plans with the Spanish at Valverde, his cavalry under Brigadier Robert Long was moving back under French pressure from Los Santos to Fuente del Maestre, then further north to Azeuchal, and then west to Santa Martha, where 'My whole force being now collected... my chief danger lay on the side of Solana, where Brigadier Madden was stationed.' Solana was 10 miles north-east of Santa Martha, and only 15 from Albuera –

the same distance as Long's direct route back to rejoin. It would seem, therefore, that he feared the enemy coming (via Solana) between him and home: over the next two days Long repeatedly sent messengers to find Madden 'to ascertain whether or not Solana was really occupied by the enemy' – even as the enemy advanced first to Almendralego (on 14 May) and then turned westwards to Azeuchal.

Long was clearly unhappy in his command. During the previous few days 'never in my life did I experience a greater anxiety of mind... the enemy advance and movements I was hourly reporting to headquarters... not a single instruction had I received, nor could I obtain, tho' repeatedly applied for; my route or point of retreat were not even pointed out. I was only desired not to commit the troops under my command against a superior force, but, at the same time, not to lose ground without necessity' (letter of 30 May).

On 14 May he had extracted from Madden a promise to send immediate warning if the French approached on his front, especially if he were forced to retreat; but further messengers had failed to find Madden. The fact that they were sent at all speaks for Long's growing concerns; he seems now to have been not simply over-anxious, but out of his depth. The fact that he 'repeatedly applied for' instructions was plain evidence that he was not suited to this level of independent command. According to D'Urban, his constant requests were 'full of difficulties, complaints, alarms and despondency'. Long's lack of confidence in his own ability to operate within Beresford's general orders must have been endlessly frustrating to the headquarters staff – and to himself. It reached the point where, on 15 May, D'Urban responded that '[The Marshal] does not see how he can well add anything to the instructions already given to you. Something must always be left to the discretion of any officer commanding an advanced corps, and to a general officer this sort of power is commonly accorded in as full a degree as possible.' This was as courteous an expression of total exasperation at Long's timidity, and as strong a hint that he should get a grip and get on with the job, as could reasonably be written.

Towards noon on the 15th, French cavalry approached Santa Martha. Long's cavalry were a mile in rear, under command of Colonel Grey, while Long and his staff were up in the village church on the high ground. 'From this height', his DAQMG, Captain Heathcote, would later write, 'when the enemy's advance guard was seen driving in the Spanish outposts, General Long sent off orders to Colonel de Grey to commence his retreat towards Albuera... General Long and the officers of his staff remained for a considerable time longer, til they had distinctly seen that a strong force of cavalry as well as infantry was advancing in several columns, and til the enemy's skirmishers were on the point of entering and passing the village below.' Long then pulled out and caught up with his regiments, by now some miles down the road to Albuera, which they reached around 2pm.

Long's ADC George Pitt, writing some twenty years later, was adamant that he 'heard Lt-Colonel Rooke, AAG, order General Long to cross to the left bank of the Albuera and take up posts (along the left bank of the river).' Colonel Leighton, commanding the 4th Dragoons, wrote in confirmation after a similar lapse in time: 'We were ordered to cross the bridge at Albuera by a staff officer.'

On the way back to the bridge Long had received an order from D'Urban at Valverde, timed at 7.30am that morning, stating 'Brig.General Long will march immediately to Albuera, where he will receive further orders... he need not leave any part of his force at Santa Martha' – because the Spanish would be given separate orders to have a squadron there.

So Long crossed the river; and in due course the French took possession of the far bank, which was undefended. This was an unfortunate start to the action: since the rising ground they now occupied was tree-clad, it was to mask subsequent French movements from British telescopes. The bitter arguments that were to rage for years between Beresford and his loyal staff on the one hand, and Long and his regimental supporters on the other, were certainly born of frictions at Campo Mayor and Los Santos, and matured during Long's querulous handling of the outpost work back to Santa Martha; but they reached critical mass on the matter of his precipitous retreat from that place, and his 'allowing' the far bank of the Albuera to be lost. This loss placed Beresford at an obvious tactical disadvantage; but equally obvious is the question of how cavalry could anyway have been expected to hold wooded terrain without infantry. What had been Beresford's plans in this regard? One suspects that the simple truth was that Soult's men arrived sooner than Beresford had expected, that he was caught out, and that Long's questionable reverse speed made him a convenient scapegoat (an animal for which the incompetent, in all walks of life, tend to keep a keener eye out than the competent).

Dozens of statements were subsequently made about the timing and speed of Long's retreat, both for and against. Apart from that already quoted above from Captain Heathcote, with which others tally, a French officer also helps us. Captain Lapene was on the staff of 5th Corps:

> On the night of the 15th May Marshal Soult was six leagues from Badajoz at Santa Martha. The French army had all arrived there. The half of General Werle's brigade only had remained two leagues in the rear at Villaba. Soult, uncertain for a part of the day if Beresford had taken up a position, was rather inclined to believe that the enemy would avoid a decisive battle and repass the Guadiana. His views, with regard to the real intentions of the allies, were soon decided by Gen. Briche, commanding the Light Cavalry of our advanced guard. He had encountered the enemy posted at two leagues from Santa Martha on the road to Badajoz, and had made them fall back before him.

These would be Otway's Portuguese, ordered by Long to take up a position at a bridge 'about half way between Santa Martha and Albuera and six English miles from either place.' Captain Lapene's statement is revealing. Not only does it show that Soult was apparently unaware of Beresford's concentration at Albuera, until he effectively reached that place; it also surely confirms that no noticeable blocking action was taken by Long at Santa Martha, nor for several miles closer to Albuera – that is, that Long does indeed look guilty of a premature retreat; and given his anxious state of mind, it is unsurprising that the pace of that retreat should have seemed unacceptably swift to those who (with hindsight) would much have preferred a slow fighting withdrawal.

It is easy to accept statements such as that from Colonel Otway, of the Portuguese cavalry: 'the march from Santa Martha to Albuera was hurried and harassing, the rear of the column being obliged to gallop most of the route'; and that of Colonel Hardinge, that 'When the allied cavalry came into our position at Albuera from Santa Martha on the evening [sic] of the 15th May, the horses from hard riding were greatly distressed.' Yet while Long's own description – 'I fell back at a walk to Albuera' – does seem self-servingly unlikely, there is also testimony from no fewer than seventeen of his loyal cavalry officers that the retreat was neither confused, hurried nor disorderly.

Where one's sympathies definitely shift towards Long is over D'Urban's accusation that he 'abandoned precipitously the right bank of the Albuera... having given up without the slightest dispute, the whole of the opposite ground to the enemy's pickets of cavalry, which immediately occupied it to the banks of the stream.' The combination of D'Urban's own order to retreat, and Rooke's direction at the bridge, make this charge quite unjust. Frankly, no competent general or his operations staff would fail to provide a firm base through which a retreating rearguard could safely pass. That firm base would take over from the rearguard, and constitute a first tripwire behind which the commander would have his proper defensive measures in place. This presupposes, of course, that the commander knows his rearguard is coming in. To be fair to Beresford, therefore, he may have intended to place infantry east of the river, but Long's early arrival pre-empted that deployment. There is a clear hint that infantry were indeed intended to have been beyond the river, in an intriguing passage in the anonymous pamphlet *Further Strictures*, almost certainly written by D'Urban in some collaboration with Beresford himself:

> The only error which appears in Lord Beresford's plans was his omitting to place some infantry in occupation of the wood on the great height beyond the Faria stream, through which the road to Santa Martha passed. *This, I understand, had been intended...* [Long's] fault ought to have been repaired. It was not; and whoever was to blame for it, this was certainly an omission. [Presumably Colonel Rooke's action, if known, was not going to be admitted.]

Be all this as it may, Long was still held to be at fault, and was superceded next morning – a scapegoat, if a worthy one; but even this was not as simple as it seemed. In fact, Long had himself signed his own demotion warrant two days earlier when, on 13 May, he had written to Beresford about the command arrangements. He was not alone in his genuine concern that the Spanish brigadier Penne-Villemur would have to command the now-united Allied cavalry, since he was senior to Long. The mere thought was horrifying to all the British officers (if disguised in discussion by the more anodine phrase 'the inconveniences arising from the collision of ranks'); and promptly the next day, Long was informed by D'Urban that 'to obviate the evil of undefined ranks and claims of command adverted to in your letter of last night, he [the Marshal] has directed Major-General Lumley to assume the command of the cavalry of this army.'

This matter of seniority provided an excellent excuse to bring in the reliable ex-Light Dragoon general, and to take out of the hot seat Robert Long – an officer perhaps hard-done-by, but clearly held to be inadequate and a continual irritant at headquarters. Yet Beresford was reluctant to act, even so: D'Urban and Hardinge both had to pressure him to make the change, even on the day of the battle when (according to D'Urban, writing in 1833) General Lumley reported to headquarters for that purpose: 'On the battle-day of Albuera... when he did [arrive]... I recollect your reluctance, even then, to displace General Long.... [so that I had to urge you] "'If you do not, Sir, the cavalry will be worse than useless, and perhaps thrown away."' It is curious that after Campo Mayor, Los Santos, and Long's constant flow of 'difficulties, complaints, alarms and despondencies' when managing the outposts since, Beresford allowed Long to command during Soult's vital final approach. That French cavalry now held the wooded slopes above Albuera was partly Beresford's fault, partly Long's; but Long should anyway have been sacked weeks earlier, and it is a puzzle why he was not.

*   *   *

Turning to the field of the battle of Albuera, one is immediately struck by its similarity with that at Fuentes d'Oñoro. There is the same broad confluence of a north–south ridge, a village on the eastern edge with a fordable stream beneath, and broken tree-covered ground to the south and south-east inviting a covered French approach. There were also two marshals who instantly adopted that approach, and two defending parties who, curiously having posted their weakest divisions on this their most vulnerable flank, were then forced to throw back their threatened right wings. Thereafter, as we shall see, the similarities ceased, with near-fatal effect for Beresford, but the general parallels were remarkable.

Fortescue's excellent pair of maps by Emery Walker draw our attention to the high ground – not that 'high' is really appropriate, since we are not dealing here with hills of substance; there are no ravines, cliffs, steep slopes or unfordable rivers anywhere relevant to pose problems for foot or horse. Indeed, the rolling, treeless terrain on the British side of the river positively cries out for cavalry action.

Soult's approach on the Santa Martha road runs downhill through the wooded slopes to the east of the Nogales stream (sometimes referred to as the Ferdia or Faria), and near its bank meets the more southerly road going to Nogales. Soult's route into Albuera then crosses a five-arched stone bridge some 300 yards above the village outskirts. At the bridge a second stream, the Chicapierna, joins the Nogales, and the joint waterway is now the River Albuera. Between the two streams before they join the land rises 130 feet or more in a series of gradual slopes, fairly steep on the east, with the road to Torre de Miguel up along most of the crest. The slopes near the village grow olives, wheat and barley, and higher up are covered with trees. The land behind this feature, in the upper part of the valley of the Nogales, is out of sight from the British features above the village. This area was well described by Colonel D'Urban, in his Report: 'The ground was covered with wood, which afforded great facility for masking... assembly for attack, particularly on [Soult's] extreme left, where it was thick, and extended down to the banks of the Feria, and where an abrupt shoulder of the tongue between the fork and that rivulet of the Albuera formed a hollow V, capable of holding a large body of troops and concealing them from any point of the opposite heights.'

To the west of the Chicapierna and the Albuera, the slopes rise to a north–south ridge, on the broad top of which five slight knolls, rising some 150 feet above the river, are all-important features; but they are only 30 or 40 feet higher than the level of the rest of the ridge, and this whole area, where the fighting mainly took place, is essentially rolling arable land, where in May 1811 the corn was high. One knoll is crossed by the Badajoz road, and the other ('Conical Hill') by that to Valverde; two more sit across the ridge a mile south and half a mile apart. Beyond by another half mile there is a kidney-shaped hill running north–south for half a mile, west of the road leading south to Almendral. Along the eastern side of the ridge, about five shallow spurs stick out, spaced about half a mile apart, and run down to the river.

To the west of the ridge the open country falls away to a faint depression, beyond which the land rises away again still further into heather-covered uplands. The bottom of the depression, in the wettest of seasons, might run freely a few feet wide, but both Oman and Fortescue agree that even then it would pose no sort of obstacle (contrary to the views of Napier and, surprisingly, of Beresford himself).

The abandoned village of Albuera was quite sizeable, with a tall-towered church and (thanks to earlier French occupations) many looted houses, lacking all roof and floor timbers and largely ruined. The village sits on a spur above and distant 200 yards from the river, where a second, much smaller stone bridge carried the road from Almendralejo to Valverde. Sherer of the 34th said the river was knee-deep, though there are references elsewhere to 'rivers... running rapidly from the late heavy rains'. The banks to the left of the small bridge 'are abrupt and uneven, and both artillery and cavalry would find it difficult to pass; to the right of the main bridge however it is accessible to any description of force.'

On the early afternoon of 15 May, Beresford's occupation of these features began to take shape. Given that Soult was marching to relieve Badajoz, it was the roads leading from Albuera towards that place – generally to the north and west – that Beresford quite logically decided to deny to Soult by sitting across them, up on the slopes half a mile above the village. The three brigades of William Stewart's 2nd Division were his prime troops, and these 5,000 men could be trusted to cover the three main routes; on their left, the road to Talavera Real would be given to Hamilton's and Collins' Portuguese, while on the British right the secondary road to Valverde would be for Blake's Spaniards. Alten's two KGL light battalions would be in the village itself. Naturally, the cavalry were to guard the flanks, especially on the right beyond the Spanish, where the land was entirely open. Cole's 4th Division was still outside Badajoz, seeing off the last of the stores, and on arrival they would be in second line to Stewart.

Marshal Beresford was utterly convinced Soult would attack the village. *Further Strictures* unequivocally states that 'General Blake was stationed on the right... simply because he came from that flank... the Marshal did not regret this... as he considered it the strongest and least likely to be attacked.'

Stewart, Hamilton and Alten marched in around 2pm, and the Spanish were expected at any time – Blake had promised at the conference two days previously to be on the ground by noon, and his troops were only 6 miles south down the road, at Almendral. But time passed, and they did not appear. Instead, between 2pm and 3pm, in rattled Long's cavalry, closely followed by the French hussars of Briche's brigade – who, having had a good look at the village from the far side of the main bridge, took themselves off through the olive groves and up the slopes beyond the Chicapierna. As instructed by Colonel Rooke, Long crossed to an apparently deserted position – the Spanish still being absent, and Stewart's battalions being over on the reverse slopes. Beresford said many years later (1834):

> Previous to the arrival of my troops, I had been over and made my observations of the ground of Albuera, and left officers to place them as they arrived. I then went a considerable distance to the left down the stream... I was not even informed [then] that [Long] had left Santa Martha. I found on my return that he had been some time at Albuera. The infantry of Sir William Stewart and Baron Alten arrived in my absence.

Brigadier Long rode to report to Beresford near the ruins of the village. They were overheard by Ralph Heathcote, Long's DAQMG, and it was clear that the marshal did not believe Long when he said he had been forced to fall back. 'Part of the conversation that passed [was] relative to the enemy's force, which Lord Beresford was unwilling to believe so considerable as stated.' Now Beresford could not post infantry across the river, thanks to Long's precipitous retreat – the French had arrived too soon. And still no Spanish... Beresford was not happy. He sent Long up on the slopes, to substitute pro tem his thousand horse for Blake's 10,000 bayonets; and sent an officer to Blake to speed his arrival and act as guide.

Marshal Soult's army was now resting and cooking at Santa Martha, apart from one brigade and Briche's cavalry, and he came forward to the latter and made his reconnaissance. He could see the green jackets of the KGL Light Battalions in the village, with Otway's Portuguese horse half a mile further north; he could see Long's dragoons south of the Conical Hill; what he could not see were any British or Spanish infantry – but then, during the day Blake had been reported by spies to be still way off to the south-west, and not predicted to join before the 17th. Soult is said to have known (quite how, is not revealed) that the 4th Division was still outside Badajoz. So the infantry of Stewart and Hamilton would be somewhere behind the hill, and between the two lots of cavalry. That would put his enemy at some 16,000 bayonets and 2,000 sabres in all – while Soult had 19,000 and 4,000 respectively. With these odds, he determined to march the 11 miles from Santa Martha at first light, and attack straightaway thereafter, before Beresford could redress the balance, and particularly before the Spanish could join him.

Soult settled on his plan of attack partly with them in mind, partly because of the other obvious attractions literally staring him in the face: he would get between Beresford and the Spanish axis of advance up the Almendral road, which lay only a mile away across the Nogales stream. The wooded hill feature in front of Briche's troopers took him straight to it. He would attack the village seriously enough to draw in Beresford's reserves, and throw his main columns, and especially his horse, on to the plain, to roll up Beresford from south to north. His cavalry would have a field day. It was in every respect a practical proposition and, like Massena viewing Fuentes a fortnight earlier, Soult was undoubtedly looking forward to the next morning's work. He had sufficient advantage in men and horses, he had an excellent plan, and his enemy had shown neither resolve in their withdrawal nor foresight in their preparations. There was also the small matter that Lord Wellington himself was many miles away; Soult therefore faced the 'second eleven', and anyway with only 7,000 or so British infantry.

*   *   *

It is not clear what anxieties William Beresford felt, if any, with respect to the flank, which, unbeknown to him, Soult now proposed to plunder. There was much subsequent discussion as to what represented the 'key' to his position on the slopes; at this early stage, suffice it to say that Beresford regarded the Conical Hill as key, for the three main routes to Badajoz passed adjacent to it and its fellow knoll a half mile to the north. He thus chose to place upon it his 5,000 British infantry. He was well aware that, in a perfect world, he should extend south to the two dominating west–east knolls 600 yards or so beyond the Spanish extremity; but then, they in turn were commanded by the kidney-shaped knoll a half mile further south. The perfect world would in that case grow from a length of line a mile and a half long, to 2 miles, and then to 2½ miles, and neither extension was thought practical with the troops available. This apparent limitation, combined with his firm assumption that Soult would anyway look to penetrate the village for access to the roads behind, made the matter academic; additionally, should the affair not prosper, Beresford's line of retreat – those very same roads – would depend utterly on his rearguard holding open the Conical Hill feature; and no prudent general could forgot the need for an open back door, just in case.

On the evening of the 15th, as if he could feel Soult's telescope upon him, Beresford seemed to change up a gear. He sent again to Blake; he sent to bring Brigadier Madden's four squadrons of Portuguese cavalry the 10 miles from Talavera Real; he sent to Lowry Cole to march the 4th Division the 16 miles from Badajoz – but, for some reason, he then forbade him to march before 2am on the 16th. The man who carried Beresford's order to Cole was Lieutenant James Crammer, 28th, who wrote: 'Employed on the night of the 15th May... to carry Despatches from Albuera to... Cole... by the prompt execution of which mission a considerable part of [his] force were enabled to reach Albuera in time to take part in the action of that day.' This implies a first order, not a subsequent hastener. Why did Beresford leave Cole so long at Badajoz? It was the omission of a man who thought he had a day in hand (which he had not). It is the more puzzling in that he did not know whether Kemmis' brigade would come with Cole from the Guadiana's far bank, nor what the French were up to beyond the Nogales.

That night the Spanish at long last started to straggle in; but they went to the wrong place in the dark. It is hard to see how, since even in daylight staff officers were on hand to guide in the various battalions, and after nightfall such arrangements were obviously doubly required. We do not know if the arrangements – or lack of them – were solely for Blake's staff to make, but that would be normal for a division on the move. Then again, we do not know why the division was eleven hours late covering the 6 miles from Alemendral. It was an unfortunate error, since nothing could be done until the morning, and in the morning all the world would be watching. Beresford later described what had happened: 'Instead of forming on the right of, and in alignment with the British 2nd Division, which was placed under and to the rear of the hill, they passed in the dark to the front of it, and formed in line with the supports of the advanced posts near the village and bridge;... retiring in the morning to take up the position that had been marked out for them.' It is likely that the arrival in the night hours of 12,000 men within a few hundred yards of the village would anyway have been reported to Soult; but come daybreak it would give him much pleasure to see confirmation – in the shape of the Spanish moving back on their markers – that the right of Beresford's line, Soult's objective, comprised Spanish troops. No doubt he was confident that they would soon give way before his assault, as they had done three months before at Gebora.

In the event, and by dint only of many blisters, the last of Beresford's troops arrived just in time. Cole's 4th Division had marched hard from Badajoz in the early hours of the morning. If, as ordered, they left at 2am, then they could not have covered the 16 miles to Albuera before about 7am, and more likely nearer 8am. That is the time recorded by D'Urban; Cole himself said it was 'as the action commenced', and most accounts put that time as the start of the battle. However, Sergeant Cooper (who had fought with the 2/7th on the Pajar at Talavera) says his battalion left the castle walls at midnight 'weary and jaded as they were after 36 hours on picket duty... [and] after marching till daylight appeared, we halted and put off our greatcoats. Everyone was complaining of want of rest and sleep.' As we shall see, they did not arrive until after the battle was well under way, and ran the last stages to the sound of the guns – Soult had come that close to catching Beresford unconcentrated.

With Cole's single brigade – Myers's Fusilier Brigade – came the 1,700 bayonets in three battalions (described by Cole's ADC Captain Roverea as 'without coats and badly armed') of Castanos's army, under D'España. They were sent to deploy with Blake, while Myers' running fusiliers fell in behind the 2nd Division.

As was customary, the British stood to their arms an hour before daybreak, and as the light came up Captain Moyle Sherer of the 34th tells us 'It was a brilliant sight, at sun-rise, to see the whole of the French cavalry moving on the plain; but in a short time they retired into the wood.' As soon as there was light enough, Beresford rode out to see what he could see:

> The Marshal reconnoitred the enemy on his right early in the morning; and he could see them forming considerable masses and with guns in the wood. But from that position it was just as convenient for them to proceed to the bridge, and the front of his position, as to attempt his right, and it was not possible for Lord Beresford to form any certain conclusion with regard to the enemy's intentions. I believe, however, that the Marshal did not as yet think, that his right would be attacked. He thought better of his adversary's judgement, or rather, perhaps, he knew the ground better. He knew that of the two it was the most difficult and hazardous point for the enemy.

Things now started to go wrong, however. In Beresford's absence (and we must hope without his foreknowledge or permission), the cavalry were ordered to go foraging, and the infantry battalions to fall out to cook. Moyle Sherer again: 'The battalion being dismissed, I breakfasted and immediately afterwards set out to walk towards the Spanish troops, little dreaming, that day, of a general action'. The 29th's breakfast was also cut short, as Lieutenant Charles Leslie recalled:

> Our brigade, after standing some hours under arms, was ordered about 6 or 7 o'clock to resume its place in the line. We had scarcely time to get a little tea and a morsel of biscuit, when the alarm was given – 'Stand to your arms! The French are advancing!' We accordingly instantly got under arms, leaving tents and baggage to be disposed as the Quartermaster and batmen best could. We moved forward in line to crown the heights in front, which were intended for our position... the army was formed... the Portuguese in blue, the English in red, the Spaniards in yellow or other bright colours... drawn up as for a grand parade, in full view of the enemy.

Breakfast for men and beasts before battle is certainly desirable; but in the case of the cavalry, to send them away at this stage – rather than having cut sheaves carried up to the lines – was extraordinarily chancy. Was there a prevailing lack of urgency – was the mood overly relaxed? Why did Sherer, a company commander, have the wrong end of the stick – were all the company commanders equally relaxed? Did Beresford himself really not expect an attack, as Fortescue says?

It could just be so – for a short while anyway, before the French crossed the Nogales on their wide left hook. The following is by Lieutenant Edward Wildman of the 4th Dragoons:

> We had as usual been under arms from a very early period of the morning, and about 8 o'clock, as well as I can recollect, the regiment I belonged to received orders to forage. The regiment was on the road to the rear for that purpose when it was recalled. The enemy must have been advancing at this time, as I hardly think it could have been more than twenty minutes, but at most did not exceed half an hour, from the period of the arrival of the regiment on the first ground it was halted on after the recall, until the commencement of the action.

D'Urban in *Further Strictures* says that

> In returning from his reconnaisance, [the Marshal] directed Major-General Long to apprize him of the least movement that took place among the French; and so certain was he of their meditating an attack, that I distinctly remember his not even sitting down to breakfast, but keeping his horses at the door, saying 'the enemy are forming on our right; but I do not think they will attack there.'

Captain Gregory, one of Long's ADCs, galloped to Beresford's headquarters:

> About 8 o'clock in the morning of the 16th, one of the 13th Light Dragoons came in from a picket on the right, with the intelligence that the enemy were crossing the Albuera. General Long immediately galloped off to the spot, when he found that *a very heavy column of infantry had already passed over. I was sent to report it Marshal Beresford*, whose headquarters were in the village of Albuera. I first made my report to one of his staff. Afterwards the Marshal himself came out to speak with me... After he had heard General Long's message, and asked me some questions as to the enemy's force that had crossed, he was turning back to enter the house, when I begged his pardon for stopping him, and told him, that the cavalry had been ordered to the rear, and that one regiment (the 4th Dragoons) had already gone off, and requested to know if he had any orders for them. He did not express any displeasure or surprise, and desired me to bring up all that might have gone to the rear, and take them more to the right than where the cavalry were before posted... I went direct to the 4th Dragoons, which regiment I found in a hollow spot some distance in rear of the position. The men were going out to forage... and those who were out were recalled by the bugle. As soon as the regiment had been collected and mounted, Colonel Leighton took them in the direction the Marshal had pointed out, and the battle had already commenced.

While Gregory was hastily getting all the cavalry back into their battle positions, the Marshal 'immediately mounted and galloped up to him [Long]. On arriving, he saw on the plain, between the wood and the bridge, two columns of infantry and a considerable corps of cavalry not less certainly than 12,000 men'.

The figure of 12,000 men quite accurately accounts for Godinot's infantry and cavalry, and Werle's large brigade. When *Further Strictures* goes on to state that 'what he supposed the principal part of the enemy's army [was seen] advancing along the plain from the wood towards the bridge', then obviously the rest of Soult's army 'were already posted in another place' – that is, as the 13th's picket had reported via Gregory, they had 'passed over the river'.

*   *   *

As to Beresford's deployment, the Allied line was laid out as follows. On the left front, half way down the slope to the river, were the eight squadrons of Portuguese horse under Colonel Loftus Otway, totalling some 850 sabres. Next to them, but back on the plain and covering the road north to Talavera Real, was Major-General Hamilton's Portuguese division in one line of 7,700 all ranks, in eight battalions; and a second line comprising the 1,385 Portuguese of Colonel Collins' Independent Brigade in three battalions.

In the centre, Beresford's 2nd Division, under the 37-year-old ex-95th Rifles officer Sir William Stewart, was deployed across the three roads running north to Badajoz and west to Valverde, with his right-hand brigade (Colborne's) on the Conical Hill. In the centre of Stewart's line was Hoghton's, and on the left Abercrombie's (which had been William Lumley's). These three brigades comprised ten battalions. Sir John Colborne had the 1/3rd (Buffs), 2/31st (Huntingdonshire), 2/48th (Northamptons) and 2/66th (Berkshires). Major-General Daniel Hoghton commanded the 29th (Worcesters), 1/48th (Northamptons) and 1/57th (Middlesex); while Abercrombie led the 2/28th (Gloucesters), the 2/34th (Cumberland) and 2/39th (Dorsets). The average bayonet strength of these battalions was 503, so most companies were but fifty strong – well below their proper strength.

The Fusilier Brigade, under 27-year-old Lieutenant-Colonel Sir William Myers, and Colonel William Harvey's Portuguese brigade, were behind Stewart, commanded by Major-General the Hon Lowry Cole. The Fusiliers comprised the 1st and 2nd Battalions, 7th (Royal Fusiliers) and the 1/23rd (Royal Welch Fusiliers), with 1,900 bayonets in all.

Long's cavalry brigade (soon to be Lumley's) consisted of the 700 sabres of the 3rd Dragoon Guards and 4th Dragoons, both under Colonel Grey, and the 600 sabres of Penne-Villemur's Spanish horse, on the plain in reserve in rear of Colborne's brigade. The 13th Light Dragoons were detached down on the river line.

The Spanish were in two lines; the first comprised the divisions of Lardizabal and Ballasteros, the second that of Zayas. Two battalions under Ballasteros (the right-hand division) were sent across the shallow dip to the knoll forward on the right, overlooking the Chicapierna. The 1,100 sabres of Loy's Spanish cavalry were further right still.

Beresford's headquarters, as we have seen, were in the village of Albuera – one would have thought, given his reading of Soult's intentions, the very last location to choose. Apart from his own security, he was entirely blind to all that unfolded on his right; no doubt he took to his horse very quickly. His thirty-eight guns were disposed as follows: a Portuguese battery of six commanded the bridge and its approach road; another six Portuguese guns supported Hamilton directly; the Spanish battery of six was with Blake; one German battery of six was on the Conical Hill, and another with Stewart; Lefebure's troop of horse artillery were with the Dragoons in rear, and another troop were marching in with Cole.

On the other side of the river, Soult had brought up the six battalions of Godinot's brigade - some 3,800 bayonets of the 16e Léger and 51e Ligne – together with Briche's cavalry brigade of 750 sabres, with two gun batteries, and they looked to be facing Baron Alten's thousand KGL light infantry in the village. On Godinot's left and facing the Spanish line, Soult allowed full view of two brigades of cavalry and Werle's large brigade of 6,000 men – thus confirming, with one sweep of Beresford's telescope, his preconceived view of Soult's plan of attack.

What he could not see, behind the tree-clad heights to his right between the Nogales and Chicapierna streams, was the area already described by D'Urban as 'a hollow V', in which Soult had earlier formed the 8,400-strong 5th Corps and eight regiments of cavalry, now well on their way to giving William Beresford a lethal surprise.

8
Albuera, 16 May: the Early Phases – Zayas, Stewart and Colborne

AT around 8am, with black clouds rolling up, General Godinot's two columns – 3,924 all ranks, of the 16e Léger and 51e Ligne, with drums beating and standards held high – approached the main Albuera bridge, with Briche's 10e Hussards and 21e Chasseurs on their right flank. Godinot's two batteries unlimbered on the slopes 600 yards above the bridge, and commenced firing overhead. The Portuguese guns of Captain Arriaga's battery responded, with fire on to the approach road; KGL skirmishers in the olive groves beyond the river began popping away, and their French opposite numbers closed up.

A small squadron of about 100 of the Polish 1st Vistula Lancers, under command of Captain Leszezynski, crossed the river above the bridge, and half of them – two platoons each of twenty-five troopers – climbed the slope towards Colborne's line; apparently, Alten's KGL nearby did not open fire. The as-yet unsuperceded Brigadier Robert Long wrote a fortnight after the battle, 'I directed the 3rd Dragoon Guards to charge and beat them back, which was done'. This was apparently unknown for many years to Beresford, who when shown Long's letter wrote: 'I am indebted for my first intelligence of an exploit achieved by the 3rd Dragoon Guards... it is asserted that they beat back a corps of French Lancers near the bridge. It was reported to me (at the time) that a small corps of French light cavalry had thrown themselves across there (near the bridge) and, after receiving some shots from our infantry, had galloped along the left bank of the Albuera... and joined their own cavalry.'

One wonders where Beresford was positioned, that he could not see this overture. There is no doubt that a cavalry clash happened, with various eyewitnesses; there is also an entirely different version of the outcome in George Nafziger's *Poles and Saxons of the Napoleonic Wars*: 'The (fifty) Polish lancers dispersed the leading British squadron (120 men) and pushed it back into the following squadrons. Attacked by the two other squadrons, the Poles withdrew towards their support, turned around and counter-attacked, breaking the dragoons for a second time. The fight developed into a melee. With the support of French batteries from the far bank, the two Polish platoons then pushed the British away from the stream.' The lancers had sixteen killed and wounded, but only two were caused by the 3rd Dragoons: the other twelve were said to be occasioned by musketry – presumably, by then, that of the KGL. The two platoon leaders, Sous-lieutenants Rogajski and Wojciechowski, were to be admitted to the Légion d'Honneur for their exploit. The 3rd Dragoons suffered an officer and nine troopers killed, nine wounded and one taken; several of the troop horses were wounded by lances.

Baron Alten's two light battalions in the village were outnumbered four-to-one by Godinot, and with Werle hovering in the background it could become ten-to-one. Beresford therefore did what Soult wanted: he sent in reinforcements. Two battalions from Lardizabal went down to give flank support; Colborne's brigade went down; Cleeve's KGL battery went down; and there is reference to Campbell's Portuguese brigade being dispatched, although this move may have come later, when Stewart moved off to the right. So at least six battalions and six guns were moved – perhaps 3,000 men; and it is hard to see what else Beresford could have done. Lieutenant Charles Leslie (29th): 'Soult must have been delighted on observing this movement: it, no doubt, was precisely what he had wished; because the columns which appeared to threaten the village and our line was only a ruse to distract our attention and neutralize the English force which he most dreaded.' Lieutenant Edward Close (2/48th), in Colborne's brigade, wrote:

> After a few cannon shots from the enemy, he began to move troops forward as if to attack the centre by the bridge. The morning was heavy and misty, and prevented us from observing the enemy's movements distinctly, in consequence of which the real point of attack was not perceived. Our brigade, however, were sent down to the protection of the bridge, which had been in our immediate front all along. The rain now fell in torrents. We remained here some time, the enemy having approached pretty near the bridge halted, whilst they pursued their attack to our right, where lay the key to our position.

As Close implied and as Oman aptly put it, the frontal threat to the village now seemed to hang fire; it was not pressed by Godinot, and nor need it be. Just by remaining there in threatening array, with his 15 per cent share of Marshal Soult's army, making the occasional movement, he held the attention not only the 10 per cent of Beresford's army actually in and around the village, but also another 50 per cent of it posted on the slopes behind. This economical arrangement allowed Beresford's other 40 per cent, the Spanish, to be tested rather more energetically by superior forces – every general's Holy Grail.

While the guns hammered away around Albuera village, two separate bodies of infantry were approaching in the rain. Myers led his Fusilier Brigade to the sound of the guns, having force-marched all 16 miles from Badajoz. He halted on the Valverde road, just to the west of Stewart's divisional line. That the Fusilier Brigade arrived at this point, albeit exhausted, is confirmed by Lord Wellington's Adjutant-General Charles Stewart in his *Narrative*: 'General Cole's division... reached the ground after the battle began.' Sergeant Cooper, 2/7th, wrote:

> Having marched a few miles further up a valley we heard distant sounds, and tho' they grew more frequent, yet we did not think that they were the noises of a battle field, as we were quite ignorant of any enemy being near. But so they proved, for in a few minutes the words 'Light infantry to front', 'trail arms', 'double quick' were given, we knew then what was astir. Being tired, we made a poor run up a steep hill in front.

The other infantry on the move were Girard's and Gazan's 8,400 Frenchmen, supported by 3,200 cavalry. They were on their way to walk over and ride down the 12,600 Spanish under Blake and Castanos on the southern extremity of Beresford's line; and before they even made that contact they would be followed by the 5,600 men of Werle's brigade – actually, a division in size.

ALBUERA
a.m. 16 May 1811

One Mile

The first intimation of Soult's left hook had come when the 13th Light Dragoons reported to Long at around 8am that 'a very heavy column of infantry had passed over the river' – that is, the crossing probably took place around 7.30am. These were Girard's 1st Division of nine battalions and Gazan's 2nd Division of ten; and although their unopposed crossing was reported, they then disappeared from the 13th's view, up into the wooded spurs beyond the Nogales, over the ridge, and down to the Chicapierna. A good deal later, after their march had developed, it is said that an ADC to General Zayas caught the dull gleam of their bayonets in the trees and, being sent to the knoll beyond the Spanish right to confirm the movement, he then carried the news to Beresford. The marshal rode forward to see for himself; and it was around this time that Briche's light cavalry, who had initially moved to the village with Godinot, turned south down the line of the river, and Werle about-turned his infantry in the same direction. The distant bayonets, and the sight of the cavalry and Werle's columns in effect turning their backs on the Allied line, confirmed that Soult was either retreating – which hardly seemed likely – or was making a very wide sweep to the south, to get up on to the plain before fighting.

*   *   *

Oman and Fortescue both imply that until Beresford was brought the report by Zayas' ADC he had no notion of Soult's design. Oman refers to 'this unexpected flank attack', while Fortescue states that 'the enemy's true intentions were now evident'. Napier, however, avers that once Godinot attacked the village Beresford, 'observing that Werle's division did not follow closely, was soon convinced that the principal effort would be on the right'. Which, considering the low opinion Napier held of Beresford, generously credits him with an enviable power of second sight. In fact, what Beresford actually displayed was at best lethargy, and at worst blindness, for there is no question but that he knew of Girard's and Gazan's march long before Zayas' ADC saw them.

The 13th Light Dragoons picket had reported to Long at 8am that a 'heavy column of infantry had already passed over', and Long's ADC Gregory was sent with the intelligence firstly to the staff, and then to Beresford himself. Before the battle commenced Beresford, in his headquarters in Albuera village, had been told this news not long after his cavalry had been sent off to forage. We have seen that he even asked Gregory 'some questions as to the enemy's force that had crossed'. This force was clearly not Godinot's, which was not yet in action. As Beresford himself wrote plainly in his Despatch:

> At 8 o'clock... [Soult's] cavalry were seen passing the Albuera considerably above our right and shortly after... [another] strong force of cavalry and two heavy columns of infantry... posted to our front... as if to attack the village and bridge... during this time he was filing the principal body of his infantry over the river beyond our right.

This 'principal body of infantry' was that of Girard and Gazan, and they had crossed unopposed well before Godinot fired the first shot. Why else did Beresford order Gregory not only to recall the 4th Dragoons from foraging, but also to take them 'more to the right than where the cavalry were before posted'? So Beresford knew that large numbers of infantry were threatening his right from very early on. Napier's account therefore makes sense, and Beresford was not exercising the power of second sight when he saw Werle appear uncommitted to the support of Godinot: he had good reason to deduce that Werle was looking to follow Soult's left hook.

Why he did not adjust the right of his line straight away we do not know. Perhaps he thought the left hook might not develop, and he was content to wait and see. If that was the case, he took the awful risk of running out of time, and presumably he knew only too well Lord Wellington's views on the inability of the Spanish to manoeuvre. Ian Fletcher, our greatest living Peninsular historian, who has studied this battle closely, says that Zayas' ADC caught sight of those bayonets among the trees about an hour and a half after the fighting at the village began; that would be about right for the distance that had to be covered. But an hour and a half is a terribly long time to wait with your line still facing east, when a very heavy enemy column had disappeared off to the south even before the fighting at the village had actually begun. And there are no accounts or references to Beresford sending out mounted patrols specifically to shadow that column and report back – the sort of reaction any competent sergeant would order. While the Long/Lumley change of command may excuse the cavalry staff themselves for not putting such an elementary precaution in hand, the apparent lack of interest by the commanding general shows a curious blindness to the urgency of the developing situation. It was as if, having decided that Soult would attack his centre, and having disposed his army accordingly, Beresford was tempted to disregard any intelligence suggesting the contrary. (In later years he continued to insist that Soult *should* have attacked his centre.)

Galvanized at last to his danger by the sight of those bayonets, Beresford now rode over to Blake, and ordered him to change front 90 degrees, and to advance to the west–east line of the two knolls some half a mile south of his present right wing – linking up, in fact, with the two battalions of Ballasteros' division who were stationed on the easterly knoll. This would open up a huge gap of nearly a mile to the present right wing of the 2nd Division; so Stewart in turn was warned to support the Spanish by moving south – and thus Colborne, in his turn, was ordered to rejoin with all haste. Leslie of the 29th, in Hoghton's brigade: 'We were suddenly thrown into open column, and moved rapidly along the heights to our right flank for nearly a mile... Colborne's brigade also, which had moved to cover the village, had been recalled and brought up in a hasty manner in column, obliquely to their right towards the heights.'

The cavalry, both British and Spanish, was brought up from the river line to take post on Blake's new right rear, except for two squadrons of the 13th Light Dragoons under Lieutenant-Colonel Muter that were sent across to reinforce the defences at the bridge. In the new cavalry location Lumley took the overall command from Long. Cole was ordered to place Myer's Fusilier Brigade, Harvey's Portuguese brigade, and the three companies present from Kemmis' brigade in rear of the cavalry. Finally, Beresford went to see Hamilton, whom he warned to move his Portuguese division to the area of the Conical Hill to replace Stewart's division.

While Beresford was still talking with Hamilton, bad news came galloping up in the form of a Spanish ADC sent by Blake. Realizing the urgent need to be at the other end of his line, Beresford quickly told Hamilton to act as he thought best, and set out to canter the mile and a half to Blake's headquarters. All was now rush and bother; how much better if all this had been put in hand an hour earlier. For French cavalry were appearing in vast quantities on the plain, and everything had speeded up, with black clouds and menace in the air.

It is said that General Zayas on his own initiative changed front without Blake's order (and he deserved Beresford's heartfelt thanks if he did), putting two battalions of the Spanish

Royal Guards on the edge of the southern forward slope in line, and in close column behind them two battalions of the Ireland and Navarre Regiments, together with a gun battery. But at this point, when only some 2,000 of his 12,600 infantry had turned to face south, Captain-General Blake 'positively refused' to do more. Henry Hardinge, Beresford's DQMG, reported later that Blake insisted that 'the attack was evidently on the front by the village. When told that the village was sufficiently occupied, he still persisted in his refusal.' Adamant in his refusal to change front, Blake sent an ADC to Beresford to stress his conviction the main attack was due on the village, and that the other eighteen Spanish battalions were staying put. One can imagine Beresford's anxious frustration during the ten minutes it took him to rush back from Hamilton – for there, 3 miles away, he could see ample proof of Soult's intent.

A glittering array 400 men wide was taking shape – the widest column ever seen in Spain. Ahead and on its flanks ten regiments of horse – 3,500 sabres and lances – formed and reformed, trumpets blaring, drums and bugles coming still faintly over the yellowing corn-fields. Blake, persuaded at last, then gave 'such tedious pedantic orders of counter-march', says Hardinge, 'that Beresford was obliged to interfere and direct the movement himself.' The Spanish army's lack of drill practice now became all too apparent, and the redeployment, under imminent threat, challenged the elementary skills of all concerned. Lardizabal had to get three battalions to the right of Zayas' line, and two more from the village; Ballasteros had to get two battalions on to the left of Zayas, and to re-form to face south his other two battalions, who were on the knoll originally but still facing east; and D'España had to send one battalion down to the bridge.

This was the imagined shape of things to come, had time not been wasted by both Beresford and Blake. Colborne was not yet rejoined, Stewart was not yet moving, and all was incomplete, when the leading brigade of Latour-Maubourg's cavalry reached the 1,100 horse of the Spanish general Loy. The French cavalry first pushed him back, then the British outposts, and, followed by a further two brigades and a battery of horse artillery, rolled over the plain to the kidney-shaped feature on the west, leaving room up the middle for the massive, crunching infantry column. Latour-Maubourg thus sat in a prime position, with 3,500 troopers facing Lumley's 1,400 and threatening to get behind his right flank. That would be check-mate in two easy moves: the open valley behind Lumley's cavalry was crossed by the vital roads to Valverde and Badajoz – Beresford's line of communications and a fortress to be relieved. It is said that Latour-Maubourg was dissuaded from such an attempt only by the appearance, up the valley sides behind Lumley, of the eight battalions of Cole's two brigades.

Three batteries of French artillery now galloped forward to the kidney-shaped knoll, to the right front of the cavalry, and commenced firing on both Lumley's squadrons and Zayas' infantry line at a range of 500 yards. This coincided with the first French infantry skirmishers closing the dip, above which the Spanish stood, mesmerized by the very sight of the huge column cresting the far slope. As it unrolled forwards without end, many were the crossings of the right hand over the heart, and mumbles of 'Jesus protect me this day!'

Behind Girard's and Gazan's two-division column came Werle's brigade, closing up fast after their counter-march from near the Albuera bridge. So Soult now had in hand a coherent mass of 14,000 infantry and 3,500 cavalry confronting just four lonely battalions of Zayas' Spanish with 2,000 bayonets – for all else was still in motion, unformed and vulnerable. No wonder General Girard, Soult's leading divisional commander, decided to go straight in. We are fortunate in having a record of Girard's attack formation, thanks to the indefatigable

Charles Oman. To understand what was about to happen, we need a mind's eye picture of his deployment, and this report, which Oman unearthed in the Paris War Ministry archives, is invaluable:

> The line of attack was formed by a brigade in column of attack. To the right and left the front line was in a mixed formation, that is to say, on each side of the central column was a battalion deployed in line, and on each of the two outer sides of the deployed battalions was a battalion or regiment in column, so that each end of the line was composed of a column ready to form square, in case the hostile cavalry should try to fall upon our flanks – which was hardly likely, since our own cavalry was immensely superior to it in number.

To enlarge on this, and to give an idea of the numbers involved, the following will be helpful. Assuming seventy-five men in a company, and six companies to a battalion, it can be seen that Girard's centre column was enormous. It comprised five battalions, one behind the other, in column of double companies, each some fifty files wide and forty-five ranks deep. On either side of this centre column was a battalion in line, three ranks deep and 150 men wide. Then, outside each of these, was a battalion in column of single companies, twenty-five men wide and eighteen ranks deep. So the entire frontage was 400 men wide, which, allowing for four gaps between the battalions – wide enough to insert guns if required – gives a final width of at least 500 yards (Oman thought possibly up to 700 yards).

This formation was a rare example of a version of Napoleon Bonaparte's famous '*ordre mixte*', his artilleryman's compromise solution to the infantry problem of whether it was better to attack in line or column. It was, however, a solution mostly famous for being carefully avoided by his generals as providing the worst of both worlds. Events would decide whether Girard's decision at Albuera was sound.

Behind this unwieldly blue mammoth came the simpler construction of Gazan's 2nd Division. This was deployed in four regimental columns, side by side, and in each column the battalions were one behind another, in column of double companies. The two outside regiments had three battalions, the two inner regiments had two battalions. So Gazan's frontage was of 200 men – but about 400 yards wide, allowing for the three much larger gaps necessary for deployment – and twenty-seven ranks deep. Although Gazan had formed up leaving a proper space behind Girard's men, the more complicated layout of the latter's column, and the inevitable bending of the two battalions in line (with subsequent corrections – 'steady on the left', 'come up on the right', and so forth), inevitably saw Gazan's front line gradually catch up with Girard's rear, and effectively merge with it. From the viewpoint of the poor devils in Zayas' three-deep line, watching the French advance towards them behind their skirmishers, all that could be seen was a blue mass more than a quarter-mile wide and (if they could see to count, through the mist and rain) some seventy-two ranks deep in the centre. The space behind the battalions in line perhaps contained bands, generals and staffs, and ammunition wagons, and there were three more gun batteries out on the left.

The whole huge, bayonet-tipped rectangle slowly progressed through the wheat, blue on yellow, a shouting mass propelled by the music, with the thudding drums predominating. No British, German or Portuguese observer of this scene had any doubt as to the outcome: their Spanish allies would run (and many would have thought, little blame to them). Like leaves before the wind, they would surely scatter at the first volley, and not stop until they got behind the British, and maybe not even then. The first British brigade (Colborne's), even now panting belatedly up the slopes from the village, had all fought at Talavera; they knew the story of Portago's four Spanish battalions that ran away, some of the 2,000 fleeing men not stopping for 20 miles except to plunder the British stores – and at Talavera they had faced nothing like this.

General Zayas' 2nd and 4th Battalions of the Spanish Royal Guards, and the two battalions of the Ireland Regiment, stood on the lip of the saddle that connected the two knolls, in three ranks, their line about 600 yards long. Girard's three batteries unlimbered on the forward slopes of the kidney-shaped knoll next to Latour-Maubourg's battery, and opened fire. In return, Blake's solitary battery came into action, from across on his left. The French skirmishers engaged, closing until the column in turn caught up, and then moved away to the flanks to harass the first arrivals from Lardizabal and Ballasteros. The column was now climbing up the Spanish side of the dip, and at 60 yards commenced volley fire, making a little ground to the front between each volley. Since their frontage of some 400 men allowed about 1,200 muskets – the first three ranks – to fire, they would have been outgunned by the 2,000 Spanish in three ranks, except for a rare occurrence: the slope being concave and the Spanish line above on the edge, many French back in the body of the column were able to fire upwards over the heads of those in advance.

So Zayas' battalions came under the lash of superior musketry and superior artillery, with nearly twice their number of enemy cavalrymen lurking on their right flank – and yet they stood. They stood or knelt in three ranks, firing, reloading and firing again into the roaring blue mass, again and again; and in the first of the day's many miracles, they stopped them – Girard's 1st Division came to a halt, about 50 yards in front of the thin Spanish ranks. If it had not been submerged beneath layers of other wonders that day, it would have transformed Spain's reputation in the eyes of all the British regiments in the Peninsula.

Quite why the French allowed themselves to be stopped, given their artillery support and musket strength, is unexplained; and so is their failure to charge that last 50 yards with the bayonet. It is a curiosity that three-quarters of the French frontage comprised three ranks in line – that is, on the same footing as their Spanish opponents – so they were perfectly positioned to emulate what the British would have done. One suspects that the theoretical advantages of Napoleon's *ordre mixte* took inadequate note of the simple practicalities of 'command and control'. The sheer size and noise of such a mass of men in battle begs the question of how the field officers were to convey their intentions. Controlling volley fire by platoons is one thing; getting a battalion in line to charge might be another – still more, two battalions plus the front of another four in column.

Whatever the reasons, the French stopped and the Spaniards held, suffering now as the dead fell and the wounded crawled back, the line closing inwards towards their Colours and with corresponding gaps widening between the battalions. It is said that they stood the French assault for more than an hour: it is to be hoped that they knew they were dying for a purpose, to win time for reinforcements to arrive. That time was in short supply was entirely the fault of William Beresford, who should have acted sooner; but before Spanish resolve could be tested beyond whatever were its new limits, reinforcements did finally arrive, in the shape of the lead brigade of the 2nd Division. Its 33-year-old commander, Lieutenant-Colonel John Colborne (52nd), later said of the impending annihilation of his brigade 'I had nothing to do with the arrangement, but merely obeyed the orders of General Stewart'. For it is William

Stewart who has been held guilty of tactics that turned out wrong, yet which – with an ounce of luck – would have brought everlasting glory.

Beresford would maintain that his intention – and Stewart's orders – were for the 2nd Division to form into line in rear, before advancing to support Zayas; but unfortunately, when Stewart rode up with Colborne, Beresford was busy placing the reinforcing battalions from Ballasteros and Lardizabal, and thus could not oversee his planned deployment. Stewart led his division forward, the brigades in column, in the order Colborne, Hoghton and Aber-crombie; the former came diagonally up the slope from the village, and the others followed on behind. Colborne marched in open column of companies. Lieutenant Moyle Sherer (2/34th), in Abercrombie's brigade, said that after the skirmishing in the village had been continuing for about an hour and a half – say at 9.30am:

> sounds which breathed all the fierceness of battle soon reached us. The continued rolling of musketry accompanied by loud and repeated discharges of cannon on our extreme right told us convincingly that the real attack was in that quarter. The brigades of our division were successively called to support it. We formed in open column of companies at half distance, and moved in rapid double quick to the scene of the action. As we moved down in column, shot and shell flew over and through it in quick succession... all was hurry.

The 2nd Division halted briefly in rear of the Spanish, suffering – as Close of the 2/48th also wrote – 'a very heavy cannonading scattering destruction amongst us at this time.' With no Beresford to hand down any orders, and casualties continuing, General Stewart cantered for-ward to read the battle. He saw all the French guns off to the right, and beyond them masses of horse; he saw the huge infantry column stretching back, still held by a Spanish line that was close to crumbling in face of such endless pounding. But the French were making no effort to manoeuvre around the Spanish flanks, and it was that realization which lit a spark in the Hon William Stewart. He was a rifleman through and through: he had commanded the 95th at the age of 26 and, with Coote Manningham at Shorncliffe, had been instrumental in the very formation and training of the Rifles. Swift movement was in his professional blood, and he was also said to be of an excitable nature. In describing what happened next, Napier used the phrase 'boiling courage overlaid his judgement'.

*   *   *

Oman says that Stewart saw that the left flank of the French grand column was quite bare and unprotected, with a clear space outside it of several hundred yards; the temptation to fill that gap with his brigade and volley into that flank was therefore great. He discounted the prox-imity of Soult's artillery and cavalry to the Allied right, for he judged the situation of General Zayas' line so serious as to make the risk acceptable. He rode back to Colborne and told him that he, Stewart, would take Colborne's brigade forward straightaway, just as it was, in column, for this was quickest; the brigade could shake out into line as they got up. John Colborne's request to form line first was denied; Stewart set off, with the 3rd (Buffs) leading a column also comprising the 2/48th, 2/66th and 2/31st. Captain Andrew Cleeve's KGL battery hurried past to unlimber four guns next to the Spanish right, opening canister fire at 90 yards. The Buffs and the 48th went past obliquely, forming into line, with the 66th struggling to make space to deploy. In a letter two days later Colborne himself wrote unhappily, 'We were brought up under very disadvantageous circumstances, and obliged to deploy under the enemy's fire'. A second request to Stewart, to keep the Buffs in column, had been denied.

Under the black and threatening sky, with the banks of dirty-white powder smoke hugging the wet, trodden crops, Latour-Maubourg's batteries began to find the range, and the redcoats must have been praying that their carefully loaded first volley of double balls would not be spoiled. The line halted long enough for two careful, devastating volleys into the French, who returned fire, before General Stewart led Colborne's men to the charge. Since Colborne wrote 'the regiments were ordered to charge before the deployment was complete', it follows that the volleys were also fired before full deployment: all very scrappy, but obviously, amid the din and smoke there was no way the fire of thirty companies could be co-ordinated (leaving the 31st out of it), still less ordered to begin at the precise moment that the left flank unit was seen to have finally deployed. The volleys would have begun on the right as each company formed, and travelled down the irregular line.

The only detailed eyewitness account suggests that Stewart led the left wing of the Buffs and the 48th's right wing directly at the front of the French left-hand column, while the 48th's left wing and the 66th's Grenadier Company were more to the front of the next battalion column along. This is how Lieutenant Edward Close, 2/48th, saw it:

> Our brigade began to form line, the Buffs on the right, 2nd/48th, and the 66th Grenadiers being all that could be said to be formed – in line they were not, our left and rear companies being in the act of forming – and the 66th moving in echelon to form. Before the 31st Regiment, which was the last of our brigade, could open out, we were bayonet to bayonet with the enemy, and the hostile armies were met to decide the fate of many, if not of the day. We found the enemy, all Grenadiers, kneeling several ranks, and pouring in a dreadful fire up the hill, for they had formed on the one side before we could effect a similar purpose on the other. Two or three shots were fired by our regiment when, irregularly formed as we were, we charged. The left column of the French became opposed to the left wing of the Buffs and our right. Their centre column faced our two left companies and the 66th's Grenadiers. Their right column, which had escaped our notice, found its way to our rear. In less time than I can write it, although we were literally cut to pieces, we stood on the hill like extended light infantry, many of the intervals filled up by the Spanish sharp shooters. The French left column was broken, and was the only part of their troops which stood the charge. They remained as if powerless until they were bayoneted by our men. The rear companies fled. The centre column, to which we were opposed, however, gave way as soon as we charged. We kept advancing until we received the order to retire, when upon facing about we beheld the mass in our rear firing away handsomely. Those of the French left and centre columns that had fled and laid down their arms, resumed the fight and commenced a murderous fire. Thus were we situated, our Colours in the interval between two columns of the enemy.

Two points immediately occur from this description, which seem not to have been covered by other commentators. Firstly, British, Spanish and French troops were becoming horribly mixed up at this early stage, with the action degenerating more into the nature of a general mêlée than the confrontation of two neat opposing lines. Secondly, Edward Close – who was in the 48th's Light Company, at the left of its line – clearly states that the left wing of the Buffs and the right of the 48th attacked Girard's left-hand column, and the two left companies of the 48th, aided by the 66th's Grenadier Company – on the right of that unit's line – charged the next column in. He says nothing about a flank attack. Our second eyewitness, Lieutenant George Crompton of the 66th, writing to his mother two days later, said:

> Three solid columns attacked our regiment alone. We fought them until we were hardly
> a regiment. The Commanding Officer was shot dead, and the two Officers carrying the
> Colours close by my side received their mortal wounds. In this shattered state, our Brigade
> moved forward to the charge. Madness alone would dictate such a thing.

Crompton was in one of the battalion companies next to the 66th's Colour Party; if he says 'three solid columns attacked our regiment', and if Close says the 66th's right-hand (Grenadier) company, the 48th and the Buffs were pitted against the two left-hand columns, then that accounts well enough for Girard's five columns. A third eyewitness in the centre of the 48th's line also considered himself to be going head-on to the French column, not down their flank. He should know, since he commanded the 48th that day: the remarkable 66-year-old Major William Brooke:

> On gaining the summit of the hill we discovered several heavy columns of French troops
> ready to receive us. The British line deployed, halted, and fired two rounds: the heads of
> the French columns returned the fire three deep, the front rank kneeling. Finding these
> columns were not to be shaken by fire, the three leading battalions of the brigade pre-
> pared to charge with the bayonet, by order of Major-General the Hon. William Stewart,
> who led them on in person to the attack in the most gallant manner. The charge being
> delivered, the French 28th Leger gave way, as did also the front ranks of the Grenadiers.
> In the latter we could see the officers trying to beat back the men with the flats of their
> swords.

Again, there is not a word about the charge being on to a flank – quite the opposite. The specific reference to the 'heads of the French columns' is quite at odds with Oman's description that the 'two battalions in column... faced outwards', and with Fortescue's paraphrase that they 'deployed to their left in three ranks' – and with all the subsequent histories that have copied Oman, and which say Colborne attacked the left flank. Yet it was Oman himself, two years before he published his great *History*, who published Brooke's journal as 'A Prisoner of Albuera' in his *Studies in the Napoleonic Wars*. In the *History* he reproduces Brooke's exact phrase 'three deep, the front rank kneeling', without acknowledgement, and without explaining why he then turned Brooke's 'heads' to 'outwards'. Incidentally, neither William Napier's account in his *History*, nor Beresford's in his Despatch, nor D'Urban's in his Report, contains any mention of Stewart's attack with Colborne's Brigade being on to the French flank – a strange omission if it was indeed into the column's side, which would have contrasted admirable British manoeuvrability with the limitations of the Spanish ally.

It appears to the present author that William Stewart's precipitous attack on Girard's flank, if made at all, was made by half a battalion, not three, and the rest was frontal. Further, it seems from Close and Crompton that considerable casualties were sustained by Colborne in the firefight and as the mêlée developed, well before the notorious intervention of the Vistula Lancers. A fourth eyewitness, Lieutenant William Woods (again from the 2/48th), was impressed by the weight of fire thrown at them before Stewart ordered the charge:

> We were soon halted and began a brisk fire, but trifling compared to that of the enemy. In a few minutes the drum beat for it to cease, and General Stewart ordered us to charge. The men huzzaed, and advanced with the greatest spirit. A column of Grenadiers of gigantic stature rendered hideous by the huge fur caps and enormous beards and mustachios which they wore, were opposed to us. When within a few yards of them, the bayonet so terrified these formidable heros that numbers dropped their arms and attempted to fly. Our men made dreadful havoc amongst them. This column was completely routed, and two others were giving way. Had another brigade been near to support us at this juncture, the fate of the day would in a few minutes have been decided. But, alas! No support was immediately near.

Another oddity unremarked elsewhere is Brooke's (and therefore Oman's) reference to the 28e Léger as the left-hand column which gave way, 'as did also the front ranks of their Grenadiers'. As we have seen, Close and Woods also refer to the enemy column they charged as Grenadiers, whose appearance could scarcely be mistaken. But the 28e Léger was a three-battalion regiment in Gazan's 2nd Division, not Girard's 1st; how came his 28e and the *Grenadiers Réunis* – corps troops, in neither division – to be at the front of Girard's division at this early stage in the proceedings?

In view of what was about to happen to Colborne's brigade, it is appropriate here to note Beresford's later suggestion, that Colborne asked Stewart to allow him to re-form the right wing of the Buffs into either square or column, in order to protect his brigade's flanks from cavalry attack, but that Stewart refused. Yet when Close coincidentally accounts for the left wing of the Buffs, he makes no mention at all of the Buffs' right wing. What was it doing?

So here we have a gigantic mêlée, with suggestions that the Buffs and the 48th were doing different things, the 66th were only partially formed, the 31st not up at all; and after a couple of quick volleys and a successful charge, the battalions reforming only to find more of the enemy to their rear, mixed up with the Spanish. It was a bloody shambles for both sides, and clearly now vulnerable to whoever could impose his will the quickest. Stewart's ad hoc assault, with the best of intentions, had lost him both men and control; but if he could yet produce his next brigade, and in better order, and hit Soult's reeling battalions, victory could be gained. Unfortunately, he was beaten to the punch, for General Latour-Maubourg now enters the picture.

*   *   *

Down by the kidney-shaped knoll, Latour-Maubourg's eye had been long enough on Beresford's back door – the valley to his front, and the eight battalions of Cole's division blocking it – to know that that prize must wait. His attention was focused therefore on the clash on the slopes to his right. He saw the British come over the crest next to and through the Spanish, and the shock of Colborne's redcoats closing on the blue of the grand column. He saw men from the rear French companies begin to flee; he saw parts of the red line penetrate the blue mass; and, as the intermittent rain turned to hail, he ordered the nearest horsemen to charge the back of the British.

Around a thousand of the 2e Hussards, 1st Vistula Lancers, and possibly a contingent of the 10e Hussards dug their heels back and rushed across the few hundred yards, levelling lances and scraping sabres from scabbards as they gathered speed. The Lancers formed nearly half of this attacking force; they were commanded by 36-year-old Colonel Jan Konopka, and were mostly mounted on Polish bays and chestnuts. Although the regiment had been present at Talavera they had taken no part in the action, and would be unfamiliar to British infantry; this was their first charge in Spain. The Vistula Lancers wore dark blue with yellow facings (both common colours among the anarchic motley of Spanish uniforms), and their square-crowned *czapska* caps were shrouded in anonymous black oilcloth; Spanish cavalry, unfortunately, also included lancer units. Behind them, and thus obscured, rode the more recognizably French 2e Hussards.

General Lumley's cavalry could perfectly well see the French crossing their front. Their inferior strength had already, and necessarily, restrained their natural urge to ride over the gun batteries on the knoll, and now it apparently continued to impose caution. John Colborne's infantry were on their own. The prevailing north wind came though Zayas' thinning ranks and Cleeve's four guns, taking their smoke on to Colborne, and further into the French, both into their faces and down the flanks. The hail was now falling hard, and muskets began to misfire. The problem of replacing damp powder in the priming pan was bad enough, and if the wet got through the touchhole into the main charge in the breech then a man was defenceless except for his bayonet for several minutes on end; in rain, his eyes and hurrying fingers would be occupied with his weapon. There can have been few eyes in Colborne's brigade idle enough to peer around through the swirling smoke at the blotted-out landscape, and the thundering beat of a thousand sets of steel-shod hooves would be lost in the continuous hammering of the cannons.

Even so, seen they were, in time for the Buffs at least to face about – one source says four ranks deep. When eventually they were spotted, the Vistula Lancers were thought to be Spanish, causing just enough momentary uncertainty before the dreadful truth dawned – and dawned on men in the middle of a firefight, facing the wrong way, many with just-emptied or just-misfired muskets. Twenty-one years later Marshal Beresford, seeking every opportunity to disagree with William Napier, dismissed the explanation of a violent downpour restricting visibility, attributing it to Napier's desire to create a dramatic effect:

> The fact is, that though the atmosphere was dark, these Lancers were observed in turn to have been stopped; and the brigade had faced to the right about with the intention of attacking them when, as they were on the point of firing, a cry was raised that they were Spanish. This occasioned a hesitation and a delay; and before any further order could be given, the enemy had made their charge.

There is no protection from a 9-foot lance when you hold a 6-foot musket, still less a 3-foot sword, except to gather men together and imitate the porcupine. And the Lancers were said to be drunk into the bargain, and thus unduly careless of giving quarter and taking prisoners – there was not much give nor take in that regard. In minutes the red lines were being swept away, leaving two dozen or so tiny company knots or 'hives' where the survivors of the first onrush had grouped roughly back-to-back, with three main groupings around the 3rd's, 48th's and 66th's Colours. Here, naturally, the fighting was fiercest, as both sides struggled over the priceless tokens of glory.

The Buffs were the first to be hit by the pounding horsemen, hesitating for fatal instants in the swirling smoke and hail; even if some muskets had sparked in the downpour, they were lost men. We must recall, too, that they had just covered the previous uphill mile at the double, and were already shattered by the continuous artillery fire, the French volleying, and the exertions of their own charge. The Buffs were a battalion well above average in strength – twenty-seven officers and 728 men (Beresford's twelve other British battalions averaged twenty-nine officers and 518 men); its two-deep line would stretch perhaps 150 paces either side of the Colours, where the commanding officer, Lieutenant-Colonel Stewart, sat his horse (which was about to be shot from under him). In the next five minutes at most, Stewart was to lose one of his Colours (albeit temporarily), twenty of his twenty-seven officers, 623 sergeants and soldiers killed, wounded or taken, leaving just ten officers and 105 men on their feet. This catastrophic casualty rate of eight out of every ten men was the worst loss in any British battalion in the entire Peninsular War. A flavour of how one of the Buffs became a prisoner is given in this extract from a letter, from an unnamed private soldier:

> I was knocked down by a horseman with his lance, which luckily did me no serious injury. In getting up I received a lance in my hip, and shortly after another in my knee, which slightly grazed me. I then rose, when a soldier hurried me to the rear a few yards, striking me on the side of the head with his lance. He left me, and soon another came up, who would have killed me had not a French officer came up, and giving the fellow a blow told the fellow to spare the English, and to go on to do his duty with those of my unfortunate comrades. This officer conducted me to the rear of the French lines and here, the sight that met my eyes was dreadful! Men dead, where the column had stood, heaped on one another; the wounded crying out for assistance and human blood flowing down the hill! I came to where the baggage was where I found a vast number of my own regiment, with a good proportion of officers, prisoners like myself, numbers of them desperately wounded even after they were prisoners!

The 3rd Foot's Regimental Colour was carried by 16-year-old Ensign Edward Thomas. When the cavalry rode down the adjacent company, wounding its commander Captain William Stevens, the boy (in Stevens' words) 'rallied my company after I was wounded and taken prisoner, crying out, "Rally on me, men, I will be your pivot" '. What happened next is taken verbatim from the regiment's *Historical Records*:

> Round the Colour Party collected a surging mass of cavalrymen which the escort had no chance of keeping at bay. In a few seconds the three sergeants were overwhelmed and cut down, and a lancer had seized the pike of the Regimental Colour, carried by Ensign Edward Thomas, a boy, barely sixteen years old. 'Only with my life!' cried Thomas when called upon to surrender his charge, whereupon he was immediately struck down, mortally wounded, and the Colour was captured.

After the battle, according to Captain Stevens, Ensign Thomas 'was buried with all the care possible by a sergeant and a private, the only two survivors of my company, which had consisted of sixty-three men when taken into action.' The history continues:

> Round Ensign Charles Walsh, who was carrying the King's Colour, there was a similar scene. The pike of the Colour had been broken by a cannon shot, and Walsh was making desperate efforts to escape with the Colour and to gain the protection of such men as were still standing near him. Lieutenant Matthew Latham, who was close at hand, seeing that Walsh was wounded and that he was about to be taken prisoner, rushed forward and seized the Colour from him. Latham, in turn, was now beset by French and Polish horsemen from whom, for a time, he was able to defend himself with his sword. At last, however, a French hussar seized the remaining piece of the Colour pike, and made a cut at him, inflicting a terrible wound which took off his nose and the side of his face. Quite undaunted, Latham continued to use his sword with effect until another blow severed his left arm. Dropping his sword, he now seized the Colour with his right hand, and still continued to struggle with his opponents, crying out that only with his life would he surrender the Colour; until at last he was thrown down, trampled on and pierced with lances. So many men were there around him, however, every man striving to gain the coveted trophy for himself, that each man impeded the efforts of his neighbour to kill the now desperately wounded Latham. So intent were they on the capture of their intended prize that they failed to notice the approach of the squadrons of the 4th Dragoons by which they were quickly scattered, and Latham was thus allowed his last few moments of consciousness in which to tear the Colour from the pike and to conceal it in the breast of his coat where, after the battle, it was found, by whom it is not known, under his apparently lifeless body.

The 3rd's Regimental Colour was later found on the battlefield by Sergeant William Gough, 1/7th, and returned. It and the remains of the King's Colour, 'which were taken and retaken three times', according to Captain Gordon, 'are now in our possession fixed on two halberds'. The Lancers did capture the two Colour pikes, complete with spearheads and cords, and since small parts of the cloth were attached they claimed the Colours had been fully captured.

The 2/48th (Northamptonshire) were next to get ridden over. They were commanded by old Major William Brooke, with thirty-two years' service, and two sons both serving under him in the battalion – William, a captain, who was to die the following year at Badajoz, and John, a lieutenant, who was severely wounded in the same bloody assault. Brooke senior's journal was published by Sir Charles Oman in *Blackwood* for 1908. His battalion comprised twenty-nine officers and 423 men. He was to lose twenty-three and 320 respectively, killed, wounded and taken – a casualty rate of nearly eight out of every ten men, only slightly less than the Buffs on his right. He was also to lose both Colours, one to a Lancer, the other to Sergeant-Major Dion d'Aumont of the 10e Hussars. Of his own capture, he wrote:

> Part of the victorious French cavalry were Polish Lancers; from the conduct of this regiment on the field of action I believe many of them to have been intoxicated, as they rode over the wounded, barbarously darting the lances into them. Several unfortunate prisoners were killed in this manner, while being led from the field to the rear of the enemy's lines. I was an instance of their inhumanity: after having been most severely wounded in

the head, and plundered of everything about me, I was being led as a prisoner between two French infantry soldiers, when one of these Lancers rode up, and deliberately cut me down. Then, taking the skirts of my regimental coat, he endeavoured to pull it over my head. Not satisfied with this brutality, the wretch tried by every means in his power to make his horse trample on me, by dragging me along the ground and wheeling his horse over my body. But the beast, more merciful than the rider, absolutely refused to comply with his master's wishes, and carefully avoided putting his foot on me.

Lieutenant William Woods was also one of prisoners taken from the 48th:

> The French General got a Regt. of Hussars, and a new species of troops armed with lances and mounted, amongst us. At this time more than half the brigade were either killed or wounded, and I found myself left with only four men of the Company, surrounded on all sides. In a minute after I was struck smartly on the right leg by a ball which had rebounded from the ground, and the next instant a number of Hussars came upon us and rode me and the four men all down together.
>
> Before I could get up a French officer came. I called out in French 'I am an English officer'. The scoundrel made no reply, but spurred his horse violently to get him over me. He was followed by several Dragoons, and I was trampled upon and bruised in several places, but not half as severely as I expected. I got up as soon as I could, and was cut at by two Dragoons in all directions. I evaded many cuts, and expected to have got away, as some of our Dragoons were coming up the hill, when someone gave me a blow on the back of my neck which brought me down again. At this instant a French officer came up and saved my life. The two villains, with horrid imprecations, robbed me of everything, pockets and all. I was then taken to the rear where, to my regrets and horror, I found Major Brooke, two Captains and five subalterns, with a number of our men prisoners, besides about 17 officers of other regiments, all but three wounded. They used us most cruelly, many of my brother officers could not get their wounds dressed; they were completely drenched in blood, which was still fast flowing from the deep cuts of the sabres.

Lieutenant Edward Close of the 48th's Light Company evaded capture by running:

> Thus were we situated – our Colours in the interval between two columns of the enemy – when their cavalry filed through the intervals of their infantry and rode through us in every direction, cutting down the few that remained on their legs. There was nothing left for it but to run. In my flight I was knocked down by some fugitive like myself, who, I suppose, was struck by a shot. This was in a road among furze bushes. Whilst on the ground I was ridden over by a number of Lancers, one of whom passing close to me was about to save me the trouble of recording this event, when a Spanish Dragoon rode up to him and struck him with his sabre, which brought him over his horse's head. I then got up and ran again, when I found myself between the French right column and the 4th English Dragoons, who were in the act of charging that body.

Major Brooke's adjutant, Lieutenant John Dixon, was attached as Orderly Adjutant to General Stewart, and, according to a regimental manuscript record, had a very narrow escape:

being pursued by several of the lancers, and had his horse shot in the back by the column of the enemy when close engaged. And at this moment the General said 'It is of no use, gentlemen, we must make the best of our way', and Mr Dixon was then closely pursued by two of the enemy's dragoons to the left of the Fusilier brigade; his poor animal, though having received his death wound, leaped a drain at the left of the fusiliers and by that means escaped, and the two dragoons fell into the hands of the fusiliers... The enemy behaved extremely badly to our officers when taken prisoners, taking all their money from them, and cutting and abusing them with their swords, the Major in particular, because he refused to give them his sword and a favourite watch which was a family concern.

The 2/66th (Berkshire) came next in the queue for the Lancers' attention. They had paraded twenty-four officers and 417 men; five minutes later they had lost fifteen and 257 respectively, or six out of every ten men. They too lost both Colours. We have already heard from Lieutenant George Crompton that they had suffered badly in the firefight with Girard's columns, unformed as they were. He goes on to say that:

at that critical period cavalry appeared in our rear. It was then that our men began to waver, and for the first time (and God knows I hope the last) I saw the backs of English soldiers turned upon the French. Our Regiment once rallied, but to what avail! We were independent of infantry; out-numbered with cavalry. I was taken prisoner, but re-taken by the Spanish cavalry. Oh, what a day was that. The worst of the story I have not related. Our Colours were taken. I told you before that the two Ensigns (Walker and Colter) were shot under them; two Sergeants shared the same fate. A Lieutenant [thought to be Lieutenant Lewis Shewbridge] seized a musket to defend them, and he was shot to the heart; what could be done against cavalry?

Crompton's fellow subaltern, 19-year-old Lieutenant John Clarke, was:

In command of a company of flankers, was struck down by a Polish lancer, taken prisoner, but escaped in a charge of cavalry... so much bruised, as to be unable to walk for a fortnight... Our men now ran into groups of six or eight to do as best they could; the officers snatched up muskets and joined them, determined to sell their lives dearly. Quarter was not asked and rarely given. Poor Colonel [sic] Waller of the Quarter-master-general's staff was cut down close to me. He had held up his hands asking for mercy but the ruffian cut his fingers off. My Ensign James Hay was run through the lungs by a lance which came out at his back. He fell, but got up again. The Lancer delivered another thrust, the lance striking his breast bone. Down he went, and the Pole rolled over in the mud beside him.

In the evening, after the battle, Hay was found sitting upright, protesting that there were many more in greater need of help. He survived, to fight another day. Captain George Goldie, commanding the Light Company, at some stage found himself commanding the battalion, and at the end 'commanding the remains of two other regiments of the brigade' as well – although this claim, made in his 1829 Statement of Service, cannot be confirmed.

Beyond the 66th lay Colborne's fourth battalion, the 2/31st (Huntingdonshire), commanded by Major L'Estrange. Since by great good luck it had not yet deployed into line, the battalion was able in good time to form square. Their bayonet hedge deterred the French horsemen who, on tiring mounts, spied easier meat to their flank – Captain Cleeve's four KGL light 6-pounders and one howitzer. Of his gun crews totalling some ninety men, the French got forty-eight, many taken to the rear as prisoners. Four days after the battle Andrew Cleeve wrote:

> We prevented the cavalry from breaking our centre; but finding no opposition on our right, they turned us, and cut and piked [lanced] the gunners of the right division down. The left division limbered up, and both guns would have been saved; but the shaft horses of the right gun were wounded, and came down, and the leading driver of the left gun got shot from his horse. Corporal Henry Finke had presence of mind enough to quit his horse, to replace the driver, and then galloped boldly through the enemy's cavalry; his own horse, which ran alongside of him, secured him from the enemy's cuts and saved the gun, which I immediately made join the fight again.

The right-hand pair of guns were evidently unable to fire on the approaching French and Polish horse because fleeing infantry were running through the gun line. Sergeants Hebecker and Bussmann were credited with getting the left pair on the move, before the right gun horses were wounded. About then Captain Cleeve was captured, but was freed quite soon afterwards – together with his lost guns – as the tide of battle moved on. (The French got away with his howitzer, and many months later it was found on the walls at San Sebastian.) The gallant Corporal Finke received a reward from Lord Wellington of 100 Spanish dollars.

The rampaging French and Polish horsemen, not content to make their presence felt among General Stewart's staff – who, as we have seen, had to withdraw for a time – aimed higher, at Marshal Beresford himself. It is recorded that having got behind Zayas' bruised line of Spaniards (and alarming that general's staff to boot), some score of riders came upon the marshal and his entourage. The gilded sabres were out all around; William Beresford dodged one ambitious thrust, seized the lancer by his coat, and by main force tipped the fellow out of the saddle – no mean feat of strength, even if the horses were moving apart.

Seeing the fragmentation of the French mounted assault, General Lumley sent the two right wing squadrons of the 4th Dragoons and the same from Penne-Villemur's Spanish to attack them, hoping to drive them out of the British lines. Lieutenant Charles Madden charged with the 4th:

> The charge of our right wing was made against a brigade of Polish cavalry, very large men, well-mounted; the front rank armed with long spears with flags on them, which they flour-ish about, so as to frighten our horses, and thence either pulled our men off their horses or ran them through. They were perfect barbarians, and gave no quarter when they could possibly avoid.

Latour-Maubourg responded by sending out a regiment of hussars to cover the Vistula Lancers' retreat; thus a confused, uncontrolled pitched battle took place among three sets of cavalry. As we have heard in several accounts, dragoons on either side seem to have been run-ning free as individuals, taking prisoners and releasing their own. Both British squadron com-manders – Captains Phillips and Spedding – were taken. The Lancers themselves lost their guidon (snatched by the Murcia Regiment of Lardizabal's Spanish infantry, and now resting in Seville cathedral) and 130 men out of 580; the 2e Hussards lost seventy out of 300 – one in every five overall. It was said of the Spanish horse that they would not press home: Colonel Light, liaison officer to Penne-Villemur, wrote 'After our brigades of infantry first engaged were repulsed, I was desired by General D'Urban to tell the Count de Penne Villemur to charge the lancers, and we all started, as I thought, to do the thing well; but when within a few paces of the enemy, the whole pulled up, and there was no getting them farther, and in a few moments after I was left to run the gauntlet as well as I could.' Still, Close of the 48th said his life was saved by a Spanish dragoon.

In so far as there was any shape to these events, the present scene could be depicted broadly as a return to French-versus-Spanish musketry, with the remnants of Colborne's brigade mixed up with French, Spanish and British cavalry both to the Spanish right flank and, to a lesser degree, in their rear. Thus by the time that William Stewart's second brigade, under Major-General Daniel Hoghton, marched up in column of companies from behind the village, led by the 29th, and started to deploy into line behind Zayas, they saw to their front coats of many colours. Their arrival clearly gave hope to those Spanish infantry whose nerve by now had all but evaporated, as Lieutenant Charles Leslie (29th) tells us:

> The Spaniards continued with some difficulty to hold their ground. Just as this misfortune [the attack by the lancers] had occurred, our brigade came up (the 29th the leading regi-ment). We closed up into quarter-distance columns, under cover of the heights, and deployed; but before the 57th and 48th regiments had completed the formation, a body of Spaniards in advance of our left flank gave way, and in making off ran in our front, and then came rushing back upon us. We called out to them, urging them to rally and maintain their ground, and that we would shortly relieve them.
>
> On these assurances, with the exertions of some of the officers and of our adjutant, who rode among them, they did rally and moved up the hill again, but shortly afterwards, down they came again in the utmost confusion – mixed pell-mell, with a body of the enemy's Lancers, who were thrusting and cutting without mercy. Many of the Spanish threw themselves on the ground, others attempted to get through our line, but this could not be permitted because, we being in line on the slope of a bare green hill, and such a rush of friends and foes coming down on us, any opening made to let the former pass would have admitted the enemy also. We had no alternative but to stand firm and, in self-defence, to fire on both; this shortly decided the business; the Lancers brought up and made the best of their way back to their own lines, and the Spaniards were permitted to pass to the rear.

The 29th (Worcestershire) was Hoghton's right of the line, and because of the continuing lancer threat around the square of the 31st, the Grenadier and No. 1 Companies were ordered to throw back their right. Colonel Inglis, commanding the 57th, takes up the story:

> After the 29th and the right wing of the 57th had formed, a body of French lancers got between the two lines [between the Spanish and the British]. The right platoon of the 29th was ordered to disperse them; the fire from this body flew rapidly to the left, and in consequence was taken up by the 57th. Colonel Inglis was at that moment wholly employed in the act of correcting an error which had occurred in the formation of the

centre of his regiment; in which owing to the rain that fell and the thickness of the atmosphere which it occasioned, joined to their having met with a piece of hollow ground, the 5th Company had lost its perpendicularity and doubled behind the 4th, whereby the centre of the regiment became crowded; Colonel Inglis having also at the same time his horse shot under him... gave the command to order arms.

He later expressed the view that probably no great harm was done to the Spanish, since the slope of the hill meant most of the 57th's balls would have passed over their heads. Major Robert Arbuthnot rode out in front of the 29th, waving his cocked hat, and gradually the message got through. The remarkable thing was that in all this confusion, by and large the Spanish continued to stand firm even though now shot at from all directions. Perhaps a few balls from the rear were a drop in the ocean of their morning's ordeal, which was now largely over. With Abercrombie's brigade having moved up to the left of Hoghton's, and the 31st taking up a line to his right, Zayas and Ballasteros were at last ordered to retire through the British.

The 2nd and 4th Spanish Royal Guards, two battalions of the Ireland Regiment, and gradually those of Ballasteros as they came up, had stood for over an hour on the lip above Girard's division, initially four battalions against (ultimately) twenty-eight. They had lost a third of their men (615 out of 2,026 all ranks), but not their honour; indeed, they had gained a new and, it has to be said, surprised respect among the British, behind whom their lines now reformed. That the Spanish had some notion of their military reputation is shown in a remark made to Sherer of the 34th, as they passed through a Spanish company: 'A very noble-looking young Spanish officer rode up to me, and begged me, with a sort of proud and brave anxiety, to explain to the English, that his countrymen were ordered to retire, and were not flying.'

Napier's intense scorn for the Spanish army generally was of a piece with his opinion of Beresford's generalship, and it is hard to credit his claim that the Spanish ran altogether; one is inclined to prefer Beresford's later statement, that Zayas' four battalions 'did not even to the end break their line or quit the field, as Napier alleges. After having suffered very considerable loss they began to crowd together in groups, and it was then that the second line (Hoghton and Abercrombie) was ordered up'. The truth of it, of course, was not that Beresford's 'second line' was held back until Zayas could do no more – which is what the marshal implies; but that the second line, like Colborne's brigade, arrived desperately late, thanks entirely to Beresford's own curious lack of urgency and forethought.

At some point adjacent in time to the British moving forward to the firing line, there was a corresponding adjustment on the French side. Marshal Soult decided to swap Girard's now blunted division for that of Gazan. One can only envy the confidence he obviously felt in his officers' ability to manoeuvre their regiments and battalions under fire in a confined area: 8,400 men in nineteen battalions, all on the move in a space of not much more than 15 acres – say six football pitches. It makes no sense to a soldier of today, and probably to precious few at the time. One suspects that the reality was a more feasible attempt to replace the cutting edge with a fresh blade – by filtering five of Gazan's best battalions, say, through the packed ranks to their front. And one does wonder, given the accounts of the French crowding forward, slowly merging and submerging the lines and columns, how their officers were able to control the fire, still less the movement, of their companies. What a nightmare it must have become by now; and the battle still had hours to run, as they stood at the bottom of that slope – facing upwards at red, not blue coats – and treading on the wounded and the corpses in the deep, churned-up red mud.

A Note on Colours, Saved and Captured; and on Lancers

This seems a logical point for the author to interrupt the narrative to comment briefly on the fate of the Colours at Albuera. There is more than one mention in the accounts of Colours being 'torn from their pikes' to conceal and save them from capture. On several ceremonial occasions half a century ago, the author carried the very elderly Regimental Colour of the 58th (Rutland); presented in 1860, this had been carried into battle against the Zulus at Ulundi in 1879, and against the Boers at Laings Nek two years later. This was therefore the 6ft by 5ft 6in Victorian Colour, not one of the modern 3ft 9in by 3ft type, miniature by comparison; the previous Colours in use in the Peninsula were only 6in larger than the Victorian in both dimensions. The author can vouch for the physical strength needed to hang on to the heavily-embroidered cloth, even when dry, in any sort of wind. To withstand the constant pressures of wind and rough handling, it is clear that no Colour was flimsy enough to be torn by hand - unless. conceivably, it was then ancient, and rotting through long use and exposure; the cloth was thick, and robustly secured around the pike. It would, however, be possible to slide the entire flag down off the pike, if one cut the cloth at the pikehead, and this is presumably what was done at Albuera.

As to those lost, the French have always claimed the capture of all six Colours of Colborne's first three battalions. This is because both the Buffs' pikes, with spearheads and cords attached as well as some small rags of cloth, were indeed carried off by the Vistula Lancers. However, this flimsy justification is quite rightly rejected by the 3rd Foot, who retained the cloth of their Colours essentially intact – they were, after all, immediately remounted on two halberds when they were discovered on the field.

The 48th's King's Colour was also taken by a lancer. After various adventures in Paris over many years, including a riot and a fire, all that remains of it is the central shield, with the legend 'XLVIII Regt.' embroidered on it and surmounted by the Crown. This fragment is now in a frame, in a storeroom of the French Army Museum in Paris. The Regimental Colour was effectively destroyed in the fire of 1851.

So too was the pike of the Regimental Colour of the Buffs. It is said that remnants of both pikes, together with the 66th's King's Colour, are suspended in the cornices of the Chapel of the Hotel des Invalides (an annexe of the Army Museum). The 66th's Regimental Colour was completely destroyed in the 1851 fire.

The 57th's Regimental Colour, such as it is – reduced to faded pieces of cloth mounted on a white sheet – is on display in the National Army Museum in Chelsea, London, next to the quarter-pound grapeshot removed from Colonel Inglis' back (*see* the following chapter).

Incidentally, after the battle Colonel Jan Konopka, commanding officer of the 1st Light Horse Lancer Regiment of the Legion of the Vistula, was promoted brigadier-general by Napoleon. On 6 April, within a fortnight of hearing that a complete British infantry brigade had been wiped out by the Poles, the Emperor ordered that a second regiment of Vistula Lancers should be raised. In mid-July he decreed that the French Army should establish six Line lancer regiments, to be converted from existing dragoon units. General Konopka became their chief instructor. Before this date the only lancer regiments in his army had been the 1st of the Vistula Legion, and the Polish Light Horse regiment of the Imperial Guard, converted to that weapon during 1809.

9
Albuera, 16 May: 11am–2pm – Hoghton, Hardinge and Cole

IT was now about 11am in the morning of 16 May. Facing the French grand column just to their south – but hidden from them by the masses of powdersmoke hanging in the damp air – Major-General Daniel Hoghton and Lieutenant-Colonel the Hon Robert Abercrombie had their brigades in one line. Including the 31st on the extreme right – sole survivor from John Colborne's destroyed brigade – General Stewart had seven battalions in line, and on their right Cleeve's battered battery of four 6-pounder guns (his howitzer had been dragged off by the French, and his other two guns were to come forward between the 29th and the 1/57th). Between the two brigades, Hawker's four 9-pounders would unlimber; so just ten guns locked arcs of fire across William Stewart's front.

The ground in front of Abercrombie's battalions on the left was a lower spur, running down in a modest slope to the Chicapierna stream. Reading from left to right, Stewart's battalions were the 2/34th, 2/39th, 2/28th, 1/48th, 1/57th, 29th and 1/31st. Stewart had 204 officers and 3,462 bayonets, less whatever casualties had been sustained by the 31st, and by the rest during their approach march. Soult had suffered losses of about a thousand to the resistance by Zayas and Colborne's counter-attack, so probably had around 7,000 bayonets, plus Werlé's 5,400 in reserve. He also had no fewer than twenty-four guns in close support to his grand column, and ten of them were the superior 9-pounders.

Zayas's mauled brigade cleared the crest, which was immediately occupied by French skirmishers, but fortunately not by the main column – presumably this was still trying to sort out its new lead formations. Soult thereby missed a great opportunity to take the high ground (modest though this feature was). General Stewart, quickly realizing the need to fill the empty space, called for three cheers and led his two brigades forward to the crest, without serious hindrance; the *tirailleurs* were pushed back without wasting a ball, whereupon, as Moyle Sherer (34th) in Abercrombie's brigade wrote,

> Just as our line had entirely cleared the Spaniards, the smoke of battle was for one moment blown aside, by the slackening of the fire, and gave to our view the French grenadier caps, their arms, and the whole aspect of their frowning masses. It was a grand, but a momentary sight, a heavy atmosphere of smoke enveloped us, and few objects could be discerned at all – none distinctly.

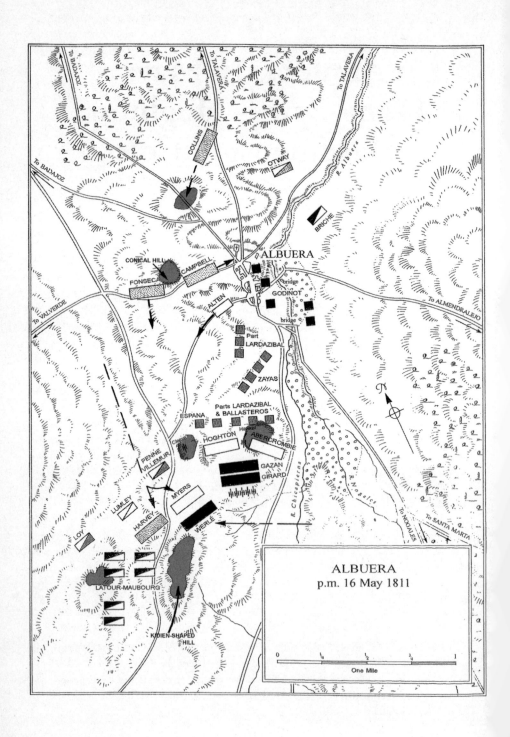

To BADAJOZ

To TALAVERA

To TALAVERA

COLLINS

OTWAY

To BADAJOZ

R. Albuera

BRICHE

ALBUERA

To VALVERDE

CONICAL HILL

CAMPBELL

FONSECA

bridge

GODINOT

ALTEN

To ALMENDRALEJO

bridge

To VALVERDE

Part
LARDAZIBAL

ZAYAS

Parts LARDAZIBAL
& BALLASTEROS

ESPAÑA

Hamlet

Chapel

HOGHTON

ABERCROMBIE

PENNE
VILLEMUR

GAZAN
GIRARD

MYERS

LUMLEY

R. Chicapierna

R. Nogales

To SANTA MARTA

HARVEY

WERLÉ

To NOGALES

LOY

LATOUR-MAUBOURG

KIDNEY-SHAPED
HILL

ALBUERA
p.m. 16 May 1811

0   ¼   ½   ¾   1

One Mile

That momentary clearing of the smoke was to be a turning point in the battle's higher direction on the French side. Just as Sherer and his comrades were able to look down on Soult's grenadiers, and doubtless ponder their chances, Soult himself was able to look up at the long red line which had miraculously replaced the Spaniards. He, too, pondered; he later wrote in his Despatch to the Emperor: 'When I ascended the heights, at the moment that the enemy's second line advanced and began to press in our front, I was surprised to notice their great numbers. Immediately afterwards I learned from a Spanish prisoner that Blake had already joined Beresford, so that I had 30,000 men to deal with. The odds were not fair, and I resolved at once to give up my original project, and to aim at nothing more than retaining the ground already won'.

We will consider the ramifications of this statement later. For the moment, it is important to bear in mind that from now on the French battalions were no longer being urged forward to push through to the Badajoz road. Victory had been re-defined: it was now merely to repel any attempt Beresford might make to drive forward – for the French, Albuera had become a defensive battle. One immediate effect was that across on the French right flank, where only skirmishers had been deployed against Ballasteros's men, and now against Abercrombie's, that purely defensive profile was to allow Abercrombie gradually to make ground forwards and inwards. Herein lay the seeds of a near-encirclement of the French, which, completed in due course by the courage of Cole's 4th Division, was eventually to send Soult's infantry reeling backwards.

Our first view of this next phase of the firefight comes from Lieutenant Charles Leslie (29th) in Hoghton's brigade:

> The formation of our brigade being now completed (after the Spaniards had cleared away) and Lumley's [now Abercrombie's] having taken post on the left, and all being now ready for the attack, Sir William Stewart rode up to our brigade, and after a few energetic words, said, 'Now is the time – let us give three cheers!' This was instantly done with heart and soul, every cap waving in the air. We immediately advanced up the hill, under a sharp fire from the enemy's light troops, which we did not condescend to return, and they retreated as we moved on. On arriving at the crest of the height, we discovered the enemy a little in rear of it, apparently formed in masses or columns of grand divisions, with light troops and artillery in the intervals between them: from the waving and rising of the ground on which some of these stood, the three or four front-ranks, in some cases, could fire over the heads of one another, and some guns posted on a bank fired over one of the columns. Notwithstanding this formidable array, our line went close up to the enemy, without even a piece of artillery to support us (at least near us there were none): we understood that the nine pounder brigade had been withdrawn in consequence of the disaster above related [the lancers]; while Soult has since stated that he had forty pieces of cannon vomiting death at this point. The 29th regiment being on the right of this line, its flank was *en l'air* and completely exposed, without any strong point to rest upon, while the Fusilier and Portuguese brigades of the fourth division, which had also been brought up to the new front, were a considerable way to our right in the plain below.

Colonel Inglis of the 1/57th, to the left of the 29th, writing in the third person: 'General Hoghton then directed Colonel Inglis not to engage till he should receive his orders to do so, and said he himself was going to the right of his brigade, and would take his hat off to Colonel Inglis as a signal to him when he wished him to commence. When the signal was given, it was returned by the Colonel, who then ordered arms to be shouldered and his regiment then threw in a very heavy and well-directed fire, by files from the right of companies.'

Leslie of the 29th again, on Inglis's right:

> This was the moment at which the murderous and desperate battle really began. A most over-whelming fire of artillery and small arms was opened upon us, which was vigorously returned; there we unflinchingly stood, and there we fell; our ranks were at some places swept away by sections. This dreadful contest had continued for some time, when an officer of artillery (I believe German) came up and said he had brought two or three guns, but that he could find no one to give him orders (our superior officers being all wounded or killed). It was suggested that he could do no wrong in opening directly on the enemy, which was accordingly done. Our line at length became so reduced that it resembled a chain of skirmishers in extended order, while, from the necessity of closing in towards the Colours, and our numbers fast diminishing, our right flank became still further exposed. The enemy, however, did not avail himself of the advantage which this circumstance might have afforded him.
>
> We continued to maintain this unprecedented conflict with unabated energy. The enemy, notwithstanding his superiority of numbers, had not gained an inch of ground but, on the contrary, we were gaining on him.

It is quite clear from this account that the 29th, at least, were well aware of their increasingly vulnerable right flank – not a difficult idea to grasp, given that Colborne's dead must have been strewn across the ground not far off. One wonders whether Latour-Maubourg sent to Soult at this stage for permission to charge again, and whether the marshal explained his new, unambitious policy?

At the far left end of Stewart's line, with the 2/34th, Lieutenant Moyle Sherer describes a confusing picture of threatening French cavalry, expenditure of ammunition, of lying down on a reverse slope and, above all, of edging forward whilst closing in to the centre. Abercrombie was trying to wrap his musketry around the right flank of the French column; nothing speaks more eloquently to the bravery and sheer resolution of his men than the constant closing to the centre – for in that very act they were acknowledging their dwindling strength. They also knew all too well that another consequence was the gap widening between their battalion and the next – and gaps attract cavalry:

> This murderous contest of musketry lasted long. We were the whole time progressively advancing upon and shaking the enemy. At the distance of about twenty yards from them, we received orders to charge; we had ceased firing, cheered, and had our bayonets in the charging position, when a body of the enemy's horse was discovered under the shoulder of a rising ground, ready to take advantage of our impetuosity. Already, however, had the French infantry, alarmed by our preparatory cheers, which always indicate the charge, broken and fled, abandoning some guns and howitzers about sixty yards from us. The presence of their cavalry not permitting us to pursue, we halted and recommenced firing

on them. The slaughter was now, for a few minutes, dreadful; every shot told; their officers in vain attempted to rally them; they would make no effort. Some of their artillery, indeed, took up a distant position which much annoyed our line; but we did not move, until we had expended every round of our ammunition, and then retired, in the most perfect order, to a spot sheltered from their guns, and lay down in line, ready to repulse any fresh attack with the bayonet. To describe my feelings throughout this wild scene with fidelity, would be impossible: at intervals, a shriek or groan told that men were falling around me; but it was not always that the tumult of the contest suffered me to catch these sounds. A constant feeling to the centre of the line, and the gradual diminution of our front, more truly bespoke the havock of death. As we moved on, though slowly, yet ever a little in advance, our own killed and wounded lay behind us; but we arrived among those of the enemy, and those of the Spaniards who had fallen in the first outset: we trod among the dead and dying, all reckless of them.

It is unclear if the French infantry still stood in their original *ordre mixte*, but it seems unlikely. Not only had the original point battalions gone, either *hors de combat* or by replacement, but since the experiment had failed against the Spanish, in these chaotic circumstances and under fire it was simply not practicable to re-form it. Jac Weller's opinion that the column was now a dense rectangle about 200 men wide by 40 deep may be too simplistic, since the 29th's writer in Maxwell referred to there being light troops and artillery 'in the intervals between...[the] masses or columns'. Fortescue wisely limits his description to 'huge masses of men and artillery'; and Oman, without a source, puzzlingly describes 'a mass of 8,000 twelve deep' – i.e. a frontage of 667 men. This is surely unlikely, since – apart from anything else – it does not adequately take into account the losses inflicted by the Spanish and by Colborne. The French grand column surely could not have numbered 8,400 after breakfast, when it set out, and still be 8,000 strong at 11am?

Given these uncertainties we cannot do a musket-count with any chance of accuracy. It is obvious from the prolonged nature of the firefight, however, that neither side had a particular edge. The casualty figures for the British confirm what several accounts state: that the French column was head-to-head with Hoghton's brigade – he had three times Abercrombie's casualties. Hoghton deployed say 1,500 muskets, perhaps 1,900 including those of the 31st; the first three ranks of the French, if now down to a width of say 300 men, would therefore produce only half their firepower. But the concave gradient allowed many muskets back in the body of their column to bring fire to bear; and then there was the French artillery. Twenty-four pieces were said to be deployed, and they would lay down a murderous fire of grape- and roundshot, all at no more than about 300 yards – 'Our ranks at some places swept away by sections', as the 29th's Lieutenant Leslie put it.

There is one word used but once in these two battle accounts: charge – and that by the 34th, only a threatened charge. It was probably aborted because of the counter-threat of hovering cavalry – an ever-present problem, which would explain the unusual absence of this staple ingredient in British tactics. After all, by 1811 it was well-established that, in bayonet charges, one side or the other almost always broke and ran before physical contact occurred. The side that ran – at Vimiero, Talavera, Busaco, Sabugal and Fuentes – had always been the French; so here at Albuera the red line would not lack the will – it was in their blood. But it may be that another, initial reason for the absence of a brisk charge was that it might not work, and the

British officers knew it – because the French were simply packed too thickly on the ground: they probably would run if they could, but it was apparent that they could not. Never before had any British officer present seen such a wall of men, so long and so thick. They might recoil, yes, or flinch away, but actually making them break and run seemed physically impossible. Once a few volleys had been fired, with the momentum for movement gone, it is easy to see how the British line became bogged down in a drawn-out, exhausting killing-match – two boxers standing toe-to-toe, trading ever-weaker punches. It would take some fresh outside impetus to break what was now a stalemate, for Soult on his side was not looking to carry the fight forward.

The sixty cartridges in the pouch on the right hip were steadily expended. Open the pan, take a cartridge, bite the top off; trickle powder into the pan and tilt the musket so that some grains enter the touchhole, close the pan; ground the butt, pour the rest of the powder into the muzzle, jam in ball and wad with your thumb, pull the ramrod out of its pipes, reverse it, ram; replace the ramrod (mind your bayonet) or transfer it to your left hand; present, cock, FIRE; butt down, open the pan, and off you go again. If you're in the second rank, mind the bloke in front. Twice a minute will do, three if you can – and your ammunition is gone in thirty minutes at most.

This face-to-face exchange of volleys, through blinding banks of powdersmoke, lasted – depending on whose account we read – for thirty, forty-five or more than sixty minutes. The senior sergeants in each company would ferry forward refills from the ammo mules in rear; but it was quicker to help yourself from the pouches of the dead and wounded – towards the end the latter were so numerous, and the survivors so few, that cartridge supply was not a problem. Pricking-out fouled touchholes and fitting fresh flints were routine jobs; but few had experienced before such jamming of locks through the expansion of hot metal parts, nor the blistering heat of the naked barrels. Many muskets were tossed aside with a curse, in favour of one snatched up from the fingers of a corpse. And all the time they could see nothing in front of their muzzles but the smoke, clinging to the wet crops, the wind from the north blowing their own smoke into the faces of the deep French ranks down the dip. It was just as well, really, not to see; the great thing was that every ball did no good to some poor bugger – if you fired a bit high, it would still catch someone back in the crowd.

Sir John Fortescue called this terrible battle of attrition a duel 'so stern and resolute that it has few parallels in the annals of war.' His memorable sentences come nearer than many to catching the grim nature of the experience; if we marvel at the fortitude of those who stood and fought, perhaps we should remember that their great-grandsons went over the top at the Somme:

> The survivors who took part in it on the British side seem to have passed through it as if in a dream, conscious of nothing but of dense smoke, constant closing towards the centre, a slight tendency to advance, and an invincible resolution not to retire. The men stood like rocks, loading and firing into the mass before them, though frightfully punished not so much by the French bullets as by grapeshot from the French cannon at very close range. The line dwindled and dwindled continually; and the intervals between battalions grew wide as the men who were still on their legs edged in closer and closer to their Colours; but not one dreamed for a moment of anything but standing and fighting to the last. The fiercest of the stress fell upon Hoghton's brigade, wherein it seems that every mounted officer fell.

Daniel Hoghton's right-hand battalion was the 29th (Worcesters), commanded by Lieutenant-Colonel Daniel White; at first it extended perhaps a hundred yards either side of his
Colour Party. Of his rank and file, only three men in every ten would end the day unscathed.
He started with 476 soldiers and thirty-one officers; eighty were killed, including five officers,
and 245 wounded, including twelve officers; and just eleven men were posted missing – taken.
So the battalion's line would have shrunk from that opening 200 yards to perhaps 60 yards,
centred on the Colours: the equivalent of two small companies. As always, the French gunners
concentrated on the centre, where both Ensign Edward Furnace (King's Colour) and Ensign
Richard Vance (the Regimental) were to perish. Furnace (whose brother William was to die
two years later with the 61st at the Nivelle) was severely wounded early on but, supported by
his sergeant, remained upright until hit again, this time mortally. Vance was in his first battle,
having been commissioned only seven months before. Fearing for the safety of his precious
charge, he is said to have torn the Colour from the pike and (like Matthew Latham of the
Buffs) hidden it inside his coat – where it was later found under his dead body, safe indeed.

The 29th's Colonel White also received a mortal wound, from which he died three
weeks later (he was buried next to Daniel Hoghton). His second-in-command, Major Gregory
Way, took over the battalion, but was promptly hit by a ball through the left shoulder
and was taken to the rear. At least, unlike at Rolica, he was not this time taken prisoner;
in fact, he received brevet promotion to the command a fortnight later, 'by special
recommendation'.

Hoghton's centre battalion was the 1/57th (West Middlesex), which inevitably became
the focal point or bull's eye for French fire of all descriptions. It was by far his largest battalion,
some 30 per cent stronger than the 29th or 48th, those on either side. The 48-year-old Colonel
William Inglis already had thirty-three years' service; he led thirty-one officers and 616 rank
and file, covering perhaps 300 yards from left to right. By the end of this murderous confrontation his 150 surviving men would stretch no more than 40 yards either side of his Colours –
like the 29th, the equivalent of two companies. One of Inglis' subalterns, Ensign Benjamin
Hobhouse of No.8 Company, wrote the next day to his father:

> During our advance in column the incessant and well-directed fire of the French artillery
> mowed down many of our poor fellows. Of course, our object was, and should have been
> sooner, to deploy into line, which we did about twenty yards in the rear of the right of a
> small body of Spaniards, who were supporting and returning the enemy's fire with the
> greatest bravery. We immediately passed in front of them, and received a most raking and
> continued cross-fire of musketry from a large body of the enemy's infantry whose heads
> were scarcely exposed above the brow of a hill. At this time our poor fellows dropped
> around us in every direction. In the activity of the officers to keep the men firm, and to
> supply them with the ammunition of the fallen, you could scarcely avoid treading on the
> dying and the dead. But all was still firm. In passing the Spaniards, the different regiments
> of our brigade were separated, and fought alone during the remainder of the action.
> Though alone, our fire never slackened, nor were the men the least disheartened. Tho' by
> closing to the right we appeared to be no more than a company, we still advanced and
> fired; and the Spaniards moved upon the left with the greatest bravery. Just before this,
> our Colonel, Major, every Captain and eleven subalterns fell; our King's Colour was cut
> in two; our Regimental had 17 balls through it, many companies were without officers,

and as the Light Company was next to me, I could not do otherwise than to take command
of it which I did, until it was my turn to take up the shattered Colours.

Major-General Daniel Hoghton had led his brigade up from behind Albuera village wearing
a green frock coat – nobody now knows why. His servant arrived with his scarlet uniform
coat as he sat his horse near the 57th's Colour Party, and he put it on without dismounting,
an act noted by Charles Leslie of the 29th: 'this public display of our national colours and of
British coolness actually was done under a salute of French artillery as they were cannonading
us at the time.'

As we have seen, Colonel Inglis' horse was hit while he was busy dressing the battalion's
line, and collapsed beneath him; he calmly stepped clear. His general also had his horse shot
from under him, causing Beresford to cry 'It is only his horse'. Hoghton scrambled to his feet
and continued in command for a brief while, before he himself was struck by three bullets and
killed, while in the act of cheering on his men. Colonel Inglis stood next to Ensign Hobhouse
and the Colours, having succeeded by seniority to the command of the brigade on Hoghton's
death; but Inglis too was hit, by a quarter-pound grapeshot below the neck which lodged in
his back against the shoulder blade – somehow missing his vital organs (miraculously, he was
to survive the day). Refusing to be carried off, he had himself laid in front of the Colours, his
rightful place of honour, from which he cried out time and again, 'Die hard, Fifty-Seventh,
die hard!' – thus giving the later Middlesex Regiment its Diehards nickname. One of his company commanders, Captain Ralph Fawcett, was mortally wounded but, following his colonel's
example, also refused to be taken to the rear; he was laid next to his dwindling company, to
whom he called out to fire low, and not to waste their ammunition.

The 57th's King's Colour was initially carried by Ensign Robert Torrens, but fell to the
ground when he was seriously wounded. Ensign James Jackson, aged 20, who was carrying the
Regimental Colour, at once told a sergeant to pick it up and, handing him in exchange
the Regimental Colour, took the King's himself. He himself had by that stage been hit three
times, in both arms and the left breast, and on receiving a fourth wound was compelled to go
to the rear. It is said that on returning from having his wounds dressed he could not persuade
his stand-in, Ensign James Veitch – who was by then also wounded – to hand back the Colour,
complete with its seventeen bullet holes and a broken pike. The 57th's Regimental Colour was
pierced by twenty-one balls, and Jackson's clothing by nine.

The left-hand battalion of Hoghton's brigade were the 1/48th, lined up between the 57th
and Abercrombie's 28th. We do not know what news had reached the 1st Battalion concerning the fate of their 2nd Battalion, but it would certainly be common knowledge that Colborne's brigade had been broken up; rumours, the wounded, and those (like Edward Close)
who had been chased back would all be making their way to the rear, eloquent enough. Men
today who have worn a regimental capbadge will understand the peculiar strength of family
feeling that extends to other wearers, the more so in times of challenge or danger. The 1st and
2nd Battalions of the 48th had fought side by side at Talavera, up on the Medelin; the resolve
that the 1st was now to show undoubtedly owed much to anger and desire for revenge. The
1st Lancers of the Vistula Legion would be well advised to steer clear of the 1/48th, from now
until doomsday.

The 1/48th paraded with thirty-three officers and 464 rank and file. No eyewitness
accounts have come down to us; we know only that the battalion was brought out of action

by a lieutenant, since the only captain still on his feet (Gilbert Cimitiere) was by then commanding the entire brigade. The commanding officer, Lieutenant-Colonel George Duckworth, was a prime example of promotion through purchase: the son of Admiral Sir John Duckworth, he was a lieutenant-colonel by the age of twenty-four. Now twenty-seven years old, he was struck by a ball in the left breast and, shortly thereafter, by another in the throat (God was not smiling on the Duckworths, since news of his death was to reach his wife the day before she had to bury their four-year-old son). On Duckworth's death Captain James Wilson took command, but was wounded; Captain Ainstie took over in turn, only to be wounded in his turn; and the un-named lieutenant then had his moment of glory. According to Edward Close, that anonymous young officer took the 1st Battalion off the battlefield with sixteen other subalterns and 100 men fit for duty – that is, fit to dig mass burial pits.

The combined butcher's bill for Daniel Hoghton's brigade was 1,044 killed, wounded and missing out of 1,651, or some 63 per cent casualties. All were lost to artillery or musket fire, with only seventeen men taken prisoner. Compare this dreadful position with that of Colborne's brigade: there (leaving out of account the 31st), the losses of 1,258 were much greater, a rate of 76 per cent of a strength of 1,648, but 479 men (38 per cent) were taken prisoner. We know from the eyewitnesses that a great many of those prisoners were wounded from lance thrusts and sabre cuts. It is easy enough to envisage the scope for mounted men to round up and shepherd away prisoners (think mounted police on crowd control duties) – and the more so when the crowd are mostly cut about the head, arms and shoulders, are streaming blood, and are fearful of further cuts and stabs.

The combined casualties for Hoghton and Colborne's brigades (again, less the 31st) therefore comes to 2,302 killed, wounded and taken out of 3,299, or 70 per cent. So those six battalions had shrunk to two, with the lucky 31st on their right still at two-thirds strength. And still they stood; and still Soult could not, or would not, order his men to run forwards 50 yards and break the now pathetically thin red line with the bayonet; and still Latour-Maubourg's under-exercised 3,500 horsemen did not rush into and over them.

*   *   *

On the left, Abercrombie's brigade of the 2/28th, 2/39th and 2/34th were suffering too, but on a much reduced scale. They were clearly not seriously threatened, since Soult had as yet taken no initiative to break what had become a lethal stalemate – despite the fact that Werle and his reserve division of some 5,400 men, who remained in rear, were untouched and by now fully rested from their approach march.

William Beresford's inactivity was also striking; by now he must surely have understood that he had to do something. General Stewart was twice wounded, though still in command of the 2nd Division; Colborne's brigade was broken; Hoghton was dead, and his replacement, Colonel Inglis of the 57th, was lying seriously wounded, not in command; Duckworth of the 48th was dead; White of the 29th, like Inglis, was seriously wounded; the replacements for these three commanding officers (a captain of the 57th, Captain Wilson and Major Way respectively) had in turn been knocked over, and so too had their replacements. So who was commanding Hoghton's brigade? We do not know – was it Colborne, or Hoghton's brigade major, or the wounded Stewart? At the end, it was Captain Cimitiere of the 48th.

Six out of every ten of the battalion officers in the line were out of action, and thus the local direction and leadership of the fighting had now descended on to the shoulders of subalterns and sergeants. Oman's careful calculations suggest that at the end of this day the 29th, 48th and 57th had between them thirty-nine officers and 568 rank and file still on their feet. But regimental sources referring to rollcalls – which perhaps took place early on, and before the return of escaped prisoners or stragglers – give totals of thirty-one officers and 346 rank and file remaining (the 29th, two captains, three subalterns and ninety-six men; the 48th, sixteen officers and 100 men; and the 57th, ten officers and 150 men). Oman's 568 bayonets are equivalent to a single battalion, and 346 scarcely a weak one; but whatever the actual pitiful numbers in their exhausted two-deep line, who can doubt the result if, towards the end, either the French cavalry or Soult's columns had charged? Flesh and blood can only do so much. The narrowed British frontage was as obvious to Soult as it was to those who stood in it. It was imperative that Beresford thicken it up and get guns to its support, and quickly. Those four widening battalion gaps to the right of Abercrombie would otherwise be filled, soon enough, but with blue. Beresford was not short of options; why was nothing on the move?

And what of the French? One can scarcely guess at the hour-long horror of that smoke-choked mass, struggling to stay upright among the sprawled corpses and reeking body parts, mixed up in the red mud with discarded packs and shakos, muskets and shoes, while hundreds of whimpering wounded dragged themselves back between the legs of the still whole, or blundered, cursing, through the ranks. There were no bands playing now, for the bandsmen were all either dead or tending the wounded in rear. Oman estimates that 2,000 Frenchmen were killed and wounded in this nightmare firefight with the brigades of Hoghton and Abercrombie. It is amazing that Soult made neither of the obvious moves to break the impasse – sending in the cavalry, or bringing forward Werle – either of which must have proved decisive. He had suffered the same leaching-away of his leaders as had Beresford: Gazan was carried off the field badly wounded, General Pepin was to die of his wounds, so too Generals Maransin and Brayer; eleven of his battalions had lost their colonels, and in some only a handful of junior officers remained upright. We shall never know if Soult would have taken either or both of his options if Beresford had not, at very long last, acted. That he was given time to do so does support those who accuse the French marshal of hesitation; Soult was beaten to the punch by Beresford, however belatedly. Colonel D'Urban takes up the narrative:

> The Marshal remained on the spot which he had occupied since the beginning of the action, having in front the line and before him the gallant 57th regiment... Perceiving that his gallant soldiers were falling fast, Lord Beresford moved to the right to inspect the state of things in that direction, and more particularly to take a survey of the enemy's left. Lt-Colonel Hardinge and some other of his staff were with him. On reaching this point he saw at once how advisable it was that an attack should be made upon that flank of the enemy; and finding several Spanish battalions in column to the rear, he exerted every mode of authority and persuasion to induce them to descend the hill, and make the desired charge.

If Hoghton was down to his last 500 men, then D'España's three battalions just in rear, with the better part of 1,700 bayonets, would be a useful stop-gap – literally. Sadly, however, these were men and leaders from a different mould to those led by José Zayas: they were the survivors of Gebora, that ghastly battle three months earlier. The hovering presence of Latour-Maubourg's cavalry reminded them all too vividly of that day, and it was more than D'Espana's battalions could bear to contemplate. They simply refused Beresford's order – request – plea to move forward; it is said the the towering Irishman literally dragged one of their commanding officers forward by his epaulettes, but that when he let go the man slunk away to the rear. These three cringing battalions were to suffer just thirty-three casualties – a rate of 2 per cent – during the whole day's work.

The next closest support was Cole's 4th Division, back behind the Spaniards' right shoulders and nearly a mile away. These eight battalions (three British, five Portuguese) had been resting now for nearly two hours after their forced march from Badajoz. Cole was behind Beresford's cavalry, so any attempt by Latour-Maubourg to disperse Lumley's fewer squadrons, to get at the Allied rear and particularly the roads to Badajoz and Valverde, would have to run the gauntlet of eight squares across the shallow valley – a powerful deterrent. Hence Beresford was understandably reluctant to consider calling forward Cole; in his present position Cole also acted as gatekeeper to the Valverde road from Beresford's own point of view – his army would need to retreat that way if, God forbid, all was lost. So Beresford sent to Major-General John Hamilton, commanding the Portuguese division. D'Urban again:

> Upon this [being unable to budge the Spaniards] the Marshal dispatched Colonel Arbuth-
> not to General Hamilton, whom he believed to be still remaining in the position that had
> been assigned to him at the beginning of the action, with orders to send, along the back
> and under shelter of the ridge, one brigade to attack the enemy's left.

Arbuthnot could not locate Hamilton for some time, since, under the discretion given him earlier, he had used his initiative and closed in support of Alten, adjacent to the village. Because the Portuguese were now partly involved in the fight with Godinot, a further half-hour elapsed before Fonseca and Collins could extricate their brigades; Campbell's brigade remained to assist Alten. By this time, Beresford was beside himself with concern. D'Urban continues:

> Lord Beresford having waited some time for the approach of the Portuguese brigade from
> Hamilton, and finding that it did not arrive, supposed some mistake must have occurred,
> and proceeded to the rear to discover the cause... Much time had now been lost; and Lord
> Beresford's anxiety under the circumstances was very great.

There is, however, an alternative scenario, which has Beresford now so reconciled to unavoidable defeat that his thoughts have turned to extricating his army. Major Dickson, commanding the Portuguese guns: 'At about the time the fourth division moved to attack, I received a verbal order in English from Don Jose Luiz de Souza (now Conde de Villa Real, an aide-de-camp of Lord Beresford) to retire by the Valverde road, or upon the Valverde road, I am not sure which.'

And D'Urban tells us plainly that his chief did more than try to get twelve guns to the Valverde road: he sent Arbuthnot to Baron Alten, with orders to 'disentangle his brigade from the village and, on the arrival of two Spanish battalions which had been ordered to relieve him, to take position on the ridge near the conical hill, *with a view of covering the Valverde road,* and being also at hand to succour the real front, or Collins' brigade as might be necessary'. D'Urban's *Further Strictures* also tell us (with the benefit of twenty-one years' hindsight) that Beresford had seen Cole begin his advance *before* he left to go to the rear. Indeed, 'it was in fact that movement which hurried him there. It occasioned him the greatest alarm and anxiety... Why, he had, at this instant, 12,000 troops who had not yet fired a musket, and who were infinitely nearer to the scene of action than that (4th) division'. But in which case, why did not Beresford, instead of going to the rear, immediately send to forbid the movement? Why did he apparently acquiesce, when he, the commanding general, was being occasioned 'the greatest alarm'? Because he had lost his commanding grip, and his next thoughts were of retreat (or what sounds infinitely better, of the prudent preparations for a withdrawal).

A little earlier Cole's ADC Major Roverea, who had been acting as liaison officer at Beresford's headquarters, galloped in, but still without any orders. Lowry Cole sent him back, specifically to 'request authority to carry his division to the support of the Troops engaged', according to Cole's DAQMG, Colonel Sir Charles Vere. This would be shortly before Beresford went to the rear. Roverea did not return; instead, Beresford's DQMG Major Henry Hardinge arrived – and in a great taking. He had been forward to visit his regiment, the 57th, or what was left of it; while there he saw the men forced to replenish ammunition from the pouches of the dead, and the culling of his brother officers. So appalled was he by the impending catastrophy that he clapped spurs to horse and went straight to Cole.

*   *   *

In later life Henry Hardinge rose to be Governor-General of India, a peer, a field marshal and Commander-in-Chief of the British Army. It is to be imagined, therefore, that at the age of twenty-six his formidable character was already well-formed, and he would not lack for the soldierly virtues. He was now to demonstrate his sound judgement and self-confidence. He was determined that positive action be commenced immediately. A factor behind his decision, we can fairly assume, was despair at Beresford's seeming lack of that very positive approach that was now so vital. We must not forget that Beresford's staff officers hitherto had not seen their master under any weight of fire. That morning he would be turning out a genuinely sad disappointment to them – for it is certain that previously, as the administrator, planner and trainer of the revitalized Portuguese Army, he would have earned their greatest respect. But here at Albuera the pressures were of a different order; as Major Roverea noted, 'Our Marshal bravely exposed himself, but gave no orders, and the officers on his staff acted as they thought best.' This is what Henry Hardinge later wrote:

> In this emergency, I could not refer to Marshal Beresford, who had proceeded to the left to hasten the arrival of the Portuguese brigade. I had witnessed his energetic but fruitless efforts, under a very heavy fire, to prevail upon the Spanish troops to move up to the right of Hoghton's Brigade. Starved and harassed by forced marches, no effort could be expected from them. Abercrombie's Brigade was in support of Hoghton's left flank, and could not be moved; the right was entirely exposed, in consequence of the Spaniards failing to move up. Alten's German brigade was engaged in defending the village of Albuera; the Portuguese division was at least two [sic] miles off, and no appearance of its coming up; the 4th Division, therefore, which had not fired a shot, was the only available force left. In this desperate state of things, not admitting of delay, but requiring an instant remedy, I rode to Sir Lowry Cole to propose to him to attack the enemy's column with his division.

Before Hardinge's arrival at his side, Cole had undoubtedly ridden forward to Hoghton's brigade to see for himself how things were going. The flow of wounded would be telling its own story, and the obvious possible task of reinforcement would naturally demand his close attention. What he saw caused him to write five days later: 'the issue at one time was very, very doubtful. So severe a combat has not, I believe, taken place this war. Those who were in Talavera and Egypt say that the fire was more tremendous than at either of them. I certainly saw nothing like it, and hope I never shall.' His DAQMG later commented that 'General Cole continued anxiously to watch the progress of the contest... [he] was impatient with being compelled to withhold support under an evident demand for succour' – and that demand now arrived with Henry Hardinge. He was quickly followed by Beresford's AAG, Lieutenant-Colonel John Rooke, who added his own view that Hoghton's brigade could not last much longer. Cole rode forward again, to confer with his fellow general William Lumley. They agreed: it was now or never. Together they decided how the cavalry would be best employed, to support the 4th Division in its advance.

For supported they must be, with twenty-six French squadrons sitting fresh and poised less than a mile away over the undulating plain. That is a distance that a decent hand canter will cover in four or five minutes – time and space enough for infantry in column or line to form square, but not leaving much spare. Cole's dilemma was the need for speed, and protection against cavalry, best gained by moving in column, coupled with the need for muskets to be in line at the other end. Given the open ground and his confidence in both Lumley's cavalry and his own infantry's drills, he chose to go initially in column. It is true that, of the few eyewitness accounts, only Lieutenant John Harrison (23rd) makes specific reference to the approach march being in column: 'our division advanced in contiguous columns of battalions at quarter distance'. This is weak ammunition against the likes of Oman, Fortescue, Weller and Fletcher, all of whom say or imply that the approach was in line from the outset. However, 4,300 men in two ranks, allowing for the six gaps between seven battalions, is a line over a mile long, and then there were the columns or squares at the flanks. Such a length of line, crossing a mile of not very smooth slope diagonally, would be hell to control, and above all it would be slow. Nor, anyway, was it necessary to be in line while still a mile away from the French; no French general would ever do it. March in column, fight in line, was the cry. Here is what General Lowry Cole said about his plan:

> The movement itself was hazardous and difficult to execute without exposing the right flank of the Fusiliers to an acknowledged great superiority of cavalry, ready to take advantage of any error that might occur. In moving forward to the attack, the Fusiliers advanced in echelons of battalions from the left – a manoeuvre always difficult to perform correctly even in a common field day; and as the Portuguese brigade in advancing had two objects to effect, namely, to show front to the enemy's cavalry, and at the same time to preserve its distance from, and cover the right flank of, the Fusilier Brigade, its movement was even more difficult to effect than the former. Thinking it desirable (with all due confidence in the Portuguese brigade), to have some British troops on the extreme right of the division, I directed the light companies of the Fusilier Brigade (including the three light companies of Kemmis's brigade) to form in column on the right of the Portuguese, where I also placed the brigade of guns, and sent the Lusitanian Legion (in column) to the left of the Fusiliers.

Lumley was to advance his somewhat weak if largely unscathed cavalry on Cole's right flank and rear.

So in brief: Myer's brigade left, Harvey's right; on the left flank a column of the latter's Lusitanian Legion of five companies, together with the four light companies of the 11th and 23rd Portuguese Line; on the right flank a column of six British light companies. Myer's left battalion was the 1/7th (Royal Fusiliers), 700 strong and commanded by Lieutenant-Colonel Myers' field officer, Major North; in the centre, the 2/7th, 570 strong and commanded by Lieutenant-Colonel Edward Blakeney; and on the right, the 1/23rd (Royal Welsh Fusiliers), 730 strong, under 24-year-old Lieutenant-Colonel Henry Ellis. The Portuguese under Brigadier-General William Harvey moved on Myers' right, two battalions each of the 11th and 23rd Regiments, some 2,300 strong. Edward Blakeney describes the scene a little earlier:

> We saw the French columns placed in echelon on our side of the hill, and the artillery – twenty-three pieces – above, and an echelon of cavalry on their left flank, covering the whole plain with their swords. The 2nd Division of British infantry was to our left and front, and had just, as we arrived, been most severely handled by the cannonade and Polish Lancers. A squadron of these Poles had moved close to us, when a British squadron charged and drove them back.

Over to the left there then developed that dreadful firefight after Hoghton's brigade moved up; the Fusiliers were mere spectators to this slaughter for an hour or more, and it was still continuing. Then, thanks to Major Hardinge's initiative, Blakeney tells us that

> At the most critical moment, Sir Lowry Cole ordered the brigade to advance. The word, coming from the left, the 1st Battalion of the Royal Fusiliers moved first; my battalion – the 2nd Fusiliers – next; and the 23rd Welsh Fusiliers on the right. We moved steadily towards the enemy.

At this point we may put ourselves in Beresford's saddle, as he watched the 4th Division move off its appointed station. His main fighting British division of three brigades is about to collapse; the Spaniards are either exhausted or mutinous; his Portuguese division is still absent; his cavalry is outnumbered; his guns are outweighed; his opponent has a whole division in reserve, fresh and nearby. He looks north-west across the plain – and suddenly he sees his remaining British brigade and its Portuguese fellow, the solid barrier he has carefully placed across Soult's approach to the Valverde road, move out of position without his order. Latour-Maubourg's 3,500 horsemen look up like cats spying the cream, and reach for their sabres. Here, then, is a Staff College scenario for budding generals, which lacks only the Four Horsemen of the Apocalypse. We must suspect that his faithful D'Urban understates the position when he tells us that his master is 'filled with the greatest alarm'. But far from ordering Cole to stop, or galloping straight over to lend his moral and personal support, or even passively watching the outcome – all rational acts – Beresford went to the rear. Perhaps he could not bear to watch? He sent Villa Real to Dickson and the now-returned Arbuthnot to Alten, to prepare for retreat, and he himself went to find the missing Hamilton.

Was this the reaction of an able commander, prudently planning ahead, or of a despondent one mentally throwing in his hand? Was this the moment that William Wellesley referred to in a letter to his brother as 'the general's loss of Head and ordering the Retreat'? We will return to this; but it is interesting that Dickson thought his orders so inexplicable that he did nothing: 'I strongly expressed [to Villa Real] words of doubts... as I could see no reason for falling back, and the infantry my guns belonged to being at hand, I continued in action'.

Altogether, Cole took forward some 5,000 bayonets to support the 2nd Division's battle against Girard and Gazan, who were by now down to about the same numbers. Unfortunately for Lowry Cole, before he could get there to add his shoulder to the wheel, another 5,400 Frenchmen were about to appear before him – Werle's division. From the ridge, Cole's movement was seen and immediately reported to Marshal Soult; and when it became clear that the 4th Division was heading for the flank of Girard's and Gazan's divisions, he at last ordered Werle forward, leaving himself with just two battalions in reserve. He also sent to Latour-Maubourg his long-awaited permission to charge. So nine fresh, experienced battalions now plodded for the muddy ridge; chinstraps were tightened, thousands of hopeful sabres rattled out of the scabbards, and left hands took a firmer grip on the reins. General Werle disdained to deploy from his three regimental columns. He advanced in columns of double companies, as the French ever seem to do, diagonally beside the 5th Corps – that is, nine companies deep or about twenty-seven ranks, with each column sixty or seventy men wide. They were seen and partly counted by Captain Hill (1/23rd), who was marching with his light company outside the Portuguese 23rd:

> The light companies were found on the right of the Portuguese in a hollow square; with this to cover its right the line moved on to carry some heights on which the enemy had posted Artillery, Cavalry, and sharp-shooters. As our line approached, their infantry crowned the heights in columns, afraid, as the prisoners informed me, to deploy in consequence of the superiority in cavalry we had manifested in the affair of Campo Mayor. From the square on the right in which I was, (which outflanked their infantry, but in return was outflanked by the enemy's cavalry), I conceived the depth of each of the columns was 9. The distance of the enemy's second line or column (which you please) was about 60 yards, in their rear again some cavalry was found.

So, at some early point near the final slope, the 4th Division battalions deployed into line. There were four small Spanish cavalry regiments out front under Loy – a thousand sabres if that – and as Cole's huge line approached the bottom of the slope, already taking casualties from the French guns, the Spanish were scattered by some of Latour-Maubourg's squadrons. Sergeant Cooper (2/7th):

> The line approached at quick step the steep position of the enemy; under a storm of shot, shell, and grape, which came crashing through our ranks. At the same time the French cavalry made a charge at the Spanish horse in our front. Immediately a volley from us was poured into the mixed mass of French and Spaniards. This checked the French; but the Spanish heroes galloped round our left flank and we saw them no more.

Lieutenant John Harrison (1/23rd) shared Cooper's view of Loy's horsemen, saying scornfully that they 'figured shamefully' in the way they allowed themselves to be driven in.

Moving up the slope, the Fusilier Brigade edged slightly ahead of the Portuguese. Captain Hill of the 23rd was still in the right flank hollow square:

Anxiously looking to the left to see how our Regiment got on, we saw them gradually ascend the slope which brought them to a ridge commanded by another, still higher, which the enemy occupied, distant about 60 yards. Here a most destructive fire of musketry was exchanged, the infantry mutually advancing; at last the enemy halted; our people continued advancing, and we had the satisfaction of seeing our Regiment on the summit of the hills on which their two lines or columns [the French] had not been able to maintain themselves. I have been speaking of our Regiment in consequence of its being on the right of the Fusilier brigade, [it] was nearer me and less covered with smoke, the other two Fusilier Regiments were in line with them to the left.

One would expect, on the usual grounds of regimental seniority, that the 1/7th would be Myers' right-of-the-line, and the 23rd the left, yet here Hill says otherwise. This layout is confirmed by the commanding officer of the 2/7th, Lieutenant-Colonel Edward Blakeney; as we have seen, he had earlier referred to 'the 23rd Welsh Fusiliers on the right':

> We moved steadily towards the enemy... the first battalion closed with the right column of the French, and I moved on and closed with the second column – the 23rd with the third column.

The French columns comprised, from their right to left, the 58e Ligne, 55e Ligne and 12e Léger (the first- and last-named being old friends from Vimiero and Talavera). Sergeant Cooper of the 2/7th went against the 58e:

> Having arrived at the foot of the hill, we began to climb its slope with panting breath, while the roll and thunder of furious battle increased. Under the tremendous fire of the enemy our thin line staggers, men are knocked about like skittles; but not a step backward is taken.

With the firefight thus developing on Werle's front, and with Harvey's Portuguese echeloned a little in rear, into the space Latour-Maubourg sent four regiments of dragoons, some 1,600 strong, in two lines. Trotting forward off the slopes to the south of Cole's division, which was heading more south-east, the French lines of horse made contact first on their left, and then successively along the front of the four Portuguese battalions. The British light companies were therefore first to engage, being then a little in advance, and they flung a fearsome series of enfilading volleys into the face and side of the green-clad squadrons as they swept past. The Portuguese infantry themselves then opened a rolling volley fire, keeping the dragoons at bay and pushing them along the line, where some tried their luck against the Fusiliers. Captain Hill's view from the light company's square was presumably rather limited, but nevertheless he wrote:

> The Fusilier Brigade, arrived on the heights, were attacked in front by cavalry who, receiving the fire of all our companies, put themselves in order and prepared to charge, thinking the whole unloaded. The spurs were in the horses's sides, they were coming on, the Grenadiers then fired on them at about 15 paces distant and the file fire recommenced from those who had first fired, when they went to the right about and galloped off. During

this some small parties of cavalry had got in our rear and took prisoners the wounded who were getting away from the fire.

Lieutenant Harrison was with the 1/23rd's No.7 Company, thus about a third of the way down the line of British battalions:

> The French cavalry, who were now in great force and looked very formidable, elated with the little success over the Spaniards, advanced *au pas de charge* on our line but observing us so unshaken and so little dismayed at their fierce appearance, when within about 100 yards, they wheeled about and we saluted their derriers with a smart fire.

By then, the dragoons were not serious. Further to the left, neither Colonel Blakeney nor Sergeant Cooper of the 2/7th make any mention of being directly threatened by hostile horse.

As the opposing infantry closed, the Portuguese in the Lusitanian Legion deployed into line on the left, joining the 4th Division to the 2nd. Harvey's battalions tended to drop back, making a more solid guard to Myers' right flank. The losses to French gunnery at close range mounted, since it was impossible to miss with grape. The British charged; the French shuddered back, to be strengthened by those behind, and the firefight of musketry recommenced at about the width of a tennis court – and at times virtually at point blank range. The fusiliers very slowly edged forward, leaving their dead and wounded behind them; the French very slowly inched backwards, leaving their casualties for the fusiliers to climb over. Colonel Blakeney of the 2/7th:

> Our firing was most incessant; the French faced about at about 30 or 40 yards from us and we kept following the enemy until we reached the second hill, and the position they had previously occupied. During the closest part of the action I saw the French officers endeavouring to deploy their columns, but all to no purpose; for as soon as the third of a company got out they immediately ran back, to be covered by the front of the column. Our loss was of course most severe; but the battalions never for an instant ceased advancing, although under artillery firing grape the whole time.

Lieutenant Harrison, with his battalion company of the 1/23rd:

> Their infantry formation was covered by their field pieces which kept up a heavy fire with grapeshot and round shot on our line at a very short distance. I am sorry to say some time elapsed before these noisy gentlemen were answered by our artillery on the left of our brigade... The French infantry were formed on an eminence and we had every disadvantage of the ground. They soon opened their fire. We returned it handsomely, came down to the charge and cheered. They faced about after a few paces and, others coming to their assistance, the contest soon became general and a most determined fire kept up on both sides, so near as to be almost muzzle to muzzle. They again drew us on by showing us their backs and we twice repeated our former treatment. This work lasted some time, they continually bringing up fresh regiments, our brigade being much broken by its loss, not above one third of our men were standing. Their infantry flanked our regiment upon the

left and were coming in on our rear, their cavalry at the same time making a desperate charge on our right and rear and I assure you we had enough to do.

The losses on both sides were terrible. As Sergeant Cooper remarked, 'Here our Colonel and all the field officers of the brigade fell killed or wounded, but no confusion ensued. The orders were, "Close up;" "Close in;" "Fire away;" "Forward!"' The carnage continued, but at least the fusiliers were not entirely bogged down; even as the line thinned, the Colour Parties moved it slowly forward – a pace here, another there – and the remains of Hoghton's brigade on their left did likewise. Leslie of the 29th wrote 'The enemy had not obtained one inch of ground but, on the contrary, we were gaining on him, when the Fusilier brigade moved up from the plain, bringing their right shoulders forward; they thus took the enemy obliquely in flank.' Nor were they bogged down across on the other side of Hoghton's brigade: the ever-active Henry Hardinge had ridden over to 'authorize' Lieutenant-Colonel Abercrombie to deploy past Hoghton's left and get on the French right flank, as Cole struck their left – that is, he should swing the 28th, 39th and 34th forward at an angle to Hoghton.

This completed the Allied line: ten British battalions and four Portuguese, strong on the right but threadbare in the centre. No more could now be done by the officers, commanders or staff; it was up to the fighting spirit of the soldiers and the low-level leadership of their corporals and sergeants – the officers were largely swept away. The endless attrition of grape and musket continued. General Lowry Cole was wounded and so were his two ADCs; Myers was dead. Blakeney, Ellis and Hawkshawe of the Lusitanian Legion were down wounded, and the replacements were themselves being replaced. These are the famous sentences that conclude William Napier's chapter on this epic struggle:

Such a gallant line [the Fusiliers], issuing from the midst of the smoke and rapidly separating itself from the confused and broken multitude, startled the enemy's heavy masses, which were increasing and pressing onwards as to assured victory: they wavered, hesitated, and then vomiting forth a storm of fire, hastily endeavoured to enlarge their front, while a fearful discharge of grape from all their artillery whistled through the British ranks. Myers was killed; Cole and the three colonels, Ellis, Blakeney, and Hawkshawe, fell wounded, and the fuzileer battalions, struck by the iron tempest, reeled and staggered like sinking ships. Suddenly and sternly recovering, they closed on their terrible enemies, and then was seen with what a strength and majesty the British soldier fights. In vain did Soult, by voice and gesture, animate his Frenchmen; in vain did the hardiest veterans, extricating themselves from the crowded columns, sacrifice their lives to gain time for the mass to open out on such a fair field; in vain did the mass itself bear up, and fiercely striving, fire indiscriminately upon friends and foes, while the horsemen hovering on the flank threatened to charge the advancing line. Nothing could stop that astonishing infantry. No sudden burst of undisciplined valour, no nervous enthusiasm, weakened the stability of their orders; their flashing eyes were bent on the dark columns in their front; their measured tread shook the ground; their dreadful volleys swept away the head of every formation; their deafening shouts overpowered the dissonant cries that broke from all parts of the tumultuous crowd, as foot by foot and with a horrid carnage it was driven by the incessant vigour of the attack to the farthest edge of the hill. In vain did the French reserves, joining with the struggling multitude, endeavour to sustain the fight; their efforts only increased the irremediable confusion, and the mighty mass giving way like a loosened cliff, went head-long down the ascent. The rain flowed after in streams discoloured with blood, and fifteen hundred unwounded men, the remnant of six thousand unconquerable British soldiers, stood triumphant on the fatal hill!

The rout of Werle's division was indeed as sudden as Napier's splendid simile of a collapsing cliff, and it was, of course, contagious. The sight of blue coats edging back from the rearmost ranks, first in ones and twos, then in groups, signalled the loosening here and there of Soult's cliff wall. It was seen inside the ranks of Girard's and Gazan's divisions. They more than any had had quite enough of these bloody red coats – a good four hours, some said, of hammering noise, horrid sights and cheating death – and the fresh pressure from Abercrombie's side became a tipping-point. Some slipped away among Werle's men; nobody wants to be the first, but once a few go back that gives excuse enough for others. And so back they flowed, down the slope, stumbling over the corpses and the debris. Sergeant Cooper:

> We closed on the enemy's columns: they break and rush down the other side of the hill in the greatest mob-like confusion... in a minute or two our 9 pounders and light infantry gain the summit, and join in sending down the slope a shower of iron and lead into the broken mass. We followed down the slope firing and hurraing, till recalled by the bugles. The enemy passed over the river in great disorder, and attacked us no more.

Leslie of the 29th: 'The enemy's masses, after a desperate struggle for victory, gave way at all points, and were driven in disorder beyond the rivulet, leaving us triumphant masters of the field.' Joining in the driving were the 150 survivors of the 57th (Middlesex), but they were called back by Beresford, who was shocked at the thought of them suffering further: 'Stop! Stop the 57th', he shouted; 'it would be a sin to let them go on'. The French ran back down to the Chicapierna stream, in front of which stood Marshal Soult's only reserve – a thousand grenadiers, in eleven companies. Through this back-stop, which lost a third of its men to the Allied guns, the remains of three French divisions continued to retreat, protected by Latour-Maubourg's cavalry. His troopers also shielded the retreat of up to forty guns, to be redeployed to the slopes beyond the stream.

   At some early point after it became apparent that the French were giving way, Marshal Beresford left his southern flank and moved up nearer the village. Alexander Dickson of the artillery spoke with him, to the right of his gun line overlooking the bridge. Asked for his state, he was ordered 'to proceed as quickly as I could with my 9 pounders to the right, which I did in time to bring them into action against the retiring masses of the enemy'. Beresford also ordered forward the Portuguese brigades of Collins and Fonseca, to join William Harvey's, and to take on the role he had forbidden the emaciated 57th. He also ordered Baron Alten's KGL Light Battalions back into the village, which was quickly secured without difficulty. General Alten:

> Just about the time... the battle had been decided in favour of the Allies, the Marshal's countermand [to his earlier order to fall back] arrived. Several companies of the 2nd Light Battalion, which were the nearest to hand, instantly faced about and retook the village,

cheering and advancing in double quick time, without meeting any serious opposition. The enemy was found to have thrown only a very few straggling Tirailleurs into the place; and even these were not met with, till the church yard, situated in the centre of the village, had been passed.

It was now after 2pm in the afternoon. Soult's gun line and Latour-Maubourg's cavalry threatened any attempt to cross the Chicapierna, and none was made. Beresford – the creator of Lord Wellington's Portuguese Army – still had in hand 96 per cent of the sixteen Portuguese battalions he had committed to the field six hours earlier. According to Oman's careful calculations, of the 9,131 all ranks in the brigades of Campbell, Collins, Fonseca and Harvey, only 345 men were casualties; and half of these were in the Lusitanian Legion – no other battalion had suffered beyond the equivalent of a half-company. Beresford also had some 9,500 Spanish infantry on their feet, most battalions indeed being untouched. Girard, Gazan and Werle crossed the Chicapierna with 10,153 all ranks. Granted, Godinot was extracting another 3,500 men from the environs of the village only a mile or so away, and then there was the French cavalry. While it would have been foolhardy to ask the Spaniards to contribute if that involved manoeuvering (and it would), one wonders if the Portuguese, supported by Lumley's horse, might not have descended on Godinot's flanks as he sought to rejoin Soult?

Such an order, or any other positive step, was never likely. Beresford had already displayed a strange lethargy on two occasions this day, and by now was doubtless only too relieved that he had got away with it. Given what Sir John Fortescue scornfully describes as his 'haunting solicitude for the means of running away', Beresford was much more apprehensive of his enemy getting a second wind and coming for him again. Exploiting his present good luck was very far from his mind. Indeed, while both sides remained unmoved that night, Beresford and D'Urban were convinced that Soult would attack next day. The army accordingly was put under arms two hours before daylight – unbreakfasted, soaking wet and miserably chilled. Sergeant Cooper (2/7th): 'Before daylight we were under arms shivering with cold, and our teeth very unsteady... We rubbed up our arms and prepared for another brush; the sun rose and began to warm us. A little rum was now served out, and our blood began to circulate a little quicker.' Beresford made what Sherer of the 34th called 'arrangements which certainly indicated anything rather than an intention to advance' – which is a nice way of saying the plan was to retreat should Soult approach again.

However, nothing happened as the light grew, and the hours passed on the morning of 17 May. Kemmis' brigade – the 2/27th, 1/40th and 97th – marched in from Badajoz via the bridge at Jerumenha: another 1,400 bayonets, but more useful as stretcher-bearers at this stage. Soult's army, too, was so totally disrupted that far from coming again, it took a major effort by the survivors to collect, succour and somehow carry off his wounded – the equivalent of a division of infantry. Sherer (34th) tells us that 'General Gazan carried four thousand wounded to Seville in safety'. Much time passed on 17 May in adapting ammunition wagons for the carriage of those unable to walk, and the emptying of nearly a hundred covered provision wagons. His ambulance train, together with the walking wounded and the marching columns (including the 550 Allied prisoners), began to move at 2am on the 18th, with a large cavalry rearguard: first 16 miles to Solana, then to Usagre via Almendralego (where, according to William Woods of the 48th, 330 French wounded were left in the convent 'recommended to our protection'). He also said that 'On the road from Albuera, which is about six leagues, we picked up more than nine hundred wounded.' Hundreds of Frenchmen with the most severe wounds, mostly amputation cases, were left in the chapel in Albuera. Of the 550 prisoners, nine out of every ten were from Stewart's 2nd Division, and eight of those nine were from Colborne's brigade. Moyle Sherer again:

> On the 18th they retired, destroying the contents of many of their tumbrils and ammunition cars, to facilitate the conveyance of their wounded; and they were followed, at a respectful distance, by our cavalry and light infantry. It was not until the nineteenth, that is three days after the battle, that we occupied the wood in which the enemy, after their bloody defeat, had been driven in discomfiture and confusion.

Beresford also had no transport to spare – it was similarly employed in convoying the huge numbers of wounded to Elvas. Soult may have received intelligence that four days earlier the British 3rd and 7th Divisions had set out from Fuentes to march south, followed and overtaken by Wellington himself, who reached Elvas on 19 May. There he was met by Beresford's ADC, Major Arbuthnot, who delivered his master's Despatch. The covering letter included the following:

> I feel much for the number we have lost. I freely confess to you I can scarcely forgive myself for risking this battle, and I as freely confess that it was very unwise, and I am convinced that I ought not to have done it... the more I reflect on the balance of good and evil from success or defeat, the more I am convinced the battle ought not to have been risked. I certainly risked all that you had been so long in gaining, and I cannot tell you how much that consideration oppressed me till all was safe. We have been fortunate and therefore all is well, and the risk we ran will not be known.

No wonder, after reading that piece of breast-beating, that Lord Wellington found the Despatch itself quite unacceptable for forwarding to London as it stood, in the words of a commander hugely down-hearted and really quite broken by his losses. Wellington was reported by Stanhope in later years to say:

> He [Beresford] wrote to me to the effect that he was delighted I was coming; that he could not stand the slaughter about him nor the vast responsibility: the letter was quite in a desponding tone. It was brought me by Arbuthnot while I was at dinner at Elvas, and I said directly, 'This won't do: write me down a victory.' So the dispatch was altered accordingly.

The trouble was that England's enthusiasm for adventures in the Peninsula was currently glowing less than brightly. This Despatch was to arrive in London on the heels of his own, ten days before, giving news of Fuentes and the loss of 2,000 men; and of the shaming news, five days before, of Brennier's escape from Almeida. The Peer could only too clearly picture the scene in the House of Commons, with the Whigs making great political capital of these losses and decrying the government's war policy. It was not the best of times to tell them of another 5,000 British casualties, without making much more positive noises as to the great disadvantages thus heaped upon the French. At 4.30am Wellington then wrote privately to Beresford, as if to lay a comforting hand on his shoulder:

> I arrived here about two this day, and received your letter of the 17th... Your loss, by all
> accounts, has been very large; but I hope it will not prove so large as was first supposed.
> You could not be successful in such an action without a large loss, and we must make up
> our mind to affairs of this kind sometimes – or give up the game.

Of course, that was written before he had ridden over the battlefield on 21 May, and had
been briefed on the action. He then formed a less generous and less supportive view of his lieutenant's stewardship, having seen the ghastly evidence of still unburied redcoats (perhaps the
57th?) 'literally lying dead in their ranks as they had stood' – a thing he later said he had never
seen before (the reference is from Lord Ellesmere). The next day he wrote to his brother Henry
in Cadiz, 'another such battle would ruin us'; and to brother William: 'As usual I shall be
abused for the loss sustained by our troops, which is certainly very great.' To Charles Stuart,
British minister in Lisbon, he wrote a request that he hold back, if he could, any early reports
to England: 'I think it very desirable that if possible no flying details of the battle of Albuera
should go home till Sir William Beresford's report shall be sent... where there are many killed
and wounded the first reports are not favourable; and it is not doing justice to the Marshal to
allow them to circulate without his [report].'

Lord Wellington also wrote to Admiral Berkeley to send a 'ship of war with [Arbuthnot,
carrying Beresford's Despatch to London] as it is desirable that he should arrive as soon as possible' – that is, before the half-truths and complaining rumours that would inevitably emerge
from officers' letters home. His brother William wrote supportively to say that such letters
would contain the truth at any event, 'even to the general's loss of Head and ordering the
Retreat etc.,' – an interesting early reference to an aspect of the battle that was clearly the subject of widespread discussion. Wellington's more comprehensive summary of events again
went to brother William, but not until 2 July:

> They were never determined to fight it; they did not occupy the ground as they ought; they
> were ready to run away at every moment from the time it commenced till the French
> retired; and if it had not been for me, who am now suffering from the loss and disorgan-
> ization occasioned by that battle, they would have written a whining report about it which
> would have driven the people in England mad.

For 'they', of course, read Marshal William Beresford.

10

'A Heavy Nauseous Smell' – the Cost of Victory

SIR William Beresford's command post during the main battle was immediately in rear of Colonel Inglis's 57th, the centre in Hoghton's bigade. He spoke from the evidence of his eyes, therefore, when in his Despatch he described the 'distinguished gallantry of the troops... which will be well proved by the great loss we have suffered; it was observed that our dead, particularly the 57th Regiment, were lying as they had fought in ranks, and every wound was in front.'

In our narrative we have several times quoted the 22-year-old Captain Moyle Sherer of the 34th Regiment. His 1823 *Recollections* are one of the very few eyewitness sources written before Napier's great but contentious *History* subsequently coloured many later eyewitness memories (and as Ian Fletcher has pointed out, Napier did not himself walk the ground). The following further extract from Sherer is perhaps a little sentimental for our taste today, but no matter – it reflects both the writer and his period:

> The roar of battle is hushed; the hurry of action is over; let us walk over the corpse-encumbered field. Look around – behold thousands of slain, thousands of wounded, writhing with anguish and groaning with agony and despair. Move a little this way, here lie four officers of the French 100th, all corpses. Why, that boy cannot have numbered eighteen years? How beautiful, how serene a countenance! Perhaps, on the banks of the murmuring and peaceful Loire, some mother thinks anxiously of this her darling child. Here fought the third brigade; here the fusiliers: how thick these heroes lie! Most of the bodies already stripped; rank is no longer distinguished. Yes: this must have been an officer; look at the delicate whiteness of his hands, and observe on his finger the mark of his ring. What manly beauty; what a smile still plays on his lip! He fell, perhaps, beneath his Colours; died easily; he is to be envied. Here charged the Polish Lancers; not long ago, the trampling of horses, the shout, the cry, the prayer, the death-stroke, all mingled their wild sounds on this spot; it is now, but for a few fitful and stifled groans, as silent as the grave. What is this? A battered trumpet, the breath which filled, this morning, its haughty tone, has fled, perhaps for ever. And here again, a broken lance. Is this the muscular arm that wielded it? 'Twas vigorous, and slew, perhaps, a victim on this field; it is now unnerved by death. Look at the contraction of this body, and the anguish of these features; eight times has some lance pierced this frame. Here again lie headless trunks, and bodies torn and struck down by cannon shot; such death is sudden, horrid, but 'tis merciful. Who are these, that catch every

moment at our coats, and cling to our feet, in such a humble attitude? The wounded soldiers of the enemy, who are imploring British protection from the exasperated and revengeful Spaniards. What a proud compliment to our country!

Less poetically, Sergeant Cooper tells us how he spent the night of 16 May:

Having returned to the top of the ridge we piled arms and looked about. What a scene! The dead and wounded lying all around. In some places the dead were in heaps. One of these was nearly three feet high, but I did not count the number in it.

What was now to be done with the wounded that were so thickly strewed on every side? The town of Albuera had been totally unroofed and unfloored for firewood by the enemy, and there was no other town within several miles; besides the rain was pouring down, and the poor sufferers were as numerous as the unhurt. To be short, the wounded that could not walk were carried in blankets to the bottom of the bloody hill and laid among the wet grass. Whether they had any orderlies to wait on them, or how many lived or died, I can't tell.

But if they were ill off our case was not enviable. We were wet, weary and dirty; without food or shelter. Respecting the wounded, General Blake, the Spanish Commander, was asked to help us with them, but he refused to send any men to carry them off.

We lay down at night among the mire and dead men. I selected a tuft of rushes and coiled myself up like a dog, but sleep I could not, on account of hunger and cold. Once I looked up out of my wet blanket, and saw a poor wounded man stark naked, crawling about I suppose for shelter. Who had stripped him or whether he lived till morning I know not.

When Kemmis' brigade marched in next morning from Badajoz, this is how one private of the 27th recorded his impressions:

Before us lay the appalling sight of upwards of 6,000 men, dead, and mostly stark-naked, having, as we were informed, been stripped by the Spaniards during the night; their bodies disfigured with dirt and clotted blood, and torn with the deadly gashes inflicted by the bullet, bayonet, sword or lance, that had terminated their mortal existence. Those who had been killed outright, appeared merely in the pallid sleep of death, while others, whose wounds had been less suddenly fatal, from the agonies of their last struggle, exhibited a fearful distortion of features.

Near our arms was a small stream almost choked with bodies of the dead, and from the deep traces of blood on its miry margin, it was evident that many of them had crawled thither to allay their last thirst. The waters of this oozing stream were so deeply tinged, that it seemed actually to run blood. A few perches distant was a draw-well, about which were collected several hundreds of those severely wounded, who had crept or been carried thither. They were sitting, or lying in the puddle, and each time the bucket reached the surface with its scanty supply, there was a clamorous and heart-rending confusion; the cries for water resounding in at least ten languages, while a kindness of feeling was visible in the manner this beverage was passed to each other.

Turning from this painful scene of tumultuous misery, we again strolled amongst the mangled dead. The bodies were seldom scattered about, as witnessed after former battles, but lying in rows and heaps; in several places whole subdivisions or sections appeared to have been prostrated by one tremendous charge or volley.

And a grisly pair of sentences by the anonymous soldier of the 71st, who arrived on the battlefield a few days afterwards:

a heavy nauseous smell assailed our nostrils; this was partly caused by the immense number of dead lying buried under the ground, and partly by the fleshy fuel of the fires, with which it was necessary to expedite the extermination of those bodies which the already engorged ground was unable to take into its cold maw. The carcasses of both men and horses were thus dragged into heaps and burned: the black and scorched sites of these sacrifices were still distinctly visible to us, covered with numerous calcined bones.

The same man returned to the field in March 1812:

When I came to the spot where the battle of Albuera had been fought I felt very sad; the whole ground was still covered with the wrecks of an army, bonnets, cartridge-boxes, pieces of belts, old clothes and shoes; the ground in numerous ridges, under which lay many a heap of mouldering bones. It was a melancholy sight; it made us all very dull for a short time.

And from Private William Wheeler (2/51st), camped on the field in April 1812:

Albuera still presents visible traces of the late bloody conflict between the army of Marshal Beresford and Soult. In some places large fires had been made, no doubt to burn the dead, again in other places are long ridges or Burrows where some have been buried – of this there can be no doubt for here and there is visible an arm or leg projecting out of the earth. The place is completely strewed with broken shells, breast plates, pouches, scabbards and caps, both of French and English.

There is one eyewitness account that gives a brief glimpse of the way officers chose to shift for themselves on being wounded. It accords with others following earlier actions; there is no specific mention of such modern ideas as aid posts or collecting stations, but rather the common-sense object of reaching the regimental baggage – the nearest source of transport. John Harrison was shot above the left knee early in the 23rd Fusiliers' approach up the slope to 'the fatal hill'. It was two days before he was seen by what he called 'one of the pestle-and-mortar' fraternity, and by then he had reached Elvas under his own steam – a full 35 miles from the battlefield. He wrote to his mother:

The nature of my wound, thank God, is not serious, the bone just grazed but no fracture... With the assistance of my sword I hobbled about half a mile to the rear when I met our Sergeant Sutler who, with the feelings and foresight of an old soldier, had brought a horse for the relief of his comrades, and conveyed me about half a mile to the rear where the baggage was then standing, where I was glad to lay down. It was now between one and two and commenced raining hard and never ceased the whole evening. The firing was all over before one o'clock.

Having laid in this state for nearly four hours and seeing no chance of conveyance, there not being more than two or three wagons employed which were obliged to attend to those in greater distress, and not admiring my berth for the night, I summoned up resolution and proposed to Castle [a fellow subaltern] to accompany me on a mule to which he consented. With some difficulty and much pain I was mounted and we set off for Valverde. The road presented a shocking scene, numbers exerting themselves to avoid the inclemency of the night from which numbers lost their lives. Not being more than two leagues, we reached Valverde soon after ten. I had previously sent my servant on to endeavour to get us an empty hovel, but this was out of the question and we pigged in with some soldiers of the Buffs. Still no 'Pill' [surgeon] was to be procured, being few in number and having many subjects.

Now my worst of all misfortunes befell me through the carelessness of my servant and the rascality of some Spaniard who stole my knapsack which was strapped behind my saddle containing my dressing gown, morocco dressing case, and all my washing apparatus, slippers, linen, trousers, and an entire change of linen. These articles would have been more than ten times their value to me in my present situation. I refreshed myself with a little tea and bread, which was all the sustenance I had that day, but notwithstanding slept pretty well on a little straw till morning when I proceeded to operations myself and cut open my overalls. As no mark was through I was afraid the ball had lodged in. It entered about three inches above the knee and luckily had past through on the under side and lodged in the overalls under the knee where I found the gentleman myself and mean to keep for a momento of the day. Just at this moment we were appraised of the probability of being taken for the enemy had made a sortie from Badajoz and were recommended to take ourselves off. We lost no time but made another start for Jerumenha where we stayed the night and reached Elvas about noon on the 18th. I should tell you of my rascally servant who left me all that twenty-four hours and lost my sword that I took such care to bring off the field. You may rely on it that he did not long stay in my service and I believe now I have an attentive good lad.

I had a close shave when we first went into action. A ball passed through the centre of my cap, taking the point of my hair and went through several folds of my pocket handkerchief which was in my cap.

William Woods was one of nine officers taken when the Vistula Lancers swooped on the 2/48th. He had been ridden down, sabred, deliberately trampled on, hit by a ricochet, robbed and hustled to the rear:

Immediately after we were taken to a wood, where all their heavy luggage remained, and where they brought their wounded. We remained here in the midst of heavy rains without any covering, but what few cloathes they chose to leave us on our backs that day, and the night, till about four o'clock of the 17th, and without anything to eat. At this time they gave us some rice and a few live goats which, when killed and divided with the rice amongst the prisoners, amounted to 4oz of meat each. At two in the morning of the 18th, we were marched off with about 4,000 of their wounded and a strong escort of artillery, infantry and Dragoons. My whole thoughts were bent on getting away, and during the march to Ribeira, which occupied the two following days, I tried three times and failed. I have not room to give you particulars.

But escape he did, at the fourth attempt, and rejoined 'what remained of our poor battalion' on 23 May. Woods was particulary angry with his French captors for their treatment of his commanding officer, Major William Brooke, who 'is a grey-headed old man 66 years of age, and although he was cut in the head severely, yet they would not allow him to ride, but even made him wade up to the middle through rivers, which were running rapidly from the late heavy rains.'

Woods did not know that Major Brooke had in fact been given a lift over the very first river, through a misunderstanding that sadly was not repeated. Brooke wrote in his 1811 journal:

Two French infantry soldiers, with a dragoon, guarded me to the rear. This last man had the kindness to carry me on his horse over the river Albuera, which from my exhausted state I could not have forded on foot. The cause of my being so carefully looked after was that my captors would not believe that I was of no higher rank than Major. I was led to some rising ground on the left rear of the French army, from which the remaining part of the action was to be seen. I was a prisoner, dreadfully wounded, and loss of blood had made me faint and weak, notwithstanding all my misfortunes, my whole heart was with my countrymen, and from the brisk fire they kept up I augured a successful end to the battle. About two o'clock I had the happiness of seeing the French run, and the English mounting the hill and giving three cheers. At this moment I was sent to the rear.

When I arrived at the French hospital, one of their surgeons, seeing me so badly wounded, left his own people and examined my head. He cut off much of my hair, and, having put some lint on my two wounds, tied up my head so tightly, to keep the scull together, that I could not open my mouth for three days, except to take a little to drink. He told me that at the expiration of that time, I might venture to loosen the bandage a little. This surgeon spoke English tolerably well, having been a prisoner in our country, and well treated, he had a respect for us. Of my final recovery he gave me little hope, as my scull had received fractures of whose consequences he was fearful. The French soldiers abused him for attending me before them: he left, promising to see me again, but I never met with him after.

Weak as I was, I reconnoitred the French guard over the prisoners in the evening: it had been reinforced, and their sentries being posted three deep, I found it impossible to get past them, although on the other side of the river I could see my friends resting on their arms after their victory. The night was extremely cold and damp: we had but few clothes left, and no blankets. We made a fire by gathering boughs from the trees near us, but could get no sleep from the pain of our wounds, the loss of blood, and our distressing circumstances.

May 17th. On the morning, and during the day following the battle, part of the dispir-ited French army was left under the command of General Gazan, who was wounded him-self, to make preparations for the evacuation of their hospitals to the rear. The French are generally well supplied with conveyances for this purpose; on this occasion they had not less than eighty or a hundred large covered wagons for the use of the worst cases, exclusive of many horses, mules, and asses. These wagons had been brought up laden with provisions to the field of battle, and after being emptied were applied to any other purpose necessary.

May 18th. About two o'clock in the morning the main convoy of wounded, amounting to nearly 4,000 in all, was put in motion. Dreadful were the cries of these poor unfortunate wretches! Had my heart been made of adamant I must have felt for the pitiable condition to which the ravages of war had brought them. It was completely daylight before the rear of the convoy had left the ground. Two or three hundred had died on the 17th, and between 600 and 700 more expired on the road to Seville. It was stated to me by a French surgeon that they left on the field some, both of their own and of the British wounded, who could not bear transport.

A strong guard, both of cavalry and infantry, some 3,500 men, was told off to guard the British prisoners, who were placed in the centre of the marching column. We proceeded on the 18th along the road leading from Albuera to Solana – four long leagues. On our arrival at the latter place the principal part of the wounded were taken into the town: the escort did not enter it, but was drawn up on some high ground, to prevent surprise by guerrillas, of whom they were extremely afraid. The cries of the wounded continued dreadful. All the British prisoners slept in an open field, with a strong guard around them. The only sustenance that we had were a few green beans (garbanzos), which the French gathered and gave to us. Indeed, this was the only food they could procure for themselves.

May 19th. Orders had been given overnight to march at three o'clock, before dawn, but from the difficulty of getting the wounded back into the wagons it was near six before escort, wounded, and prisoners marched for Ribera. We passed through Almendralego, where the French troops took care to plunder the inhabitants of everything they could lay their hands upon.

Old Major Brooke escaped nearly two months later, from Seville, and rejoined the Colours in mid-August after a three-month journey 'of upwards of 400 miles in Spain and Portugal'. He went home sick, rejoining the 48th in time to be severely wounded at Badajoz in April 1812.

*   *   *

Before considering the horrendous casualty figures, it would be an act of humility to turn to the end of this book, and the three pages of Appendices listing the British and German officers killed, wounded and missing. The pages are facsimile copies from the *Narrative of the Peninsular War* by Charles Stewart, later Lord Londonderry, who as brigadier-general and Lord Wellington's Adjutant-General rode with him on 21 May over the corpse-strewn field. There is something cold about listing, as we must, the plain figures; putting names to regiments, and in particular to the long lists of subalterns, is a poignant antidote to that coldness. Remember that many ensigns were aged sixteen years or even less; remember that for every captain named, there goes an infantry company bereft of its leader; remember that either as a point of honour, or to avoid causing undue fear among loved ones at home, many severe wounds were reported as slight, and many slight wounds were not reported at all.

Now, as to the cold figures, we all – even Sir John Fortescue – take Oman as our bible. He unravelled the French losses, as far as is possible given Marshal Soult's shameless return of only 2,800 in his Despatch. Oman estimated French casualties at a total of 8,262 all ranks; in arriving at this total, however, a large measure of projection was involved, and while we may accept his remark that this was 'very near the real figure', no one now will ever know the true number of Frenchmen knocked over. As a proportion of the troops deployed (24,000), Oman's estimate of 8,262 is a casualty rate of one in three.

It is plain, of course, that Girard and Gazan took the heaviest loss, some 4,000 men down, or one in every two. Girard's division, as the lead formation, suffered most, then Gazan's, then Werlé's, then Godinot's and the cavalry in diminishing order. The latter two commands, with around 10 per cent casualties, were well capable of fighting on if required, as were all Soult's artillery. Just two of Latour-Maubourg's cavalry regiments lost markedly, at around a quarter of their strength: the ever-thrusting Vistula Lancers and the 2e Hussards, who between them laid so many of Colborne's brigade in the mud.

So Soult's losses of some 8,000 out of his army of 24,000 left him with 16,000 Frenchmen under arms on the wooded slopes beyond the Chicapierna. On the west side of the river, Beresford had nearly 30,000; but of these only 5,000 were British and 1,300 German, for they had carried the burden of the day. By 3pm on the 16th no less than 70 per cent of the Allied casualties wore red and green coats, notwithstanding the fact that at 8am they had comprised only 30 per cent of the whole.

This is not to say that the wearers of Portuguese blue and Spanish motley had been spared. Of the latter, obviously General Zayas' battalions suffered worst, and their honour was indeed satisfied – an overdue outcome that all Spaniards could recall with immense pride for years to come. Oman did have trouble measuring their loss, but concluded that of Zayas' nine battalions and total casualties of 681, no fewer than 615 were among his two battalions of the Spanish Royal Guards and two of the Ireland Regiment. These four battalions, with increasing help from Lardizabal and Ballasteros, fought in line for over an hour against Girard's mixed columns, and those who fell to the French cannons and musketry represented a 30 per cent loss from their opening strength of 2,026.

Given that the majority of them were never put into the line, the Portuguese losses were an insignificant 400 out of their 10,000 present. The Lusitanian Legion, on the left flank of Myers's Fusilier Brigade, accounted for half of these. The remainder of Harvey's brigade, four battalions on the right of the Fusiliers, got off very lightly, with just thirty-two casualties from 2,355 men. Hamilton's division of eight battalions, and Collins' brigade of three, each lost the equivalent of only a company during their brief moments under fire.

The Germans in the village fought Godinot all morning, with some help. Alten's thousand-odd light infantry lost 100 men, the same proportion exactly as his direct opponents. These figures were nowhere near the butcher's bill for the street-fighting in Fuentes a fortnight earlier, and mark the contrast between Massena's seriousness of intent in that earlier battle and Soult's gesture or feint at Albuera village.

Nor, in comparison with Fuentes, did Beresford's cavalry come to much harm – Otway's 800 Portuguese not at all, and Grey's 1,100 British dragoons only losing the equivalent of a small squadron – forty-eight men, or 4 per cent. At Fuentes the Allied horse had suffered more than twice as many casualties, so Lumley's baptism of command was blessed, largely through enforced inactivity. Being so outnumbered on such splendid cavalry going – fifteen squadrons against twenty-six – he was obliged to stay concentrated. Yet even as a standing threat his lurking presence surely imposed some constraint on the enemy – foot and horse alike – given the fighting reputation already acquired by the British cavalry. Latour-Maubourg sat long hours opposite this weaker foe, with Soult's hesitant hand upon his bridle. It was as well for Lumley that

Latour-Maubourg did not take a leaf out of Cole's book on insubordination, and give in to temptation. Had the numbers been reversed, one suspects that Lumley would have turned pretty quickly to his trumpeter. Latour-Maubourg's main apprehension, of course, must have been that should he make a wide left hook for the baggage and the road to Valverde, then Lumley and the 4th Division would promptly throw themselves at the left flank of Soult's infantry.

As to the losses in General Stewart's 2nd Division, we have seen that the desperate dismemberment of John Colborne's brigade reduced his strength from 2,066 to just 653 men – 69 per cent loss in a matter of minutes. Of this remnant, 263 or four in ten were in the lucky 2/31st; so the other 390 survivors were spread over the other three battalions. It is no wonder that after the battle the 2/48th's 109 men were absorbed – easily – into their 1st Battalion; nor that the remaining Buffs, Berkshires, Diehards, Worcesters and Huntingdons were brought together in a single bandaged provisional battalion, under John Colborne.

Hoghton's brigade was similarly reduced, if more slowly, over an hour and more. If Colborne lost seven of every ten men, Hoghton lost six; if the former at the end had 653 men on their feet, Hoghton's eventual stand-in, Captain Cimitiere, led just 607. Side by side, therefore, these once proud seven battalions now stood with a strength of just two. Only Colonel Abercrombie's men, especially those of the 34th and the 39th, brought the numbers up anywhere near a half-decent average. These two battalions, by chance, took post away to the left of that merciless cauldron of shot and shell that concentrated on the 29th and 57th. They each lost about two companies, and the 28th three, but together they were still recognizable as a brigade of infantry, nearly fully officered.

Overall, however, General Stewart's division could no longer be considered a fighting formation. The total loss of 2,868 out of 5,460 more than halved his ranks and nearly halved his officers: the whole might now usefully re-form as a five-battalion brigade, until fresh drafts from home allowed a resumption of separate identities – and that prospect was weeks away.

The story of William Myers' Fusilier Brigade has been told, but not the cost. A snapshot would be that when Captain Stainforth's company of the 23rd came out of action, it was commanded by a corporal named Thomas Robinson. The reason was sadly familiar. During their approach march up the long, bare slope to confront Werle's columns the fusiliers suffered badly from Soult's artillery, and thereafter from short-range grapeshot; yet what really thinned the three battalions was that half-hour of close-quarter battle. One in every two fusiliers fell; the 2/7th in the centre fared worst, with 61 per cent casualties, like their counterparts in the centre of Hoghton's brigade. By the time that Werle's battalions turned and ran, more than 1,000 fusiliers lay scattered across the muddy plain.

The figures accumulate in the mind's eye into an appalling scene. A thousand fusiliers on the ground, 1,500 of Colborne's, another 1,000 of Hoghton's on top of 700 of Zayas' in the centre; 400 of Abercrombie's across the other side: say 1,000 corpses in all, and 3,000 maimed – and then there were the French... So many thousands, all in the space of a few football pitches – 'a heavy and nauseous smell... immense numbers of dead lying buried... the carcasses of both men and horses dragged into heaps and burned'. The anonymous redcoat who wrote that might perhaps have taken some heart had he heard Marshal Soult's bemused complaint 'They could not be persuaded they were beat... They were completely beat: the day was mine but they did not know it and would not run.'

*   *   *

Today we can take pride in that honourable mention-in-despatches from a gallant, defeated foe; but in May 1811 there was little preening, only relief at survival. As the extent of the losses became plain, and the story spread of the botched redeployment to face right, so too grew a sense of the poor generalship of the Allied army that day.

'Whore's ar Arthur?', Sergeant Cooper was asked by Private Horsefall as the Fusiliers marched forward: 'I said, "I don't know, I don't see him."' He rejoined, "Aw wish he wor here." So did I'. And so did many others.

11
Reflections

THE wounded Lieutenant John Harrison of the 23rd, writing two days after the battle from Elvas – and therefore out of touch with any news firmer than rumours – said: 'I cannot tell you which [army] was victorious, only that we gained the ground we fought on... both armies have suffered most dreadfully... we [the 1/23rd] lost about fifteen officers killed and wounded.' Two days later his critical faculties had kicked in, and he had no doubt been listening to later comers when he wrote to his mother quoting what were probably common views: 'Had we been brought into action sooner, the events might have been less disastrous to the brigade on our left... I believe every soldier did his duty but there is not much doubt a great want of generalship was evinced throughout the whole affair, otherwise our success must have been more complete.'

Tomkinson of the 16th Light Dragoons was a little more specific in his criticism: 'Considerable blame was attached to Beresford for the way he fought, having neglected to occupy the key to the position... Colonel D'Urban, QMG to Beresford, was the person who did everything... The Marshal lost his head when the enemy gained the hill, on which he was for an immediate retreat.' This is an interesting comment, since it is the second reference made by eyewitnesses to two aspects of Beresford's handling of the battle: that he (effectively) issued no orders, and that he lost his head and ordered a retreat.

John Mills of the 1/2nd (Coldstream) Guards, near Elvas, gave evidence of ripples on a wider scale when he wrote on 27 June:

> We are all here much surprised at the Vote of Thanks to Genl. Beresford – Good John Bull, how easily art thou duped. Genl. Beresford is the most noted bungler that ever played at the game of soldiers, and at Albuera he out-bungled himself. Lord Wellington riding over the ground a few days after with Beresford observed that there was one small oversight: that his right was where his left should have been.

This last is a curious but felicitous choice of words; it repeats the phrase attributed to Wellington by Charles Stewart, his Adjutant-General, following their doubtless thoughtful battlefield tour on 21 May. It appeared in a letter written by Stewart the following day to Lord Castlereagh:

> Beresford, on the evening of the 15th, seems not to have attempted to take up the ground in the manner which might have rendered it very formidable, but – like a Spanish army and officers – as the high road led from Albuera to Badajoz, he placed his army across it, as if this alone could stop the foe. From this period to the commencement of the battle, his right seems to have been placed where his left should have been.

Charles Stewart further commented that the highest points on the ridge should have had gun batteries installed, protected by earthworks; and Fortescue is convinced that this too came directly from Wellington's lips, for Charles Stewart 'is not likely to have thought of such a thing himself'.

John Mills' letter to his mother shows that Wellington's views were widely known, and therefore widely accepted as the prevailing judgement on Beresford's choice of the vital ground. We may be sure that the Military Secretary, FitzRoy Somerset, was echoing his master's voice when he wrote a week later to his brother that 'Beresford does not appear to have managed the battle with much skill'.

Nine months later, John Mills of the Coldstream was still writing venomously about Beresford: 'We passed over the field of Albuera. The numerous bones and remnants of jackets still tell the tale and I cannot help wondering that so nefarious a military delinquent should still wear his head, and regretting that it should be in the power of a fool to throw away the lives of 6,000 men. The ground he chose convicts him. He had the choice of two positions 200 yards distant from each other, chose the worst and lost his men in taking up the other after he had perceived his error.'

Having thus thrown a little mud at Marshal Beresford's generalship, we ought to attempt some formal assessment of his exceedingly bloody few hours at Albuera. Readers will bring their own views, which will vary between Beresford's having made the best of a bad job and being let down by others, through phrases such as 'inept but unlucky', to the more unequivocal condemnations inspired by William Napier, which go a good deal beyond accusations of mere blundering.

*   *   *

To begin with, we may consider Marshal Jean-de-Dieu Soult, Duke of Dalmatia, Colonel-General of the Imperial Guard – like Napoleon and Wellington, then aged forty-two years. He perfectly demonstrated at Albuera Lord Wellington's opinion that while well able to get his troops to battle, thereafter he left them lacking decisive leadership. There is no question but that Soult's rapid approach – over the Sierra Morena and up through Zafra and Santa Martha – left Beresford desperately short of time to close his formations on Albuera. There is still less to question in his plan of attack and his early execution of it, whether or not he was telling the truth when he said that he did not know Blake's Spaniards had joined. (Surely 12,000 men moving, in the dark, to the immediate left of his outposts on the Chicapierna, could not have gone unreported? – and they would anyway have been seen when they redeployed at first light.)

Whether Soult knew that he would be attacking Beresford's weakest formation, or truly thought that he was inserting himself between an unjoined Blake and Beresford, no matter: his early possession of the wooded slopes between the Chicapierna and the Nogales naturally hid an approach to the open southern plain, on which Latour-Maubourg's superiority could bear. Presented with that gift, he correctly judged that the road to Badajoz through Albuera village was fit only for a feint, and was very much second-best as the main assault axis. Soult made his feint successfully; Beresford necessarily reinforced Alten at the village; and Soult launched a left hook of huge force – 14,000 infantry and 3,500 horsemen. He got his guns well forward, and his cavalry, and Girard and Gazan's columns closed on that virtually empty ridge. Astonishingly, however, that effectively was that – the advance of the grand column seems to have marked the end of Soult's contribution to the battle.

There was his army, brilliantly arrived at the vulnerably open side door of Beresford's entire position. Not a bayonet, not a sabre, had yet stirred in an Allied hand to foil this unfolding masterpiece (it seems unduly critical to mention that Soult wasted four hours of daylight, following dawn at 3.30am). By all martial justice, the day should have been his: that huge mass, Werle following Gazan following Girard, three gun batteries shooting them in, three whole divisions 400 men wide, and in front of them – still not yet fully formed – all of four Spanish battalions. How could Soult have failed?

We cannot argue, as we do so often elsewhere, that it was again a question of the superiority of line over column. If Girard was truly formed in mixed order, as we are told by a French source, then three-quarters of his front – two battalions in three ranks – were advancing in line, with 900 presentable muskets; that is, Girard was already mostly deployed to produce musket volleys. The Spanish could indeed level more pieces – say 2,000 to his total 1,200; but the French column's ranks in depth were able to fire overhead. It looks as if the French point battalions just did not have it in them to press home their assault. This fits the sense one gets, as Colborne's battalions arrived and poured in their volleys and the bayonet charge, that Girard nearly gave way. The Vistula Lancers transformed that scenario; yet Girard failed to grasp his second opportunity, to come again. Hoghton thus had time to form and stabilize the chaos, while the grand column was re-ordered to bring Gazan's battalions to the front and take Girard's back. We do not know who decided on that manoeuvre, but presumably it had to be Soult himself, since it involved two divisions.

Neither do we know if it was at this stage that he learned from the Spanish prisoner that Blake had joined, and hence – the odds no longer being fair – 'I resolved at once to give up my original project, and to aim at nothing more than retaining the ground already won.' Presumably this passage in his Despatch is meant to explain his defeat: 'I thought I was attacking 20,000; if I had known they were 30,000, I wouldn't have attacked; on finding out, I stopped attacking and went on the defensive; unfortunately they were too many to hold.' Soult's subsequent lack of positive activity accords with such a change in approach, for thereafter nothing pro-active was done, either with his reserve or his cavalry. Yet had he ventured either force during that dreadful half-hour before Myers marched, the day must have been his. Soult stands accused, therefore, of not reading the battle, of missing his opportunity; and thus, he did not deserve to win.

But then, neither did Beresford. If they were boxers, Soult in the blue corner had the nifty footwork and a strong left hook, and had battered and dazed his opponent, who was about to fall. The least push would do; but Soult did not push. The man in the red corner, of course, must also be considered: with his extra weight, and having had ample time to study the ring, how did he come to such a pass, where a half-decent jab would have floored him? We will first deal with the school of thought that holds – to continue the boxing analogy – that he was let down by his seconds.

Our perhaps over-lengthy paragraphs on whether or nor Robert Long fell back too quickly from Santa Martha, and thereby prevented a planned occupation by Beresford's infantry of the wooded slopes opposite the Albuera ridge, reached no conclusion other than that Long's celerity made him a convenient scapegoat. D'Urban's Report says that Alten's and Stewart's formations came forward from Valverde on the morning of the 15th, and were in position about noon; and that Long's cavalry rode in, all hot and bothered, at 'about three o'clock.. rather more briskly than had been looked for'. He continues that when Beresford returned in due course from his reconnaissance, he 'found that [the enemy] had already crossed the rivulet [the Nogales] and that the whole of the opposite bank was in possession of... the enemy... This mistake once made, it was too late to repair it.'

But what about the three hours between noon and 3pm? Surely occupying the woods further out should have come before putting Alten into the nearby, closely-observed village? In *Further Strictures*, as we have seen, D'Urban said 'This, I understand, had been intended... whoever was to blame for it, this was certainly an omission'. It sounds very much like a simple omission by a careless staff officer.

Yet did it really matter – could infantry occupying those woods have denied them to Soult when his own infantry closed up? Surely not for long; and to what purpose? Instead, since Soult used those woods merely as temporary cover, and the ground was not vital in its own right, it would have been far better to breach the cover by deploying cavalry outposts to spy and report on the type and numbers of French troops behind it, and when they looked like moving. But there are no accounts of any such reconnaissances. The first report mentioned arrived at 8am on the 16th, more than four hours after first light, when the 13th Light Dragoons saw the French cross the river. Not for the first time, Robert Long attracted more odium than he deserved.

Joachim Blake, on the other hand, is a general who definitely let his ally down, and nobody has a good word for him. The following extract from D'Urbans's Report points the official finger:

> These dispositions were promptly and precisely carried into effect, with the exception of that of General Blake, whose delay in executing it had very nearly led to the most fatal consequences; for so much time had been lost, that instead of being prepared upon the ground he was to hold, his troops had scarcely placed themselves there when the enemy fell upon them... Even late as it was, Sir William Beresford was obliged to move and post them in person, no orders having been sent to that effect by General Blake, who impressed with an idea that the real attack was upon the centre, took upon himself to delay the execution of the first order he received to front to his right, and sent to Sir William Beresford to say so; thus losing nearly half-an-hour of time that was very precious.

It has been fairly said, however, that Lord Wellington – had he been in command – would not have sent the order to Blake and then disappeared north to talk with General Hamilton, but would himself have taken Blake precisely to his ground, and pointed it out, and watched the deployment get under way. Surely the priority, if one can only do one thing at a time, is to do that which has primary importance while sending others with orders to cover secondary needs. Blake was clearly deluded and a menace, and just possibly scared enough to want someone else to fill that right-hand slot; but the half-hour would not have been lost if Beresford had been on the spot, instead of relying upon, but not supervising, a Spanish general.

Strangely, the third general said to have let Beresford down – William Stewart – also did so apparently in Beresford's absence elsewhere. (We must therefore be thankful that the next - fourth – time Beresford went absent at the vital time and place, General Cole had the strength of character to take responsibility for the necessary decision himself.)

Stewart's crime was to deploy his division 'on the hoof', as it were, one brigade at a time, and in the case of his first (Colborne's) brigade, one battalion at a time. His orders were to form his division behind Zayas, in a second line; upon completion of that deployment he was to move through the Spanish units. It is a little unclear whether he had discretion over stepping forward in line, or whether Beresford himself was to set the 2nd Division off. Stewart was accused, in the absence of Beresford (said to be bringing up more Spaniards to aid Zayas), of going straight into the attack piecemeal with his first brigade, and compounding his excess zeal by not allowing Colborne to get his battalions in line; Stewart took them forward in column, before deploying into line literally as they came in contact. Further, Stewart then denied Colborne's second request to keep his right battalion in column or square, to guard against the cavalry that they knew were somewhere to the right, hidden by the smoke and rain.

Defenders of Stewart say that sight of the exposed French flank, and the terminal state of the Spanish line, justified the immediate launch of Colborne without Beresford's word; and also that having Hoghton and Abercrombie in line to the left was anyway irrelevant to seizing that flank opportunity. The author has attempted, however, to show cause to doubt that Stewart's attack *was* on the flank, bar probably five companies of the Buffs: Oman (and all who have come after) for some reason turned Major Brooke's words 'the *heads* of the French columns returned the fire three deep, the front rank kneeling' into 'the two battalions in column... *faced outwards*... three deep, the front rank kneeling'. So if the fleeting opportunity for a flank attack was not, in the event, seized anything like fully by Stewart, his piecemeal deployment is even less justified; and certainly, there can be no defence for refusing Colborne his change of formation to defend against cavalry. A measure of guilt can perhaps be detected in the letter Stewart wrote the next day to Beresford:

> You are probably aware, Sir, that the 1st Brigade was suddenly attacked in flank and rear by a body of the enemy's cavalry, while it was engaged in the most desperate effort of charging the whole of the attacking force of the enemy. The form of the hill up which that brigade was so ably led to the charge by its commander, and the obscurity occasioned by the smoke of musketry and a heavy squall of rain, prevented the enemy's cavalry from being either seen or sufficiently early resisted.

(So please don't blame Colborne or me; blame the weather and unexpected musket smoke.)

Stewart had bad luck; he saw an opportunity as well as a desperate need, but what he did not see was his commanding general. Again, at the crucial moment, Beresford was somewhere else. So Stewart showed initiative – that quality above all that riflemen treasure and act upon. Unfortunately, its proper reward was blotted out by hail and rain – for without the elements, the Vistula Lancers would have received a far warmer welcome.

*   *   *

It is time to turn to command faults of varying seriousness, but which may confidently be laid at Beresford's own doorstep.

The first in time was his surprising lack of urgency at the outset. The cavalry's being sent off to forage at an inappropriate period could have been on the orders of a staff officer; the movement order to Cole outside Badajoz was not, and it was sent too late. Taken together, if Soult had launched his attack an hour or so earlier (and with first light at 3.30am, Soult's 7.30am start scarcely suggests that he was up with the lark), then the shallow valley behind the Albuera position would have been empty of Lumley and Cole, and

Latour-Maubourg would instantly have been on the Valverde road. It was a curious decision to tell Cole not to march before 2am on the morning of 16 May. Fusiliers having at last to 'run to the sound of the guns' has a somewhat amateurish ring to it; no wonder they missed 'our Atty'.

Beresford's most serious misuse of time, however, also occurred before contact. We have castigated Blake for the near-fatal loss of half-an-hour in getting Zayas to face right; but this was as nothing compared to the delay in ordering Blake to change face in the first place. We know that Beresford's appreciation was that Soult would attack the village, to secure the roads to Badajoz and Valverde, and we know that the Allied formations were deployed accordingly. The decisions based on this appreciation then seemed to become irrevocable; presented with intelligence suggesting that they were wrong and now inappropriate (the 13th Light Dragoons' 8am report), Beresford's staff did nothing for well over an hour. It was as if the intelligence was just not acceptable to an inflexible mindset, and therefore need not be acted upon. It took the appearance of Zayas' ADC an hour and a half after the fighting in the village began, reporting the flash of approaching bayonets on the right, to galvanize Bereford at last. His lengthy lethargy is surprisingly excused by Oman, who refers to 'this unexpected flank attack'; and also by Fortescue, when he generously states that 'the enemy's true intentions were now evident'. The rush thereafter – the redeployment of guns, cavalry and brigades of infantry, from the village, to the village, along the ridge, across the ridge, and into the valley behind – these are not measured acts of generalship, but panicky stop-gaps.

Beresford should have turned back his right flank immediately he received the 13th Light Dragoons' report, and faced south; but something stopped him. Whatever it was, it led to the death and maiming of a very great number of his men, and for this they were to judge him a blunderer. His fixation with the Albuera–Valverde, Albuera–Badajoz roads was the root cause of his apparent reluctance to shift. It was the reason for his initial deployment, and for the emphasis on what he saw as the key feature – the so-called Conical Hill. That feature and the slopes around it stopped both egress from the village and access to the Badajoz and Valverde roads; but it was irrelevant to any approach from the south – Soult's choice, against which Beresford had failed to insure himself by thorough reconnaissance. Beresford's Despatch admits that 'the heights the enemy had gained raked and entirely commanded our whole position'. As John Mills said, 'The ground he chose convicts him. He had the choice of two positions two hundred yards distant from each other, chose the worst, and lost his men in taking up the other after he had perceived his error.' In fact rather more than 200 yards, but essentially that is a correct summary; and it is one Lord Wellington shared, since he later wrote 'all the loss sustained by the troops was incurred in regaining a height which ought never for a moment to have been in possession of the enemy'.

It is said – via Charles Stewart – that Wellington would have kept his line hidden behind the ridge, with batteries on the crest protected from cavalry by earthworks. That assumes, of course, a red line of 'that astonishing infantry' – in other words, that Wellington would never have attempted to defend his vulnerable flank with troops renowned for their inability to manoeuvre; one certainly suspects that he would have had Hamilton on his right, rather than Blake. Beresford seems to have chosen to keep Blake on his right flank merely because it was adjacent to the Spanish approach route from Almendral, and could be reached without marching across the front of any other formation. His decision reinforces the view that he saw the right flank as safe from Soult.

We now come to the grim situation of Hoghton's shrinking brigade, and the desperate search for support. We can only conjecture about the scene: Beresford failing to get D'España's three battalions forward to plug the gap; sending to Hamilton for a Portuguese brigade, without success; then, supposing 'some mistake must have occurred, proceeded to the rear to discover the cause... Beresford's anxiety was very great'. Indeed; but D'Urban tells us that *before* he went back, he saw Cole move forward, which 'movement hurried him there. It occasioned him the greatest alarm and anxiety... Why, he had at this instant 12,000 troops who had not fired a musket, and who were infinitely nearer to the scene of action than that [4th] Division.'

Then why did Beresford not stop Cole? There surely was ample warning; after Cole conferred with Lumley, the 4th Division had to be reconfigured, with Harvey's Lusitanian Legion crossing to the left of Myers' brigade, whose light companies crossed singly to the right to reform as the new flank battalion; each of the other six battalions would necessarily adjust their spacing, to allow the approach-march columns room to deploy eventually into line. Surely these manoeuvres and their implication could not have escaped notice by Beresford's staff? – his headquarters was less than a mile away, up a bare slope.

One thing is certain: not even Beresford's 'great alarm' as to the survival of his 2nd Division had proved enough for him to order the 4th Division to their rescue, and it had to be done for him by Henry Hardinge – a mere major. His own reluctance to commit his reserve in those dire circumstances strongly suggests that Beresford regarded Cole's batalions as other than a usable reserve, and in some way untouchable. Because they blocked the Valverde road? When he saw with 'the greatest alarm and anxiety' that they were on the move, at Hardinge's instigation, was he overwhelmed by the fear that all might be lost, and that he must move Alten and Dickson back to cover a retreat? It is otherwise hard to credit that a commander would ride away to the rear at such a moment. He denied ordering a retreat, of course; but that was the widespread opinion among his officers, who moreover believed that he did so because he had 'lost his head' – one of the most demeaning accusations any English officer could level at another.

Somebody – Pakenham? – said scathingly that Beresford was an anxious man. The drawing by Heaphy in the National Portrait Gallery, thought to be an excellent likeness (though it conceals his dead eye), confirms that view quite stunningly: here, surely, is a man under stress, apprehensively looking out for the next problem to be thrown at him. All his military life – twenty-six years – William Beresford had served under a higher authority. Latterly that was Lord Wellington, until only two months ago, when in Hill's absence he was given independent command and detached south from the Field Army. Few armchair generals would care for such a role, especially if answerable to Wellington of all people. He would naturally be anxious to do well, to gain his approval; and the author believes that in William Beresford's case this anxiety excessively coloured the decisions he made throughout his detachment.

His generalship as a result became, effectively, incompetent, because he became averse to taking what he saw as risks; caution is not, of course, necessarily a bad trait, but it is often inappropriate in a general whose role is to take the fight to the enemy. War, as Wolfe noted, is choice between difficulties, and things go wrong. The competent rise above misfortune, or turn it to their own advantage. It seems that Beresford's caution led his imagination to foresee trouble at every turn, and persuaded him to fight shy.

We can see elements of some of the above, firstly, in Beresford's unwillingness to use Grey's dragoon brigade on the road to Badajoz, after it was plain that he had – without firing a shot – achieved his aim of capturing Campo Mayor. It is true that since his arrival forced Latour-Maubourg to quit the town, he really had no need to do more. But Brigadier Long and Colonel Head got involved, successfully, and had a right to expect to be seconded; a little effort on Beresford's part would have been enough to put the 100e Ligne neatly in the bag, to say nothing of Latour-Maubourg himself. But he would not make that effort because – as he admitted – of the perceived risk to Grey's horsemen. A far more important example of this caution, in keeping the 4th Division out of battle at Albuera, very nearly proved catastrophic. Beresford's seeming obsession with the possibility of retreat, and his tactical reluctance to deploy far from his line of retreat, suggest that he was in fear of the ultimate failure of collective capture. It was very nearly a classic example of a man's guarding his back door so persistently that he lets the burglar in the front.

A half-brother to risk-aversion is disinclination to change a plan once it is settled, and therefore a tendency to ignore any intelligence that arises later if it casts doubt upon the wisdom of the plan. This results in passivity or lack of urgency in prosecuting events, and a preference for reacting to them. In seriously anxious people the fear of failure is never far away, and their mantra is 'Whatever you do may be wrong, so do very little'. At Albuera, Beresford's slowness to react to early signs of the French southern hook, by ordering Blake to re-form right, was also near-fatal. The battle against the French 5th Corps would have been entirely different if Stewart's 2nd Division had been waiting in a well-settled second line behind Blake. But Beresford was convinced that Albuera village and his precious road past the Conical Hill were the target, and it suited his retreat plan to sit across that road. He did not want Soult to attack Blake, because it upset his plan; therefore the 8am report that a strong force of infantry had crossed the river must be wrong, or certainly not to be acted upon hastily, without confirmation in due course – confirmation that he made no attempt to obtain. Beresford was in denial.

His general defensiveness, born of anxiety, is evidenced not only by the scapegoating of Robert Long (not without some small cause), but overwhelmingly by the bitter paper warfare that he waged in later years. The voluminous writings in response to Napier's charges, and to the accusations of Brigadier Long's nephew, Charles Long, have to be read to be believed. They would not have emanated from a secure and balanced man. It is laughable – beyond laughable – to think of Lord Wellington ever descending to such a level; but neither is it credible of Thomas Graham, say, or Rowland Hill. Wellington himself acknowledged his lieutenant's weakness when writing in December 1812 to Lord Bathurst: 'They tell me that when I am not present, he wants [lacks] decision; and he certainly embarrassed me a little with his doubts when he commanded in Estremadura.' However, throughout the rest of the campaigns in Spain, Wellington continued to regard Beresford as his successor; the latter's proven competence when dealing at government level was unique among Wellington's generals, and it seems clear that he was quite a different officer when acting under his master's orders. In that letter to Bathurst, Wellington also said 'I am quite certain that he is the only person capable of conducting a large concern.' But had Lord Wellington had been killed, and had Beresford taken command, would his doubts have diminished, or multiplied? Thankfully, that remains an academic question.

*   *   *

This sad catalogue of Beresford's faults as a field commander is in stark contrast to the impressively soldierly qualities shown by his men. Beresford did indeed not deserve to win, any more than Soult; yet both marshals led amazingly robust armies, who stood toe-to-toe for hours, exchanging death and hideous wounds without wavering, despite the constant visual evidence of the dreadful, inevitable attrition scything through their thinning ranks. Survivors of that day's work knew they were lucky men. The subsequent burning and burying of stripped and bloating corpses would continue to remind them of it for the next three days, while the routine muster parades rubbed in just how few they were. And not a man who had stood in that Allied line would doubt that the affair had been mismanaged. 'Oh, old 29th, I am sorry to see so many of you here!' said Lord Wellington to some wounded Worcesters in the hospital at Elvas; 'Oh, my Lord, if you had only been with us, there would not have been so many of us here!'

It has often been asked why, about a hundred years later on the Somme, men went 'over the top' to certain death. Albuera has faded far into the past, so nobody now asks why the Worcesters or the Buffs or the Northamptons stood their ground, and faced a similarly certain death from grapeshot or shell or ball. The collective spirit necessary for such resilience sprang not from belief in the cause of their country, nor from fear of the consequences of running – and certainly they did not fight for Marshal Beresford. They stood together as they had marched together, a regimental family wearing a special numbered badge and their own coloured jacket-facings. For two years they had marched many miles through Spain and Portugal, enduring the grilling sun and the freezing nights, the rains and the hunger; and in that time they had got to know one another. The infantry company – of sixty or so men, one captain, two subalterns, some older sergeants and corporals (and plenty more of both busted back to private) – all pulled as a team. Mix them up in a crowd, and they would seek to find one another, and congregate together. The same applied to the battalion, of which they were a tenth part; and often it was helped by the character of their leaders.

The officers of all ages – from Major Brookes at sixty-six, to a squeaky-voiced fifteen-year-old ensign – were set apart from their men by class, education and relative wealth. In home barracks they were distant figures, but on campaign they were a daily presence, and they shared almost all the hardships of their men. Company officers enjoyed – at best – a horse, a pack mule, a batman and a soldier servant; but those privileges did not keep off the sun, rain and snow, or make the rocky roads any smoother, or ward off disease. A purse of silver might buy private rations in well-provisioned towns, but they spent much of every year far from such places. Above all, neither rank nor wealth moved aside the path of a bullet or sabre. True, it was still very much an age of social deference (on our side of the Channel); but soldiers made a simple demand in return – an officer had to be physically fearless in performing his duty. As long as he stood his ground to give encouraging leadership in battle, then they asked little more; if he gave more, in terms of a decent care for his men's welfare, then they repaid it with loyalty, even affection. Their own words make clear that they did not regard flogging, in itself as an instrument of tyranny, so long as punishment was inflicted in accordance with their sense of natural justice. Stern discipline was accepted provided that it was not applied by martinets in a mean or 'nagging' spirit. The rare officer who was a dithering coward or a mean spirited slave-driver might have reason to fear for his chances of survival in a confused firefight but in any case, the mores of the officer class ensured that such men seldom lasted long in fighting battalion.

Within the ingrained customs of social distance, good officers were regarded as father-figures, and teenage ensigns as younger brother-figures. Infantry regiments were (and still are) largely family-officered, in those days by the land-owning gentry and squires of the county; aristocrats were rare in Line regiments. Fathers, sons and brothers commonly served together, or successively; this was naturally well known by the soldiers, and well taken. It showed that their officers thought highly enough of their regiment – theirs, not any other – to devote their lives to serving in it. A man can enjoy no greater and more pleasurable compliment than that his son should wish to follow in his footsteps, and it showed to the soldiers another aspect of that regimental spirit that bound all together. In my own regiment in the Peninsula – the 48th – there soldiered together the three Brookes, three Donellans, the Johnstone brothers, the Peacockes, Tonyns, Wemys, Bells, Erskines, Gibbs, Donovans and Morrisons, and no less than five Campbells. The sense of desirable continuity thus shown by their leaders strengthened the soldiers' belief that they were part of something good, and this powerful sense of belonging was embodied by the Colours. Often this proud family spirit was celebrated, when out of the line, by inter-regimental brawling and competitiveness. In battle it became a determination to win, and what other regiments did or did not do was their own affair.

At Albuera, where something had obviously gone deadly wrong, this regimental spirit was what kept the men shuffling sideways towards the Colours, stepping over the groaning, bloody gaps; it kept the right hand going down for another cartridge; it kept them facing front. For it had come down to a very simple proposition – to the life and good name of their Regiment – and so long as they could see from the corner of their eye the Colours still flying, they must endure. As individuals, they could not possibly let down the regimental family; and it was that spirit which won them the great battle at Albuera.

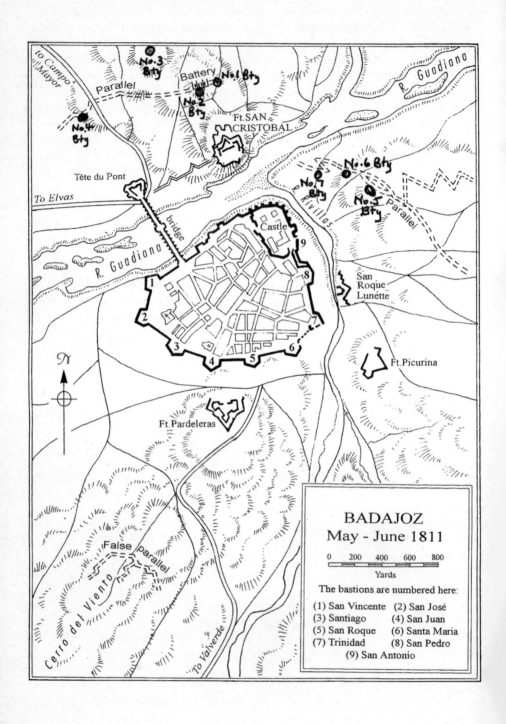

to Campo Mayor

Parallel

No.3 Bty

Battery   No.1 Bty

No.2 Bty

Ft.SAN CRISTOBAL

No.4 Bty

R. Guadiana

No.6 Bty

Tête du Pont

No.7 Bty   R. Rivillos   No.5 Bty

To Elvas

Parallel

bridge

R. Guadiana

Castle

9

8

San Roque Lunette

1

2

3   4   5   6   7

Ft.Picurina

N

Ft.Pardeleras

False parallel

Cerro del Viento

To Valverde

BADAJOZ
May – June 1811

0   200   400   600   800
Yards

The bastions are numbered here:

(1) San Vincente   (2) San José
(3) Santiago   (4) San Juan
(5) San Roque   (6) Santa Maria
(7) Trinidad   (8) San Pedro
        (9) San Antonio

12
Back to Badajoz,
29 May–5 June

IT is unclear whether William Beresford suffered some sort of breakdown after the battle. A month later his principal ADC, Major William Warre, wrote to his father that 'The Marshal is somewhat better, though he will require some time of quiet body and mind to put him quite right again'. The 'and mind' is perhaps the telling phrase. A week later there is another reference to the need for rest 'of both body and mind'; while five months later 'He requires in his present state every indulgence... still very weak... His complaint is a low fever and great debility, which has been hanging about him for some months' – in other words, ever since Albuera. Debility speaks possibly of a mental state, but the protective Warre does not enlarge.

Six days after he saw the field of battle, that is on 27 May, Lord Wellington relieved Beresford of the command of his southern wing, taking it himself while Rowland Hill was on the final stage of his journey back from England; only four days later, on 31 May, Hill was in turn given command both of his old 2nd Division and, as in the past, the overall command of the rest of this detached wing – the 4th Division, Alten's small brigade of the KGL, and Lumley's cavalry. It is curious that Wellington chose not to leave Beresford undisturbed in the command for those four days, unless he had real concerns for his deputy's fitness. So Beresford left for Lisbon, and the quieter challenges of the Portuguese Army's paperwork. Or, as Wellington had put it to Liverpool: 'I must confine Beresford to the management of the detail of the Portuguese army.'

Wellington reckoned that he had a month to take Badajoz, no more. Soult was limping slowly away south towards the Sierra Morena. He could realistically come back only when reinforced from Sebastiani and Victor, and that would not be soon. He had sent Gazan with a brigade to escort the wounded, separately, to Seville; his own force was therefore down to just 14,000 men. They had reached near to Llerena by 22 May; by that date the exhausted British 2nd and 4th Divisions, and Baron Alten, had only got to Villalba and Fuente del Maestre, 8,000 strong and with Lumley's cavalry out ahead. Hamilton's and Collins' Portuguese had gone the other way, to gather around Badajoz once more and cover the southern approach to the fortress. The 3rd and 7th Divisions marched down to Badajoz the following week, the latter investing the north bank and the former joining the Portuguese. Some 14,000 men now prepared to test Governor Phillipon once more, and ground was broken on 29 May. The news of the return of the British, much reinforced, to the siege of the fortress, was the final proclamation to the world and to his Emperor of Soult's defeat at Albuera: that he had not achieved his purpose of relieving Badajoz.

Lord Wellington had left General Brent Spencer as his watchkeeper of the northern frontier around Ciudad Rodrigo, with the 1st, 5th, 6th and Light Divisions, and two Portuguese brigades – some 26,000 infantry and nearly 2,000 horse. It was nearly impossible that after

Fuentes d'Oñoro on 5 May the new French commander, Marshal Marmont, could move the bruised Army of Portugal one foot in front of another for several weeks. Nonetheless, Wellington had left Spencer (as we might expect) detailed instructions, listing his actions should the impossible happen. Lord Wellington was no doubt mindful of the surprisingly quick riposte made by Massena after Sabugal, as well as of the limits to Spencer's natural military skills – which no-one regarded highly.

Unsure of the Allies' intent, and thus how far he need withdraw, Soult sought information on his pursuing enemy's progress by sending Latour-Maubourg and his cavalry division back up the Badajoz road. This force of around 3,000 sabres in ten regiments, together with a field battery, was far too powerful to be intended simply to reconnoitre the opposition, and was surely sent with aggressive intent. It bumped two squadrons of Penne-Villemur's Spaniards (commanded temporarily by Loy) on advanced piquet near Villa Garcia, and pushed them back 5 miles to Usagre, where they came upon Lumley. And there the British cavalry proceeded to arrange as nice an affair as could be wished, particularly since the players are our friends from Campo Mayor and Los Santos (although this time we are spared too much involvement by Robert Long): the 3rd Dragoon Guards, 4th Dragoons, 13th Light Dragoons, and Otway's and Madden's Portuguese horse.

*   *   *

This action was what Oman called 'the most satisfactory of its kind that the British horse in the Peninsula had been engaged in since the combats of Sahagun and Benavente', and Fortescue, 'altogether a pretty little fight'. It is Ian Fletcher, however, who gets nearer the point when he writes in his *Galloping at Everything* that 'The action at Usagre is a wonderful example of the planning and execution of a trap, the likes of which the British cavalry have generally been accused of being incapable of mounting.' Here we see rare evidence of British cavalry brainpower, exercised for once alongside their customary brawn and dash. At a cost of just twenty casualties, Lumley took prisoner six officers (including a colonel) and seventy-two men, and killed and wounded more than 250. This joyful result added yet another to the growing list of triumphant tales for his subalterns and troopers to chuckle over around their evening campfires, armouring their confidence for the next time they faced French horse.

Usagre has a stream on its north edge, running along a steep-sided ravine. A bridge takes the Badajoz road out of town through a walled lane, and over a low ridge 200 yards away. The approach to the bridge, the bridge itself and the exit defile are all narrow, the former being the town's main street. The river is fordable about a mile away on each flank. All this Lumley had noted on the previous evening, and the potential of the position did not escape him.

Hearing of the approach of the French, he withdrew the 3rd Dragoon Guards and 4th Dragoons behind the ridge, and sent forward over the eastern ford Otway's Portuguese – four weak regiments totalling only some 850 men – and Head's 13th Light Dragoons with another 400 sabres, while over the western ford he sent Madden's Portuguese – all to join up with Loy's Spanish horse. When the French horse artillery opened up on them, Loy withdrew through the town and the others over their fords, to disappear behind the ridge. Seeing this, and eyeing the rather cramped way forward over the river bridge, Latour-Maubourg prudently decided first to turn the Allies' flank, beyond the ridge. He sent Briche's brigade of light horse to the right, to cross at Otway's eastern ford and get behind him; when this had been achieved his other three brigades would advance straight up the middle.

Unfortunately for him, when Briche, with the 10e Hussards and 21e Chasseurs to hand, found Otway ready to dispute what looked like a fairly defendable crossing place, he passed on eastwards in search of another – but without sending back a progress report to his general. Briche failed to cross, and got further entangled when he stubbornly pressed on through rougher going. After an hour had slipped away Latour-Maubourg could wait no longer. Assuming that Briche by now must be somewhere on the other side of the river, he ordered Bron's dragoons – the 4e, 20e and 26e – to pass through the town and over the bridge.

The 4e and 20e reached the open ground beyond the river, the 4e leading – 400 strong and forming line, at the halt, a little to the right. The 20e Dragons crossed behind them in column, and were coming up their left side, not quite 300 strong, preparatory to forming line themselves. In another several minutes they would have the 26e in rear, as second line, and could set off in good and proper order to climb the slope, find the enemy, and join Briche in a satisfactory day's work. It was at this moment that Lumley's glorious trap yawned open in front of an appalled Latour-Maubourg.

Beyond the skyline 200 yards in front a growing thunder first attracted their ears; there then rose over the crest 700 raised right arms in red sleeves, holding aloft glittering blades, then 700 horsemen pouring down the slope towards the startled Frenchmen. To cover 200 yards at a decent canter takes all of thirty seconds; there was scarcely time to take a shorter rein and tug out the sabre. The 4th Dragoons raced appropriately straight for the French 4e, the 3rd Dragoon Guards curling in on their left just as the French 20e were starting to form line. Seven hundred against 650 was an even match, but one side was stationary while the other had rushing impetus; the clash bowled the French over and down and back, straight on to the lead squadron of Latour-Maubourg's 26e Dragons, who were just beginning to file across the bridge. All was chaos around the blocked bridge as the red coats closed on the crowd of green, forcing the French tighter and tighter like a pack of hounds cornering their fox, cutting away. Others chased fugitives who were fleeing along the river bank in desperate but vain search of any place to cross; others still were already starting to escort back their prisoners, or catching loose horses – and there were plenty of those for the taking, as many Frenchmen flung themselves out of the saddle to make their escape across the ravine on foot.

Latour-Maubourg could do nothing. Dismounting troopers to fire their carbines across the river made some impression, but with the Portuguese and Spanish by now joining in the French only managed to clear the bridge when they eventually brought artillery to bear. In turn, however, Lumley successfully deployed Lefebure's troop of six 6-pounders, to trump the French gunners and round it off. Charles Madden rode with the 4th Dragoons:

> We charged them with great rapidity, having a good descent in our favour; we broke them with the shock and they retired in the greatest confusion. Those in front of the 3rd endeavoured to get over the wall, and were nearly to a man cut down or taken prisoners; the 4th cut them down in the lane leading to the bridge, till it was blocked up with men and horses. Numbers made their escape by leaping off their horses and getting over a high wall into an olive grove.

It had been perfectly timed. It is clear that Lumley had his two regiments lined up ready on the reverse slope, in splendid imitation of Wellington's infantry tactics. There was, however, some question that only one regiment was meant to go forward initially – predictably Robert Long shoved his oar into the tale; but this time we will pass over Long, and settle happily for

Lumley's summary in his report that it was 'a simultaneous movement, directed most judiciously by the Brigadier-General... it decided the point.' It certainly did; the trivial cost of twenty casualties indicates the complete extent of Lumley's little victory. He had taken out the equivalent of three squadrons – nearly a regiment's worth of good horsemen. Once again, French cavalry had been bested; and the 4th Queen's Own Dragoons had the rare treat of charging and overturning the Emperor Napoleon's 4th Dragoons – a feat rightly celebrated by the regiment for many years to come.

Latour-Maubourg now knew who he was up against: the reconnaissance in force was not repeated, and Usagre was as far as he was to get for a couple of weeks.

*   *   *

Seventy-five miles away, up the main road at Elvas, Lord Wellington was contemplating the odds. That same day Houston's 7th Division had reached the northern approaches to Badajoz. Governor Phillipon's stores held but a fortnight's normal rations, which would only stretch so far, and an early attempt at relief could be expected. Marmont's Army of Portugal was coming to the end of its major reorganization after Massena's retreat following Fuentes, and could soon hit the road with some 28,000 bayonets and 2,500 horse; Soult might gather another 25,000 – a formidable combination. On 29 May, Lord Wellington wrote to his brother Henry: 'We break ground at Badajoz tomorrow, and we hope to get the place in a few days. If we do not succeed in a few days, we shall not succeed at all, as the seventeen or nineteen battalions and some cavalry of the 9th Corps are on their march to join Soult, and I think will reach him by the second week in June.'

Two days later and 200 miles away around Salamanca, Marmont indeed gave his chief lieutenant General Reynier five divisions and sent him south via the pass at Banos, while he himself went west to resupply Ciudad Rodrigo, terrify Brent Spencer around Almeida, and then turn south via the pass of Perales.

But that anticipates events at Badajoz, where it was already plain that, just as three weeks earlier, the capture of the fortress would have to be another rushed job in the face of an approaching relief force. At least this second try progressed – twice – to the stage of infantry actually attempting the breaches before time ran out; and their 500 casualties would be only a pale foreshadowing of the hellish events that would be revealed by the morning light of 7 April 1812.

It all would turn on the guns. Alexander Dickson again had to rely on the seventeenth century museum pieces from the walls of Elvas. Perhaps quantity could make up for quality: this time he provided twice as many – thirty brass 24-pounders with 600 rounds of ammunition, four 16-pounders with 300 rounds, four 10in howitzers with 200 shells each, and eight 8in with 350 shells each. Over a week's repair work was necessary, however, since the previous journey back from Badajoz had seen the carriages damaged; consequently Dickson could not get his convoy assembled until 29 May, and even then six iron ships' guns from Lisbon were still en route. He also had twice as many gunners this time, 500 Portuguese and a 100-strong British artillery company from Lisbon (brought forward the last 25 miles at the best speed of a mounted mule convoy). Dickson, using the sort of cheerful language proper when writing to a gunner general at Woolwich, declared himself 'very sanguine of success', as his convoy rumbled and squeaked its way to the two depots set up on either side of the river. He knew only too well that the ancient brass cannon would inevitably droop their barrel after prolonged firing, that vent holes would blow, and that ill-fitting balls would wobble unpredictably up too-large bores, but what other choice did he have? His sapper opposite number, Captain John Jones, committed the understatement of the year to his journal on 22 May, when he wrote 'The experience of the late attack... created considerable doubts of the sufficiency of the Portuguese brass ordnance for the meditated operation.'

On the engineering side, Lieutenant-Colonel Fletcher had twenty of his own Corps' officers, with eleven volunteer assistants from the Line battalions, together with 265 infantrymen doubling as carpenters and general labourers – there were only twenty-five real sappers present. Fletcher stockpiled 3,500 picks and shovels, 60,000 sandbags, and 600 each of gabions and fascines. Where the ground was too hard to dig, filled gabion baskets and sandbags would, in theory, absorb solid shot; but in practice they were only as good as they were hard-packed in the first place – and tired infantrymen hate shovelling soil. Unfortunately, on the rocky surface north of Fort San Cristobal the soil had already been removed by the active Governor Phillipon's working parties, in anticipation that the British might try the same approach again.

He was right, and for the same reason: the British lacked time for any other way. An unhurried textbook approach to the southern walls was the guaranteed solution which no-one disputed, and the uncertain prospects of another hurried attempt on Fort San Cristobal were something to be accepted only with gritted teeth. The theory was that with the fort on the north bank of the Guadiana in British hands, the castle 500 yards away across the river was ultimately untenable; under immediate dropping fire from the guns then to be sited at San Cristobal, the old Moorish walls were likely to be breached after only three or four days' battering. Captain John Jones summed it up in his journal: 'Fort Cristobal being reduced, and powerful batteries erected in and near it, no body of troops could stand in the castle for the defence of a breach in its walls' without a great deal of work and expenditure of time. Further, the castle walls were 'apparently of very bad masonry.'

This begged a number of questions. What lay under the visible masonry? What was the guarantee that Dickson could provide the necessary 'powerful batteries'? And before these questons even arose, what about the rocky site for the guns of the besiegers of San Cristobal, and the time required to blast out the requisite firing platforms? On these erroneously optimistic assumptions the sappers pressed their solution on Lord Wellington who, within the fortnight, was to regret what his Despatch self-critically described as 'entertaining a belief that the means of which I had the command would reduce the place before the end of the second week of June... [but] I was unfortunately mistaken in my estimate of the quality of these means' – or more truly, but unspoken, the quality of his sappers' and gunners' mistaken estimates.

The plan was to be an improved version of the earlier attempt, revised particularly in that the artillery assault on the castle walls should commence alongside that on San Cristobal rather than being dependent upon its prior capture; in this way Phillipon's response would be divided rather than concentrated. There would again be a false attack on Fort Pardaleras. Further, given the greater quantity of pieces, there should this time be counter-battery fire in concert with a heavier fire upon the breaches. Finally, the three batteries immediately north of San Cristobal were to be linked by a parallel trench, to prevent any repetition of the significant previous losses to a French sortie: this time the batteries would be properly protected by covering troops *in situ*. These would be provided by Houston's 7th Division, the 17th Portuguese Line and two Portuguese militia regiments, while the castle would be the objective for Picton's 3rd and Hamilton's Portuguese divisions: some 5,000 men for the fort, and twice that for the castle (and – given success – for clearing the town). Picton had arrived from Fuentes by easy marches, and Ensign William Grattan, whom we last saw leading his company of the 1/88th in the critical counter-attack into that village, tells us that:

> The 28th, 29th and 30th [May] were taken up in marking out our camp, and constructing huts; and as the weather was beautiful, and our camp abundantly supplied by the peasantry, we passed a very agreeable time of it. The river ran within a few yards of us; its marshy banks being thickly covered with plantations of olives, afforded a delightful shade to us when we either went to fish or bathe. Its breadth at this point might be about sixty *toises* [paces], and it is well stocked with fine mullet. We had expected several expert fishermen amongst us, and they contrived not only to supply their own tables with fish, but also to increase the comforts of their friends.

We shall hear further from the eighteen-year-old Connaught Ranger; for now it suffices to quote his heartfelt comments on the infantryman's dislike of siegework: 'There is no duty which a British soldier performs before the enemy that he does with so much reluctance – a retreat excepted – as working in trenches... an inglorious calling... full of danger... attended with great labour [and] with a deal of annoyance, for the soldiers are at least partially commanded by officers, those of the Engineers, whose habits are totally different from what they have been accustomed to... a life lost in the trenches is looked upon as one thrown away and lost ingloriously... the soldier is obliged to stand to be shot at, with a pick-axe or shovel in his hand... this is a trying situation for a soldier.'

To draw attention away from the chosen targets, carelessly concealed digging was begun before Fort Pardaleras on the night of 29/30 May. This position was nearly a mile from the main fortress walls, on the long ridge running away to the south, and perhaps 1,100 yards from Pardaleras. Three hundred picks and shovels reopened the trenches used here in Beresford's earlier false attempt, and this work was continued during the following daylight hours. Overnight a patrol had gone forward to check the bank of the Rivillas river – running along the eastern walls – and also its depth, and the approaches on the other side right up to the castle walls. All was found acceptable.

Lieutenant-Colonel Fletcher marked out the line for the trench linking the three batteries, which was to run between 500 and 800 yards from the castle. A covering party of 1,200 men – one bayonet for every yard of trench – was placed 30 yards in advance, with piquets and light troops ahead in their turn; while four parties each 400 strong plied the picks and shovels that had been collected (no doubt with blasphemy) from the engineer park. Two of the parties worked on a separate approach trench some 1,000 yards long, zig-zagging in from the east, and the other two on the slightly longer parallel in front, which would link the three planned batteries. It took nearly three hours of darkness to deploy the men and detail their tasks; then six hours' labour produced by first light a trench 3ft wide and deep, with a 3ft parapet of packed soil. As the morning light spread the French garrison brought six guns to bear, but did not unduly interrupt the widening of the trench: by the end of daylight on 31 May it was 6ft wide, and the trench guard of 1,200 men moved in, reasonably safe from fire while unexposed. Ensign Grattan commanded one of the working parties opposite the castle:

> Nothing so astonished me so much as the noise made by the engineers; I expected that their loud talking would bring the enemy's attention towards the sound of our pick-axes, and that all the cannon in the town would be turned against us – and, in short, I thought every moment would be my last. I scarcely ventured to breathe until we had completed a respectable first parallel, and when it was fairly finished, just as morning began to dawn, I felt inexpressibly relieved.
>
> As soon as the enemy had a distinct view of what we had been doing, he opened a battery or two against us, with, however, but little effect, and I began to think a siege was not that tremendous a thing I had been taught to expect; but at this moment a thirty-two pound shot passed through a mound of earth in front of that part of the parallel in which I was standing (which was but imperfectly finished), and taking two poor fellows of the 83rd (who were carrying a hand-barrow) across their bellies, cut them in two, and whirled their remains through the air. I had never before so close a view of the execution a round shot was capable of performing, and it was of essential service to me during this and my other sieges. It was full a week afterwards before I held myself as upright as before.

Across the wide Guadiana, unfortunately, the early work on the hill beyond Fort San Cristobal made little progress, and that quite costly. It quickly became obvious that so much of the thin topsoil had been carted away, and dumped over their cliff by the defenders, that more would need to be carted in to stuff the gabions. For the gun platforms to be sunk and levelled into the rock was an activity now beyond mere pick-axes. The infantry progressed well enough with the connecting trench; but the four battery sites, even by nightfall on the 31st, had inadequate parapets only 2ft high. The French had opened an immediate heavy fire from the fort, and across the river from the castle, the former at a range of only 400 yards from two of the four batteries. Not surprisingly, the gabions went down like skittles, the casualties mounted, and eventually the workmen were withdrawn from the batteries.

The next forty-eight hours saw non-stop effort opposite the castle, with the development and completion of the main breaching battery (No.5). The parallel itself and the approach trench were finished, and the guns and howitzers installed: fourteen 24-pounders, two 10in and four 8in howitzers, the howitzers to be used as mortars against the castle's defences. Dickson allocated four officers and 300 gunners (of whom 250 were Portuguese). The garrison replied steadily throughout, but doing no great harm; and all was ready to commence the bombardment of the castle walls the next morning, after just three days and nights of labour. It must be noted, however, that the breaching battery was some 800 yards from the portion of the wall it was to batter: the time factor forbade the development of a further parallel to get closer, just as it had earlier encouraged the decision to dig out quickly the loose soil from Beresford's original spadework – accepting therefore a site really quite distant for the purpose.

Above San Cristobal the two batteries (Nos.1 and 2) on the left of the parallel, and only 400 yards from the fort, suffered increasing casualties. The sappers resorted to gunpowder to deepen and level the platforms, behind protective earth- and brushwood-filled gabions, which in turn were screened by fascines. But the French had judged the range to a nicety, and employed large 16in howitzers or mortars to drop explosive bombs over the top of the gabions and into the works – with destructive effect; fortunately, those bombs which missed the earthworks rolled away down the ridge to explode harmlessly. Protection improved with the arrival from Elvas of woolpacks (bales of fleeces), which made a more resilient and portable absorber of shot than the gabions that required such labour to fill. As a result the work progressed more rapidly; the gun platforms and splinter-proof magazines were completed, and the ammunition parties hastened to fill the latter. The ordnance was installed; and at 9.30am on 3 June firing commenced both from the four batteries on the ridge, and from No.5 Battery below. The latter contained fourteen 24-pounders, and Nos.1, 2 and 3 Batteries a total of twelve others, with four more in reserve.

Over the next ten hours, until the light went at around 7.30pm, the steady fire was continuous, at a rate of one round every five minutes from each of the 24-pounders and one every twelve minutes from the howitzers. The noise rolled around the slopes and buffeted back from the walls, with a similar racket crossing from the right, over the Guadiana. As the range to the castle was found, and an accurate fall of shot developed, hopes were raised: the old Moorish facing stones began to crack and fall. Ominously, however, by last light two guns were out of action – one with an exploded vent hole, the other's barrel drooping at the muzzle. The same fault rendered unserviceable another 24-pounder over the river, where the French also knocked over one of the howitzers with a lucky shot from the fort. Another suffered a broken carriage, from the continuous effect of the concussion in the breech and an excessive angle of fire. Fletcher reported to Lord Wellington: 'Much of the wall of the Castle has fallen, but there is yet nothing like a practicable breach. On the whole I think the guns employed are so uncertain in their efforts that it may become necessary to push yet further forward... the breach in San Cristobal was not considered to be sufficiently practicable this evening to attempt an assault.'

A flavour of life for the covering party on that day is given by William Wheeler of the 2/51st:

> The day our Batteries opened on Fort San Cristobal I was on covering party and stationed in the trench in front of No.4 Battery. The first hour the shock of the guns would almost lift us off the ground, but we soon became so used to it that we could sleep as comfortable as if we had been in a feather bed. The duty in the trenches by day is very fatiguing, almost suffocated for want of air and nearly baked by the sun, parching with thirst, with a beautiful river close to us but might as well be an hundred miles off – for if anyone only indulged the eye with a peep, bang goes half a dozen muskets at his head. Then we are kept in constant motion by swarms of flies, to say nothing of the vermin that have stationed themselves inside our clothes, who are as busy as possible laying siege to our bodies, while we cannot bring a finger to bare on them.

Once darkness fell the effort switched to repairing damaged gabions and refilling the magazines. Expenditure had been around 120 rounds a gun and fifty shells a howitzer – say a total of 3,600 and 600 respectively for the day's work. Major Dickson got together 160 mules and 115 bullock carts for the two resupply convoys, and this became the routine for the next several nights. Wheeler recalls other nightly routines – fire-balls and grapeshot:

As soon as the enemy hear the pick-axe they give us a light by throwing out a quantity of fire balls. This would be very accommodating on their part if they did not open as many guns as they can bring to bear on the place. These balls give a great light around the place where they fall and enable them to point their guns with greater precision. The other night we began to brake ground in a fresh place, they very politely gave us a light by sending out six very beautiful fire balls, the word 'down' was given, but before we had time to stretch ourselves on mother earth they discharged a volley of round and grape shot. One of the round shot must have passed pretty near my cranium, I thought I was wounded, my head ached violently. I felt the pain a long time and it was with difficulty I could perform my duty. Had I been working in a place where there was no danger I certainly would have given up, but here I was ashamed to complain, lest any of my comrades should laugh at me.

In the early hours of 4 June the availability of spare manpower allowed another battery (No.6) to be marked out some 400 yards to the right of No.5, with a range to the breach of 650 yards, and big enough for seven pieces. The next day the 24-pounders continued to hammer away at the castle, but with no great change visible to the bank of earth at the breach; the balls seemed to slam into the packed clay mass, a tremendous impact repeated over and over but with small reward. And the venerable brass guns continued to suffer: two more drooped at the muzzle, the French got another, and three howitzer carriages were disabled. Because of the 'droop' effect, it was decided to allow a longer cooling time for the brass between shots, and an interval of eight minutes was set for the remaining nine serviceable 24-pounders.

In addition to the heat of the firing, of course, the barrels were also cooking under the sun of a Spanish June – Private Wheeler again:

> It is astonishing with what rapidity our works advance, in a short time we had four batteries ready. When off duty, in our camp we are exposed to the scorching heat of the sun, we have no tents, not a tree or bush to shelter us, we have to fetch every drop of water we use at the distance of three miles, we must be ready at a moment's notice should the enemy sally. The other day an accident of an alarming nature occurred, a fire broke out in our camp, the ground being covered with a sort of thistle that was completely dried out by the sun, and caused the fire to spread alarmingly. It was making rapid progress to the spot where the whole of the ammunition was deposited. Fortunately we subdued the fire before it caused any mischief.

Up on the ridge, 4 June also saw a slower firing pattern, for the same reasons. One 24-pounder drooped at the muzzle, one suffered carriage damage, and two howitzer carriages became unusable due to the high angle of fire (the fault, according to Dickson, of 'a brute of a Portuguese Captain'). By the end of the day the four batteries were down to eleven 24-pounders, four 16-pounders and three howitzers. However, according to Captain Jones' journal, the breach in the wall of Fort San Cristobal was seen to be 'much injured'. That at last gave some encouragement to Nos.1 and 2 Batteries; they had also tried their hand against the castle, but at a range approaching 1,200 yards, and given the excessive windage in the ancient barrels, accuracy was not to be expected. William Grattan is worth reading at this stage:

By ten o'clock in the morning our line of batteries presented a very disorganized appearance; sand-bags, gabions, and fascines knocked here and there; guns flung off their carriages, and carriages beaten down under their guns. The boarded platforms of the batteries, damp with the blood of our artillerymen, or the headless trunks of our devoted engineers, bore testimony to the murderous fire opposed to us, but nevertheless everything went on with alacrity and spirit; the damage done to the embrasures was speedily repaired, and many a fine fellow lost his life endeavouring to vie with the engineers in braving dangers, unknown to any but those who have been placed in a similar situation.

It was on a morning such as I am talking of that Colonel Fletcher, chief officer of Engineers, came into the battery where I was employed; he wished to observe some work that had been thrown up by the enemy near the foot of the castle the preceeding night. The battery was more than usually full of workmen repairing the effects of the morning's fire, and the efforts of the enemy against this part of our works were excessively animated. A number of men had fallen and were falling, but Colonel Fletcher, apparently disregarding the circumstances, walked out to the right of the battery, and, taking his stand upon the level ground, put his glass to his eye, and commenced his observations with much composure. Shot and shell flew thickly about him, and one of the former tore up the ground by his side and covered him with clay; but not in the least regarding this, he remained steadily observing the enemy. When at length he had satisfied himself, he quietly put up his glass, and turning to a man of my party who was sitting on the outside of an embrasure, pegging in a fascine, said, 'My fine fellow, you are too much exposed; get inside the embrasure, and you will do your work nearly as well.' – 'I'm almost finished, Colonel,' replied the soldier, 'and it isn't worth while to move now; those fellows can't hit me, for they've been trying it these fifteen minutes.' They were the last words he ever spoke! He had scarcely uttered the last syllable when a round shot cut him in two, and knocked half of his body across the breech of the gun. The name of this soldier was Edmund Man; he was an Englishman, although he belonged to the 88th Regiment. When he fell, the French cannoniers, as was usual with them, set up a shout, denoting how well satisfied they were with their practice!

In 1902 Sir Charles Oman edited the first reprint of Grattan's *Adventures* (1847), and made a point in his Preface of praising the 'very considerable talent for describing battles' shown by Grattan. Having followed his gripping account of the street-fighting in Fuentes village one can only agree, and it is clear that his memories of Badajoz were equally vivid.

Next morning, 5 June, No.6 Battery opposite the castle received seven of the 24-pounders previously in No.5, and these opened up at 10am. Now No.5 Battery had just three 24-pounders and five howitzers, so the new battery in effect became the main breaching battery. During the day a battalion-strong working party hurried to put up traverses, since at last the defenders in Fort San Cristobal had seen fit to relocate a gun backwards, to plunge fire down over the river, enfilading both the parallel and the batteries. At 650 yards to the castle breach the fire from No.6 was accurate, but disappointing in effect: the bank of earth remained surprisingly upright. Which was more than could be said of the Portuguese ordnance: two more barrels drooped, though the one which had previously blown its vent hole was repaired and returned to duty. William Wheeler was in the covering party yet again on 5 June:

About midday I was in the trench in front of No.2 Battery. An old Portuguese had just arrived with a car loaded with ammunition drawn by two oxen, he had just got his load deposited in the Magazine when the enemy favoured us with a shell from the 'big Tom of Lincoln' (the name we have given to one of their tremendous mortars). I watched its progress and saw it burst a few feet over the oxen, they were cut to pieces with the car. When the cloud of dust and smoke had cleared away we observed the old fellow running like a deer, he had miraculously escaped unhurt. Besides killing the oxen, one of our guns in the Battery was dismounted. Another was soon mounted, but it caused some trouble as they dapped [dropped] another shell into the battery and wounded several men.

Above the fort that day, while the breach grew and the French defensive fire waned somewhat, another two barrels had drooped, and it had become clear that things could not long continue in this way. Alexander Dickson went to Lord Wellington to obtain consent to fetch up six iron Portuguese Navy 24-pounders from Elvas, where they had newly arrived from Lisbon. Captain Cocks recalls overhearing the Peer say to Dickson, 'If we succeed with the means we have it will be a wonder.'

A new battery (No.7) was marked out to the right and forward of No.6, and only 520 yards from the castle breach. A large party of 1,400 men set to work that night, and rather fewer next morning on 6 June, to make the new battery and the approaches to it ready in all respects. 'The heavy grape which the garrison showered down from the castle annoyed the workmen extremely, and caused many casualties', noted Captain Jones, and of course the fort joined in with its plunging fire – another gun and a howitzer were brought to bear on Nos.6 and 7 Batteries. The breach in the castle wall, however, at last began to show results, the ramp of earth increasing to the extent that, according to Jones, it was thought 'practicable for a man to get up'; Dickson said 'for a single person by night', which was not quite so encouraging. Prospects had also improved at San Cristobal, where a close reconnaissance had been made the previous night by Lieutenant Forster, RE. On the strength of his report and the further improvement since then, a decision was taken by Lord Wellington to assault the breach that very midnight. An unenthusiastic Fletcher had repeated the warning given on the 3rd; but with the French armies now closing in, the attempt had to be made.

Before describing what happened, the mention of Forster's night reconnaissance allows us to enjoy more from Grattan. He too was to venture forward towards the walls and meet up with another sapper officer, also on reconnaissance:

> On the evening of the 5th I was sent in advance with a covering party of forty men; we were placed some distance in front of the works, and as usual received directions to beware of a surprise. Our batteries were all armed, and a sortie from the garrison was not improbable; the night was unusually dark, and except an occasional shell from our mortars, the striking of the clocks in the town, or the challenge of the French sentinels along the battlements of the castle, everything was still.
>
> A man of a fanciful disposition, or indeed of an ordinary way of thinking, is seldom placed in a situation more likely to cause him to give free scope to his imagination than when lying before an enemy on a dark night; every sound, the very rustling of a leaf, gives him cause for speculation; figures will appear, or seem to appear, in different shapes;

sometimes the branch of a tree passes for a tremendous fellow with extended arms, and the waving of a bush is mistaken for a party crouching on their hands and knees.

I don't know why it was, but I could not divest myself of the idea that an attack upon our lives was meditated. I cast a look at my men as they lay upon the ground, and saw that each held his firelock in his grasp and was as he should be; half an hour passed away in this manner, but no sound gave warning that my suspicions were well founded. The noise of the workmen in the trenches lessened by degrees, and as the hour of midnight approached there was, comparatively speaking, a death-like silence. I went forward a short distance, but it was a short distance, for in truth – to say the least of it – I was a little 'hipped'. I even wished the enemy would throw a shot or two against our works to give a fillip to my thoughts. Heavens! How I envied the soldiers, who slept like so many tops and snored so loud. I went forward again, but had not proceeded more than about one hundred paces when I heard voices whispering in my front, and upon observing more minutely in the direction from whence the sounds proceeded, I saw distinctly two men. The uniform of one was dark; the other wore a large cloak, and I could hear his sabre clinking by his side as he approached me.

At the instant I do not know what sum I would have considered too great to have purchased my ransom and placed me once more at the head of my men. I need scarcely say that I regretted the step I had taken, but it was too late. The figures continued to advance towards the spot where I was crouched, and were already within a few paces of me. I did not know what to do; I dreaded remaining stationary, and I was ashamed to run away – there was not a moment to lose, and I made up my mind to sell my life dearly. I sprang up with my drawn sabre in my hand, and called out as loud as I could (and it was but a so-so effort), 'Who goes there?' My delight was great to find, in place of two Frenchmen (the advance, as I expected, of several hundred), Captain Patten of the Engineers attended by a sergeant of his corps; he held a dark lantern under his cloak, and he told me he had been on his way to reconnoitre the breach in the castle wall, but that he thought it as well to return to the first covering party he should meet with, in order to get a file of men which he proposed taking with him to within a short distance of the breach. I was just then in that frame of mind from my own little adventure to approve highly of his precaution, and I gave him a couple of what our fellows (the Connaught Rangers) used to call lads that weren't easy or, so to speak without a metaphor, two fellows that would walk into the mouth of a cannon if they were bid to do it.

Previous to this I had passed an uneasy night, but I was now filled with much anxiety for the fate of Captain Patten and my own two men. They had left me about a quarter of an hour when a few musket-shots from the bastion nearest the breach announced that the reconnaissance had not been made unnoticed by the enemy: and shortly after, the return of my soldiers confirmed the fact.

It appeared that upon arriving within pistol-shot of the wall Captain Patten motioned to the men to lie down, while he crept forward to the breach; he had succeeded in ascertaining its state, and was about to return to the soldiers, when some inequality of the ground caused him to stumble a little, and the noise attracted the attention of the nearest sentinel, whose fire gave the alarm to the others. One of their shots struck Captain Patten in the back, a little below the shoulder, and he survived its effects but a few hours. Thus fell a fine young man, an ornament to that branch of the service to which he belonged, and a branch which in point of men of highly cultivated scientific information, as well as the most chivalrous bravery, may challenge the world to show its superior.

13
The Assaults on
Fort San Cristobal,
6 & 9 June

WHAT happened at Fort San Cristobal around midnight on 6/7 June, and again three nights later, can largely be told through eyewitness accounts. Three men watched from outside, and of course picked up the talk afterwards from those involved at the breach itself. These were Ensign William Grattan of the 88th (in Mackinnon's brigade); Captain John Jones, the sapper brigade-major, whose journal gives us so much detail; and the gunner Major Alexander Dickson – though for once his letters are sadly sketchy. There was also one witness who was in the very thick of it: Private William Wheeler of the 2/51st, in Sontag's brigade. This may seem thin gruel for the historian, compared with the rich literary pickings from the great assault of April 1812, but it is more than adequate to allow us to picture this present scene. These witnesses are fortunately distributed: the engineer and the gunner officer can guide us authoritively through many of the arrangements, while Private Wheeler not only took part in both assaults, but his words were written within days, and therefore owe nothing to others or to the distortions of time. William Wheeler was, as Basil Liddell Hart wrote in the 1951 Preface to his newly-discovered *Letters*, 'a good story-teller [with] a remarkably observant mind' (and incidentally, like Grattan, he reveals a deep and attractive pride in his regiment).

*   *   *

Thanks to John Jones we have General Houston's orders for the first attack. The two grenadier companies of the 2/51st and 2/85th were augmented to a total strength of 180 men, the 17th Portuguese Line and the Chasseurs Britanniques contributing, the whole to be commanded by Major Macintosh of the 85th. The assault company comprised four divisions or platoons, each of twenty-five men (three platoons from the 51st, one from the 85th), with one of the former under Ensign Dyas forming the 'Forlorn Hope'. Dyas was to be accompanied by Lieutenant Forster, the sapper subaltern who had previously reconnoitred the breach and declared it practicable. A gap of one hundred paces was to separate Dyas' party from the next. Forster was to take two ladders (and presumably four or five sappers to carry them), while the main assault party was to take ten ladders.

The reserve company of grenadiers would seek to divert the garrison 'by a brisk fire of musketry' from the edge of the glacis, adjacent to the breach on the east face of the fort. They would also be conveniently placed there to support the assault force, either at the breach or exploiting inside the fort when entry had been gained. To prevent interference from the garrison of the *tête du pont*, the trench guard – not less than 300 men – were to go forward to the ravine between the fort and No.2 Battery, with a company of fifty men sent down beyond the western glacis, to block the trench approach from the bridgehead. Another company, with two guns, was to go down by the river, to disrupt any waterborne reinforcements. It was stressed, somewhat optimistically, that until the French opened defensive fire the assault party should use only their bayonets.

There was also a follow-up plan, for two companies armed with pick-axes and shovels, all carrying gabions, to enter the fort once it had been won. Their job was primarily to make the breach practicable for the entry of artillery; they were also to put in a covered cannon-proof trench across the inside of the fort – the object of the whole operation, after all, was to get guns and ammunition to the far ramparts overlooking the castle.

The French garrison of San Cristobal comprised a single company of the 88e Ligne commanded by Captain Chauvin, just seventy-five strong but well supplied with additional muskets. Governor Phillipon's sappers had made a ready supply of hand grenades to hurl down on the attackers; there were cannon standing by loaded with grapeshot, and the breach itself was blocked by upturned carts and protected by *chevaux-de-frise*. Above all, however, Chauvin had had the wit after last light to clear the ditch of rubble – that is, the debris of the collapsed wall no longer lay in the ditch, forming a ramp. There was now a vertical 7ft wall – a giant step – edging the ditch, with the battered breach sloping away above it.

The commander of the Forlorn Hope, Joseph Dyas, had a good reputation in his regiment. Private Wheeler describes him as 'a young officer of great promise, of a most excellent disposition, and beloved by every man in the Corps – an Irishman by birth and whose only fortune was his sword'. He was sent off around midnight by Major Macintosh, with the second detachment following a moment or two later. The men crossed the rocky slopes, covering the 400 yards quickly and quietly, under cover of the guns opening diversionary fire on the fort. The glacis was soon reached. Private Wheeler: 'Not a head was to be seen above the walls, and we began to think the enemy had retired into the town.' Captain Jones: 'The pallisades had all been destroyed by the fire of the batteries, and the counter-scarp proved no obstacle, being at that re-entering spot only four feet deep.' William Grattan continues:

> The handful of men that formed the forlorn hope, led on by their brave young commander, jumped into the ditch, and proceeded along the curtain of the breach... They had scarcely arrived at its foot when the officer of Engineers was mortally wounded, and Ensign Dyas was in consequence the only person to direct the men at the breach.

Captain Jones takes up the tale of those frustrating minutes:

> On attempting to mount the breach, it was found perfectly impracticable, the garrison having removed the rubbish from the foot of it during the period between dark and the attack, and the escarp standing clear nearly seven feet high.

The twelve ladders, 15ft long, were back with the main assault party, who had not yet appeared. After vainly attempting to clamber on to the breach slope, Dyas sensibly called his men off. We may assume his adrenaline promptly took him to find the missing

Major Macintosh, and above all the ladders. Unfortunately, they were about to be used elsewhere, as Wheeler tells us:

> We entered the trench and fixed our ladders, when sudden as a flash of lightning the whole place was in a blaze. It will be impossible for me to describe to you what followed. You can better conceive it by figuring in your minds eye a deep trench or ditch filled with men who are endeavouring to mount the wall by means of ladders. The top of this wall crowded with men hurling down shells and hand grenades on the heads of them below, and when all these are expended they have each six or seven loaded firelocks which they discharge into the trench as quick as possible. Add to this some half dozen cannon scouring the trench with grape. This will immediately present to your imagination the following frightful picture. Heaps of brave fellows killed and wounded, ladders shot to pieces, and falling together with the men down upon the living and the dead. Then ever and anon would fall upon us the body of some brave Frenchman whose zeal had led him to the edge of the wall in its defence, and had been killed by their own missiles or by the fire of our covering party.
>
> But in the midst of all these difficulties, great as they were, we should have taken the fort but for an unforeseen accident that could not be remedied – it was the ladders were too short. Several men who had gained the tops of the ladders could not reach the top of the wall with their firelocks.

It is not clear what had gone wrong, but Major Macintosh, who had not been able to make his own reconnaissance, seems not to have kept close enough behind Dyas' party. Getting over the glacis and finding some damaged part of the wall, which he assumed to be the breach, and assuming further that the Forlorn Hope had been overwhelmed, he set his men to a scaling attempt with the ladders. Grattan tells us what presumably was the common belief, that Macintosh had found 'nothing more than an embrasure – a dismantled bastion – which had been a good deal injured by the fire of our batteries'. The French garrison having cleared the rubble, 'the ladders were in consequence not of a sufficient length... a quarter of an hour had now elapsed...[in] several fruitless attempts to enter the fort.' Private Wheeler wrote that 'as soon as this was discovered, all hopes of gaining possession were abandoned, and the order was given to retire'.

Dyas now arrived at that spot, but Macintosh had gone; Grattan tells us that Dyas 'having reached the spot where his companions had been so uselessly, yet fatally employed, found it occupied only by the dead and wounded... finding himself unsupported by the storming party, at length quitted the ditch, but not until he heard the enemy entering it by the sally-port'.

Charles Oman states to the contrary in his account (but without sources): his version is that Macintosh was told by the Forlorn Hope, as they withdrew, that the breach was impracticable; and that he then deliberately sought alternative scaling places, only to find his 15ft ladders faced by 20ft ramparts. One would have thought he should first have tried Dyas's 7ft obstacle at the foot of the breach – which in this version of events Dyas presumably told him about; this was, after all, their given task, and Macintosh had not yet attempted it.

The loss was put at Lieutenant Forster and twelve others killed, and eighty-two wounded and missing – ninety-five casualties in all, or around 50 per cent of those involved. Captain Chauvin's company of the 88e Ligne lost one killed and five wounded. Inside the town the next day (according to the diary of a Spanish resident), the French announced that the English 'only got as far as the ditch of San Cristobal, where they left two hundred dead.'

This débâcle – for such it was – arose out of a mixture of failings: the rubble being actively cleared away, and Chauvin being given four hours of darkness in which to do it; the officer in command not accompanying Forster's and Dyas' reconnaissance; the sappers misjudging the proper length of ladder; and the sapper subaltern wrongly declaring the breach practicable when it was blocked and protected – though again, Chauvin may have moved in the carts and other obstacles after nightfall.

What sat squarely on Lord Wellington's shoulders, however (and we may assume that he gave Houston a broad indication of what to do and how to do it, if not a detailed order), was the very limited manpower employed. The two reinforced assault companies, the trench guard, and the two companies of workmen allocated to the fort once secured, did not amount to more than 580 men together – a mere battalion, when Wellington had 14,000 men on call, of whom 5,000 were Houston's on the north bank, within striking distance of San Cristobal. Chauvin's company of the 88e Ligne, in a roughly square emplacement with sides a hundred paces long, could not possibly have prevented multiple escalade attempts on those 20ft walls, if they were well spaced out and had ladders of the correct length. (One cannot help pondering the similarity with the siege of 1812, when two weeks of battering breaches, followed by forty unsuccessful and bloody assaults up them, saw a final solution provided by Picton's 3rd Division, simply by placing their 30ft ladders against the thinly-defended castle walls.) This present half-hearted effort did not deserve to succeed; its very lack of ambition showed – unsurprisingly – British inexperience in siegecraft.

*   *   *

Taking advantage of a two-hour truce on the morning of the 7th to evacuate the wounded from the ditch, the breach was observed close to, and the late Lieutenant Forster's opinion on its practicality was widely rejected. During the day the digging continued; No.7 Battery was completed, at a range of 520 yards from the castle, and three 24-pounders were emplaced. Six others were in No.6, and only howitzers now fired from No.5 – the original breaching battery. The earth wall continued to resist all efforts; but the arrival of the six iron naval guns from Elvas, which were set up in No.7 Battery, materially improved progress the following day. By darkness on 8 June the ramp at the base of the castle breach was readily observable, and now ran to within a few feet of the top of the wall; 'By the evening the breach appeared as if several people could scramble up abreast' (Dickson). Efforts were made to prevent the nightly clearance of rubble from the ditch, partly by using superior grapeshot fetched up from Elvas.

At Fort San Cristobal, however, the design of the counter-scarp largely blocked any view from the batteries on to the base of the breach. It was therefore difficult to judge the success of this fire, and the only sure way to do that was by close reconnaissance at night.

By late on the afternoon of 9 June the fire on the fort was being delivered by only eight guns, and on the castle by twelve. The rate of fire – necessarily, to allow cooling – was down to about one round every ten minutes, or ninety rounds per gun during the day. But both breaches were again looking favourable and, as Grattan has told us, on the night of 5/6 June the sapper Captain Patten had reported – with his last breath – that the fords over the Rivilla and the approach to the castle breach were without hindrance. But it was observed on the morning of the 9th that despite the sweeping of the ditch with grape- and case-shot during the night, the defenders had again cleared the slope of debris from the foot of the breach.

With this in mind, Wellington now decided to assault Fort San Cristobal that night of the 9th/10th, but not the castle. This time the officer in command, Major Alexander McGeechy of the 17th Portuguese, carried out a quick reconnaissance after last light with Joseph Dyas, who was again to lead the Forlorn Hope; clearly, this lieutenant without wealth or connections was determined to 'make his fortune with his sword' or die in the attempt. Grattan gives us his version of what was discussed during the reconnaissance – which, since McGeechy was killed an hour later, was therefore what Dyas reported had been said. Somewhat unattractively, Dyas told a tale against his dead superior's judgement:

> They made a detour by the edge of the river, and succeeded in reaching unperceived to within a short distance of the fort. Under cover of some reeds, they carefully examined the breach which, to Major MacGeechy appeared a practicable one, but Dyas better informed from experience, combated all the arguments of his companion, and desired him to watch attentively the effects of the next salvo from our Batteries, he did so, and appeared satisfied with the result, 'Because the wall', he remarked to Dyas, 'gave way very freely.' 'Yes' replied Dyas, 'but did you not observe how the stones fell without rolling, rely on it if there was any rubbish about the base, or face of it, the stones would roll and not fall.' The observation was not lost on Major MacGeechy, but it having been decided that the attack was to be made that night, both the leader of the forlorn hope and the Commander of the storming party at once made up their minds for the trial.

(In passing, readers will note this further if trivial example of a common feature of military incompetence – the deliberate or subconscious ignoring of new intelligence that casts doubt on a plan already settled.)

McGeechy was given command of the assault party, comprising two detachments or reinforced companies each of 100 men. The plan this time was for a double attempt – Oman says that there were two breaches, a large one and a small one; Jones talks of 'the breach', with a second escalade at 'the salient angle of the work'. Each detachment should be preceded by a subaltern and twenty-five men – in theory making two Forlorn Hopes, but again Jones speaks only of Dyas' party. Another thirty men, all marksmen, were to keep up a brisk fire against the parapet between the breach and salient angle. Seventy men would go down to the road along the river, to watch out for any waterborne reinforcement; and a hundred men were to harass the western parapets while sealing off the approach from the *tête du pont*. Another thirty, from the main trench guard, would similarly keep up a brisk fire on the northern parapets, while the trench guard itself was to be in reserve, as required. Finally, another fifty men from the trench guard of No.4 Battery were to go forward to fire upon the *tête du pont* parapets. As before, two companies carrying small gabions and picks and shovels would follow up success, to make the breach accessible for the guns.

So taking the strength of the trench guard again at about 300, that makes some 880 men committed to this attempt – a large increase. But still the assault party itself numbered just 200 now, against 180 the first time round; thus all the extra men were indeed extras, filling the supporting roles. And anyway, Phillipon had reinforced Chauvin: a second company had crossed over, and all were issued with three muskets per man, live shells with short fuses, hand grenades, illuminating fire-balls, barrels of powder with matches fastened to them, and even rocks for hurling. The breach was built up with an artificial parapet of sandbags and wool packs, with *chevaux de frise* blocking the rubble ramp, and the debris at the foot of course cleared away after last light, despite the preventative fire from the batteries. Ninety minutes later Chauvin's men were ready and waiting, when around 9pm Major McGeechy gave the nod.

The troops had formed up in the ravine behind the batteries. Immediately they emerged on to the slopes they came under fire from the garrison, who greeted this new attempt with the confidence gained three nights before. Their cheers and ribald invitations rang out as the first parties, already thinned as they climbed the rocky surface, came to the terraced glacis. Major McGeechy was struck down, so too the sapper conducting officer, Lieutenant Richard Hunt. Grattan tells the story as he heard it:

> Two hundred men moved forward to the assault, Dyas leading the advance. He made a circuit until he came exactly opposite to the breach. Instead of entering the ditch as before, a sheep path, which he remembered in the evening while he and Major McGeechy made their observations, served to guide them to the glacis in front of the breach. Arrived at the spot the detachment descended the ditch and found themselves at the foot of the breach, but here an unlooked for event stopped their further progress and would in itself have been sufficient to have caused the failure of the attack. The ladders were entrusted to a party composed of a foreign Regiment 'the Chasseurs Britanniques'. These men, the moment they reached the glacis, glad to rid themselves of their load slung the ladders into the ditch. Instead of sliding them between the palisadoes, they fell across them, and so stuck fast, and being made of heavy green wood, it was next to impossible to move much less to place them upright against the breach, and almost all the storming party were massacred in the attempt.
>
> Placed in a situation so frightful, it required a man of the most determined character to continue the attack. Every officer of the detachment had fallen, Major McGeechy one of the first, and at this moment Dyas and about five and twenty men were all that remained of the two hundred. Undismayed by this circumstance, the soldiers persevered, and Dyas although wounded and bleeding, succeeded in disentangling one ladder, and placing it against what was considered the breach. It was speedily mounted, but on arriving at the top of the ladder, instead of the breach, it was found to be a stone wall that had been constructed in the night, and which completely cut off all communication between the ditch and the bastion, so that when the men reached the top of this wall, they were, in effect, as far from the breach as if they had been in their own batteries.

In his letter home ten days later, Private Wheeler enlarges on his own experience:

> This second attempt was attended with the same ill success as the first. It is true we had profited by the discovery of the ladder being too short, but the old fox inside was too deep for us. He had caused all the rubbish to be cleared out of the trench. This again placed us just in the same predicament, our ladders were again too short and if possible we received a warmer reception than before. The ladder I was on was broken and down we all came together, men, firelocks, bayonets, in one confused mass, and with us a portion of the

wall. After some time the fire slackened, as if the enemy were tired of slaughter, when an officer Lieutenant Westropp came running up from the western angle of the fort calling out to retire – the enemy were entering the trench by the sally port. We then began to leave the trench. Poor Mr Westropp was assisting a wounded man in getting out, when he was shot dead just as he had effected his purpose.

I now saw Ensign Dyas calling to the men to leave the trench and retire to our rallying post. As we were retreating down the glacis, a misfortune befell me and I had a narrow escape of being made prisoner, being cut off from my comrades by the party who sallied. There were eight or nine in the same mess. These the enemy obliged to go into the fort. However, I hit upon an expedient that answered well. I threw myself down by a man who was shot through the head and daubed my white haversack with his blood. I showed this to the enemy when they ordered me to get up and go into the fort. From the appearance of the blood they must have thought I had a very bad wound in the hip, so they all left me – except one, who searched my pockets, took off my shirt, boots and stockings... The enemy having retired within the fort, the moon rose, which cast a gloomy light round the place. Situated as I was this added fresh horrors to my view, the place was covered with dead and dying, the old black walls and breach looked terrible and seemed like an evil spirit frowning on the unfortunate victims that lay prostrate at its feet. As the moon ascended it grew much lighter and I began to fear I should not be able to effect my escape, for the enemy kept a sharp look out and if anyone endeavoured to escape they were sure to discharge a few muskets at him. I soon perceived that as often as our batteries fired they would hide behind the walls. I made the most of this by sliding down as often as I observed a flash from our works. By daybreak I had got to the plain below the fort. I had nothing to do but have a run for it across the No.1 Battery. This plain, like our camp, was covered with small dry thistles. The enemy discharged two guns loaded with round shot, and several muskets at me. My comrades cheered me and I bounded across like a deer, the Devil take the thistles. I felt none of them until I was safe behind the Battery.

Captain Douglas gave me a drop out of his bottle, and I made for camp where I arrived just in time to have my name struck out of the killed and wounded list, 'sans shirt, sans boots and sans stockings'. Lieut Dyas was in camp. How he had escaped unhurt is a mystery. He was without cap, his sword was shot off close to the handle, the sword scabbard was gone, and the laps of his frock coat were perforated with balls. Indeed everyone who returned bore evident marks where they had been. Their caps, belts, firelocks etc were more or less damaged. I had three shots pass through my cap, one of which carried away the rosehead [cockade] and tuft, my firelock was damaged near the lock, and a ball had passed through the butt.

t is not difficult to imagine Joseph Dyas' intense frustration at finding the ditch rubble-free, nd again presenting a sheer step or edge to the breach; it only confirmed the accuracy of his arlier observation. He would therefore have turned expectantly this second time for the rranged ladders. However, here too he was out of luck, thanks to the carrying party from the Chasseurs Britanniques. (By now only the officers of this unit were highly motivated French migrés; the ranks were filled with multi-national riffraff, including recent French prisoners, d the rate of desertions was astronomical.) Captain Jones tells us that the ladders were 25ft to 30ft long, and Grattan that they were of heavy green wood: hooked over the timbers in the palisade, and hanging down into the ditch, they would be ferociously hard to free. Perhaps it was shame at his men's near-deliberate carelessness that drove their officer, Lieutenant Dufiel, to risk his life on one ladder that was pressed into service. He was observed by the defenders climbing a ladder and calling out '*Je monte, suivez-moi!*' At the top he ran forward a few steps up the ramp, followed by two or three men, only to be bayoneted. This scene repeats and multiplies in the mind's eye, as one reads Jones' description:

> The second detachment of 100 men advanced with the same steadiness as the first, and descended into the ditch without much loss. They then applied the ladders to the scarp, and succeeded in rearing most of them. The men ascended the ladders with great readiness, but everyone who succeeded in reaching the parapet was instantly bayonetted down, and the garrison after a little while mounted on the parapet, upset the ladders. At this time the two assaulting columns were completely mixed together, and united in many strenuous endeavours to replace the ladders at various points of the front; but the enormous quantity of large shells, hand-grenades, bags of powder and combustibles, which the garrison threw into the ditch, rendered their perseverance and gallantry unavailing.

A short paragraph from William Napier's *History* provides a final description:

> The troops with loud shouts jumped down into the ditch, but the French scoffingly called to them to come on, and at the same time rolled the barrels of powder and shells down, while the musketry made fearful and rapid havoc. In a little time the two leading companies united at the main breach, the supports also came up, confusion arose about the ladders, of which only a few could be reared, and the enemy standing on the ramparts, bayoneted the foremost of the assailants, overturned the ladders, and again poured their destructive fire upon the crowd below. When a hundred and forty men had fallen the order to retire was given.

The Spanish diarist in the town noted that 'the firing lasted until eleven. In the morning of the following day, the French displayed in the plaza an English officer, another Portuguese, and a soldier, saying they had captured them in the breach.'

And that was that; for the next morning brought the news Lord Wellington was expecting. A captured letter, from Soult to Marmont, indicated a juncture of the Armies of Portugal and Andalusia within the week, around Merida (two 20-mile marches from Badajoz). Soult would have been joined by General D'Erlon, and together the two marshals might then field 60,000 men. So Wellington called his commanders together at noon on 10 June, ordering an immediate end to the siege, and giving instructions for a rapid withdrawal. The castle breach that morning was deemed practicable, but he now had no time in hand to repair it behind him even should an assault succeed. In any event, such an assault, necessarily across 700 paces of open ground and vulnerable to flank fire from the fort – which also commanded the foot of the breach – was far from guaranteed success. It was likely to be bloody, and Lord Wellington had lost enough men in ditches for now. The first attempt on 6 June had suffered 50 per cent losses, this second one nearer 70 per cent – 139 men killed and wounded out of the 200 in the two assault companies. Including the losses in the batteries and the working parties, Jones reckons that the two attempts cost 485 men in all, of whom 125 were killed. Seventeen brass 24-pounders were disabled, fifteen of which were by their own fire, 'the vents of the other thirteen brass 24-pounders being much enlarged and in a very bad state'.

By lunchtime on 10 June, Phillipon knew that he had won by the shortest of heads, which made it all the sweeter. His council of war's earlier recommendation to postpone, for five days more, his plan for a night breakout across the bridge was now redundant. His garrison was on half-rations, with enough for ten more days in hand (the last resupply had come in before Beresford's first envelopment in April); but now he only had to sit it out. The British marched away on 16 June, and Marshals Soult and Marmont came marching up on the 20th.

*   *   *

It is easy to list the misfortunes and errors that attended these attempts: the optimistic range at which the breaching batteries were sited; the inadequacy in numbers, and quality, of the guns available – and of the gunners to serve them; the shortage of trained engineers and sappers, and their errors of judgement; the wall that, beneath its ostensibly feeble masonry, turned out to be a natural bank of earth; the half-hearted size of the assault parties; the garrison's nightly activity in clearing their ditches; and the lack of adequate close-range musketry on to the parapets.

More fundamental, with the British siege train still languishing in Oporto, was the repeated decision to seek access to the castle via Fort San Cristobal. The rocky ground and the time factor forbade the rulebook approach of covered roads right up to the glacis, short-range battering and close infantry assaults. Given this known impediment to engineering perfection, and the known weakness of artillery and sapper resources, the attempts in May and June 1811 were examples of professionals pushing their luck with fingers crossed. Wellington and Colonel Fletcher had little alternative to chancing their arm in this way, given their circumstances; but it was neither man's finest hour. 'Next time I shall be my own engineer', Wellington was said to have muttered; what Fletcher muttered is not recorded. Captain Jones, true to his capbadge, wrote cheerfully that 'This attempt to recover Badajoz, although bold and hazardous in the extreme, and contrary to all rule, had much merit as a feasible expedient and deserved a happier result.' The gunner Dickson gently implied that the sappers had got it wrong: 'the Engineers had hopes... it was thought that... the supposed weakness of the Castle walls... on the Cristobal side the wall was found to be uncommonly tough, and much higher than we were informed' (by the sappers). But, polishing his own capbadge, Dickson stoutly maintained that 'every thing that artillery could do was done, considering our miserable means... [but] our batteries were too far off' (because the sappers couldn't sap us any closer).

As to the broader picture, it is not hard to weigh up the failure of this second mini-siege of the fortress in the context of the near-failure down the road at Albuera three weeks earlier. That battle was fought specifically to keep Soult from relieving Badajoz – to fend off his interference with the first siege, so that it could be resumed. For that resumption now to have failed seems to negate all the sacrifices of bloody Albuera. Here we go again (you might say through gritted teeth), as you shoulder your musket and step out to beat of drum on 16 June; so goodbye Badajoz, goodbye damned picks and shovels – and goodbye Tom, and Paddy, and all the others left naked and torn in the Albuera lime-pits and on the funeral pyres. We didn't stop Soult, we just delayed him by a month – and was that worth the price we paid?

So was William Napier right to say Beresford should not have fought Soult at all – that it a waste of brave men, dying to no purpose? Napier answered himself when he later wrote the deeper truth: 'Marmont's army was conscious of its recent defeats at Busaco, at Sabugal, at Fuentes d'Oñoro; the horrid field of Albuera was fresh; the fierce blood spilt there still reeked in the nostrils of Soult's soldiers.' To this thought we might add Victor's lesson learned at Barrosa, and before that at Talavera, and before that Junot's at Vimiero. Is it any wonder that thereafter Napoleon's marshals so very rarely risked attacking 'our Atty's' men in a defensive position? (The exceptions were at Sorauren in the Pyrenees in 1813, and at Waterloo – and much good that did them.)

The French death toll at Albuera, and the unconquerable spirit displayed there by the British infantry under the worst punishment imaginable, gained for Wellington's Peninsular Field Army a remarkable moral ascendancy. From then on, French generals were to look twice at any red coats glimpsed on a forward slope, for fear of what lay behind; they had learned the terrible strength in a little two-deep line, its quick pair of volleys, the cheer and the charge. In short, as Charles Oman summed it up when writing of the position in June 1811: 'the offensive spirit was gone: the French armies in Spain found themselves thrown upon the defensive; and so things were to remain for the rest of the Peninsular War. The offensive, though it was hardly realized as yet, had passed to Wellington.'

That is the true measure of his campaign of 1811. Oman's point was immediately proved when, a week after quitting Badajoz, Marshals Soult and Marmont chose not to attack Wellington on the Caia; and again when Marmont and Dorsenne chose not to attack him at Fuenteguinaldo; and yet again when he was behind the Coa, at the end of September. They were all in thrall to a greater power, a demonstrable master of their own craft. Of course, as good Frenchmen, they did not let this matured respect for the Rosbiffs either diminish their own gallantry or sap their determination to rise to the challenge: but it created a sensible caution, all the more crippling for its novel contrast to previous French military practice.

14
El Bodon,
25 September, and the
Final Manoeuvres

IN mid-1811, Lord Wellington's strategic aims remained unchanged: firstly, the removal of the French garrisons from Ciudad Rodrigo and Badajoz, where their presence facilitated any new mischief Napoleon might launch into Portugal. Secondly, with a future exit route secured to his rear, he sought to cut the imperial artery linking the brothers Bonaparte in Madrid and Paris. Along that road, hundreds of miles away as it disappeared north-east into the haze, rose the temptation of the long grey line of the Pyrenees – what in December he was to call 'the most vulnerable frontier of France'. But first he had to own both the gateway fortresses between Portugal and Spain: Ciudad Rodrigo would not by itself give him strategic freedom – with the French in Badajoz still dominating the southern route into Portugal, any thrust eastwards from Ciudad Rodrigo would itself be exposed.

So the events of the second half of 1811 were essentially manoeuvres to lead his lordship forward to the stirring events of 1812: the capture of the two border fortresses, the mighty clash of 100,000 men at Salamanca, the fleeting entry into Madrid, the failed siege of Burgos and the withdrawal back to Ciudad Rodrigo – a frustrated campaign, which nonetheless was to leave the southern half of Spain completely free of the occupier, and Wellington pondering a blitzkrieg through northern Spain to a place called Vitoria.

If these were his long-term aims, the immediate need was more mundane: to concentrate his divisions under his own hand again, however temporarily. His northern force led by Brent Spencer had been moving south during the second week of June, paralleling Marshal Marmont's march to meet Soult. Spencer rejoined the new 12-mile line which stretched from Elvas north-east over the Caia, and through Campo Mayor north to Oguella, a small fortified town on the Gebora. For the first time in many weeks Lord Wellington commanded his army again, with no detachments. According to Oman, he had 46,000 infantry – two-thirds of them British, with 17,000 Portuguese – and 5,000 cavalry. (The Spanish armies had gone south, rather ambitiously to make threatening gestures towards Seville, since Soult had now stripped out much of its French garrison for his field army.)

Between them Marshals Soult and Marmont could field 60,000 men. A reconnaissance in force was carried out across the Guadiana on 22–23 June, and identified at least two British divisions on the ridge north from Campo Mayor (the 3rd and the 7th). It is not clear if the other divisions were spotted, or if the general strength of the position was appreciated: it had rattled flanks, concealed lateral roads in rear, good reverse slopes and a signalling system. As Wellington wrote on the 26th, 'They have been looking at us for a week and the more they

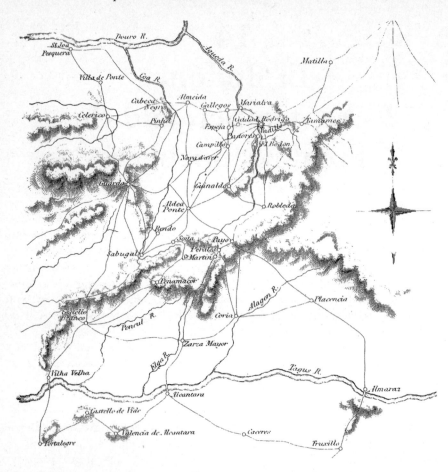

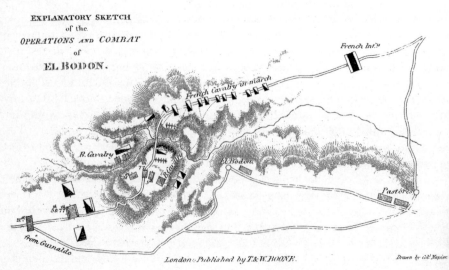

EXPLANATORY SKETCH
of the
OPERATIONS AND COMBAT
of
EL BODON.

London: Published by T.& W. BOONE.

Drawn by Col. Napier

look the less they like us.' The next day Soult heard that the Spanish had marched south; that was more than enough to cool any ardour he might have felt for offensive action. His concern – once again – was for Seville; Graham at Barrosa had fetched him back there three months ago, now it was the guerrillas and Blake. The threat of the latter's troops would once have occasioned dismissive French laughter, but after Girard's experience with Zayas at Albuera a little attention might be in order.

So, leaving the 5th Corps and Latour-Maubourg to help mask Badajoz, on 28 June Soult set out for Andalusia, with Godinot's and Conroux's divisions and Briche's cavalry brigade. Before drawing off, Godinot had blown in the walls of Olivenza; this report, together with news on the 29th of his subsequent march towards Los Santos, gave Lord Wellington the clearest expectation that Soult would not now attack him. A fortnight later, after repairing and fully provisioning Badajoz, Marmont in his turn drew off north and east beyond Truxillo, and D'Erlon south towards Zafra, in the perpetual French search for food. Wellington was keen to quit the unhealthy Caia and the dreadful Guadiana fevers, and on hearing of Marmont's movement he went into scattered cantonments between Estremoz and Castelo Branco, his own headquarters relocating briefly to Portalegre. Not for a moment did he contemplate a return to the walls of Badajoz: his bent brass guns were back in Elvas, and the two French generals were capable of combining in ten marches. He had had enough of sieges with inadequate resources and lack of time; he was all afire now to do things properly, starting with Ciudad Rodrigo. He sent for Major Dickson on 19 July:

> His Lordship informed us that it was his intention to attempt the siege of Ciudad Rodrigo, and after talking over the necessary means of transports, &c., he told me he wished I should proceed to Oporto by way of Almeida, and to superintend the conveyance of the English battering train up the Duoro to Lamego, and from thence by land to Trancoso, from whence it would also be conveyed by land to its ultimate destination. Two companies of British artillery have been ordered from Lisbon to Oporto to be employed on this service under my orders.

Reaching Oporto after a blazing hot journey of fourteen days – punctuated by bouts of fever, the inspection of various stocks of large-calibre ammunition and the testing of the state of roads and bridges – Dickson expended prodigious amounts of energy to shift the train up the Duoro to Lamego, using 160 barges; and thence, in 900 carts hauled by 4,170 pairs of bullocks, to Villa da Ponte up in the hills, which he reached by the end of August. The story of his Herculean labour to organize and transport the battering train is set out in the greatest detail in his letters in *The Dickson Manuscripts*, and makes fascinating reading for those intrigued by such technical problems.

Wishing to shift his operations northwards with a view to blockading Ciudad Rodrigo, Lord Wellington moved his headquarters in mid-August to Fuenteguinaldo, 20 miles southwest of the fortress and the same distance below Fuentes d'Oñoro. He left Rowland Hill responsible for the Badajoz area, with the same force Beresford had previously commanded. Crouched like a ring of slip fielders, the Light Division were to the south of the fortress, around Martiago, the 3rd Division to the west around Carpio (in front of the Fuentes battlefield), and the guerrilla Julian Sanchez dominated the northern approaches. The rest of the army lay to the south of the old battlefield, covering some 50 miles as the crow flies, with the

5th Division forward across the border towards the Sierra de Gata. However, the blockade was scarcely formed before Marmont joined with Dorsenne's Army of the North (formerly led by Bessières) – 60,000 men altogether; and on 24 September a supply convoy from Salamanca reprovisioned the garrison in Ciudad Rodrigo. Marmont had heard the previous week of a siege train making its way from Oporto, and had drawn his own conclusions.

With such numbers opposed, and with Marmont pushing forward keen to find evidence of preparations for a siege, Wellington should have fallen back towards the mountains. However, he was loathe to close up his divisions, believing that Marmont had no ambitions other than the revictualing of the fortress – which was correct, but did not allow for the Frenchman's curiosity. Whether or not the British planned a siege, and if so how advanced were the early preparations – the stockpiling of timber, the manufacture of gabions and fascines, the movement of heavy artillery – were questions clearly requiring a different reaction from that to a mere blockade. Marmont wanted to know. So his cavalry ran into Major-General Thomas Picton's 3rd Division, dispersed over some 6 miles, and a perilous scenario rapidly developed around El Bodon.

*   *   *

Picton had troops in Pastores, in El Bodon, on the high ground crossed by the Ciudad Rodrigo–Fuenteguinaldo road, and to the west: four separate groups of two or three battalions each, over 6 miles of front, with large uncovered gaps. This arrangement puzzled Marmont, as well it might, and he understandably assumed that there was more to Wellington's design than met the eye. Not looking for any major action, he accordingly dispensed with his slower-moving infantry, but sent General Louis Pierre Montbrun forward with seven cavalry regiments. What followed threatened (briefly) disaster for General Picton.

Montbrun struck at his centre on the El Bodon ridge. Penetration over it would have cut off the 74th and three companies of the 5/60th Rifles in Pastores 6 miles to the east, and the 1/45th and 1/88th with Picton himself in El Bodon, 2 miles to the east. Fortunately, Lord Wellington was on the spot (although as Grattan truly noted, 'the spot was a large one, with but few troops to cover it'). He had a clear and early view from the ridge, and the rising dust clouds revealed in his telescope supplied the answer that was urgently needed: there were two roads from Ciudad Rodrigo to Fuenteguinaldo – which was Montbrun taking? The minute that he judged the Pastores road was not the one, Wellington sent to Colonel Trench there to withdraw the 74th (Highland), and similarly to Colonel Wallace in El Bodon. He called forward the 77th (East Middlesex), who were a little in rear, to reinforce the 2/5th (Northumberland) on the ridge, and the 21st Portuguese, who came up somewhat later. He took all of Alten's available horse: three squadrons of the 1st Hussars KGL and two squadrons of the 11th Light Dragoons, and a Portuguese brigade of six 9-pounders and six 6-pounders, under Major Arentschildt (said by Grattan to be drawn by mules). The strength of the five Allied squadrons is stated by all but one of the sources to have been 500; the exception, however, the authority that would have known the exact ration strength – the commissary of the 1st German Hussars, August Schaumann, whose journal states that 'our cavalry brigade amounted only to 330 men'.

The 77th Regiment had only been in Portugal for two months, and were exceedingly short from Walcheren fever. They had been brought up to strength with young recruits, but continuing sickness had again reduced them to some 440 all ranks. The guns took post in centre, with the 77th on their left, with the two dragoon squadrons and one from the German Hussars. On their right were Major Henry Ridge with his 2/5th and the other two German squadrons. A total, then, of 330 sabres, 1,000 bayonets (some say less) and a dozen guns – a thin force to face 2,500 Frenchmen.

Montbrun had five regiments of light horse: Lamotte with the 1er and 3e Hussards, and Fournier with the 7e, 13e and 20e Chasseurs. Ensign Grattan, with the 88th along the ridge, watched them come:

> [He] came thundering over the plain at a sweeping pace; ten of his squadrons dashed across the ravine that separated them from Arentschildt's battery, which opened a frightful fire of grape and canister at point blank distance... once fairly over the ravine, they speedily mounted the face of the causeway, and desperately, but heroically, charged the battery. Nothing could resist the torrent – the battery was captured and the cannoniers massacred at their guns.

Wellington had made plain to his commanders that they were there to buy time for Picton to extricate his exposed battalions. That meant keeping the French horsemen below the crest, for once they managed to push any of their number beyond it they could too easily take the defenders in rear. August Schaumann sat his horse with the 1st Hussars KGL:

> Close to me, in the rear of the sand-hills, stood our regiment, brigaded with the 11th Light Dragoons, commanded by General Victor v.Alten. In front of the hills there was a brigade of English infantry and a Portuguese battery. The Portuguese gunners took refuge under their guns, while the French, cutting the traces, attacked the English brigade, which had formed square. At the same time (probably in order to discover whether there were any troops in the rear) the enemy dropped howitzer shells over the sand-hills among our cavalry brigade, which, being short of several squadrons, amounted only to 330 men.

An anonymous officer of the 77th, writing home five days later, tells us what the infantry did:

> Lord Wellington came riding up, and immediately saw the point the enemy meant to attack, where the 5th Regiment and guns were posted, and directly ordered us off to its support. Shortly after we got there the enemy charged our guns: they had at the same time five field pieces and a howitzer playing from an opposite hill on us. The greater part of our regiment had never seen a shot fired: they behaved most nobly. We remained until the enemy came within about twenty yards of us, the front rank kneeling, their bayonets pointing towards the cavalry, and we and the 5th in two squares; when the rear rank gave them such a volley that they tumbled down the hill in great style. Two squadrons of the 11th Dragoons and one of the German Hussars charged after them and cut them up terribly. The Germans gave no quarter.

apier, Oman and Fletcher all tell us that the capture of the guns followed a lengthy riod of charge and counter-charge. But Schaumann, Grattan, the 77th's officer and

Captain Childers of the 11th Light Dragoons (*see* below) are plain that the capture was the first thing that happened – that is, that it immediately preceded the prolonged period of desperate charging. Indeed, Schaumann says the cavalry were actually in rear of the ridge, in dead ground, when the guns were attacked.

When Napier says that 'the danger [being] then imminent, suddenly the 5th regiment led by Major Ridge, a daring spirit, darted into the midst of the French cavalry and retook the artillery', it is likely that the 77th – being new to the country and full of raw recruits – stayed put, the 5th alone exploiting forward. The curiosity is how Ridge was able to 'dart' at all with a square; we must assume that the 5th and 77th were in square all the time, notwithstanding that Oman famously has Ridge in line to charge cavalry – an act of heroism not recorded before or since. However he did it, it was a vulnerable moment for the gallant Ridge, so aptly named. It needs only a dozen horsemen to go hard at the end of a line two ranks deep in order to roll the men over and smash it completely. Henry Ridge therefore took a huge risk, but he got away with it: the French cavalry were both astonished by his audacity, and unbalanced by his attack. No longer in a coherent line, and anxious to sort themselves out, they gave way individually and sheered off. Ridge halted and retired; the Portuguese gunners ran out to their guns; and grape and canister again spewed down and across the slopes. Captain Michael Childers commanded one of the 11th's squadrons:

> We waited on a height where there was a fine plain... with the infantry and some Portuguese guns... a strong column of cavalry was advancing, charging the guns that were on the edge of the high ground to our right. They also charged the 5th and 77th who drove them down the hill like a flock of sheep and retook the guns.

Young Grattan was also watching:

> The regiments of the right brigade [at El Bodon] were posted on a height parallel to that occupied by the 5th and 77th. We had a clear and painful view of all that was passing, and we shuddered for our companions; the glittering of the countless sabres that were about to assail them, and the blaze of light which the reflection of the sun threw across the brazen helmets of the French horsemen, might be likened to the flash of lightning that preceded the thunder of Arentschildt's artillery – but we could do nothing. A few seconds passed away; we saw the smoke of musketry – it did not recede, and we were assured that the attack had failed; in a moment or two more we could discern the brave 5th and 77th following their beaten adversaries, and a spontaneous shout of joy burst from the brigade.

August Schaumann went on to say that, the guns and squares being attacked, the French began to shell the reverse slope where the cavalry stood:

> This was the signal for our brave fellows. At a slow trot they advanced through a hollow between two sand-hills, and then, accelerating their speed, ultimately seemed to merge with a loud cheer into the black mass of the French cavalry. Again they appeared, and after having formed once more in the hollow, returned to the charge with a loud cheer. Incredible as it may seem, it is nevertheless true that for three-quarters of an hour they

continued these tactics and charged in all eight times, and with such success that, where they made their thrusts, the French flew asunder, leaving great gaps in their ranks.

But they came on again, and again. Fortunately it was a case of 'Hey diddle diddle, straight up the middle', for if Montbrun had had the wit to go round the flank all would surely have been lost. His continued frontal assaults are a puzzle today, but were a blessing at the time. The Germans and the 11th had clearly already laid fresh claim to that moral ascendancy established at Campo Mayor, Los Santos and Usagre; there is little doubt that Montbrun's troopers were 'shy', as the courteous slander of the day had it. It is said that when the trumpets sounded for one last advance, the Allies saw the regiment at the head of the column refuse to move off. Captain Childers again:

> They then came to our front and rather to our left, and the Brigade... was ordered to charge them as soon as they made their appearance upon a part of the hill that was more accessible to the rest. The Hussars were ordered to charge and the 11th to support [and] as we got the order some time before it was put in execution, we were complaining that we were not sent first; but we soon found there was game enough for both parties. We both instantly charged and drove them down the hill where there was an immense column. We of course did not follow them down the hill, but retired about 100 yards, they immediately followed us and we charged and drove them down again. This continued for a long time, I should think an hour at least, in which it was reckoned we charged eight times, each time five or six times our number.

The colonel commanding the KGL Hussars agreed; he wrote later that each of the five Allied squadrons must have charged eight or nine times, the enemy coming on nearly forty times in all – but not once did they cross the crest.

In the precious hour that had been bought, Thomas Picton had got the 45th and 88th Foot out of El Bodon. Colonel Trench in Pastores was also making for Fuenteguinaldo, sensibly far to the south of El Bodon; and therefore, when at around 2pm Wellington spied French infantry closing at last, he ordered the retreat. Arentschildt went first with his mules and some cavalry; then the 21st Portuguese in square – they had remained in reserve on the reverse slope throughout the action – followed by the 5th and 77th in a single square. The rear was covered by two German squadrons and at least one of the 11th. Montbrun watched the guns limber up and go, and immediately sent squadrons on to the ridge towards El Bodon. The main body surged up the hollow and over the top the moment the German Hussars finally turned for good. Two and a half thousand horsemen flowed forward, as at a signal gun, as Captain Childers tells us:

> The last charge we made with not more than twenty men. We got so mixed up with them as they stood firm, and advanced on both flanks at the same time, that we were obliged to retreat at a good gallop, with them at our heels – in fact I saw them stab one of our men, who like a fool was not looking behind him. We galloped I should think about three quarters of a mile when we came up with a solid square of infantry of the above named regiments [5th and 77th], and as we passed within sixteen yards of them they opened their fire on our pursuers and knocked a good many over, who we turned back and sabred. We

were so mixed up with the French that when the infantry fired they killed one of ours and a hussar. The conduct of the infantry was admirable.

So the large marching square of red coats now became the focus of French efforts. Napier's admiring eloquence for once seems a trifle overexcited:

> Then the fifth and seventy-seventh, two weak battalions formed in one square, were quite exposed, and in an instant the whole of the French cavalry came thundering down upon them. But how vain, how fruitless to match the sword with musket! To send the charging horsemen against the steadfast veteran! The multitudinous squadrons, rending the skies with their shouts, and closing upon the glowing squares, like the falling edges of a burning crater, were as instantly rejected, scorched, and scattered abroad; and the rolling peals of musketry had scarcely ceased to echo in the hills, when bayonets glittered at the edge of the smoke, and with a firm and even step, the British regiments came forth like the holy men from the Assyrian's furnace.

Montbrun put his squadrons at three sides simultaneously, only to be held by the volleys punching out at short range, and the German Hussars swooping back to clear the local disorder along the sides of the square. Montbrun's horse battery came into action briefly, before the squadrons again rushed forward to try their luck, but the ranks held firm and tight-spaced, and the French horse were never going to break in.

The two squares had by now caught up with the 45th and the 88th, the latter's Ensign Grattan telling us that:

> Montbrun at the head of fifteen squadrons of light horse pressed closely on our right flank, and made every demonstration of attacking us with the view to engaging our attention until the arrival of his infantry and artillery... For six miles across a perfect flat, without the slightest protection from any incident of ground, without artillery, and I might say without cavalry (for what were four or five squadrons to twenty or thirty?) did the 3rd Division continue its march. During the whole time the enemy's cavalry never quitted them; a park of six guns advanced with the cavalry, and taking the 3rd Division in flank and rear, poured in a frightful fire of round-shot, grape and canister. Many men fell in this way, and those whose wounds rendered them unable to march were obliged to be abandoned to the enemy.
>
> This was a trying and pitiable situation for troops to be placed in, but it in no way shook the courage or confidence of the soldiers; so far from being dispirited or cast down, the men were cheerful and gay, the soldiers of my corps telling their officers that if the French dared to charge, every officer should have a *nate* [neat] horse to ride upon.
>
> General Picton conducted himself with his accustomed coolness; he remained on the left flank of the column, and repeatedly cautioned the different battalions to mind the quarter distance and the 'tellings off'. 'Your safety,' added he, 'my credit, and the honour of the army, is at stake: it all rests with you at this moment.' We had reached to within a mile of our entrenched camp, when Montbrun, impatient lest we should escape from his grasp, ordered his troopers to bring up their right shoulders and incline towards our column: the movement was not exactly bringing his squadrons into line, but it was the next

thing to it, and at this time they were within half pistol-shot of us. Picton took off his hat, and holding it over his eyes as a shade from the sun, looked sternly, but anxiously at the French. The clatter of the horses and the clanking of the scabbards were so great when the right half squadron moved up, that many thought it the forerunner of a general charge; some mounted officer called out, 'Had we not better form square?' – 'No,' replied Picton; 'it is but a ruse to frighten us, but it won't do.'

At this moment a cloud of dust was discernable in the direction of Guinaldo; it was a cheering sight; it covered the 3rd Dragoon Guards, who came up at a slinging trot to our relief. When this fine regiment approached to within a short distance of us they dismounted, tightened their girths, and prepared for battle; but the French horse slackened their pace, and in half an hour more we were safe within our lines.

The retreat of the marching squares from El Bodon was similar to the Light Division's fighting withdrawal to the lines at Fuentes d'Oñoro: the same discipline in the ranks of foot and horse, the same frustration for the French cavalry. Montbrun deserved his lack of success, for not developing an indirect, wider approach; had he done so from the outset, however, Wellington would surely have suffered an embarrassing reverse, strung out and vulnerable as his battalions undoubtedly were that morning. It had been a nasty few hours for them all. Fortunately the casualty figures were trivial – 160, half in the cavalry, to 200 French – a cheap price that did not begin to reflect the risk involved. Given how nearly the action at El Bodon must have come to troubling his lordship, apparently he showed no sign of it, or not to the anonymous officer of the 77th:

> To describe Lord Wellington is impossible; his coolness, his decision in the midst of a hot fire from the enemy were eminently conspicuous; he has the eye of a hawk. He was close in our rear, and exclaimed: 'Well done, the 77th,' when he saw our men behave so well.

The next twenty-four hours were also to be uneasy for the commander-in-chief. At Fuenteguinaldo he now had just 16,000 men, in an excellent position, but Marmont was gathering together some 40,000 and a hundred guns. That night Crauford's Light Division was supposed to march in, whereupon Wellington, and Thomas Graham 12 miles to the north, could safely have withdrawn. But Crauford disobeyed, not moving until next morning, and throughout 26 September the outnumbered Wellington was forced to sit waiting – either for Crauford or Marmont, whoever should come first. As Graham was to write, 'it was all very pretty – but spun rather fine. Had the enemy behaved with common spirit on the 26th we should not have got off so easily from Guinaldo.'

When Robert Craufurd arrived at last, Wellington greeted him with 'I am glad to see you safe'. 'Oh, I was in no danger, I assure you', replied Crauford, in an off-hand manner. 'No, but I was, through your conduct', came the icy reply. 'He's damned crusty today', muttered Crauford, still uncomprehending. As Wellington's Judge-Advocate, Larpent, wrote: '[Crauford] at times perplexed Lord Wellington considerably, who never could be sure where he was... [and at other times] never knew what he would do... It was surprising what he bore from him at times... [yet] Lord Wellington knew his merits and humoured him.' Indeed; and when four months later 'Black Bob' died on the Lesser Breach at Ciudad Rodrigo, Wellington called 'the bitterest blow of the war'.

In the event, Marmont shirked attacking Wellington at Fuenteguinaldo. When the Allies moved west to concentrate on formidably strong ground behind the River Coa, he sensibly shirked it again, preferring to go into winter quarters around Salamanca, 60 miles beyond Ciudad Rodrigo. That fortress was thus once more isolated, and therefore tempting to the British. In early October the Allied divisions also settled into proper winter quarters. The 3rd, 4th and Light Divisions went forward to within 15 miles of Ciudad Rodrigo, observing rather than blockading, with the cavalry and Julian Sachez's guerrillas operating to the east, across the Salamanca road. The men were set to making gabions and fascines, at a rate of 4d and 2½d respectively. The battering train, which had already been moved up to Villa da Ponte, moved in late November to Almeida – now repaired, and a safe sanctuary only two days' march from Ciudad Rodrigo.

With impeccable timing for the British cause, there then came astonishing news from Paris to Marshal Marmont. It arrived with him on 13 December: he was immediately to send 12,000 men to aid Suchet's march on Valencia, and another 3,000 were to go to secure the lines of communications. For Napoleon was of the firm opinion (in the words of his chief-of-staff Berthier) 'that the English army has 20,000 sick, and barely 20,000 able-bodied men with the colours, so that they cannot possibly try any offensive enterprise'.

At the turn of the year Marmont thus lost a third of his army – two infantry divisions and one of cavalry. The troops moved eastwards on 15 December, the first hint of it reaching Lord Wellington on Christmas Eve. At first it was a puzzle, however welcome: 'I cannot understand these marches and countermarches', he wrote to Graham on Christmas Day. But he soon received a fuller report, and a memorandum of the 28th noted that 'The movement of Marmont's army towards Toledo, to aid Suchet as is supposed, have induced us to make preparations for the siege of Ciudad Rodrigo'. To modern ears, this phrasing hides the satisfaction the news had brought to headquarters. It was in fact a stunningly welcome surprise – Wellington was in the joyful position of a burglar watching a house he hopes to rob, only to see the occupiers leaving on holiday.

An extra Christmas present arrived on 29 December, with the intriguing news that all the cavalry of the Imperial Guard were marching for France, and that the two infantry divisions of the Young Guard were also going north from Valladolid. Wellington initially thought these deployments were connected to some further need to support Suchet; time would show him that it was Russia that now consumed the Emperor's mind, beyond his concerns for a small army in Portugal. The orders for the siege of Ciudad Rodrigo were issued on New Year's Day, 1812. So it was that at the beginning of a memorably bad year for Napoleon, the first omen was summoned up on 19 January when Wellington secured the fortress of Ciudad Rodrigo and thereby control of the core strategic northern route into Spain. After the tortuously unsuccessful attempts on Fort San Cristobal and the Badajoz castle in May and June, the speed of the twelve-day reduction of Ciudad Rodrigo left Marmont aghast and disbelieving – and left the British looking forward with renewed optimism to a third try at Badajoz. But that most bloody of encounters, and the subsequent events around Salamanca, are another story.

*   *   *

It is customary, in final chapters, for historians of the Peninsular War to summarize the campaign, to pull together the detailed sub-plots and thus to present a concluding overview. This custom flows from the length of the war, which saw the snows of six winters, which naturally tend to chop the story into annual chapters – or, in the case of great historians like Napier and Oman, annual volumes. Not counting the sieges, and the actions in the Pyrenees in the winter of 1813/14, all the major battles took place in the summer months, when new grass fed the horses, and a new harvest provided bread and biscuit. In the winter, generals laid plans; in the summer their soldiers marched again, to try to put them into effect – as had been the pattern of European warfare for centuries.

The importance of the 1811 campaign lies in its pivotal role, its fulcrum position in the shifting British/French balance. Out of Wellington's strategic masterpiece of ultimate defence – the Lines of Torres Vedras – came the strategic weakening through starvation of Massena's army, and his subsequent withdrawal, with huge losses, up to and beyond Sabugal. Soult had accordingly moved north to his aid (and in the process, amazingly snatched Badajoz); to do this he had borrowed much of Victor's force from around Cadiz, which allowed Graham to earn his reputation at Barrosa – which in turn pulled the elastic on Soult, to drag him back. That in turn allowed Beresford the space for the first attempt at Badajoz, while his master dealt with a resurgent Massena at Fuentes d'Oñoro; and so back bounced Soult again, to try to save Badajoz, and to thwart him Beresford committed his command to the bloody confrontation at Albuera.

The important events of the first half of the year thus all have causal relationships; but beyond the individual episodes, there can be seen emerging an interesting and ultimately decisive shift in the initiative towards Lord Wellington. The French marshals were beginning to dance to his tune – and dance, moreover, with a deal more circumspection than previously. Their new reluctance to engage became more noticeable in the second half of the year, and is of a piece with the changed scenario: the commander-in-chief was now going for the two fortresses and, beyond them, aggressively to carry operations into Spain. The year 1811 therefore sees the gradual change from defence to offence.

The author's detailed opinions and prejudices have already been expressed in the chapters dealing with the major actions. There are, however, four concluding areas upon which he wishes briefly to enlarge.

Among the various lessons of the year, the superiority of British and German cavalry must stand high. Forever outnumbered, their right arms proved stronger at Campo Mayor, at Los Santos and in the brilliant ambush at Usagre – and strong enough against a far more numerous enemy to buy time at Fuentes d'Oñoro, Albuera and El Bodon. The year saw no cavalry disaster; the odd picket was embarrassingly surprised here and there, but that laxity of control so often levelled against their officers was largely invented by Sir Charles Oman in his ungenerous treatment of Campo Mayor. Succeeding historians have tended to accept his view, but that affair is more truly described by Ian Fletcher in his *Galloping at Everything* – a properly generous treatment of our cavalry in the Peninsula – as 'a pivotal action which set the tone of future battles between British and French cavalry'. Long, Head and Otway performed a splendid feat of exhuberant horsemanship that day, in the proper style and tradition for cavalry; that it was sadly unexploited was the fault of the cripplingly cautious Beresford, an infantryman.

William Beresford himself must also be considered among the major points of interest thrown into high relief by that year's campaigning. He was in many respects an extremely able leader, but a curious personality; he obviously inspired deep loyalty from men like D'Urban and Warre, yet 1811 revealed his lack of that decisive confidence in the field so essential to higher commanders. No more revealing light can be shone on his belated and near-fatal reaction to Soult's move around his right at Albuera than the contrast of his chief's far swifter reaction to Massena's equivalent threat ten days before at Fuentes. If it had not been for Henry Hardinge, Sir Lowry Cole and the Fusiliers, all the grim sacrifices by the men of Zayas, Colborne, Hoghton and Abercrombie would have been in vain, and no thanks to William Carr Beresford. His many fine qualities seemed to diminish, even to evaporate, when he was confronted by the enemy while in independent command.

As admitted already, however, few of us would remain free of anxiety when conscious of Wellington's appraising eye gazing on our efforts from the background; and his lordship himself had his difficult moments. Something unquestionably went wrong at Sabugal, and not just Erskine's ill-handled turning movement; in the fog over the river neither the 3rd nor 5th Divisions got forward as they should, and Reynier's 2nd Corps escaped – a failure both galling and unnecessary. At Fuentes d'Oñoro he allowed only a thin margin for error on that right flank, and further invited disaster by his selection of Houston's new 7th Division, which should never have survived that day – any more than Picton's scattered battalions should have got off from El Bodon. There, too, Lord Wellington perhaps underestimated his enemy – though not (quite) his own soldiers' ability to march and manoeuvre, to their limit. But as always, we find little enough with which to charge the Peer, and much more to admire.

In particular, since the campaign was one of constant movement, we see his superiority in logistics – getting provisions of all sorts to where they were in demand. He had brought his Indian experience up to date in the European context, and was thus mindful of his relationship with both Portugal and Spain. That which did not come courtesy of the Royal Navy, and a fleet of ox-carts at 15 miles a day, he bought locally, and paid for it well and promptly – unlike the French, whose methods Jac Weller memorably called organized thievery. This was not simply a question of seeking local co-operation by behaving decently to the civilian population, but one of realistic observation. Napoleon was mistaken, during his brief visit, not to pay more attention to the geography and climate of the Iberian Peninsula, which would not long support an army living off the land in Revolutionary fashion.

The Lines of Torres Vedras showed Wellington's strategic understanding in this regard: he saw the vulnerability of the French, and the starvation of Massena's army was the aim and the result. And unlike his enemy, whose tactical movements were several times influenced by the need to find food, in this campaign the Peninsular Field Army never went seriously hungry: 'I know of no point more important than closely to attend to the comforts of the soldier: let him be well clothed, sheltered and fed. How should he fight poor fellow if he has, beside risking his life, to struggle with unnecessary hardships.'

If the commissariat was kept firmly under Wellinton's eye and thumb, his intelligence service was kept under his hat. A flow of information came from his spies, his observing officers, the interrogation of prisoners and deserters and from captured despatches, and it all went directly into his head alone. As we have seen, he was thus able to judge nicely the approach and possible concentration of his opponents. The French marshals, on the other hand, thanks to their cruelties to the populace and the resulting guerrilla reaction, lived in an intelligence vacuum; their couriers were routinely caught and killed, and their messages willingly exchanged for Wellington's gold by their killers.

Wellington's gathering of intelligence, as of provisions, was the result of the energetic attention he always paid to these prime areas of generalship, throughout the entire war. They are areas particularly worthy of mention, however, in connection with the 1811 campaign, since

Massena, Soult and Marmont so obviously neglected them, and suffered for it. These self-inflicted wounds stemmed, it would seem, from some arrogant memory of past successes; as in the case of their column tactics, they did not see a need to change.

*　　*　　*

In reading eyewitness accounts, time and again we have marched into the volley-smoke: up the hill at Barrosa, over the river at Sabugal, into the streets of Fuentes, and along the ridge above Albuera – the grapeshot whistling past our ears while we fumble for the next cartridge and, in the act of biting it, look across at the man in the blue coat, similarly engaged, often catching his eye. Time and again we have dropped our bayonet-point, clamped the butt against the right hip, cheered, and charged – expecting not only to see the back of his coat but also his abandoned knapsack, with the usual food, drink or plunder. Wellington's soldiers led primitive lives, open to the elements; a man must usually have been pre-occupied with his stomach, his feet in deteriorating shoes, his lost blanket, his toothache and his blisters.

These men were led in the main by young gentlemen, sometimes boys in their teens, to whom they deferred in the natural order of things, and whose will – if not always done readily, out of the usual respect for their betters – was nonetheless done, for fear of harsh punishment. We know from those like William Grattan, Robert Blakeney, William Woods, Edward Close, Moyle Sherer and Charles Leslie that young officers were not only expected to keep a sensible distance from their other ranks, but also to encourage in their soldiers that pride in the regiment which would be the cement in their two-deep red wall. Read Appendix I, 'The 29th at Albuera', and you are reading a man for whom the 29th is the best regiment in the British Army. Sir John Fortescue, writing his great *History* during the First World War, tried to explain what he called the constancy displayed on the ridge at Albuera:

> Whence came the spirit which made that handful of English battalions – for not a single Scots or Irish regiment was present – content to die where they stood rather than give way one inch? Beyond all question it sprang from intense regimental pride and regimental feeling... The regimental officers can hardly have failed to perceive that Beresford was making a very ill hand of the battle, but that was no affair of theirs. The great point to each of them was that his battalion was being tried, and that in the presence of other battalions, by an ordeal testing its discipline and efficiency to the utmost. Sergeants and old soldiers... took the same view... And hence it was that when one man in every two, or even two in every three, had fallen in Hoghton's brigade, the survivors were still in line by their Colours, closing inwards towards the tattered silk which represented the ark of their covenant, the one thing supremely important to them in the world.

This pride was indeed never more amply demonstrated than on that dreadful day of 16 May 1811. Two centuries on – with no automatic deference as of right, and certainly no punitive sanctions – we must hope that our present junior leadership and regimental spirit again proves superior to that of our future foes; and that it will be roundly cheered by the gaunt ghosts in faded red coats, doubtless watching with a keen eye as they lean on their firelocks.

Appendix I
'The 29th at Albuera'

The following article, by an unknown author, appeared in 'Firm', the regimental magazine of the Worcestershire Regiment, in 1928; it is reproduced with the kind permission of the Trustees of The Worcestershire Regimental Museum. It is preceded here by a description of the 29th by Moyle Sherer of the 34th, also present that day on the ridge at Albuera:

'Nothing could possibly be worse than their clothing; it had become necessary to patch it; and, as red cloth could not be procured, grey, white, and even brown had been used, yet, even under this striking disadvantage, they could not be viewed by a soldier without admiration. The perfect order and cleanliness of their arms and appointments, their steadiness on parade, their erect carriage, and their firm and free marching, exceeded anything of the kind I had ever seen. No corps of any Army or Nation, which I have since had an opportunity of seeing, has come nearer to my idea of what a regiment of infantry should be, than the old Twenty-Ninth.'

* * *

Dawn of May the 16th, 1811. It has been raining in the night, and a damp mist hangs low over the countryside. Slowly the mist lifts, revealing dense masses of sleeping soldiers huddled in their cloaks and greatcoats close to the lines of their piled muskets. Propped against the nearest pile are longer weapons – three sergeants' pikes, and above them two cased Colours. Around that pile are sleeping the two subalterns and the three sergeants who are to carry and guard the honour of the Regiment through the coming day.

Far off a bugle sounds. One after another, bugles and trumpets take up the note, and the army wakes to life. Men shake themselves awake, stiff and cold after their night in the rain; there is shouting along the lines and a boiling of camp kettles. The ordered piles of muskets are broken up, and are presently replaced by ordered lines of men. Company by company, battalion by battalion, brigade by brigade, the army falls into its ranks for battle.

The mist thins away, showing on all sides the wide landscape of southern Spain – an empty land, with but few houses or cottages to mark the brownish rolling hills and dark woods. We are on a low ridge between two small streams. Far off to front and rear the ground swells upward, and on our right it rises more sharply to a low rounded hill.

Along the ridge our army is forming up. On our right, foreign uniforms of brown, blue and yellow mark the brigades of the Spanish Army – our allies. Close at hand are our own British troops in their red coats – ten battalions in all, in three brigades; and the right flank battalion of the centre brigade is our own Regiment: the Twenty-Ninth.

The Regiment is old in war. Three long years of camping, marching, and fighting have left the red uniforms worn and faded, mended and patched in many places with variegated cloth of many colours. The iron-grey trousers are torn and muddy. Pipe clay has been to seek, an the heavy white cross-belts are dingy and stained. But most of those in the ranks are old soldiers of long service, who know the essentials of War. The long heavy muskets are serviceable and clean, the thin triangular bayonets and the broader blades of the sergeants' pikes are like streaks of silver even after a night of rain, and the snap of the ordered movements after the sharp commands tell of the proud discipline which has been rigidly maintained.

The Colours are uncased, and take post in the centre of the battalion. Great heavy squares of silk, these Colours, unfringed and almost without ornament, save that in the centre of the pale silk of the Regimental Colour is embroidered our badge – the Royal Lion above the number 'XXIX' with, sprawling above it, added by a half-skilled craftsman of Lisbon, the single name 'ROLEIA' – the name of that desperate battle three years ago where fell the gallant Colonel Lake and so many of his men.

The two ensigns carrying the Colours are mere boys. Ensign Furnace carrying the King's Colour is a lad of only 17 years. Ensign Vance carrying the Regimental Colour is but little older. Both are fresh to the war – the latest from home who have joined the veteran battalion. Their hair, long and curling after the Byronic fashion of the day, their slight side whiskers, high stocks, and white frill at the breast, their new coatees, with swallow tails rather longer than the regulation knee length, the careless knotting of their sashes, all betoken the latest fashion of the young 'bucks' of the Regency. Both are stirred by the thrill of their first battle; and their young eagerness is matched by the grim calm of the three colour-sergeants. Grizzled veterans these last, who can recall the wild melee of Rolica, the adventurous passage of the River Douro, and the great charge of bayonets and pikes upon the crumbling French line at Talavera.

From the front comes the boom of a gun and the dull rattle of musketry. Smoke rises into the still morning air from a house burning in the red-roofed village on the river bank half a mile in front. On the gentle slope beyond the village, dark masses twinkling with steel are marching and wheeling – the squadrons and battalions of the enemy. Orderlies gallop to and fro, and the distant fusilade spreads and grows. Presently a nearby battery opens fire, and the distant view is obscured by its drifting smoke. Through the smoke come howling the enemy's shot. Like giant cricket balls at utmost speed the cannon balls pitch and bounce along the ground. The massed battalions stand easy in their ranks, waiting the order to advance, and idly watching the mounted officers riding along the line. One of them, our Brigadier, Hoghton, has been wearing an un-dress frock coat of dull green. His servant comes up with his full-dress coat of scarlet and gold, and without quitting his saddle the Brigadier exchanges his coat under the enemy's fire, while the ranks cheer him in great good humour, knowing him for a fighting man after their own heart.

The angry firing in front spreads and grows. Colborne's Brigade on our right is ordered forward, and his battalions tramp, with drums playing, down the gentle slope – solid masses of dull red and glittering steel, with their paired Colours rising proudly in their midst. Our Brigade as yet stands fast, and the enemy in front do not seem to be pressing their advance.

Away to the right the masses of the Spanish forces are changing their formation. Their battalions are wheeling and facing round, moving away towards their further flank. Mounted officers pass galloping. Rumour spreads down the ranks. The French attack in front is but a feint. The mass of the enemy has encircled our right flank, and are even now climbing the far side of the hill which dominates our position. The Spaniards are moving hurriedly to stay their advance.

Our burly General, Sir William Beresford, gallops down the ranks towards the threatened flank, his staff clattering in his wake. Firing and white smoke rising on the hill show that the danger is real. The whole array of our army is set in motion. Our Battalion shoulders arms, wheels to the right, and marches off, with drums and fifes playing proudly at the head. In front of us the four battalions of Colborne's Brigade are likewise advancing. Close behind us are the rest of our own Brigade, our friends the Forty-Eighth and Fifty-Seventh. On our left flank the feint attack around the village seems dying down. The dull day has grown duller, and lowering clouds give warning of rain.

On the hill in front the firing grows heavier, and through the drifting smoke we can discern the Spanish masses surging to and fro. The fight must be on the very crest. The battalions of Colborne's Brigade are crossing a shallow valley and then breasting the slope of the hill beyond, showing as solid blocks of red amid the batteries and baggage behind the Spanish line. The storm clouds seem to hang lower, the wind rises, and the sky grows dark.

Of a sudden the storm breaks in a rush of hail and rain, rain which drives down in sheets, veiling the slopes beyond. Through the hail comes a low drumming sound shaking the earth, and dimly we see a dark wave travelling at utmost speed – French cavalry, which have swung right round the hill, charging Colborne's Brigade from their exposed right flank.

Through the rain we see Colborne's battalions breaking their solid order in a desperate effort to form square – too late. Before they can form, the racing cavalry crashes into and over the crowded battalions. The hillside in front becomes a swirling mass of galloping horsemen dimly seen through the rain, circling and wheeling, striking with sword and lance among disordered fugitives. Away to the left one battalion has succeeded in forming square, and is beating off the horsemen by rapid musketry. Further off, the roar of firing on the hill in front continues unabated.

Our drums cease to play. With sharp orders our Battalion halts, orders arms, and with a hard rattle of ramrods the muskets are loaded. Then the long bayonets leap upward again as arms are shouldered. Our drums have wheeled round from the front, and are posted close to the Colours behind the second company. Another sharp order, and in silence the Battalion tramps forward.

Towards us come running a crowd of broken Spaniards, with French lancers cantering and thrusting savagely among them. The Battalion halts and our front company gives fire with rapid successive volleys of platoons. As the smoke clears the survivors of the horsemen are galloping away out of range. Again we tramp forward.

As we cross the little valley and breast the hillside the rain continues, chilling us, and making the long grass slippery to tread. The French horsemen, now scattered and exhausted, are drawing off to rally and reform; but again and again our leading companies disperse their wheeling squadrons by sharp volleys. The ground is strewn with fallen horses and men – Spanish and English intermixed, killed or wounded by lance and sword.

Down the slope come streaming crowds of retreating Spaniards, stumbling past us as we press forward. The battle on the hill is going badly. The rain thins and ceases. Steadily the companies tramp up the slope, in silence and grim resolve. The musketry in front is close now, and acrid smoke comes drifting through the ranks. We are about to meet the French the French whom we have beaten time and again. We will not fail now.

We reach the top of the slope. The firing is close at hand. From the smoke in front mounted officer comes cantering back – our own Major Gregory Way who has gone forwa to reconnoitre. He reins his great horse 'Black Jack' by the side of our Colonel, and gestures eagerly as he explains. Orders are shouted. Through the smoke the last brave Spaniards are filing back to reform behind us. Our drums crash out again, breaking into our fighting tune, our own March – 'Royal Windsor'.

The leading company halts. Swiftly, company by company, the battalion deploys into line, while the drums and fifes hammer out their defiant tune amid the firing and the shouted orders. As our Colours wheel up into the centre of the line we see for a moment the proud young faces of the two ensigns backed by the grim old colour-sergeants. Our line has been formed on the edge of a small ravine or sunken lane. A sudden gust of wind blows aside the smoke and shows on the far side of the ravine, not fifty yards away, a dense oncoming crowd of bayonets, plumed shakos and dark coats – a massed battalion of the enemy.

At once their leading rank breaks into a rapid independent fire. Their dark mass vanishes in a haze of smoke stabbed by sparkling flashes, and the bullets crack around our ears. Orders ring sharp and clear. 'Ready!' – the ramrods rattle along the line, and our front rank drops on the knee. 'Present!' – the bayonets flash out horizontal. 'Fire!' and our front rank is blotted out in driving smoke.

Volley after volley, platoon by platoon, the firing blazes up and down our line. With the perfect fire-discipline of long practice our soldiers handle their arms, pouring storm after storm of bullets into the enemy's ranks. At intervals a breeze rends the smoke and lets us dimly see the dense dark crowd surging on the far side of the sunken lane. Their men have fallen in heaps, but more come crowding up from behind, although in their packed column only the foremost can answer the fire of our thin line.

In the desperate urgency of our rapid fire we have no time to count how fast our men are struck down. As each man falls, his comrades close in to keep the platoon line intact – close in continually towards the centre, where the Colours form the Battalion's rallying point. Glancing through the smoke we see the lifted Colours sway and reel as bullet after bullet tears through the wavering silk.

Through the smoke in front comes the blaze and crash of a field gun, brought into action in the enemy's front line – then another and another. A hail of grape-shot strikes down ten men at once, and the enemy's cannon-shot come howling and tearing through our ranks. But ever those left standing close inwards towards the centre, firing swiftly and grimly at the blaze of the guns.

The Colours are the enemy's best aiming mark, and two of the colour-sergeants are down. The King's Colour sways and falls as Ensign Furnace is hit. But the surviving colour-sergeant props up the boy, and with desperate effort he again raises the heavy flag aloft. A subaltern from the nearest company rushes up, begs him to hand over the Colour and go back; but with clenched teeth the boy refuses. The honour is his, and he will keep it to the last.

Our ranks are thinning under the deadly fire from the guns close in front. More of our men are down than are on their feet. The fierce platoon volleys are dissolving into a ragged independent fire from the little groups left standing, still instinctively closing inwards.

In the centre has been the grimmest slaughter, and the Colour party now stands isolated amid a circle of wounded and dead. The Regimental Colour falls as Ensign Vance is struck down. The last colour-sergeant crashes down by his side. The boy Furnace stands tottering under the King's Colour alone.

Mortally wounded, Ensign Vance raises himself and looks for aid. The drifting smoke hides everything, and he can see no one to save the Colour which is his to guard. At any moment the enemy may be upon him. *The French must not have the Colour.*

All about him are dead. The responsibility is on him alone. Dying, he wrenches desperately at the head of the staff, tearing the heavy silk from the pole. *The French must not have the Colour.*

Beside him Ensign Furnace, struck a second time, falls to his knees, then crumples in a heap, the King's Colour sinking over him like a pall.

Suddenly through the mist to our right comes a clamour of firing. The enemy's musketry in front ceases, the smoke thins, and those who are still standing see the crowds of the enemy breaking their ranks, facing round to meet a new attack upon their flank. Volley after volley, and then a line of bayonets, fur caps and red coats gleaming through the smoke – fresh British battalions of fusiliers breaking in on the enemy's shattered array.

The French masses give way and reel backwards before the charge, while such of our men as are still standing leap forward cheering, with bayonets levelled to complete their rout.

*   *   *

Dusk, under a chill drizzle of rain. Small parties with lanterns are searching along the line, numbering the heaped bodies of dead and succouring the wounded, who in our companies far outnumber those left unhurt. A cry – 'Captain Gell, sir – here are our Colours!'

Reverently the torn King's Colour is lifted from the dead hands of Ensign Furnace. Beside him Ensign Vance lies face downwards, the pole of the Regimental Colour by his side. The Colour itself cannot be seen; but later, on lifting his body, the precious silk is found crumpled close into the breast of his coat.

Appendix II

No. XXVII.

Return of Killed, Wounded, and Missing, of the Army under the Command of His Excellency Field-marshal the Marquess of Wellington, K. B., in the Affair at Fuente Honore.

	Killed											Wounded											Missing											Total										
	Lt. Colonels	Majors	Captains	Lieutenants	Ensigns	Staff	Serjeants	Drummers	Rank and File	Total	Horses	Lieut. Colonels	Majors	Captains	Lieutenants	Ensigns	Staff	Serjeants	Drummers	Rank and File	Total	Horses	Lieut. Colonels	Majors	Captains	Lieutenants	Ensigns	Staff	Serjeants	Drummers	Rank and File	Total	Horses	Lieut. Colonels	Majors	Captains	Lieutenants	Ensigns	Staff	Serjeants	Drummers	Rank and File	Total	Horses
Royal Horse Artillery											1											1											1												1
14th Light Dragoons											1											1										1												3	
16th Do. Do.											1																																	1
1st Hussars K. G. L.									1	1	1			1						4	5	5														1						4	5	5
5th Foot 2nd Battalion									1	1					1					4	4	4														1	1					4	4	4
24th Do. 2nd Do.																		1		5	5	4																	1			5	9	4
42nd Do. 2nd Do.														1	1						2	7									2	2				1	1					2	9	7
45th Do. 1st Do.														1							1															1							1	
50th Do. 1st Do.			1						3	3					1					9	9														1	1					20	22	
60th Do. 5th Do.				1					6	6					2		1	1		31	38	5														1	3	1	1	3		43	52	
71st Do. 1st Do.									1	1				1	1					17	20															1	1					10	26	
74th Do. Do.									5	5										9	9																					10	10	
79th Do. 1st Battalion																		2		9	9																		2		12	12	
83rd Do. 2nd Do.																				6	6																				5	5	
88th Do. 1st Do.															1					9	10																1					6	6	
88th Do. 2nd Do.									3	3								1		2	3																		1		3	10	
92nd Do. 1st Do.															1					9	10	3															1					2	3	
94th Do. Do.															1					5	6																1					9	10	
95th Do. 3rd Battalion																		1		3	4																		1			7	7	
1st Light Battalion K. G. L.									2	2										2	4																				4	4	
2nd Do. Do.									1	1										4	4																				4	4	
1st Line Do. Do.														1	1			1		3	3															1	1			1		4	4	
2nd Do. Do.																																												
5th Do. Do.																		1		3	3																		1		3	3	
7th Do. Do.															1			1		3	3																1			1		3	3	
Total British			3	1			1		19	22	4	1		3	7	3	1	10		145	171	6									21	21	1	1	4		8	3	2	11		185	214	11
Do. Portuguese				1			1		13	14				1	3	2	1	1		25	33																	3	1	1	3		38	48	
General Toaal.			4	1			2		32	36	4	1		4	10	5	2	11		170	204	6									21	22	1	1	5		11	5	2	14		223	262	11

3rd May, 1811.

Appendix III

No. XXIX.

Return of Killed, Wounded, and Missing, of the Army under the Command of His Excellency General Lord Viscount Wellington, K.B. on the 5th May, 1811.

5th May, 1811.

Regiments.	Killed													Wounded														Missing														Total													
	Gl. Staff	Colonels	Lt. Cols.	Majors	Captains	Lieuts.	Ensigns	Staff	Serjeants	Drums.	Rk. & File	Total	Horses	Gen. Staff	Colonels	Lt. Cols.	Majors	Captains	Lieuts.	Ensigns	Staff	Serjeants	Drums.	Rk. & File	Total	Horses		Gen. Staff	Colonels	Lt. Cols.	Majors	Captains	Lieuts.	Ensigns	Staff	Serjeants	Drums.	Rk. & File	Total	Horses		Gen. Staff	Colonels	Lt. Cols.	Majors	Captains	Lieuts.	Ensigns	Staff	Serjeants	Drums.	Rk. & File	Total	Horses
General Staff																																									2													2	
Horse Artillery																																																						
Foot Do.																																																						
1st Royal Dragoons												5	8																												2											2	6
14th Light Do.											4	5	9						2					18	21	9							3				36	37	24		2					5					40	26	30
16th Do. Do.											4	4	18						2					36	37	21											24	24	2							4					41	41	42
1st Hussars K. G. L.											3	4	5						2			1		16	19	22											3	3							2					33	38	30
Coldstream Gds. 1st Bn.											7	7	4											10	13	13																									27	27	11
3rd Foot Guards, 1st Do.											7	6	6						3			2		50	58	20																			6			2		37	45	26

		Total British											
Total British				2	1	7	1		8	2	129	148	45
Do. Portuguese					1				5	1	44	50	
Grand Total.				3	1	7	1		13	3	173	198	45

e

Appendix IV

XXXIX.

Return of Killed, Wounded, and Missing, of the Army under the Command of His Excellency Field-marshal the Marquis of Wellington, K. B. at the Battle of Albuera.

16th May, 1811.

Regiments.	Killed — Total	Killed — Horses	Wounded — Total	Wounded — Horses	Missing — Total	Missing — Horses	Grand Total	Grand Total — Horses
General Staff			7				8	
Royal British Artillery	3	3	10	7			15	20
Do. German Do.		9	16	11		1	48	34
3rd Dragoon Guards	9	24	17	10		3	20	19
4th Dragoons	2	10	6	6		4	27	23
13th Lt. Dragoons	3	11	15	20		2	1	
3rd Foot 1st Ba.			222		29		591	
7th Do. 1st Do.			263		1		326	
7th Do. 2nd Do.			269				315	
23rd Do. 1st Do.			282		161		310	
27th Do. 3rd Do.			5		179		8	
28th Do. 2nd Do.			137				149	
29th Do.			245		6		304	
31st Do. 2nd Do.			126				155	
34th Do. 2nd Do.			95		11		128	
39th Do. 2nd Do.			81				98	
40th Do. 1st Do.							11	
48th Do. 1st Do.			183				247	
48th Do. 2nd Do.			82		2		297	
57th Do. 1st Do.			339		6		343	
60th Do. 5th Do.			16				17	
66th Do. 2nd Do.			91		96		237	
97th Do.			1		101		1	
1st Lt. Do. K. G. L.			55				61	
2nd Do. Do.			28		2		32	
Total British	815	53		226	544	17	4158	97
Do. Portuguese	98	10		10	26		389	18
General Total	913	63		236	570	17	4547	115

Appendix V (i)

Names of the Officers Killed, Wounded, and Missing, at Albuera, 16th May.

Killed.

British.	Regiments.	Portuguese.	Regiments.
Maj. Gen. D. Hoghton	3rd Dn. Guards	Staff-surgeon Boolmau	
Lieutenant Fox	3rd Foot, 1st Bn.	J. P. J. Jose Muntro	
Captain Burke	Do.		
Lieutenant Herbert	Do.		
Ensign Chadwick	Do.		
Thomas	Do.		
Captain Erck	7th Do. 1st Bn.		
Lieutenant Archie	Do.		
Captain Montague	23rd Do. 1st Do.		
2nd Lieutenant Hall	Do.		
Captain Humphrey	29th Do.		
Lieutenant Duguid	Do.		
Ensign King	Do.		
Furnace	Do.		
Vance	Do.		
Captain Gibbons	34th Do. 2nd Bn.		
Lieutenant C. Castle	Do.		
Ensign Sarsfield	Do.		
Lieutenant Beard	39th Do. 1st Do.		
Lieut. Col. Duckworth	48th Do. 1st Do.		
Lieutenant Page	Do.		
Ansaldo	Do.		
Lieutenant Lisdon	48th Do. 2nd Bn.		
Loft	Do.		
Drew	Do.		
Ensign Rodiwell	57th Do. 1st Bn.		
Major Scott	Do.		
Captain Fawcett	66th Do. 2nd Bn.		
Lieutenant Shewbridge	Do.		
Ensign Coulter	Do.		
Lieutenant Whitney	Do.		

Wounded.

British.	Regiments.	Remarks.
Maj. Gen. the Hon. G. L. Cole	34th Regt.	Slightly
Hon. W. Stewart	103rd Do.	Do.
Capt. Egerton	Do.	Severely
Waller	Sicilian Regt.	Do.
Rouveria, A.D.C. to Major Gen. the Hon. G. L. Cole	42nd Do.	Do.
Waite	2nd Do.	Slightly
Baring, A.D.C. to Maj. Gen. Allen	1st Lt. Bn. K. G. L.	Do.
Capt. Hawker	Royal Artillery	Severely
Lieut. Thiele	Do. Ger. Do.	Slightly
Capt. Holmes	4th Dragoons	Do.
Lieut. Wildman	Do.	Do.
Adjt. Chantry	Do.	Do.
Capt. Marley	3rd Foot, 1st Bn.	Severely
Gordon	Do.	Do.
Stevens	Do.	Do. and taken prisoner
Cameron	Do.	
Lieut. Juxon	Do.	Slightly
Shepherd	Do.	Do.
Hooper	Do.	Do.
Latham	Do.	Do.
Wright	Do.	
Woods	Do.	
Houghton	Do.	Severely
Titlow	Do.	Do.
O'Donnell	Do.	Do.
Ensign Walsh	Do.	Slightly
Lieutenant-colonel Sir W. Myers Bn.	7th Do. 1st Do.	Severely (since dead.)
Capt. Cholwick	Do.	Slightly
Singer	Do.	Do.
Crowder	Do.	Do.
Lieut. Provost	Do.	Severely
Manltry	Do.	Do.
Ellis	Do.	Do. (since dead.)
S. B. Johnstone	Do.	Severely
Mullens	Do.	Slightly
Henry	Do.	Severely
Jones	Do.	Do.
Morgan	Do.	Do.

Appendix V (ii)

No. XLI.

Continuation of the Names of Killed and Wounded at Albuera.

Wounded.

Rank and Names.	Regiments.	Remarks.	Rank and Names.	Regiments.	Remarks.
Lieut. R. Johnson	7th Fusileers, 1st Bn.	Slightly	Lieut. Popham	29th Fusileers	
Gibbons	Do.	Do.	Briggs	Do.	Severely
Moses	Do.	Severely (since dead)	Ensign Lovelock	Do.	Slightly
Br. Lt. Col. Blakeney	7th Do. 2nd Bn.	Severely	Kearney	Do.	Severely
Capt. M'Ginnes	Do.	Left arm amputated	Lovelock	Do.	
Orr	Do.	Severely	Adjt. Wild	Do.	Severely
Tarleton	Do.	Slightly	Capt. Flemming	31st Do. 2nd	Do.
Lieut. Erwin	Do.	Severely	Knox	Do.	Slightly
Healy	Do.		Lieut. Butler	Do.	Do.
Wray	Do.	Severely	Gethin	Do.	Do.
Orr	Do.		Cashell	Do.	Do.
Seaton	Do.	Severely	Ensign Wilson	Do.	
Penrice	Do.		Nicholson	Do.	
Lorentz	Do.	Slightly	Capt. Weddrington	34th Do. 2nd	
Holden	Do.	Do.	Wyatt	Do.	
Fraser	Do.	Do.	Lieut. Hay	Do.	
Acting Adjt. Meagher	Do.	Do.	Walsh	Do.	
Lieut. Col. Ellis	23rd Do. 1st Bn.	Do.	Capt. Brine	39th Do. 1st	Severely
Capt. Hurford	Do.		Lieut. Hart	Do.	Do.
M'Donald	Do.		Pollard	Do.	Do.
Stainforth	Do.	Slightly	Ensign Cox	Do.	Do.
1st Lieut. Harrison	Do.	Do.	Capt. Wilson	48th Do. 1st	Slightly
Booker	Do.	Severely	French	Do.	Do.
Treeve	Do.		Bell	Do.	
Thorpe	Do.		Morrisot	Do.	Slightly
2nd Lieut. Castles	Do.	Slightly	Parsons	Do.	Severely
Harris	Do.		Lieut. Crawley	Do.	Slightly
Ledwith	Do.		Sterring	Do.	
Adjt. M'Lean	Do.		Wright	Do.	Slightly
Capt. Gale	28th Do. 1st Bn.	Severely	O'Donoghue	Do.	Do.
Carroll	Do.	Slightly	Duke	Do.	Do.
Lieut. Crummer	Do.	Do.	M'Intosh	Do.	Do.
Cottingham	Do.	Do.	Vincent	Do.	Do.
Shelton	Do.		Ensign Collins	Do.	Do.
Ensign Ingram	Do.	Slightly	Adjt. Steele	Do.	Do.
Lieut. Col. White	29th Do.	Severely	Capt. Watkins	48th Do. 2nd	Do.
Major Way	Do.		Waugh	Do.	Do.
Capt. Hodge	Do.	Slightly	Drought	Do.	
Todd	Do.		Wood	Do.	
Nestor	Do.	Slightly	Lieut. Johnson	Do.	Slightly
Lieut. Stannus	Do.	Severely	Vandermeuliu	Do.	Do.
Brooke	Do.		Shea	Do.	

Appendix V (iii)

Names of Officers Continued. Killed and Wounded at Albuera.

Rank and Names.	Regiments.	Remarks.	Rank and Names.	Regiments.	Remarks.
Wounded.			**Wounded.**		
Lieutenant Sharp	48th Foot 2nd Bn.		Portuguese.		
Ensign Norman	Do.		Colonel Collins		
M'Dougall	Do.		Adjutant Jose de Mello	2nd Regiment	
Lieutenant Col. Inglis	57th Do. 1st Do.		Ensign P. Broquet	4th Do.	
Major Spring	Do.	Slightly	Captain Jose de Mattos	5th Do.	
Captain Shadforth	Do.		James Johnson	Do.	
M'Gibbon	Do.		Lieutenant Jose Miranda	Do.	
Jermyn	Do.		Ensign J. S. Vasconcellas	Do.	
Stainforth	Do.		Lieutenant J. P. de Carvalhos	11th Do.	
Hely	Do.		B. de Napoles	Do.	
Kirby	Do.	Severely	Captain A. P. D. Aragas	23rd Do.	
Lieutenant Evatt	Do.	Do.	Lieutenant-colonel Hawkshaw	1st Bn. L. L. L.	
Baxter	Do.	Slightly	Major J. Paes	Do.	
M'Lachlane	Do.	Do.	Captain F. Jacob	Do.	
M'Farlane	Do.		J. P. Rosado	Do.	
Dix	Do.	Slightly	Licut. Ant. Carlos	Do.	
Patterson	Do.	Severely	Andrew Camacho	Do.	
Hughes	Do.	Slightly			
Sheridan					
Vietch					
Myers					
M'Dougall					
Ensign Torrens					
Jackson		Slightly			
Lieutenant Ingerleben	60th Do. 5th Do.	Do.			
Captain Ferns	66th Do. 2nd Do.				
Lieutenant Hicken					
Harvey		Slightly			
L'Estrange					
Chambers					
M'Carthy		Slightly			
Codd					
Hand		Severely			
Crompton					
Ensign Walker					
Hay		Severely			
Mack		Slightly			
Major Hartwig	1st Lt. Bn. K. G. L.				
Ensign Smalkenson					
Adjutant Taple					
Captain J. Herse	2nd Do. Do.				

Eyewitness Sources

Regimental Histories of the 11th, 13th and 14th Hussars; the Rifle Brigade (Verner); the 3rd, 5th, 7th, 28th, 29th, 43rd, 48th, 52nd, 57th, 66th and 79th Regiments of Foot; and the King's German Legion (Beamish)

Alten, Baron Victor von, quoted in Beamish

Anon. private, 3rd, letter in Regimental History

Anon. private, 27th, letter in United Services Journal (1830)

Anon. private, 71st, 'T.S. Soldier of the 71st' (1828)

Anon. officer, 77th, letter in RUSI Journal

Anon. officer, 13th LD, letter in the 'Courier'

Anon., 'Strictures and Further Strictures' on Napier's History (1831/1832)

Beresford, Sir Wm., correspondence with C.E. Long (1832–1835)

Blakeney, LtCol Ed., 7th, letter in USJ (1841)

Blakeney, Lt Robt., 28th, 'A Boy in the Peninsula War' (1899)

Brooke, Maj Wm., 48th, 'Journal' (1811), reprinted in Oman's 'Studies'

Brotherton, Capt Thos., 14th LD, 'Peninsula Reminiscences' (1986)

Burgoyne, Lt John, RE, 'Life of etc' (Wrottesley) (1873)

Cadell, Capt Chas., 28th, 'Narrative of the Campaigns of the 28th' (1835)

Childers, Capt Michael, 11th LD, letter quoted in Regimental records

Cleeve, Capt Andrew, RA, letter quoted in Beamish

Close, Lt Ed., 48th, 'Journal'

Clarke, Lt John, 66th, quoted in Fraser's 'Soldiers Whom Wellington Led'

Cocks, Capt Ed., 'Letters & Diaries' (1986)

Colborne, LtCol John, quoted in Moore-Smith's biography (1903)

Cole, Sir Lowry, 'Memoirs' (1934) and USJ (1841)

Cowell, Ensign John, 1st Guards, 'Leaves from a Diary' (1854)

Cooper, Sgt J.S., 7th, 'Rough Notes etc' (1869)

Costello, Rifleman Ned, 95th, 'The Peninsular Campaign' (1841)

Crammer, Lt James, 28th, journal quoted in Regimental History

Crompton, Lt Geo., 66th, letter in Journal of Society for Army Historical Research (1922)

Dalbiac, Col Chas., quoted in Beresford/Long correspondence (1832–35)

Dickson, Capt Alex., RA, 'The Dickson Manuscripts', also quoted in Napier

Doyle, Capt Carlo, 87th, quoted in B/L correspondence

Doherty, LtCol Patrick, 13th LD, quoted in B/L correspondence

Doherty, Lt Geo., 13th LD, quoted in B/L correspondence

Donaldson, Sgt Jos., 94th, 'Eventful Life of a Soldier' (1852)

Douglas, Sgt John, 'Tales of the Peninsular'

FitzClarence, Lt Geo., 10th LD, 'Memoirs'

Gabriel, Capt, ADC to Gen Stewart, quoted in B/L correspondence

Garrety, C/Sgt Thos., 43rd, 'Memoirs of a Sergeant of the 43rd'

Grattan, Ensign Wm., 88th, 'With the Connaught Rangers' (1902)/ 'Reminiscences' USJ (1831/1834)

Graham, MajGen Thos., 'Life of Lord Lynedoch' (1868)

Gordon, Capt, 3rd, quoted in Buffs Historical Record

Gough, Maj Hugh, 88th, biography by R.S.Rait (1903)

Gregory, Capt, ADC to Gen Long, quoted in B/L correspondence

Hall, Lt Francis, 14th LD, 'Recollections'

Hamilton, Sgt Anthony, 43rd, 'Hamilton's Campaign with Moore and Wellington'

Hardinge, Maj Henry, 57th, letters in USJ (1840)

Harrison, Lt John, 23rd, letters in JSAHR

Hartmann, Maj, KGL, quoted in B/L correspondence

Heathcote, Maj Ralph, Long's DAQMG, quoted in B/L correspondence

Henegan, Sir Richard, 'Seven Years Campaigning' (1846)

Hill, Capt, 23rd, letter in JSAHR

Hobhouse, Ensign Benjamin, 29th, letter to his father (17 May 1811)

Hopkins, Lt John, 43rd, quoted in Regimental History

Inglis, LtCol Wm., 57th, letter in USJ (1832)

Jeffries, Lt, 13th LD, quoted in B/L correspondence

Jones, Maj John, RE, 'Journals of the Sieges' (1813)

Kincaid, Lt John, 95th, 'Adventures'

Knowles, Lt Robt., 7th, 'Letters' (1913)

Knox, Lt Wright, 87th, letter (7 March 1811)

Lawrence, Sgt Wm., 40th, 'Autobiography' (1901)

Lapene, Capt, Soult's 5th Corps, letter in Oman

Leslie, Lt Chas., 29th, 'Military Journal' (1887)

Light, Col, quoted in B/L correspondence

Long, Brig Robt., 'Peninsular Cavalry General' (1951)/ C.E. Long's vindication

Macalister, Capt, 13th LD, quoted in B/L correspondence

Madden, Lt Chas., 4th Dragoons, 'Diary etc' (1914)

Massena, Marshal, his Despatches

Maxwell, W.H., 'Peninsular Sketches (1844)

Mielmann, Capt, KGL, quoted in Beamish

Mills, Ensign John, 1st Guards, letters in 'For King and Country', Fletcher (1995)

Nightingall, MajGen Miles, letters in JSAHR (1973)

Otway, LtCol, quoted in B/L correspondence

Pelet, J.J., 'The French Campaign in Portugal' (1973)

Roverea, Capt, ADC to Gen Cole, journal quoted in 'Memoirs of Lowry Cole etc' (1934)

Schaumann, Asst Comsy August, KGL, 'On the Road with Wellington'

Sherer, Lt Moyle, 34th, 'Recollections' (1834)

Simmons, 2/Lt Geo., 95th, 'A British Rifleman' (1899)

Somerset, LtCol Lord FitzRoy, letter to his brother

Soult, Marshal, his Albuera Despatch

Squire, Capt, RE, letter of 17 May 1811 quoted in Napier

Stevens, Capt Wm., 3rd, letter in Buffs Historical Record
Stewart, Brig Charles, 'Narrative of the Peninsular War' (1828)
Stothert, Capt Wm., 3rd Guards, letter of (15 April 1811)
Surtees, Wm., 'Twenty-five Years in the Rifle Brigade'
Tomkinson, Capt, 16th LD, 'Diary of a Cavalry Officer' (1894)
D'Urban, Col Benjamin, 'The Peninsular Journal' (1930)
Villa Real, Count de, quoted in B/L correspondence
Warre, Capt Wm., 'Letters from the Peninsula' (1909)
Watson, LtCol Henry, quoted in B/L correspondence
Wheeler, Pte Wm., 51st, 'Letters etc' (1951)
Whittingham, Sir Sam., 'Memoirs and Letters etc' (1868)
Wildman, Lt Ed., 4th Dragoons, quoted in B/L correspondence
Woods, Lt Wm., 48th, letter of 29 May 1811

Further Reading

With few exceptions, the ninety or so eyewitness accounts above are available in the Reading Room of the National Army Museum in Chelsea, London. Anything published after about mid-1840, however, should be read in the knowledge that the author would have had at his elbow William Napier's six-volume *History of the War in the Peninsula*, for the next sixty years the pre-eminent general history, which naturally inspired many veterans' memoirs. It also provided a ready-made solution for veterans with memory loss concerning particular events, such as those at which they were not actually present, and Napier's words were accordingly well borrowed – frequently verbatim.

However, with no disrespect to Napier, Sir Charles Oman's seven-volume *History of the Peninsular War*, first published between 1902 and 1930, must remain the academic bible of ultimate reference. Volume III covers Busaco and Torres Vedras, Volume IV the events of 1811. Oman's immense research into sources and battlefield investigations produced a massive definitive work, which surely (warts and all) will never now be superceded by a single author. His nearest rival is his contemporary Sir John Fortescue, whose thirteen-volume *History of the British Army* devotes no fewer than seven volumes to the Peninsula – Volume VIII covers 1811. His excellent maps form the basis for those in this book.

So Napier, Oman and Fortescue are the undisputed general historians. As to the year 1811 and the particular events I have examined in detail, an extremely useful essay on Albuera was published in 1996 by Philip Haythornthwaite; and thirty years earlier Jac Weller covered Fuentes and Albuera with all-too-short chapters in his remarkable *Wellington in the Peninsula*. Deeper coverage had to wait until Ian Fletcher's *Bloody Albuera* (Crowood) in 2000, and Mark Thompson's *The Fatal Hill* in 2002. Both are insightful books, if generous to Beresford's generalship. Since Thompson had previously republished in 1993 all 550 pages of the Beresford/Long correspondence, he must also be the acknowledged guide to crossing that prickly carpet of accusation and counter-accusation.

Writing these words sore from a day's hunting, I am reminded also to mention Ian Fletcher's *Galloping at Everything* (1999). He does long-overdue justice to the British cavalry so unfairly slighted by Oman. Fletcher covers all the many mounted actions throughout the seven individual Peninsular campaigns, of which 1811's Campo Mayor, Los Santos, Usagre and El Bodon are but splendid examples; and he shows how neglected the cavalry have become in Peninsular battle studies, especially in the smaller affairs.

Both *The Dickson Manuscripts* and Jones' *Journals of the Sieges* are available in facsimile reprints from Ken Trotman Ltd, and cannot be beaten for getting a 'feel' for siegework, especially when read alongside the letters of men like Private Wheeler and Ensign Grattan, who climbed the ladders and dug the parallels.

Grattan, Schaumann and Kincaid all make entertaining as well as informative reading, combining a huge enjoyment in the actual story-telling with endlessly rewarding factual descriptions; but for the minutiae of a battle nothing can beat a chair in the Reading Room in the National Army Museum, facing a pile of *Journals of the Society for Army Historical Research,* or those of *the United Services Institute.*

After that, for entertaining light relief based on serious research, I commend the Richard Sharpe novels by Bernard Cornwell. The adaptations for television have provided a splendid visual feast for all us Peninsula addicts; may they soon be repeated.

Index